DOUGLAS GREENWALD   *Consulting Economist and Former Head of the Department of Economics, McGraw-Hill Publications*

In collaboration with:

HENRY C. F. ARNOLD   *Professor, Seton Hall University*

DAVID M. BLITZER   *Chief Economist, Standard & Poor's Corporation*

WILLIAM J. BROWN   *Professor of Finance, College of Business, Northern Illinois University*

LEWIS I. KOFLOWITZ   *Director of Economic Analysis, National Association of Recycling Industries*

GUENTER H. MATTERSDORFF   *Cochairman, Graduate Program in Public Administration, Lewis and Clark College*

EDWARD G. MAYERS   *Cofounder and Full Partner in Mayers-Pitcairn Management Associates*

The Concise
McGraw-Hill
DICTIONARY OF
MODERN
ECONOMICS

*A Handbook of Terms
and Organizations*

An abridged version of *The McGraw-Hill
Dictionary of Modern Economics*, Third Edition,
by Douglas Greenwald & Associates.

McGraw-Hill Book Company

*New York   St. Louis   San Francisco   Auckland   Bogotá
Hamburg   Johannesburg   London   Madrid   Mexico   Montreal
New Delhi   Panama   Paris   São Paulo   Singapore
Sydney   Tokyo   Toronto*

Library of Congress Cataloging in Publication Data

McGraw-Hill dictionary of modern economics.
  The Concise McGraw-Hill dictionary of modern economics.

  "An abridged version of The McGraw-Hill dictionary
of modern economics, third edition, by Douglas Greenwald
& associates."
  1. Economics—Dictionaries. I. Greenwald, Douglas
II. Title.
HB61.M32 1984   330'.03'21   83-25589
ISBN 0-07-024387-5 (pbk.)

1 2 3 4 5 6 7 8 9 0   BKP/BKP   8 9 8 7 6 5 4

ISBN 0-07-024387-5

The editors for this book were William A. Sabin and
Nancy Warren, the designer was Elliot Epstein, and the
production supervisor was Thomas G. Kowalczyk. It was
set in Bembo by Waldman Graphics, Inc.

Printed and bound by The Book Press.

This paperback edition, first published in 1984, is an abridged
version of *The McGraw-Hill Dictionary of Modern Economics, Third Edition.*

2224478

Contents

Preface

The Concise McGraw-Hill Dictionary of Modern Economics provides definitions of about 1,100 terms from the fields of economics, econometrics, marketing, and statistics, and descriptions of fourteen federal and international economics organizations. All these definitions and descriptions are exactly the same in content and length as those given in the unabridged edition of the dictionary (published in 1983). There are only two significant differences between this *Concise Dictionary* and the complete work from which it derives. First, the *Concise Dictionary* does not contain most of the section that describes a number of public and private economics and research organizations. We have, however, retained entries for a few key economics and statistical organizations. Second, the *Concise Dictionary* does not contain about 250 terms which were, for the most part, related to the accounting profession and to the insurance industry.

In this dynamic period for the economics profession, long-accepted definitions of economics terms have been drastically altered, old terms have been discarded completely, and new terms have entered the language. These major changes are all reflected in this concise edition. In addition, the bibliographical references that accompany the definitions have been thoroughly updated as an aid to the reader who wants to learn more about a particular subject.

We have tried to explain clearly and concisely the key points of each concept. We have also tried to write simple and lucid definitions of the technical and econometrics terms that form the basis of much theoretical and mathematical analysis currently being propounded.

The *Concise Dictionary* (like the larger work from which it is derived) is a joint product of economists who were connected at one time or another with the economic departments of McGraw-Hill. It does not, however, embody any formal or official expression of McGraw-Hill policy. The authors are solely responsible for the selection of the individual terms and the definitions that accompany them.

I would like to thank William Sabin of McGraw-Hill's Professional and Reference Division for his support in getting this *Concise Dictionary* published. I would also like to thank Anna Shaler and Nancy Warren for their editorial help in preparing this book for publication. I must also thank my wife, Mickey, for her support and encouragement. And finally, I would like to express appreciation to the teachers of economics and readers of economics throughout the nation and overseas whose suggestions over the years have been incorporated in *The Concise McGraw-Hill Dictionary of Modern Economics*.

Douglas Greenwald

What the dictionary provides

1 A simple definition of approximately 1,100 frequently used modern economic terms.

2 A detailed description of a few public agencies and organizations concerned with economics, including a few outside the United States.

3 References to both current and original sources of information which provide a more detailed explanation of the terms

4 References to sources of economic data.

5 Tables and diagrams when necessary to enhance the definitions.

6 Whenever possible, description of both sides of any issue that might be subject to controversy.

Who can use the dictionary

1 Students who need an auxiliary reference work for courses in economics and business.

2 Students who are working in applied courses and whose background in economics may be limited or out of date.

3 Students of American history and government.

4 College engineering students who are taking a first course in economics.

5 Heads of household and investors who must understand financial and economic reports.

6 Libraries.

7 Instructors.

8 Foreign students who are unfamiliar with American practice and terminology.

9 High school students.

10 Students who are taking evening courses.

11 Editors of newspapers and periodicals of all types.

12 Business executives.

13 The average individual who would like to know a little bit about a lot of economics.

How they can use it

1 Teachers, students, and the general public can consult it as a reference work.

2 Readers can use the dictionary to develop increased interest in economics and to stimulate a desire to learn more about a specific area of economics.

3 Students and nonstudents of economics can use it to bring their economic thinking up to date.

Contributors

Douglas Greenwald A consulting economist to governments and to several corporations. When he retired from the McGraw-Hill Publications Company in 1978, he was Vice President, Economics, and head of its internationally known Department of Economics. He is chief editor and a contributor to the *Encyclopedia of Economics* and coauthor of *New Forces in American Business*. He contributed the chapter "Forecasting Capital Expenditures" in the first edition of the National Association of Business Economists' *How Business Economists Forecast*. He was a member of the board of directors of Standard & Poor's Inter Capital Fixed Income Fund. He is a fellow of the American Statistical Association (ASA) and the National Association of Business Economists. He was a member of the board of directors of the ASA, chairman of the Business and Economics Statistics Section of the ASA, and a president of the New York chapter of the ASA. He was a president of the Metropolitan Economic Association and vice president for economists in the Business Advisory Professions Society. He was one of the organizers of the Federal Statistics Users Conference, was chairman of the conference, and is currently ex officio adviser to the conference. He was a member of the Regional Accounts Committee sponsored by Resources for the Future; and adviser to the National Wealth Planning Committee sponsored by George Washington University; a member of the Census Advisory Committee of the ASA; a member of the Business Research Advisory Committee to the Bureau of Labor Statistics; a member of the Advisory Committee on Statistical Policy to the Statistical Policy Division of the Office of Management and Budget; and a member of the Advisory Committee on setting up a new program for the teaching of Economic and Statistical Research in Business, Industry, and Government at Columbia University's Teachers College. He is currently an economic adviser to the Congressional Budget Office.

Henry C. F. Arnold B.B.A. and M.B.A., University of Michigan; Ph.D., Graduate Faculty of the New School for Social Research. Dr. Arnold is currently teaching at Seton Hall University. Prior to joining McGraw-Hill Publications' Department of Economics, he worked in the research departments of the Federal Reserve Bank of New York and the New York Stock Exchange. After leaving McGraw-Hill, he worked as an economist for the Chase Manhattan Bank and then as a teacher of economics at Rutgers University in Newark, New Jersey. Prior to his current teaching position, he taught at Iona College. He is a member of the American Economic Association, the American Finance Association, and the Royal Economic Society. He is a contributor to the *Encyclopedia of Economics*.

David M. Blitzer B.S. in environmental systems engineering, Cornell University; M.A. in economics from George Washington University; Ph.D. in economics from Columbia University. Dr. Blitzer is currently chief economist for Standard & Poor's Corporation. He moved to S&P from its parent company, McGraw-Hill, Inc., where he was staff economist. Earlier he was a senior analyst for National Economic Research Associates and did work in economics for the New Jersey Department of Environmental Protection, the Natural Resources Defense Council, and the National Committee on Materials Policy.

William J. Brown A.B., Bowdoin College; M.A., University of Chicago; Ph.D., New York University. Dr. Brown is currently Professor of Finance at Northern Illinois University. He was Senior Financial Economist, Office of the Comptroller of the Currency, and before that an economist for the American Bankers Association. Prior to that, he was an economist in the McGraw-Hill Publications' Department of Economics. He serves as a consultant for both private industry and government agencies. He is a contributor to the *Encyclopedia of Economics* and is the author of numerous scholarly and popular articles in the field of economics.

Lewis I. Koflowitz M.B.A. in business economics, Columbia University Graduate Business School. Mr. Koflowitz is an honors graduate in economics from New York University. Prior to joining the McGraw-Hill Publications' Economics Department, he was economics editor on *Engineering News-Record*, a McGraw-Hill publication. Before moving to McGraw-Hill, he was a research assistant specializing in management for Business International, Inc. After leaving McGraw-Hill, he was an economics editor for *Metalworking News*, a Fairchild publication. Currently, he is Director of Economic Analysis for the National Association of Recycling Industries. He is a contributor to the *Encyclopedia of Economics*. He is a member of the New York Association of Business Economists, the American Economic Association, and the Metropolitan Economic Association.

Guenter H. Mattersdorff Ph.D. in economics, Harvard Graduate School of Public Administration. Before coming to McGraw-Hill Publications' Department of Economics as senior economist, Dr. Mattersdorff was an instructor at Yale University, the University of Massachusetts, and Connecticut College. He has been a professor at Lewis and Clark College and chairman of the Department of Economics. He is cochairman of Lewis and Clark's Graduate Program in Public Administration. In 1982, he was visiting professor of economics at Haverford College. He is a contributor to the *Encyclopedia of Economics*.

Edward G. Mayers B.Sci.B.A., M.A. in economics, Ohio State University. He is currently cofounder and full partner in Mayers-Pitcairn Management Associates. He was a senior economist in the McGraw-Hill Publications' Department of Economics. Prior to joining McGraw-Hill, he was an associate economist at American Cyanimid Company and associate professor of economics at the U.S. Merchant Marine Academy. He is a contributor to the *Encyclopedia of Economics* and is the author of two monographs commissioned by the Joint Council on Economic Education. He has contributed to several textbooks on business and economics and is a member of the American Statistical Association.

Part One
TERMS

A

ability-to-pay principle of taxation   The theory that the tax burden should be distributed according to the individual's ability to pay. It is based on the assumption that those who possess more wealth than others should contribute a relatively larger amount to the support of the government. The obligation to pay is seen as a social or collective responsibility rather than as a personal one. Employing the concept of a diminishing utility of income, the ability-to-pay principle tries to equalize the sacrifice made by each individual in paying taxes. The determination of a tax base capable of measuring an individual's ability to pay is a major problem of this theory. Generally, net money income (with deductions for minimal survival needs) is used as the best measure of this ability. This measure ignores differences in financial commitments, in expectations of future income, and in habits of consumption, however, and thus may not reflect the individual's real ability to pay the tax. Another problem is the determination of a rate schedule which truly equalizes the sacrifices involved in paying a tax. The concept of diminishing marginal utility indicates that a tax based on the ability to pay should be progressive (or at least proportional), but there is no way of determining how steep rate increases should be. Furthermore, the application of a uniform rate to all taxpayers ignores differences among persons in the utility of income. The ability-to-pay principle, regarded by many as the most equitable and just theory of taxation, is incorporated into most of the important U.S. taxes, such as the progressive personal income tax and the inheritance tax. For additional information, see Richard A. Musgrave and Peggy B. Musgrave, *Public Finance in Theory and Practice,* McGraw-Hill, New York, 1975.

absolute advantage   The ability of a particular country, firm, or worker to supply a product or service at a cost lower than that of a competitor. Most of the world's trade is carried on because of differences in absolute advantage: bananas are bought from Honduras instead of Canada, nylon is purchased from Du Pont rather than General Motors, and even in a small village the watchmaker buys bread from the baker instead of making it. This division of labor is generally advantageous because it forces every country, firm, and worker to specialize and thus to acquire cost-cutting skills. Nevertheless, competitors faced with the prospect of going out of business sometimes react by requesting government regulations that give them a new lease on life. Such regulations, which reduce the gain obtained from an absolute advantage, are sometimes defended in the name of the infant-industry argument. According to this argument, a protected industry, if allowed to live and grow even when at a competitive disadvantage, may have a chance to develop new markets and new methods that will give it an absolute advantage in the future. See C. P. Kindleberger and P. H. Lindert, *International Economics*, Irwin, Homewood, Ill., 1978.

accelerated depreciation   A faster-than-historical rate of depreciation of a fixed asset for income tax purposes. It is a method of depreciation that makes the depreciation allowance, and hence the tax allowance, available earlier in the life of the asset. By using the liberalized provisions for computing depreciation allowances introduced in the U.S. Internal Revenue Code of 1954, a business can recapture almost 50% more of its investment in a new fixed asset during the first half of the asset's useful life than it could when it was limited to straight-line depreciation. In addition, rapid tax amortization certificates, introduced during World War II and the Korean conflict to stimulate defense and defense-supporting investment, permitted companies to depreciate within five years assets that would normally have been depreciated over a longer period. Accelerated depreciation in any form does not increase the total tax-free allowance for capital consumption. For additional details, see Norman B. Ture, *Accelerated Depreciation in the United States, 1954–1960*, National Bureau of Economic Research, New York, 1967.

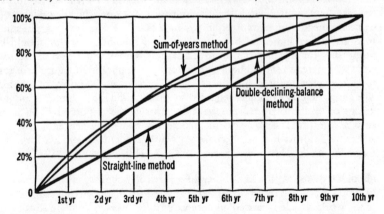

accelerator theory   The theory that a change in the demand for goods induces a change in the amount of machinery needed to produce those goods. Let us assume that a manufacturer of radios needs $3 of capital for $1 of

production, and that annual replacement costs equal 10% of the manufacturer's preceding year's capital stock. The table below shows that the output
rises between periods 1 and 2 by $5, and that the manufacturer must expand
capacity by spending $15, plus a replacement cost of $30. Thus, a 5% rise in
demand induces a 50% increase in investment spending. The accelerator can
also cause a violent collapse of investment spending, as shown between periods 3 and 4.

Period	Output of goods	Capital stock required	Addition to capacity	Replacement	Total spending for investment
1	100	300	0	30	30
2	105	315	15	30	45
3	115	345	30	32	62
4	110	330	−15	35	20

The accelerator is particularly important in assessing the business outlook
when industry is operating near capacity. At such a time, a small increase in
demand can raise investment spending enormously. Five limitations to the
accelerator theory should be considered before applying it to practical problems. (1) The theory assumes full-capacity operation at all times. This assumption is obviously untrue in practice, and this is one of the main reasons
that capacity statistics have been developed for the economy. (2) The theory,
as stated, breaks down because it assumes that gross investment can fall below
zero, which is impossible. When the derived demand for capital equipment
falls so rapidly that depreciation does not dispose of all the equipment not
needed, excess capacity is created. (3) The model does not explicitly include
expectations as a factor which may raise or lower capital investment. (4) All
the foregoing are limitations to be borne in mind, but they do not destroy
the theory. More important is the fact that investment sometimes requires
years to be completed, a fact that the theory ignores. Because of this time
factor, actual investment may fluctuate less markedly than the theory allows
when business goes through the cycle. (5) The principle assumes fixed proportions between output and capital stock. This may not necessarily be true
if capital can be worked three shifts during periods of unusually heavy demand instead of the normal one shift. The accelerator principle was introduced by John M. Clark in 1917 to explain proportionately larger variations
in investment over the course of a business cycle than had occurred in the
output of consumer goods. Interest in the accelerator as a theoretical tool
increased after 1936, when it was discovered that it could be combined with
the Keynesian consumption function to formulate self-generating models of
the business cycle. For further discussion, see John M. Clark, "Business Acceleration and the Law of Demand: A Technical Factor in Economic Cycles,"

Journal of Political Economy, vol. 25, no. 3, March 1917, reprinted in *Readings in Business Cycles,* McGraw-Hill, New York, 1951; Thomas F. Dernburg and Duncan M. McDougall, *Macroeconomics,* 5th ed., McGraw-Hill, New York, 1976, pp. 272–280.

accord, Treasury-Federal Reserve An agreement by the U.S. Secretary of the Treasury and the Board of Governors of the Federal Reserve System on the "debt management and monetary policies to be pursued in furthering their common purpose to assure the successful financing of the government's requirements and, at the same time, to minimize the monetization of the public debt." The announcement on March 4, 1951, that the Treasury and the Federal Reserve had reached "full accord" in these matters marked the official end of one of the most controversial disputes on monetary policy in the Federal Reserve's history. This dispute concerned the continuation into the 1950s, at the Treasury's behest, of the World War II policy of supporting at par the prices of U.S. government bonds. Before the accord, financial institutions wishing to expand their private lending operations were able to sell their accumulated government bond holdings to the Federal Reserve at par. As a result, the Federal Reserve's ability to employ monetary policy as a weapon against postwar inflation was severely restricted. The additional inflationary pressures created by mobilization for the Korean conflict led to the announced accord and to a decision to abandon the unconditional support of government security prices. For a discussion of the basic questions involved in the controversy, see Lester V. Chandler and Stephen M. Goldfeld, *The Economics of Money and Banking,* 7th ed., Harper & Row, New York, 1977; for an account of events surrounding the accord, see Herbert Stein, *The Fiscal Revolution in America,* University of Chicago Press, Chicago, 1969, chap. 10.

acquisition The taking over of one firm by another. The acquisition of a corporation is usually carried out by the purchase of a controlling portion of its common stock. The acquisition form of merger differs from consolidation, which is a joining of firms into a single consolidated company. It is easier to merge small firms by acquisition, since the capital needed for the takeover is within the resources of the acquiring firm. Consolidation is more common in the merger of large firms, especially since new sources of capital may sometimes be required in merging the given firms into a more highly capitalized corporation. A series of acquisitions by one company may be part of an attempt to secure market control, particularly if legal or other restrictions prevent the consolidation of a large number of firms at one time. For additional details, see Betty Bock, *Mergers and Markets: 7,* Conference Board, Studies in Business Economics, no. 105, New York, 1969.

adjustable-rate mortgages *See* **mortgages, nontraditional.**

administered-price theory A theory that the prices of goods or services are allegedly established by agreement among the executives of large firms and maintained despite changes in market conditions. Thus, the market forces of supply and demand play little or no role in determining prices. When the demand for a particular product declines, prices remain the same. Because economic activity no longer declines sharply in recession periods, those persons who supposedly administer prices are not under strong pressure to reduce them. Rather, the incentive is to maintain prices, since the pressures from cost-push and from the demand side are generally prevalent. Before World War II, the inflexibility of administered prices was accepted by some economists and government authorities, but it was not until after the war that this inflexibility was considered to be closely related to the degree of market concentration. For further discussion, see Gardiner C. Means, *The Corporate Revolution in America,* Crowell-Collier, New York, 1962.

administrative budget The traditional method of budgeting federal expenditures and receipts in the United States until 1969. The administrative budget includes the collection and distribution of all funds of which the government considers itself the sole owner. The administrative budget concept is roughly consistent with the concept of federal debt subject to limitation and the federal funds part of the unified budget. There are a number of trust accounts, such as those used to finance social security programs, of which the government does not consider itself full owner, and transactions for these accounts are not included in the administrative budget. Certain highway and housing trust funds are also regarded as outside the administrative accounts and are excluded from the administrative budget. The result of these exclusions is that the administrative budget does not present a complete picture of federal government transactions. For additional details, see Gerhard Colm, *The Federal Budget and the National Economy,* National Planning Association, Washington, D.C., 1955.

ad valorem tax A levy based on a fixed percentage of an item's dollar value. Ad valorem is a Latin term meaning "depending on the value of the item." The great advantages of an ad valorem tax over a specific tax (for example, 4 cents per gallon of gasoline) are that it does not erode during inflationary times and that its direct relationship to an item's value makes it more equitable. A disadvantage is that the need to determine the value of the taxable item makes this tax more difficult to compute. Ad valorem taxes include sales taxes, property taxes, and the majority of import duties. See Richard A. Musgrave and Peggy B. Musgrave, *Public Finance in Theory and Practice,* McGraw-Hill, New York, 1975; Robert H. Haveman, *The Economics of the Public Sector,* 2d ed., Wiley, New York, 1976.

advertising A method of providing private consumers, businesses, and governments with information about specific goods, services, or opportunities with the ultimate goal of increasing sales. Advertisements convey news about goods and services, including details to show what they are, what they are used for, where they are, and what they cost. Advertising has become an important sales aid, especially for nationally and internationally distributed items. It may be considered one step in the process of automated selling, in which fewer sales personnel are needed to inform consumers about a product. The dollar volume of advertising in all media in the United States in 1980 exceeded $50 billion, or 2% of the dollar volume of all goods and services produced. Most business executives believe that advertising helps move billions of dollars' worth of goods and services off the shelves of manufacturers, wholesalers, retailers, and service establishments to the consumers of the world. On the other hand, some economists believe that advertising results in a misuse of resources, that it creates undesirable wants at the expense of public needs, and that its benefits rarely justify the costs involved. Despite a popular belief prior to the 1950s that advertising contributes to economic instability, postwar evidence suggests that it may be a stabilizing economic force. In the business recessions of 1948–1949, 1953–1954, 1957–1958, 1970, and 1974–1975, advertising did not follow the downward course of business activity, and in the recession of 1960–1961 it declined much less than general business. See Simon L. Julian, *Issues in the Economics of Advertising,* University of Illinois Press, Urbana, 1970; Stanley I. Ornstein, *Industrial Concentration 2nd Advertising Intensity,* American Enterprise Institute, Washington, D.C., 1977.

affiliated company A company related to another by virtue of stock ownership. When the ownership proportion is substantial but less than 50%, the owned company is referred to as an affiliate. An affiliate should be distinguished from a holding company, which controls the voting power of one or more other corporations. For additional information, see Jerome B. Cohen, Edward D. Zinbarg, and Arthur Zeikel, *Investment Analysis and Portfolio Management,* rev. ed., Dow Jones–Irwin, Homewood, Ill., 1973, pp. 197–201.

affluent society A wealthy nation in which most persons enjoy an abundance of material things. Popularized by John Kenneth Galbraith in *The Affluent Society,* the term is frequently used to describe the United States, where, at the end of 1970, 67 million families and individuals owned more than 89 million automobiles, 90 million television sets, 59 million vacuum cleaners, and 20 million home freezers. The United States had grown so prosperous, Galbraith argued, that it no longer needed to increase the output of consumer products, but it could and should improve the quality of life by shifting emphasis from the private to the public sector of the economy. For example, resources could be used to create better schools, cleaner streets, a greater number of parks, and a variety of other social services. Many U.S. economists disagree with this argument. They reject the idea that most consumer wants have been satisfied and oppose the promotion of government services at the expense of private consumption. For Galbraith's view, see J. K. Galbraith, *The Affluent Society,* Houghton Mifflin, Boston, 1958.

aggregative model   An econometric model involving variables whose individual observations represent aggregates. For example, total income and total expenditures are both aggregates. Similarly, an index number may depict the behavior of groups of individual observations. It follows that peculiarities of the individual observations that are grouped as well as the peculiarities of possible subgroups are not encompassed by such models. For additional information, see Lawrence R. Klein, *Introduction to Econometrics*, Greenwood, Westport, Conn., 1977.

agricultural revolution, modern   The rapid rise in farm output per worker-hour and in crop output per acre, accompanied by a sharp decline in the number of farm workers, since the 1940s. Because of the introduction of new and improved agricultural machinery, the development of better soil-utilization methods, and the marked improvement in farm chemicals, such as fertilizers, weed killers, and insecticides, farm production per worker-hour rose by 453% and output per acre by 64% between 1950 and 1980, while the number of farm workers declined from 9.9 million to 3.8 million. Although the main impact of the modern agricultural revolution has been felt in the United States, its effects have been worldwide. For statistics showing the magnitude of the agricultural revolution in the United States, see *Changes in Farm Production and Efficiency*, U.S. Department of Agriculture Bulletin 561, September 1978.

allocation of resources   The distribution of resources among different uses and users. A basic problem of every economic system is the means of achieving an allocation of resources that will result in maximum efficiency. Resources must be channeled into the production of goods that consumers want most and must be prevented from entering the production of goods that consumers want least. In addition, they must be allocated to the most productive industries. The optimum allocation of resources is achieved through the workings of the free-price system, in which resources move from less profitable to more profitable uses and from less important to more important uses. A necessary condition for an optimum allocation of resources is that the marginal product of any resource be the same for all its alternative uses. With pure competition in all product and resource markets, an optimum allocation is achieved automatically, but monopoly or monopsony leads to different marginal products with different uses and thus to misallocation. Other impediments to optimum resource allocation are ignorance of profitable opportunities, sociological and psychological factors (e.g., lack of factor mobility), and institutional restrictions (e.g., labor unions and patents). For further information, see Richard H. Leftwich, *The Price System and Resource Allocation*, 6th ed., Dryden Press, Hinsdale, Ill., 1976; D. S. Watson and Mary A. Holman, *Price Theory and Its Uses*, 4th ed., Houghton Mifflin, Boston, 1976.

alpha coefficient A method of measuring risk. The alpha coefficient is used to account for change in a stock's price not attributable to the beta coefficient. It measures the various residual nonmarket influences unique to the beta coefficient. For example, if you add more stock to your portfolio, you tend to diversify away both the chances of obtaining a positive alpha as well as the risk of getting a negative alpha. As a result, your portfolio's volatility will become very much like that of the whole market. For additional information, see Marshall E. Blume, "On the Assessment of Risk," *Journal of Finance*, vol. 26, no. 1, March 1971, pp. 1–10; Marshall E. Blume and Irwin Friend, "A New Look at the Capital Asset Pricing Model," *Journal of Finance*, March 1973; Michael C. Jensen (ed.), *Studies in the Theory of Capital Markets*, Praeger, New York, 1972.

alternative costs *See* opportunity costs.

annual improvement factor A provision written into a collective bargaining agreement for wage increases tied to increases in productivity. Often called the productivity clause, the annual improvement factor provides for wage increases in addition to those resulting from the operation of an escalator clause, which keeps real wages in line with rising consumer prices. The annual improvement provision originated in the contract agreement signed by General Motors and the United Automobile Workers in 1948. The annual improvement factor is based on the theory that employees should periodically receive wage or salary increases in addition to those connected with promotions. In the *Economic Report of the President* of January 1962, an administration for the first time advanced guidelines for noninflationary wage increases. These equated the rate of increase in wage rates (including fringe benefits) in each industry to the trend rate of overall productivity increases. By the end of 1967, the Council of Economic Advisers no longer thought it appropriate to set the trend of productivity as a numerical target for wage increases. See Lloyd G. Reynolds, *Labor Economics and Labor Relations*, 7th ed., Prentice-Hall, Englewood Cliffs, N.J., 1978.

anticipation survey A survey of the expectations of business firms and consumers. The use of anticipations data from surveys has become an important element in the forecasting of short-term business conditions. Anticipations data are divided into two broad classes. First, there are expectations relating to the future behavior of business as a whole, such as sales or the climate of the financial markets, which are beyond the individual firm's control. These expectations are called market anticipations. Second, there are anticipations about the future actions of the economic unit (firm or household), such as plans to install capital equipment or to make certain consumer purchases. These anticipations, over which the individual or firm has control, are known as intentions or plans. The two types of expectations are closely related, since business or consumer intentions are highly dependent on the relevant market anticipations. Since World War II, the systematic collection of anticipations data through survey methods has greatly expanded, and information on many aspects of consumer and business expectations is now compiled periodically. Perhaps the most useful anticipations data collected are those of capital spending plans and sales expectations. The two main sources of these data are the *Annual Survey of Business Anticipations in Plant and Equipment Expenditures,* compiled by the U.S. Department of Commerce, and the McGraw-Hill Department of Economics surveys, *Business' Plans for New Plants and Equipment.* The two principal sources of information on consumer anticipations of purchases, finances, etc., are the Survey Research Center of the University of Michigan and the Conference Board. For additional details on the use of anticipation surveys in forecasting, see National Bureau of Economic Research, *The Quality and Economic Significance of Anticipations Data,* Princeton University Press, Princeton, N.J., 1960; Conference on Research in Income and Wealth, *Short-Term Economic Forecasting, Studies in Income and Wealth,* vol. 12, Princeton University Press, Princeton, N.J., 1955; Robert Eisner, *Factors in Business Investment,* Ballinger, Cambridge, Mass., 1978.

antitrust legislation   Legislation that prohibits monopoly, restraints of trade, and conspiracies to inhibit competition. Laws of this type are based on common law originating in the opposition of British courts to illegal grants of monopoly by the crown during the seventeenth century, and on the long-standing resistance to conspiracy and to contracts that restrict the freedom to choose and pursue one's trade. The first U.S. antitrust laws were enacted in Kansas in 1889; some forty states now enforce them. The first federal law, the Sherman Antitrust Act of 1890, outlawed monopolies, restraints of trade, and every contract, combination, trust, or conspiracy to achieve them, but without defining these terms. It was followed by the Federal Trade Commission Act of September 26, 1914, which created the Commission and empowered it to prevent persons, partnerships, or corporations (except banks and common carriers otherwise controlled) from using unfair methods of competition and unfair deceptive acts or practices in commerce. This law was strengthened by the Clayton Antitrust Act of October 15, 1914, which outlawed price discrimination, exclusive or tying contracts, intercorporate stockholdings, interlocking directorates, and, by amendment in 1950, direct or indirect acquisition of a competitor's assets if this action substantially lessened competition. The Robinson-Patman Act of 1936 amended the Clayton Act with regard to price discrimination. Specifically, it prohibited suppliers from soliciting business from large customer firms, such as chain stores and mail-order houses, by offering terms more favorable than the real savings in cost that would result from handling a large order. It also enjoined large integrated companies from making traditional charges (such as brokerage fees, advertising allowances, and fees for other services) unless the costs were actually incurred. This act, which is often said to aim as much at preserving small firms as at curbing restraints of trade, symbolizes the dilemma of the Antitrust Division in the Department of Justice and of the Federal Trade Commission. They must find the means to prevent a firm from acquiring great market power without destroying its incentive to prosper and grow more than its competitors, and also to avoid penalizing a large firm, which can often be much more efficient than its smaller competitors. See Robert H. Bork, *The Antitrust Paradox: A Policy at War with Itself,* Basic Books, New York, 1978; Jerrold G. Van Cise *The Federal Antitrust Laws,* American Enterprise Institute, Washington, D.C., 1975.

applied research   Scientific investigation aimed at discovering new products and processes, usually with specific profit-making objectives. Applied research differs from basic research, which has no specific profit-making objectives, chiefly in terms of economic purpose. In methods and procedures, however, it is often difficult to distinguish between the two. Statistics on applied research are published by the National Science Foundation, Washington, D.C., in its periodic *Reviews of Data on Research and Development.*

appreciation   An increase in the market value of an asset (stocks, bonds, plant and equipment, real estate, and the like) above its value at some prior period. It is the opposite of depreciation. Generally, appreciation is not recognized until it has actually been realized through the sale of the asset. For example, a private home in a fine location was purchased for $75,000 in 1970, but within a decade the value of the location and the house appreciated until it was worth $200,000. When the owner sold the house for $200,000 in 1980, the appreciation on the original investment was $125,000. Current accounting practice frowns on the writing up of business assets. For current accounting practice, see Walter B. Meigs and Robert F. Meigs, *Accounting, the Basis for Business Decisions,* McGraw-Hill, New York, 1980.

appropriation, federal   A financial grant by the Congress of the United States for a stated purpose, such as permitting a federal agency to place an order, to award a contract, or to buy goods and services and thus to commit the government to expenditure in the future. The rates at which appropriations are obligated and expenditures carried out are determined by the various federal departments and agencies, subject to the control of the U.S. Office of Management and Budget. The appropriation is the most important form of new obligational authority. For details of the process by which the federal government reaches decisions on expenditure, see Arthur Smithies, *The Budgetary Process in the United States,* McGraw-Hill, New York, 1955; see also Murray L. Weidenbaum, "The Federal Government Spending Process," in U.S. Joint Economic Committee, *Federal Expenditure Policy for Economic Growth and Stability,* 1957.

a priori estimates   *See* **extraneous estimates.**

arbitrage   The act of simultaneously purchasing foreign exchange, securities, commodities, or other goods in one market and selling them in another market at a higher price. The following example, using foreign exchange, best shows the operation. Let us suppose that at a given moment one British pound (£1) is trading for $1.96 in London and that at the same time £1 is trading for $1.92 in New York. This difference in exchange rates (prices) between the two markets allows a nimble arbitrager to buy pounds in New York at $1.92 per pound and sell them in London for $1.96, thus making a profit of 4 cents per pound, less any costs arising from the transaction. An arbitrager can profit whenever the price differential between the two markets exceeds the cost of the transactions. Generally, the act of arbitraging tends to decrease any price differential between the two markets. See Lester V. Chandler and Stephen M. Goldfeld, *The Economics of Money and Banking,* Harper & Row, New York, 1977.

arbitration   The settlement of differences between two parties—usually labor and management—by a third party known as an arbitrator. Arbitration in labor disputes is divided into two types. The first, called arbitration of rights, involves a dispute arising during the life of a contract between union and management. This type of arbitration is provided for in more than 90% of all U.S. collective bargaining agreements. Unions and managements are willing to accept this kind of arbitration because it involves only the interpretation of the principles and rules governing the relationships between them, which have already been established in the collective bargaining process. This type of arbitration often involves workers' claims that they have been treated unfairly in promotion or layoff procedures. The second type, called arbitration of interests, consists of the negotiation of a new contract. In such an arbitration, which is much less common, wages and working conditions are usually at issue. The arbitration in 1963–1964 of featherbedding on railroads by a committee composed of public, private, and interested parties brought this type of arbitration into prominence in the United States. See Lloyd G. Reynolds, *Labor Economics and Labor Relations,* 7th ed., Prentice-Hall, Englewood Cliffs, N.J., 1978.

assessment bond   *See* **revenue bond.**

asset   A physical property or intangible right, owned by a business or an individual, that has a value. An asset is useful to its owner, either because it is the source of future services or because it can be used to secure future benefits. Business assets are usually divided into two categories, current and fixed. Current assets, which are those that can readily be turned into cash, include cash on hand, accounts receivable, inventories, and marketable securities. Fixed, or noncurrent, assets, which are those that cannot readily be turned into cash without disrupting the business operations and which are generally held for more than one year, include land, buildings, equipment, and long-term investments. Another type of fixed assets, called intangible assets, consists of certain nonmaterial rights and benefits of a firm, such as patents, copyrights, trademarks, and goodwill. For additional information see Harold Bierman, Jr., and Allan R. Drebin, *Managerial Accounting*, 3d ed., Dryden Press, Hinsdale, Ill., 1978.

atomistic economy   An economy in which many small independent producers compete in each industry. In an atomistic industry, the theoretical models of pure competition are approximately valid. The individual sellers are so small that they accept the selling price for their goods as more or less given and adjust their output to this market price. No seller (or buyer) acting independently in an atomistic industry can perceptibly influence price, and the large number of firms rules out the possibility of collusive restraint of output. The United States had a more or less atomistic economy in the first half of the nineteenth century before the widespread emergence of large-scale production and big business. Among industries that have approached the atomistic model in recent times are agriculture, coal mining, and cotton textile manufacturing. For additional information, see Joe S. Bain, *Industrial Organization*, 2d ed., Wiley, New York, 1968.

Austrian school   The name applied to a group of late nineteenth-century Austrian economists, led by Karl Menger, Friedrich von Wieser, and Eugen von Böhm-Bawerk, who adopted a more subjective approach to economics than earlier economists had, emphasizing the concepts of demand and utility and changing the previous emphasis on production and supply. Basic to their analysis was the theory of diminishing marginal utility, whereby a diminishing quantity of satisfaction is derived from successive units of a good, given an unchanging demand. These economists believed that the value of a good depends on the pleasure or utility derived from it and thus varies directly with the strength of the demand and inversely with the supply of the good. Besides its theory of value, the school was noted for its theory of interest and capital. Böhm-Bawerk, the principal exponent of the theory, treated capital as a commodity and interest as the price paid for the use of capital. The rate of interest was determined by consumers' preferences for present over future goods, and by the possibility of increasing the productivity of a given process through an increase in its roundaboutness, or period of production. Later generations of the Austrian school, including Ludwig von Mises and Friedrich A. von Hayek, taught for many years in England and America and exerted great influence on their audiences. For additional details, see Joseph A. Schumpeter, *History of Economic Analysis*, Oxford University Press, New York, 1954; Mark Blaug, *Economic Theory in Retrospect*, Cambridge University Press, Cambridge, 1978; Eugen von Böhm-Bawerk, *The Positive Theory of Capital*, G.E. Stechert, New York, 1923.

autocorrelation A situation in regression analysis that exists when the historical actual data that constitute a *dependent* variable are not randomly distributed around the calculated regression line. In practice, in the case of the equation $\hat{Y} = a + bX$, it is not required that observations constituting the independent variable X be random. Neither is it required that successive values of the dependent variable Y be random. However, deviations of actual from computed values (Y minus $\hat{Y}$) should be random if the squared standard error of estimate $\overline{S}^2_{yx}$ and the coefficient of determination $\overline{R}^2_{yx}$ are to be unbiased. Autocorrelation, when detected, can be reduced or eliminated by converting the dependent variable to first differences. For additional information, see Karl A. Fox and Tej K. Kaul, *Intermediate Economic Statistics,* Krieger, Melbourne, Fla., 1980.

automatic stabilizer (built-in stabilizer) An economic shock absorber that helps smooth the swings of incomes and prices without constant changes in government policy. Personal and corporate income taxes and unemployment insurance are among the most important automatic stabilizers in the United States. When business begins to sag, the government's income tax receipts immediately decline by a larger proportion than personal income, and payments to the unemployed rise. Thus, consumer buying power is strengthened, and recessionary pressures are tempered. Social security and farm-aid programs also act as built-in stabilizers. In combination, these stabilizers have been credited with a key role in the prompt reversal of U.S. recessions since World War II. This point is discussed by M. O. Clement, "The Quantitative Impact of Automatic Stabilizers," *Review of Economics and Statistics,* February 1960; see also Thomas F. Dernburg and Duncan M. McDougall, *Macroeconomics,* 5th ed., McGraw-Hill, New York, 1976, chaps. 5 and 18.

automation The use of advanced mechanical equipment, especially in combination with high-speed computers and other self-regulating controls. The word, which is an abbreviation of "automatization," was first used by D. S. Harder in the General Motors Fisher Body Division in 1935, when he set up an automation engineering department and a manufacturing department in the Grand Rapids plant. Automation includes almost every operation that dispenses with human assistance or control, whether because of the newly developed control machinery or because of mechanical improvements on the assembly line. Although automation is credited with much of the increase in productivity that industrial nations throughout the world have experienced since World War II, its full economic impact is difficult to assess. On the one hand, its introduction has permitted significant cost reductions and made feasible tasks that would have been impractical without it. On the other hand, it has helped aggravate the problem of unemployment by reducing the need for labor, especially unskilled labor. For further discussion of the problems and potentials of automation, see John Diebold, *Automation: The Advent of the Automatic Factory,* Van Nostrand, New York, 1953; Herbert A. Simons, *The New Science of Management Decisions,* rev. ed., Prentice-Hall, Englewood Cliffs, N.J., 1977.

autonomous investment Investment that is determined independently of existing economic conditions, such as the level of national income or consumption. Induced investment, in contrast, depends on existing and anticipated economic conditions. The development of new products and new production techniques is a major force underlying autonomous investment. Investment induced by sociological, psychological, and political conditions also is considered autonomous. Thus, investment in western railroads in the United States in the nineteenth century was investment of the autonomous type. See D. Hamburg and Charles L. Schultze, "Autonomous Investment vs. Induced Investment," *Economic Journal,* Royal Economic Society, London, March 1961.

autonomous variable A variable in statistics and econometrics that is not wholly dependent on economic factors. Its movement cannot be predicted from a correlation with business activity. Usually, it is a variable the structure of which does not change freely in the short run. Investment expenditures are generally considered an autonomous variable.

autoregression The possibility that the error term in an econometric equation may be correlated with one or more lagged endogenous variables included in the equation. The lagged endogenous variables are, in effect, predetermined values, each standing in a regression relationship with one or more of the immediately preceding terms. Econometric equations involving lags of an endogenous variable are called autoregressive. The inclusion of such variables nullifies any assumption that the error inherent in the estimating equation is not correlated with any predetermined value. For additional information, see Lawrence R. Klein, *An Introduction to Econometrics,* Greenwood, Westport, Conn., 1977.

autoregressive transformation The procedure whereby the original variables in an autoregressive system where there is autocorrelation in the error term are restated in such form that the error term is uncorrelated. For example, the conversion of variables to first differences may have the desired result. For additional information, see Lawrence R. Klein, *An Introduction to Econometrics,* Greenwood, Westport, Conn., 1977.

B

backdoor financing A method of financing federal programs by bypassing usual congressional appropriations procedures. It eliminates review by appropriations committees. Known also as the public debt transaction, the device authorizes a government agency to borrow from the Treasury rather than depend on congressional appropriations. The justification for this method is that it merely involves a lending program; since the Treasury will be repaid, there is no need for outright appropriations. Theoretically, the borrowed sums must be repaid, but in the past Congress has canceled the larger part of a debt when an agency has been unable to repay it. Backdoor financing was first used in the depression of the 1930s, when the Reconstruction Finance Corporation (RFC) was established to revitalize business. To accelerate operations, Congress gave the RFC borrowing power and thus avoided the necessity for yearly appropriations. Originally, loans were to be repaid, but by the time the RFC closed its books in 1957, Congress had canceled $12.8 billion of the $26.6 billion that the RFC had borrowed from the Treasury. Since then the technique has spread rapidly.

backlog of unfilled orders An accumulation of orders received by manufacturers for products to be shipped at a later date. Manufacturers' backlogs depend on both the rate at which new orders are received and the rate at which they are shipped. To the business economist, short-run fluctuations in backlog volume are an important tool for forecasting short-term business trends. A rapidly growing backlog suggests a steadily rising production level; a declining backlog suggests cutbacks. The level of unfilled orders for major industries is reported in U.S. Department of Commerce, *Survey of Current Business*, monthly.

backwash effect An unfavorable condition arising in underdeveloped countries as a result of the emphasis placed on export trade (usually only raw materials) at the expense of the growth of domestic manufacturing and the industrialization of rural areas. Some economists claim that the backwash effect of trade has been stronger than the spread effect. By slowing down much-needed industrialization in underdeveloped countries, the backwash effect presents a major obstacle to development and results in increasing disparities in productivity between advanced and underdeveloped countries. For additional information, see Gunnar Myrdal, *An International Economy: Problems and Perspectives*, Greenwood, Westport, Conn., 1977.

bailout An attempt to use corporate funds to provide payments to shareholders which are taxable at favorable capital gains rates and do not adversely affect the shareholders' relative interest in the corporation. Among types of bailouts are additional stock dividends and debt financing.

balanced budget The equalization of revenues and expenditures over a period of time. Traditionally, the annually balanced budget has been the basis of sound government fiscal policy, since it serves as an important check to irresponsible action and promotes business confidence. Whereas political support for increased government spending and lower taxes is easy to secure, adherence to a balanced budget limits the use of these steps. Seen in this light, the balanced budget has come to mean any surplus of government revenues over expenditures. Although balancing the budget is the long-standing method of ensuring fiscal responsibility, according to many economists it runs counter to the goal of economic growth and stability. During a period of recession, tax revenues fall; taxes may be raised and/or expenditures reduced, or both may take place, to eliminate the resulting deficit. Such measures generally aggravate the recession, however, causing income and tax revenues to fall still further. Similarly, during a period of inflation, a balanced-budget program requires that rising tax revenues be offset by lowered taxes or by increased government expenditures, both of which steps accelerate inflation. For this reason, some economists argue that the conventional wisdom of the balanced budget is outmoded and that government deficits and surpluses ought to be used as part of a planned compensatory fiscal policy to stabilize the fluctuations of the business cycle. For additional information, see Walter Heller, *New Dimensions of Political Economy*, Harvard University Press, Cambridge, Mass., 1966; Herbert Stein, *The Fiscal Revolution in America*, University of Chicago Press, Chicago, 1969.

balanced growth A program of coordinated growth of all sectors of the economy. Usually, developing countries plan a balanced growth for their economies. Thus, in an underdeveloped nation, the success of a program of capital formation depends on complementary production. Goods produced by the new production facilities must be demanded by consumers, and the productive factors required for expanded manufacturing must be available. Balanced growth requires that investment take place in clusters. For example, a plan for the construction of a steel mill should include coal and iron ore mines, a transportation system, and a market for the finished output. The basic purpose of a program of balanced growth is to minimize the occurrence of bottlenecks and gluts in the various sectors of the economy. It usually requires some planning by the central government to ensure the undertaking of the necessary projects. For further information, see Benjamin Higgins, *Economic Development,* Norton, New York, 1968.

balance of payments   A systematic record of all the economic transactions between one country and the rest of the world in a given period, usually one year. Among the principal international economic transactions are the movement of goods, services, interest and dividends, gifts, and short- and long-term investments, currency shipments, and gold movements. Each transaction gives rise either to a foreign claim for payment, recorded as a debit (e.g., from imports, capital outflows), or a foreign obligation to pay, recorded as a credit (e.g., from exports, capital inflows). Each debit transaction in the balance of payments of one country is automatically accompanied by a credit entry in that of another. By totaling all debit and credit transactions between the residents (individuals, business firms, and government) of one country and the residents of all other countries, a statement of the international economic relationships of an individual country is provided. The balance of payments is generally divided into three accounts: current, capital, and gold. The current account includes the flow of goods and services and thus represents payments for and receipts from imports and exports, including interest and dividends. The capital account, which includes the transfer of short- and long-term investments, represents all additions to or subtractions from a stock of investment. The third major account is that of compensatory gold movements. In recent years, the U.S. balance-of-payments presentation has focused on two official definitions of the overall surplus or deficit—the balance on liquidity and the balance on official reserve transactions. In 1971, the presentation was altered to give emphasis to six balances: the balance on goods and services; the balance on goods, services, and remittances; the balance on current account; the balance on current account and long-term capital; the net liquidity balance; and the official reserve transactions balance. As an accounting method, the balance of payments must balance over a given period; because of its double entry nature, debits must always equal credits. If a country's receipts (credits) fall short of its payments (debits), it has a balance-of-payments deficit and must export gold to meet its obligations for the remaining payments. If, on the other hand, credits exceed debits, the country has a balance-of-payments surplus, and an inflow of gold will take place to bring the accounting statement into balance. For quarterly data on the U.S. balance of payments, see U.S. Department of Commerce, *Survey of Current Business,* March, June, September, and December issues; for a more comprehensive collection of balance-of-payment data for different regions and countries, see International Monetary Fund, *Balance of Payments Yearbook,* Washington, D.C.; see also Fritz Machlup, *International Payments, Debt and Gold,* Scribner, New York, 1964, part I.

balance of trade (merchandise balance)   The difference between the value of the goods that a nation exports and the value of the goods that it imports.

The balance of trade differs from the balance of payments in that it excludes capital transactions, payments for services, and shipments of gold. When a country has an export surplus, its balance is favorable; when it has a deficit, its balance is unfavorable. The balance-of-trade concept is losing much of its usefulness because of the growing volume of capital transactions and payments for services. For example, in every year during the 1950s and 1960s, the United States enjoyed a surplus in its balance of trade but suffered an almost uninterrupted succession of deficits in its balance of payments. Merchandise trade statistics for western countries are reported in Statistical Office of the United Nations, *Monthly Bulletin of Statistics,* New York; those for the United States are reported in great detail in *Department of Commerce Report FT110* (for imports) and *Department of Commerce Report FT410* (for exports).

balance sheet A statement of a firm's financial position on a particular day of the year; as of that moment, it provides a complete picture of what the firm owns (its assets), what it owes (its liabilities), and its net worth. The balance sheet should not be confused with the income statement, which is a record of a year's operations. Assets are customarily divided into two parts, current assets and fixed assets. Current assets include cash on hand, investment in government securities, accounts receivable (the amount owed to the company by its customers), inventories, and other short-term investments. Fixed assets include land, buildings, and equipment. Liabilities are divided into current obligations, which fall due within a year, and long-term debt. Current liabilities consist of accounts payable (what the company owes to its suppliers), short-term loans, interest, and accrued taxes. Long-term liabilities include such items as long-term bank loans, bonds, and mortgages. By subtracting total liabilities from total assets, a company's net worth or a stockholder's share in the business may be ascertained. Net worth is the value of all outstanding stock, usually listed at par value or the issue price, plus any surpluses. A balance sheet always balances in total, but no individual item necessarily matches another. See G. Shillinglaw, J. J. Gordon, and J. Ronen, *Accounting: A Management Approach,* Irwin, Homewood, Ill., 1979.

bank credit proxy A rough daily estimate of movements in commercial bank loans and investments. This is a measure of bank credit from the liability side. The proxy is composed of all deposits at member banks and is adjusted to include nondeposit liabilities such as bank-related commercial paper, loan participations and sales, and Eurodollar deposits. The bank credit proxy was developed to assist the Federal Reserve operate monetary policy. Some economists view bank credit as having a more direct effect on spending than money or money-related variables. Since credit can be identified with outlays by particular economic sectors, the use of the bank credit proxy allows analysis of the quality and distribution of credit.

bank debits The total dollar value of checks which depositors write on their bank accounts during a certain period. Because the ratio of bank debits to demand deposits measures the use of deposit money, it is an important indicator of business activity. The figures on the volume of bank debits and demand deposits are compiled by the Federal Reserve System from reports by approximately 1,600 banks in 232 centers in the United States (New York City, where bank debits are heavily weighted by securities transactions, is not included). Excluded from this statistical series are debits to U.S. government accounts and interbank transactions, which are not directly related to business activity. For statistics on ratios of debits to demand deposits, see *Federal Reserve Bulletin,* Washington, D.C., monthly.

bank deposit   The money in an account of a depositor (either an individual or a firm) in a bank. A bank deposit arises when (1) an individual or a firm puts cash in a bank, (2) some other asset is sold to a bank, or (3) a bank lends money to an individual. It is a bookkeeping item, constituting an asset for an individual and a liability for a bank. There are two types of bank deposits: demand deposits (money payable on demand) and time deposits (money payable after a fixed period of time). See John J. Klein, *Money and the Economy,* Harcourt Brace, New York, 1978; for statistics on the amounts and kinds of bank deposits, see *Federal Reserve Bulletin,* Washington, D.C., monthly.

banking school   The name given to a group of nineteenth-century economists who argued that a mixed currency (bank notes and demand deposits) would expand and contract with the needs of business. Whereas the currency school held that only gold and redeemable notes were money, the banking school, led by Thomas Tooke and J. Fullarton, stressed the variety of sources of credit and emphasized the aspect of demand deposits as part of the money supply. Adherents of the banking school considered it more important to control the lending policies of the central bank, and so influence the quantity of demand deposits, than to try to limit the quantity of currency in circulation. They also adhered to the real-bills doctrine, which held that if banks limited their loans to self-liquidating commercial paper (real bills), the money supply would adjust itself so as to be exactly adequate for business needs. If the banks ignored the policy of real bills only, the resulting rise in prices would lead to a *pari passu* increase in the money supply, so that there was no possibility of an inflation produced by the overexpansion of bank credit. For additional details on the controversy between the currency and banking schools, see Jacob Viner, *Studies in the Theory of International Trade,* Harper & Row, New York, 1937; see also Thomas Humphrey, "The Quantity Theory of Money: Its Historical Evolution and Role in Policy Debates," *Economic Review,* no. 60, Federal Reserve Bank of Richmond, Richmond, Va., May–June 1974, pp. 1–19.

banking system   The establishment of a group of financial institutions which foster a flow of credit and money that will facilitate orderly economic growth. Early banking systems served mainly as depositories for funds, while the more modern systems have considered the supplying of credit their main purpose. A system of banks now serves three main functions: (1) It lends money, (2) it accepts money on deposit, and (3) it creates and lends its own credit. The National Banking Act, passed on February 25, 1863, and amended many times thereafter, has served as the basis for the national banks of the United States. Because of the defects and inefficiencies of the decentralized nation-state system, the act was further amended on December 23, 1913, when President Woodrow Wilson signed the Federal Reserve Act, establishing the Federal Reserve System and requiring all national banks to become members of it. For information on the Federal Reserve System, see *The Federal Reserve System: Purposes and Functions,* Board of Governors of the Federal Reserve System, Washington, D.C., 1964; see also John J. Klein, *Money and the Economy,* Harcourt Brace, New York, 1978.

bankruptcy A condition, legally declared by a court of law, of insolvency of individuals, partnerships, or corporations. Its purpose is to discharge the debtor from all debts and to protect the debtor's creditors by providing an orderly procedure for liquidation. The bankrupt debtor relinquishes all property to a court-appointed receiver, who then transfers the assets to an elected trustee for disposal for creditors' benefits. Bankruptcy proceedings are of two types: (1) voluntary, in which the debtor submits to a federal district court a petition requesting to be declared bankrupt; and (2) involuntary, in which the creditors take the initiative and submit the petition to the court requesting that the debtor be declared bankrupt. Under the bankruptcy law, an individual, a partnership, or a corporation (except railroads, municipalities, and financial corporations) may be voluntary bankrupts. Any person (except farmers and wage earners) and any corporation (except railroads, municipalities, and financial corporations) can be declared an involuntary bankrupt.

bargaining agent A union chosen by the employees of an appropriate bargaining unit to act as their representative and certified as such by the National Labor Relations Board. Controversies have arisen over the selection of a craft or an industrial union as the bargaining agent. Prior to the early 1940s, the board had shown a preference for industrial unions over craft unions, but subsequently it has permitted skilled crafts to vote separately whenever they have wished to do so. This policy has not, however, been applied to steel, aluminum, and other mass-output industries, where the board has maintained that production is so highly integrated that separation of crafts is not practical. For a general discussion of bargaining agents, see Lloyd G. Reynolds, *Labor Economics and Labor Relations,* 7th ed., Prentice-Hall, Englewood Cliffs, N.J., 1978.

bargaining theory of wages A theory which holds that wages are determined by the relative bargaining strength of employers and employees. When workers join unions, wages rise because the relative strength of the labor rises. On the other hand, as the size of business enterprises grows, wages are pushed below the level which they would otherwise attain because the strength of employers rises. In general, the bargaining theory attempts to explain how wages are determined in the short run and not how they are determined over long periods of time. For a classic statement of the theory, see John R. Commons, *History of Labor in the United States,* Macmillan, New York, 1951.

barriers to entry   Obstacles that prevent or deter a potential new business from entering the industry. Industries perform best (resulting in the lowest prices, greatest amount produced, and maximum productivity) when there is a high degree of competition in the industry; entry, or threat of entry, into a business by new firms can enhance competition. However, a potential entrant into a business may encounter a number of obstacles: There may be high capital requirements, the minimum size for efficiency may be very large, or existing firms may undertake actions to prevent new firms from entering the industry, to name a few. Thus, a barrier to entry results from an asymmetry between economic environmental pressures on a potential entrant into an industry and the established firms in that industry, giving the established firms a competitive advantage. See F. M. Scherer, *Industrial Market Structure and Economic Performance,* Rand-McNally, Chicago, 1970; Robert H. Bork, *The Antitrust Paradox,* Basic Books, New York, 1978; E. W. Eckard, "Antitrust Policy and the Market Concentration Doctrine: A Static View of a Dynamic Economy," *Business Economics,* vol. 15, no. 1, January 1980, pp. 31–34.

barter   A system of exchange in which goods and services are traded without the use of money as a medium of exchange. Bartering predates the use of money and international trade. As market economies developed in both domestic and international settings, the direct exchange of goods and services without the use of a financial medium became extremely cumbersome, and was used only minimally in industrial countries. In recent years, a revival of bartering has begun. One reason for this has been the desire to reduce inflationary pressures that develop as goods and services in the general marketplace go through several stages of manufacture and distribution on their way to their ultimate consumer. If an individual who wants to acquire a certain commodity or service can find another person willing to offer that good or service directly in exchange for another good or service which the first individual can provide, then the direct exchange of such commodities or services will yield many cost savings. In addition to providing savings due to reduction or elimination of channels of distribution, barter operations also provide individuals with a means of avoiding or bypassing various taxes and other costs of doing business in the general marketplace. The increased interest in bartering has led to the establishment of a substantial number of firms that facilitate the matching of buyers and sellers of various goods and services.

basic research   Original scientific investigation undertaken for the advancement of knowledge rather than immediate financial return. Basic research differs from applied research, which usually has specific profit-making objectives, in terms of economic progress. In methods and procedures, however, it is often difficult to distinguish between the two. Statistics on basic research expenditures are published in National Science Foundation, *Reviews of Data on Research and Development,* Washington, D.C., periodically.

basing-point system   A pricing system in which the seller sets a price by adding to a list price transportation costs between a fixed base, which is not necessarily the seller's plant, and the buyer's plant. An extreme illustration of this practice is the Pittsburgh-plus system formerly used by steel producers. Under this system, the price of steel was set by taking the Pittsburgh price and adding the cost of freight from Pittsburgh to the market regardless of the location of the shipping plant. If, for example, the price of a ton of steel in Pittsburgh was $100 and the freight to a Chicago customer was $20, the delivered price in Chicago was $120 no matter whether the steel came from a Chicago mill or a Pittsburgh mill. The basing-point system was most effective in industries in which transportation costs were high in relation to price. The arguments against the system are that it eliminates price competition, introduces geographical price discrimination, and results in wasteful crosshauling and uneconomic location of plants. Some economists disagree, suggesting that the practice is only one element in a complex economic system. For further information, see Fritz Machlup, *The Basing-Point System: An Economic Analysis of a Controversial Pricing Practice,* McGraw-Hill, New York, 1949.

basis point   A unit of measure used to express interest rates and bond yields. One basis point is equal to one-hundredth of a percent. Small-point differences in percentage rates of return are extremely significant in the bond markets because huge sums of money are involved. A 10% rate on a $100-million bond issue means that the borrower must pay $10 million a year in interest charges. An increase of only 15 basis points to 10.15% brings the interest cost to $10.15 million, an increase of $150,000. That is why yields are generally expressed in graduations of one-hundredth of a point.

Bayesian statistics   The translation of subjective forecasts into mathematical probability curves. Traditionally, statisticians use probabilities based on exhaustive empirical research. For example, if a coin were flipped an infinite number of times, the proportion of heads should be 0.5. In many business situations, however, there are no probabilities available because the process in question has not been in operation. Instead of a firmly tested probability, then, Bayesian statistics uses the best estimate of the given circumstances as if it were a firm probability. Named for Thomas Bayes, an eighteenth-century English clergyman who invented the first formula for using subjective probabilities, Bayesian statistics has become an important decision tool for modern business. For further information, see Arnold Zellner, *An Introduction to Bayesian Inference in Econometrics*, Wiley, New York, 1971.

bear   A person who believes that the prices of stocks, bonds, commodities, or foreign exchange are going to decline and generally acts on this belief by selling short and hoping to buy back (cover) at a lower price. The term dates back to the early eighteenth century, when dealers on the London Stock Exchange were called bears if they thought the trend of stock and bond prices was down and bulls if they thought it was up. Why the more pessimistic dealers were called bears is difficult to say, but there are two plausible stories. First, the old proverb "to sell a bear's skin before one has caught the bear" describes what bears on the stock exchange are doing, because short sellers do not own the stock they are selling—they have borrowed it. Second, "bear" may be a perversion of "bare," so that "bear" sellers are "bare" of the securities they have sold.

bear market   A market in which the prices of most of the items traded are declining. The term generally refers to falling stock, bond, or commodity markets. No precise origin of the term is known, but it is likely that someone coined it to refer to the London Stock Exchange when the "bears" (dealers who thought that prices were going to fall and sold stocks or bonds short) were dominant.

beggar-my-neighbor tactics   Methods of increasing the exports of one country at the expense of those of other countries. Such actions as unnecessary currency depreciation or unprovoked tariff increases, especially in times of domestic unemployment, are generally considered beggar-my-neighbor tactics. It is argued that such tariff increases or currency depreciations increase domestic income and employment by causing a rise in the demand for domestic products since imports are reduced. However valid such an argument may be theoretically, in the real world beggar-my-neighbor policies induce swift retaliation by foreign countries who see their markets shrinking. Thus, beggar-my-neighbor tactics rarely produce much good and often result in competitive tariff increases or currency depreciation, causing a decrease in total world trade. For additional details, see Joan Robinson, "Beggar-My-Neighbor Remedies for Unemployment," in American Economic Association, *Readings in the Theory of International Trade*, Irwin, Homewood, Ill., 1950.

behavioral economics   The study of the economic behavior of people, and of groups of people, by means of the scientific method of controlled observation or experimentation. Behavioral economics analyzes such psychological antecedents of economic activities as the motives, attitudes, and expectations that influence decisions in economic matters. Its starting point consists of empirical investigations of the behavior of businesspeople and consumers. Generalizations about behavior emerge gradually by comparing behavior observed under different circumstances. Next, it focuses on the study of the decision-making process in spending, saving, and investing. Finally, the study of the human factor plays an important role in behavioral economics. Thus, behavioral economics differs greatly from classical economics, which deduces principles of economic behavior from features of human nature assumed to have identifiable values at all times. Consumer behavior has been the most common subject of behavioral studies, which make use of case studies and of laboratory as well as field experiments. The measurement of expectations through questioning representative samples has been undertaken for several decades and has been used extensively for the purpose of forecasting major expenditures and the course of the entire economy. See George Katona, *Psychological Economics*, Elsevier, New York, 1975.

behavior equations   These are based largely on what economic theory indicates that an individual or group of individuals acting as agents will do when faced with an economic decision. Theory suggests first which variables should be included in the analysis (that is, the conditions surrounding the decision) and second, given the conditions, the direction that the decision will take. Behavior equations may be contrasted with institutional equations where the pattern of action is prescribed by law, rule, or custom. For additional information, see T. C. Koopmans (ed.), *Statistical Inference in Dynamic Economic Models*, Cowles Commission Monograph no. 10, Wiley, New York, 1950.

benefits of large-scale production   Economies in the productive process made possible because of the large scale on which the firm operates. For example, small firms must buy in less-than-carload lots, while larger firms may buy in carload lots or possibly in trainload lots, both of which lessen the transportation costs of purchased factors of production. In addition, technological methods which may be impractical at low levels of production become economically beneficial at higher levels. Small amounts of by-products may not be economically salable, but large and continuous quantities may find a ready market. Large purchasers of labor and other productive factors may find themselves in a position to dominate the economic lives of their suppliers and thus bargain for prices which smaller purchasers could not obtain. One of the most familiar advantages of large size is the ability to issue unsecured promissory notes to the public (known as commercial paper), on which the interest cost is considerably less than it is on commercial bank loans. None of these pecuniary benefits are to be confused with returns to scale in production, which involves the firm's production function. See William G. Shepherd, *The Economics of Industrial Organization*, Prentice-Hall, Englewood Cliffs, N.J., 1979, chaps. 11 and 12.

benefit theory of taxation   The principle that tax payments should be based on the amount of benefits received from government services. Thus, the cost of government services should be apportioned among individuals according to the relative benefits that they enjoy. Although the benefit theory may be applicable to certain fields in which the government functions as a commercial enterprise (e.g., the postal system, public power projects, etc.), it is generally very difficult to allocate the costs or benefits of the majority of government services among citizens with any degree of accuracy. Most services of modern governments are provided in the interest of group rather than individual welfare; thus, the cost of these activities cannot be divided and assigned logically to the recipients of the benefits. For example, there is no fair way of dividing the cost or benefit derived from the operation of a police force or from the workings of the judicial system. The benefit theory would also restrict the performance of certain socially desirable government services, such as relief to the needy and free public education, since the primary beneficiaries cannot afford the full cost of these programs. Application of the benefit theory of taxation is not widespread today, but it is used in such taxes as highway tolls, gas taxation, fishing and hunting licenses, and property taxation. For further information, see John F. Due and Ann F. Friedlaender, *Government Finance*, 6th ed., Irwin, Homewood, Ill., 1977.

beta coefficient   A method of measuring risk, relating the volatility of a stock or a portfolio to the market as a whole. A beta coefficient should anticipate what will happen to a stock or portfolio of stocks given a fluctuation in the whole market. A high-risk stock thus has a high beta, a low-risk one a low beta. If it is more volatile than the market, its beta is above 1; if it is relatively stable, its beta is below 1; and if a stock moves exactly as the market moves, its beta is 1. According to beta theory, there are two possible methods of obtaining above-average portfolio performance. The first is to forecast the market as a whole more accurately and adjust the portfolio's beta accordingly. The second method of obtaining superior performance is to achieve a positive alpha, or excess return. The reason why one stock has a higher or lower rate of return than another stock with the same beta is because of the alpha factor, which measures the various residual nonmarket influences unique to each stock. For additional information, see Marshall E. Blume, "On the Assessment of Risk," *Journal of Finance*, vol. 26, no. 1 March 1971, pp. 1–10; Marshall E. Blume and Irwin Friend, "A New Look at the Capital Asset Pricing Model," *Journal of Finance*, March 1973; Michael C. Jensen (ed.), *Studies in the Theory of Capital Markets*, Praeger, New York, 1972.

bias   In forecasting, the situation that exists when a set of forecasts typically understates or overstates the corresponding actual values. A strong pessimistic bias would be demonstrated by forecasts that consistently underestimated the actual level or changes for a series. A strong optimistic bias would be illustrated by forecasts that consistently overshot the actual level or changes for a series. A simple measure of bias is the mean error. A measure of the overall accuracy of forecasts, which can be used to separate the bias from the remaining error, is the mean square error. For additional information, see Victor Zarnowitz, *An Appraisal of Short-Term Economic Forecasts*, National Bureau of Economic Research, Occasional Paper 104, Columbia University Press, New York, 1967.

bilateral negotiations and agreements Transactions and agreements between two parties. The term is generally used to refer to trade agreements between two countries. There are bilateral clearing agreements, bilateral payments agreements, and bilateral trade agreements. Bilateral trade and payments agreements are substitutes for more efficient and economical multilateral trade. Except for limited advantages in periods of disturbance, bilateral agreements are usually harmful to world trade and to the countries participating in them. When trade between any two countries is conducted through bilateral agreements, it tends to be reduced to a level at which the value of goods moving in one direction exactly equals the value of goods moving in the other direction. As a result, less effective use is made of the world's resources, since there are fewer opportunities to take advantage of international specialization. Moreover, trade is diverted from its normal channels into channels that are determined by the control system and not by market forces. Many countries lacking foreign exchange seek bilateral agreements to overcome this shortage. Once bilateral trade begins, it has a tendency to spread. Thus, nations placed at a disadvantage because of exchange controls adopt controls themselves as a means of striking back at other countries. For additional information, see C. P. Kindleberger and P. H. Lindert, *International Economics*, Irwin, Homewood, Ill., 1978.

bills-only policy The policy of confining Federal Reserve open-market operations to short-term securities, especially ninety-one-day Treasury bills. The Federal Open Market Committee felt that limitation of its transactions to Treasury bills would have less of a disrupting influence on the money market, since the market for short-term securities is more fluid than other markets. It believed that the policy of bills only would increase the "depth, breadth, and resiliency" of the government bond market, whereas intervention in all maturity sections of government securities might destroy the private market in these securities, leaving a market in which the Federal Reserve alone would establish prices and yields. It has been argued, however, that the actual operation of the policy has not had the desired effects on the government bond market. Furthermore, critics assert that the interest structure of government securities is an important tool of monetary policy and should be influenced more effectively by the Federal Reserve. In reply, the Federal Open Market Committee has stated that it is the central bank's business to control only bank reserves and the money supply, leaving the determination of interest rates to the free market; the bills-only policy has enabled it to do that.

In 1960 the committee relaxed its bills-only stand to a policy of bills preferably, opening the way for possible Federal Reserve transactions in longer-
term government securities. For additional details, see Ralph Young and
Charles Yager, "The Economics of Bills Preferably," *Quarterly Journal of
Economics,* Cambridge, Mass., August 1960, p. 341; Lawrence S. Ritter and
William L. Silber, *Principles of Money, Banking and Financial Markets,* 3d rev.
ed., Basic Books, New York, 1980.

bills-preferably policy   *See* bills-only policy.

block trading   A securities transaction of 10,000 shares or more. A block
trade is usually initiated by an institution that wishes to purchase or sell a
large quantity of stock and will accept a discount from the current market
price in order to sell or pay a premium in order to buy. There are usually
fewer participants on the side that initiates the trade (active side) than on the
other side (passive side). Thus, the key to assembling a block trade is to find
the orders on the passive side. Theoretically, a block trade cannot be executed
in the exchange auction market in the normal course of events. However,
studies have shown that about 65% of the total volume in transactions of
10,000 or more shares of common stock listed on the New York Stock
Exchange is executed on that exchange. Block trading became an important
market factor on the New York Stock Exchange only in the late 1960s. For
additional information, see Alan Kraus and Hans Stoll, "Price Impacts of
Block Trading on the New York Stock Exchange," *Journal of Finance,* June
1972; Richard R. West and Seha M. Tinic, *The Economics of the Stock Market,*
Praeger, New York, 1971.

bond   A written promise to pay a specified sum of money (principal) at a
certain date in the future or periodically over the course of a loan, during
which time interest is paid at a fixed rate on specified dates. Bonds are issued
by corporations, states, localities (municipal bonds), foreign governments,
and the U.S. government, usually for long terms (more than ten years). The
quality of bonds of U.S. and foreign governments rests on the ability of these
entities to tax citizens to gain revenue. State and local government bonds,
which are exempt from federal income taxes, can be classified as general or
limited-obligation bonds. The former rest on the "full faith and credit" of
the issuer, that is, the taxing ability; the latter depend on the revenue gained
from a specific asset, such as a bridge or a tunnel, for payment of interest
and principal. Corporate bonds may be unsecured (debenture) or secured by
the assets of the corporation. In the latter case, the corporation usually exe-
cutes a mortgage to a trustee who represents the rights of the bondholders.
In all cases, the safety of a corporate bond depends on the earning power of
the corporation. For further information, see Jules I. Bogen (ed.), *Financial
Handbook,* 4th ed., Ronald, New York, 1968; J. Fred Weston and Eugene F.

Brigham, *Essentials of Managerial Finance,* 5th ed., Holt, Rinehart and Winston, New York, 1979.

bond yield The rate of return on an investment in bonds. The yield of a bond is one of the principal determinants of its attractiveness. Concepts of yield used to judge bonds include yield to maturity and nominal current yield. Yield to maturity, the most common measure of yield on good bonds, is the percentage which the combined annual gain bears to the average investment. It is used when the purchase price of a bond differs from its maturity value, and the computation of yield must therefore take into account any changes in the size of the principal at maturity. To compute the net yield at maturity, the amortization of the increase or decrease in the average annual investment must be added to the basic interest rate. Generally, longer-term bonds have a higher yield, and the more speculative the bond, the higher its rate of return. The nominal yield, or the coupon rate, is the ratio of interest to principal, as expressed on the face of the bond. The current yield generally used in describing speculative bonds whose repayment at maturity is doubtful expresses the annual interest payment as a percentage of the actual purchase price of the bond (not its face value). For additional details, see Burton Malkiel, *The Term Structure of Interest Rates,* Princeton University Press, Princeton, N.J., 1966; Marcia Stigum, *Money Market Calculations, Yields, Swaps, and Breakeven Prices,* Dow Jones–Irwin, Homewood, Ill., 1982.

book value The value of a corporation according to its accounting records. It is computed by subtracting all debts from assets; the remainder represents total book value. Total book value is also referred to as net assets. If a corporation has assets of $300,000 and debts of $100,000, its total book value is $200,000. In reports of corporations, the book value is usually represented on a per-share basis. This is done by dividing the total book value by the number of shares. In the example given above, if the corporation had 10,000 shares outstanding, its book value would be $20 per share. The book value differs from the par value of the shares and also from the market value. For information concerning the relation of book value to security analysis, see Lyman Keith, *Accounting: A Managerial Perspective,* Prentice-Hall, Englewood Cliffs, N.J., 1980.

boom A rapid expansion in business activity to new high marks, resulting in low unemployment, high profits, and high stock and commodity prices. Since booms cannot be sustained for long periods of time, busts may follow them. The U.S. economy has experienced few booms and no busts since World War II.

boom year A year in which the physical volume of goods and services and industrial production rises sharply (more than 4.5%), when consumer money income after taxes increases more than 10% per year, and when unemployment drops below 5.5% of the labor force. In a boom year, there are very large purchases of consumer durable goods and capital goods. The criteria given above are now generally used by many business economists in describing a boom business year.

Box-Jenkins forecasting method   A statistical method for forecasting a time series based on its own past history. This is an alternative to regression analysis, where the forecast is based on other independent variables. The Box-Jenkins approach, also called ARIMA (autoregressive integrated moving average) considers the time series as a group of random variables obeying an underlying probability distribution. By analyzing the relations among the variables, the method aims to estimate the distribution and forecast the series. For additional information, see Robert S. Pinclyck and Daniel Rubinfeld, *Econometric Models and Economic Forecasts,* 2d ed., McGraw-Hill, New York, 1981; G. Box and G. Jenkins, *Time Series Analysis: Forecasting and Control,* Holden-Day, San Francisco, 1976.

boycott   An organized effort to refrain from conducting business with a particular seller of goods or services. The purpose generally is to force, or encourage, the firm or business being boycotted to accede to demands made by the boycotting group. Such demands might include lower prices, higher quality, better working conditions, etc. The limited boycott of beef consumption as prices skyrocketed in the 1970s resulted in a sharp reduction in demand, and a resultant, although temporary, decline in prices. In recent years, television viewers have boycotted, or threatened to boycott, products sold by companies who sponsor certain television programs containing excessive sex and/or violence. These efforts have persuaded some companies to withdraw their sponsorship from such programs, or moved the companies to insist on reduced levels of such objectionable material in programs they sponsor. Unions striking various companies and industries have encouraged boycotts of those firms' products by the general public, in order to exert pressure on their employers to yield to the unions' demands.

branch banking   The operation of one or more suboffices by a single bank. Unlike many other countries, such as Great Britain and Canada, in which a few large banks with hundreds of branches dominate the financial scene, the United States has traditionally relied on independent banking units. Nevertheless, branch banking has expanded in the United States. The number and location of branches are regulated by state laws; sixteen states severely limit branches, and fifteen prohibit them altogether. The advocates of branch banking claim that it offers great credit mobility (funds can flow from one branch to another) and permits individual banks to grow large enough to serve large corporations. Those opposed to branch banking believe that it leads to a dangerous concentration of economic power. For branch banking data, see *Federal Reserve Bulletin,* Washington, D.C., usually the April issue.

breakeven point The specific volume of sales with which a firm neither makes nor loses money. Above this point, a firm begins to show a profit; below it, a loss. Breakeven point analysis is used to compute the approximate profit or loss that will be experienced at various levels of production. In carrying out this analysis, each expense item is classified as either fixed (constant at any reasonable level of output) or variable (increasing as output increases and decreasing as output declines). (See accompanying chart.) For a more comprehensive analysis of breakeven point examples, see Clifford Harris, *The Breakeven Handbook: Techniques for Profit Planning and Control*, Prentice-Hall, Englewood Cliffs, N.J., 1978.

Breakeven Point Analysis

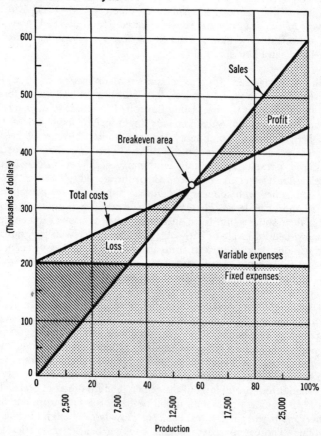

Bretton Woods Conference A conference held between July 1 and July 20, 1944, at Bretton Woods, New Hampshire, at which forty-five nations agreed to a comprehensive arrangement that would govern the world trade and payments system for 27½ years. Even though discussions at Bretton Woods touched on sensitive national and regional issues, no insurmountable obstacles emerged. Concerns about accumulated war debts and volatile export earnings of nations producing raw materials were set aside. The participating nations agreed upon an international payments system to be administered by a newly created International Monetary Fund (IMF) and a supporting institution, the International Bank for Reconstruction and Development (IBRD). The IMF was responsible for supporting fixed exchange rates and the IBRD was intended to have a limited role of primarily guaranteeing private short- and long-term loans. For the first time in history, a world agreement was written which explicitly stipulated the rules of an international monetary system, as well as the means to execute and maintain its principles. In order to meet the requirements for a global economic resurgence, nations relinquished some degree of economic sovereignty. The Bretton Woods Conference facilitated the eventual expansion of world trade and income. However, the uneven growth of world economies, divergent monetary and fiscal policies, and international liquidity constraints caused the demise of the Bretton Woods system in 1973. See Armand Van Dormeel, *Bretton Woods: Birth of a Monetary System*, Holmes and Meier, New York, 1978; Leland B. Yeager, *International Monetary Relations: Theory, History and Policy*, 2d ed., Harper & Row, New York, 1976.

budget A schedule of all the revenues and expenditures that an individual, group, government, or organization expects to receive and plans to spend during some future time period, usually the following year. Budgets range from very simple and casual ones, like the typical family budget, to extremely complex and sophisticated ones, like the federal government's annual 14-pound endeavor. All contain estimates of anticipated revenues from sales, taxes, gifts, and so on, and they specify what expenditures are planned during the time period. If revenues exceed expenditures, a budget surplus is expected. If, on the other hand, expenses are expected to be greater than revenues, a budget deficit must be confronted, and some method of financing it must be planned. A budget usually is used to control the allocation of revenues so that spending is rational. For additional information, see J. K. Lasser, Tax Institute, *J. K. Lasser's Managing Your Family Finances*, Doubleday, Garden City, N.Y., 1968; J. Fred Weston and Eugene F. Brigham, *Essentials of Managerial Finance*, 5th ed., Holt Rinehart and Winston, New York, 1978.

budget deficit An excess of expenditures over revenues. Although no individual or business firm can incur deficits over an indefinite period, some economists believe that the federal government is in a different category and that budget deficits year after year are acceptable and sometimes recommendable. They point out that a balanced budget is unstabilizing in recessions, aggravating the effects of a drop in national income, and suggest instead a deliberate unbalancing of the budget to create a deficit. This will increase total spending, which, in turn, will increase national income. Because of the operation of the national income multiplier, the increase in income will be larger than the deficit. The budget deficit can be achieved by lowering taxes, raising government expenditures, or adopting both measures. Although an increase in government spending may be more effective in raising national income, since it has a higher income multiplier, a tax cut may be preferable, since it can be made effective more quickly. Government budget deficits are generally financed by borrowing through the sale of bonds. The sale of such bonds to Federal Reserve banks and private commercial banks tends to maximize the expansionary effects of the deficit, while the sale of bonds to individuals and nonfinancial business firms has less of an expansionary (and, possibly, an inflationary) effect. For one view, see Herbert Stein, *The Fiscal Revolution in America,* University of Chicago Press, Chicago, 1969.

budget surplus   An excess of revenues over expenditures. The use of the government budget surplus is an important part of countercyclical fiscal policy. During periods of inflation, it is desirable to reduce total spending in the economy, diminishing the excess demand which is forcing up prices. At such times, the government budget can be adjusted to produce a surplus and achieve the desired lowering of income. This may be accomplished by lowering government expenditures, raising taxes, or adopting both measures. The reduction of government expenditures is more effective than a tax increase as an anti-inflationary measure, since its negative income multiplier is greater, but it is generally harder to put into effect, especially when the budget consists of many large items. For the budget surplus to be effective, the surplus money must not find its way back into the spending stream. The surplus funds may be used to retire part of the outstanding federal debt or to build up the balance of the Treasury account. If debt retirement is undertaken, the purchase of government bonds held by banks has a greater anti-inflationary effect than the refunding of bonds held by private citizens and nonfinancial business firms. For further information, see Herbert Stein, *The Fiscal Revolution in America,* University of Chicago Press, Chicago, 1969.

building cycle   An alternate expansion and contraction of fairly long duration in building construction activity. It may be caused by a sharp increase in population, speculation, or the lifting of building restrictions which had been imposed in wartime. In each of these cases, a relatively sudden increase in the demand for new buildings leads to construction of boom proportions that gradually declines as building needs are filled. Some authorities have estimated the duration of building cycles in the United States at about eighteen years, but others deny the existence of a regular pattern of fluctuations in construction activity. For a fuller treatment of building cycles in theory and fact, see Clarence D. Long, Jr., *Building Cycles and the Theory of Investment,* Princeton University Press, Princeton, N.J., 1940; for a discussion of the causes and consequences of fluctuations in building activity and a critique of Long's findings, see Miles L. Colean and Robinson Newcomb, *Stabilizing Construction: The Record and Potential*, McGraw-Hill, New York, 1952.

built-in stabilizer   *See* automatic stabilizer.

bull   A person who believes that the prices of stocks, bonds, commodities, or foreign exchange are going to rise and generally acts on this belief by buying and hoping to sell at a higher price. The term dates back to the early eighteenth century, when dealers on the London Stock Exchange were called bulls if they thought the trend of stock and bond prices was up and bears if they thought it was down. Why the more optimistic dealers were called bulls is difficult to say, but one story is that the way in which a bull tosses things up with its horns describes the action of the bull on the exchange.

bull market   A market in which the prices of most of the items traded are increasing. The term usually refers to rising stock, bond, or commodity markets. No precise origin of the term is known, but it is likely that someone coined it to refer to the London Stock Exchange at times when the "bulls" (those dealers who thought the prices were going to rise and bought stocks or bonds) were dominant.

business   Any organization whose major purpose for existence is to earn a profit for its owners, including corporations, partnerships, and proprietorships that provide goods and/or services to their customers. Because earning a profit—an excess of revenues over expenses—is considered to be a primary goal of a business firm, businesses are often characterized by attempts to increase the productivity—or the amount of output for each unit of input—of the various resources used in producing the goods or services sold by the firm. Increasing productivity helps reduce the overall cost of producing a unit of output, and thus increases the firm's profit margin—or the return on revenues. In recent years, other concerns of business, aside from increasing profits, have been thrust upon firms by external forces. These new considerations have included such areas as the relationship of business to its local community and to society generally; the costs to society of industrial air, water, and solid waste pollution; the desire of a firm's employees for a more satisfying work experience (which has influenced the development of firms' human resources); corporate responsibilities to contribute to social goals, such as the arts; corporate concerns for health, such as drug and alcohol rehabilitation programs; and the responsibility of business for job retraining.

business barometer   A weighted average of a variety of economic indicators, such as steel production, coal production, oil production, electric power generation, and carloadings, that measures the level of general business activity. A business barometer provides relatively current information on business activity which can be directly related by executives to their own operations.

There are weekly, monthly, and quarterly business barometers. The *Business Week* index is an example of a weekly business barometer widely used by the business community.

business cycles An alternate expansion and contraction in overall business activity, evidenced by fluctuations in measures of aggregate economic activity, such as the gross national product, the index of industrial production, and employment and income. A business cycle may be divided into four phases: expansion, during which business activity is successively reaching new high points; leveling out, during which business activity reaches a high point and remains at that level for a short period of time; contraction, during which business volume recedes from the peak level for a sustained period until the bottom is reached; and recovery, during which business activity resumes after the low point has been reached and continues to rise to the previous high mark. Unlike many cycles observed in nature, business cycles are not uniform in frequency, amplitude, or duration. Joseph A. Schumpeter classified business cycles into three categories on the basis of their duration: Kondratieff cycles, or long waves, lasting from fifty-four to sixty years; Juglar cycles, having a duration of nine to ten years; and Kitchin cycles, spanning a forty-month interval. The National Bureau of Economic Research, which has carried out extensive investigations of the empirical evidence of business cycles, counts thirty distinct business cycles in the United States during the period 1854–1980, measured from trough to trough; their average duration is fifty-one months. (See accompanying table.) Many theories have been advanced to explain business cycles. Some economists blame inadequate levels of investment or consumption. Schumpeter saw a principal cause in the disruptions created by such major innovations as railroads. Wesley C. Mitchell's analysis centered around the prices, costs, and profits theory. He also took the position that fluctuations are due to the very nature of the free-enterprise business system but that no single explanation of their causes is adequate. Other economists have felt that fluctuations in the stock of money cause business fluctuations. In attempting to postulate theories of the business cycle, economists have not as yet been able fully to explain the variety of factors that underlie business fluctuations, but most of them have made valuable contributions to the understanding of the cycles that business undergoes. Among the many works on business cycles are Geoffrey H. Moore, *Business Cycles, Inflation and Forecasting,* Ballinger, Cambridge, Mass., 1980; Wesley C. Mitchell, *Business Cycles and Their Causes,* University of California Press, Berkeley, 1959; Joseph A. Schumpeter, *Business Cycles,* 2 vols., McGraw-Hill, New York, 1939. An excellent general text is Thomas F. Dernberg and Duncan M. McDougall, *Macroeconomics,* 5th ed., McGraw-Hill, New York, 1976.

business failures The cessation of operations by a business concern because of involvement in court procedures or voluntary actions which will

Business-Cycle Expansions and Contractions in the United States: 1834–1981

Dates of peaks and troughs						Duration in months			
By months		By quarters		By calendar year		Con-traction (peak to trough)	Expan-sion (trough to peak)	Cycle	
Trough	Peak	Trough	Peak	Trough	Peak			Trough to trough	Peak to peak
				1834	1836		24*		
				1838	1839	24*	12*	48*	36*
				1843	1845	48*	24*	60*	72*
				1846	1847	12*	12*	36*	24*
				1848	1853	12*	60*	24*	72*
Dec. 1854	June 1857	4Q 1854	2Q 1857	1855	1856	24*	30	84*	36*
Dec. 1858	Oct. 1860	4Q 1858	3Q 1860	1858	1860	18	22	48	40
June 1861	Apr. 1865	3Q 1861	1Q 1865	1861	1864	8	46	30	54
Dec. 1867	June 1869	1Q 1868	2Q 1869	1867	1869	32	18	78	50
Dec. 1870	Oct. 1873	4Q 1870	3Q 1873	1870	1873	18	34	36	52
Mar. 1879	Mar. 1882	1Q 1879	1Q 1882	1878	1882	65	36	99	101
May 1885	Mar. 1887	2Q 1885	2Q 1887	1885	1887	38	22	74	60
Apr. 1888	July 1890	1Q 1888	3Q 1890	1888	1890	13	27	35	40
May 1891	Jan. 1893	2Q 1891	1Q 1893	1891	1892	10	20	37	30
June 1894	Dec. 1895	2Q 1894	4Q 1895	1894	1895	17	18	37	35
June 1897	June 1899	2Q 1897	3Q 1899	1896	1899	18	24	36	42
Dec. 1900	Sept. 1902	4Q 1900	4Q 1902	1900	1903	18	21	42	39
Aug. 1904	May 1907	3Q 1904	2Q 1907	1904	1907	23	33	44	56
June 1908	Jan. 1910	2Q 1908	1Q 1910	1908	1910	13	19	46	32
Jan. 1912	Jan. 1913	4Q 1911	1Q 1913	1911	1913	24	12	43	36
Dec. 1914	Aug. 1918	4Q 1914	3Q 1918	1914	1918	23	44	35	67
Mar. 1919	Jan. 1920	1Q 1919	1Q 1920	1919	1920	7	10	51	17
July 1921	May 1923	3Q 1921	2Q 1923	1921	1923	18	22	28	40
July 1924	Oct. 1926	3Q 1924	3Q 1926	1924	1926	14	27	36	41
Nov. 1927	Aug. 1929	4Q 1927	3Q 1929	1927	1929	13	21	40	34
Mar. 1933	May 1937	1Q 1933	2Q 1937	1932	1937	43	50	64	93
June 1938	Feb. 1945	2Q 1938	1Q 1945	1938	1944	13	80	63	93
Oct. 1945	Nov. 1948	4Q 1945	4Q 1948	1946	1948	8	37	88	45
Oct. 1949	July 1953	4Q 1949	2Q 1953	1949	1953	11	45	48	56
May 1954	Aug. 1957	2Q 1954	3Q 1957	1954	1957	10	39	55	49
Apr. 1958	Apr. 1960	2Q 1958	2Q 1960	1958	1960	8	24	47	32
Feb. 1961	Dec. 1969	1Q 1961	4Q 1969	1961	1969	10	106	34	116
Nov. 1970	Nov. 1973	4Q 1970	4Q 1973	1970	1973	11	36	117	47
Mar. 1975	Jan. 1980	1Q 1975	4Q 1979	1975	1979	16	58	52	74
July 1980	July 1981	2Q 1980	2Q 1981	1980	1981	6	12	64	18
Averages									
5 cycles, 1834–1855						24*	26*	50*	48
16 cycles, 1854–1919						22	27	48	49
6 cycles, 1919–1945						18	35	53	53
8 cycles, 1945–1975						11	45	59	55
35 cycles, 1834–1975						19	32	51	51

Source: National Bureau of Economic Research.

*Based upon calendar-year dates.

result in loss to its creditors. The statistics of business failures compiled by
Dun and Bradstreet include only firms involved in court procedures, such as
receivership, reorganization, and assignment, or voluntary actions which will
result in loss to their creditors. They do not take into account firms which
were liquidated, merged, or sold to avoid loss. For the most part, these
statistics cover commercial and industrial businesses. The Dun and Bradstreet
series differs from that of discontinued businesses, which refers to all firms
that go out of business for any reason. The number of business failures is a
significant indicator of overall business activity, classified by the National
Bureau of Economic research as one of its leading indicators. Business failures
generally increase when business recedes and decrease when business expands.
For cyclical changes in business failures, see Victor Zarnowitz and Lionel J.
Lerner, "Cyclical Changes in Business Failures and Corporate Profits," in
Geoffrey H. Moore (ed.), *Business Cycle Indicators,* Princeton University Press,
Princeton, N.J., 1961, chap. 12.

business forecasting The art of predicting future business conditions.
Short-term forecasts run from one to as many as six quarters ahead, and
long-term forecasts from five to fifteen years or more. Only a few U.S.
companies make medium-term forecasts covering from two to three years.
Short-term forecasts, which are strongly influenced by current business levels,
usually serve to support decisions on inventory purchasing, operating rates,
and sales activity; their vista is too short to form a good basis for capital
investment plans. In long-term forecasts, on the other hand, the potential
growth of the economy is the important consideration. These forecasts form
the basis for an intelligent financial plan, in which decisions on capital investment can be made with regard to new capacity and the distribution of
the new capacity among new products and regions of the nation and the
world. For methods of business forecasting, see William F. Butler, Robert
A. Kavesh, and Robert B. Pratt (eds.), *Methods and Techniques of Business
Forecasting,* Prentice-Hall, Englewood Cliffs, N.J., 1974.

business investment in new plants and equipment A major component
of gross private domestic investment which includes expenditures for new
structures and new machinery and equipment. New structures and additions
include all nonresidential construction and major alterations, land improvements, and exploratory and development expenditures chargeable to fixed-
asset accounts. New machinery and equipment includes all automobiles, trucks,
tractors, etc.; furniture and fixtures, office machinery; and all other new
equipment. Where motor vehicles or other capital is purchased both for personal and business use, only the portion allocated to business is included.
Expenditures for all items charged off as current operating expense, including
costs of maintenance and repairs, new facilities owned by the federal government but operated under contract by private companies, and plant and
equipment furnished by communities and organizations, are excluded. Ex-

penditures are generally reported in the various surveys of business investment as payments are made, and on an ownership basis rather than a use basis. In airlines and railroads, where there is extensive leasing of equipment, however, the total value of the equipment is counted as an expenditure at the time it is leased. The surveys of both the Commerce Department's Bureau of Economic Analysis and the McGraw-Hill Department of Economics are of companies, not establishments, with expenditures allocated to industries on the basis of the primary industry of all of each company's production. Despite the fact that business investment in new plants and equipment is a lagging indicator, it is closely watched by economists and forecasters as an important and sensitive cyclical indicator and for its relation to long-term growth. It is somewhat influenced in the short run by liquidity considerations and the availability of internal funds from both profits and external sources of finance, and in the long run by the relative cost of capital and other inputs of production. A major portion of business investment generally involves the modernization of old capital which has worn out or outlived its usefulness. An overwhelming influence on business investment is the general state of the economy and, in particular, the pressure of demand on existing capacity and the rate of growth of output. For additional information, see Robert Eisner, *Factors in Business Investment,* National Bureau of Economic Research, Ballinger, Cambridge, Mass., 1978.

business loan   A loan to a commercial or an industrial enterprise for business purposes. Such a loan is used to increase the volume of production and the distribution of goods or to accumulate inventories. Business loans are distinguished from loans to financial institutions and other noncommercial enterprises. The amount of such loans is studied closely as an indicator of business activity. For further discussion, see J. Fred Weston and Eugene F. Brigham, *Essentials of Managerial Finance,* 5th ed., Holt, Rinehart and Winston, New York, 1979; for current weekly or monthly data, see *Federal Reserve Bulletin,* Washington, D.C.

bust   A drop in business activity to an extremely low level, resulting in high unemployment, low incomes, low profits, and low stock and commodity prices. Historically, busts have usually followed booms. Automatic stabilizers have helped prevent the U.S. economy from experiencing a bust during the postwar years.

buyers' market   A market situation in which, at current prices that would cover a representative producer's average costs, supply is greater than demand. Because of the excess short-run supply, buyers have a bargaining advantage, and prices are forced below average costs. To reduce their excess stocks, sellers must accept lower prices. The existence of a buyers' market determines the direction of longer-run movements in production and price, indicating a fall in production or price or a combination of the two.

buy-now campaign A plan, urged usually by the national government or part of the business community, to spur recovery through an increase in current consumer purchases. Timed correctly, a buy-now campaign can give a depressed economy the needed impetus to start it moving upward.

C

call An option, or contract, which gives the holder the right to buy a certain amount of stock at a specified price for a designated time period. It is the opposite of a put. There are four parties to every call: the holder (buyer); the maker (seller); the broker who brought them together; and the endorser, a New York Stock Exchange member firm, which guarantees that the maker will comply with the agreement. Calls are usually written for thirty, sixty, or ninety days or for six months, but any time period longer than 21 days (a New York Stock Exchange rule) to which the parties agree is acceptable. For the right to buy the stock, the buyer pays a premium to the seller of the call. The seller, in turn, pays a small commission to the put and call broker. Four factors affect the price of a call: (1) the period covered by the contract, (2) the price of the stock at the time the call is written, (3) the ability of the call to be exercised at that price or at a higher price, and (4) the volatility of past price movements of the stock. For further information, see George L. Leffler and L. C. Farwell, *The Stock Market,* Ronald, New York, 1963, pp. 310–329; William F. Sharpe, *Investments,* Prentice-Hall, Englewood Cliffs, N.J., 1978.

callable loan (call loan) A commercial bank loan payable on demand by the lender and repayable at any time by the borrower. The greater part of broker borrowing has been on a call-loan basis, repayable on demand in clearinghouse funds on one day's notice. Stocks, bonds, and other forms of property are put up as collateral for a call loan. The call-loan agreement between the bank and the broker stipulates the margin, or the difference between the market value of the pledged securities and the amount of the loan; provides for the substitution of collateral deemed adequate to the bank; and empowers the bank to sell the securities in case of default or failure to keep collateral at the required level of margin. Because the call loan tends to deter rational business planning, it is rarely used by manufacturers or distributors. Before the 1930s, the callable loan market was the most important segment of the New York money market because commercial banks used call loans as secondary reserves. Individual banks considered these loans highly liquid and had no compunction in demanding repayment. After the 1929 market crash had shown how illiquid these loans actually were, however, banks no longer regarded them in the same light. For further information, see D. K. Eiteman, C. A. Dice, and W. J. Eiteman, *The Stock Market,* 4th ed., McGraw-Hill, New York, 1966, pp. 310–327; Lawrence S. Ritter and William L. Silber, *Principles of Money, Banking and Financial Markets,* 3d rev. ed., Basic Books, New York, 1980.

Cambridge school A school of economic thought of the late nineteenth and twentieth centuries, based largely on the works of Alfred Marshall, Arthur C. Pigou, and D. H. Robertson. The Cambridge school, so named because many of its adherents taught at the University of Cambridge, borrowed much from earlier schools of economic analysis, combining the classical concepts of real cost as the basis of value, rent, and the basic theory of money and foreign trade with the German historical approach of the institutional study of economic forces and the contributions of the marginal-utility theorists. Economists of this school concentrated their study on value and distribution theory, analyzing the pricing and allocative processes of the economic system while largely neglecting the problems of aggregative output, income, and economic growth and development. The unifying factor in the approach was the concept of economic equilibrium. Their basic tool was partial-equilibrium analysis, or the analysis of phenomena in one industry at a time, holding all other prices, outputs, and demands unchanged. The value of a particular commodity was determined by the equilibrium of the forces of supply and demand. The theory of money and foreign trade was treated in a similar manner, by studying the equilibrium of supply and demand. For fuller details on the approach of the Cambridge school, see Alfred Marshall, *Principles of Economics,* 8th ed., Macmillan, London, 1922; Mark Blaug, *The Cambridge Revolution: Success or Failure?,* Institute of Economic Affairs, London, 1975; G. C. Harcourt, *Some Cambridge Controversies in the Theory of Capital,* Cambridge University Press, New York, 1972.

Cambridge school of thought, modern A convenient grouping for a highly varied body of notions associated with a number of economists at the University of Cambridge, England, who either worked with Keynes or were deeply involved in the Keynesian revolution of the 1930s, such as Nicholas Kaldor, Joan Robinson, and Piero Sraffa. They address the long-run problems of growth and income distribution that Keynes largely neglected. Keynesian economists are more easily defined by what they are against than by what they are for. They are opposed to what is known as neoclassical microeconomics, that is, the maximizing of economic agents, rapid responses to price changes, emphasis on competitive equilibrium outcomes, Pareto optimality, and the income-expenditure, 45°-diagram interpretation of Keynesian macroeconomics. Both Kaldor and Robinson have developed distinct growth models based on Keynesian primacy of investment (itself the product of business confidence rather than prices) and the return to factors of production and the use of two saving functions, one for capitalists and the other for workers. The American members of the Cambridge school, calling themselves post-Keynesian economists, recently published a new *Journal of Post-Keynesian Economics*. For additional information, see J. A. Kregel, *The Reconstruction of Political Economy: An Introduction to Post-Keynesian Economics*, Macmillan, London, 1973. For an unsympathetic view, see M. Blaug, *The Cambridge Revolution, Success or Failure?*, Institute of Economic Affairs, London, 1975.

cameralism A form of mercantilism popular in Germany and Austria in the middle of the eighteenth century. It was a broad system of public administration, technology, and the management of financial affairs. In contrast to the western mercantilists, the cameralists stressed domestic industrial centralization rather than commercial expansion. Their aim was to foster home industry and a self-sufficient economy. They favored a growing population as a means of increasing national production and encouraged the consumption of domestic products. They also designated the revenues of the cental government as the most important index of a nation's wealth. See A. Small, *The Cameralists: The Pioneers of German Social Polity*, Burt Franklin, New York, 1909.

canons of taxation Principles or maxims used in the establishment or evaluation of a tax system. Adam Smith, the celebrated eighteenth-century British economist, was one of the first to set forth such principles. He said that taxes should (1) be levied on individuals according to their ability to pay as reflected by income, (2) be certain as to amount and condition of payment, (3) be payable at a time and in a manner convenient to the taxpayer, and (4) be collectible at a low cost. Later writers changed the emphasis on these principles, and greater attention is now generally paid to considerations of (1) equity between taxpayers, (2) the effect of the tax system on economic growth and efficiency, and (3) its effect on economic stability. For Adam Smith's classic statement, see *The Wealth of Nations*, Random House, New York, 1937.

capacity The largest output that a firm or industry can produce while operating on its customary schedule and using existing plants and equipment. The concept of capacity is different for each industry. It may vary with the number of shifts customarily worked and with allowances for repairs and maintenance. For example, continuous-processing industries, such as paper and steel, work around the clock, while most other industries operate on a one- or two-shift basis. Capacity figures expressed in such units as tons, barrels, pounds, and yards are available for basic industries, including primary aluminum, refined copper, cotton yarn, synthetic fibers, cement, wood pulp, paper, petroleum products, and coke. Capacity indices for major manufacturing industries from 1950 on are found in *Annual Surveys of Business' Plans for New Plants and Equipment,* McGraw-Hill Department of Economics, New York; for various measures of capacity and evaluations, see *Measures of Productive Capacity, Hearings before the Subcommittee on Economic Statistics of the U.S. Joint Economic Committee,* May 14, 22, 23, and 24, 1962, Washington, D.C., 1962.

capacity utilization rate   *See* operating rate.

capital   The designation applied to all goods used in the production of other goods, including plants and machinery. It is one of the four major factors of production, the other three being land, labor, and entrepreneurial ability. In a business sense, capital is the total wealth or assets of a firm and thus includes not only capital goods (tangible assets), but also trademarks, goodwill, patents, etc. As an accounting term, it represents all the money secured from stockholders, plus all earnings retained for use in the business. For a fuller discussion of capital and capital formation, see Simon Kuznets, *Capital in the American Economy,* Princeton University Press, Princeton, N.J., 1961; F. A. von Hayek, *Pure Theory of Capital,* Macmillan, Toronto, Canada, 1941; G. C. Harcourt and N. F. Laing (eds.), *Capital and Growth,* Penguin, Harmondsworth, Middlesex, England, 1971.

capital account, balance-of-payments   A group of entries appearing in the balance-of-payments account which provides a measure of all international capital transactions. The term refers to the long- and short-term loans that private citizens make or receive from foreign private citizens and the long- and short-term loans and credits that the government makes through various direct or intermediate channels. The capital account is shown in terms of net increases or decreases in assets and liabilities. Assets represent the reporting country's investments abroad; liabilities, the invesment of foreigners in the reporting country. Increases in assets and decreases in liabilities indicate an outflow of capital (debit); decreases in assets and increases in liabilities, an inflow of the capital (credit). It is the transactions in this account that presented the United States with the greatest difficulties in balancing its international payments in the 1957–1964 years. The deficits in capital movements abroad have more than offset the surpluses on current account, thus placing pressure on U.S. gold reserves. For additional information, see International Monetary Fund, *Balance of Payments Manual,* Washington, D.C., January 1950.

capital appropriations   The term applied to a firm's plans to buy new plants and equipment which have been formally approved by its board of directors or other responsible officials. Cumulative appropriations figures serve as a yardstick of future investment, but the measure is only approximate, since appropriations may be advanced or canceled. On the average, nine months elapse from appropriation to actual expenditure. The Conference Board collects and publishes quarterly data on the capital appropriations of large U.S. manufacturing corporations and utilities; see *The Conference Board Business Record,* Conference Board, New York.

capital budget   That part of a firm's budget which is concerned with the planning and control of capital expenditures. The budgeting of capital outlays is usually undertaken as part of a long-range program and is then transformed into an annual planning budget. Basic considerations in capital-outlay budgeting are the need for capital expenditures during the period in question; the money available for investment, including sources of financing; the rationing of funds among projects; and the timing of capital expenditures in relation to general business conditions. Each project is considered a separate venture and evaluated on the basis of total expenditure involved, the income required to cover the expenditure, the ultimate gain to be derived from the project, and the degree of urgency of the project. Among the steps involved in capital-outlay budgeting are general approval of the project, an estimate of cost and profitability, budget authorization of the project, and a follow-up study to determine the benefits derived from the capital expenditure. For additional details, see J. Fred Weston and Eugene F. Brigham, *Essentials of Managerial Finance,* 5th ed., Holt, Rinehart and Winston, New York, 1979.

capital coefficient   *See* capital-output ratio.

capital consumption allowance   An entry in the national income accounts that reflects the depreciation suffered by business production equipment and plants in a given period. It also includes the value of capital equipment accidentally destroyed and certain expenditures incurred in finding new resources, such as the cost of gas and oil well drilling. The allowance is based primarily on tax reports of depreciation, although these do not necessarily approximate the physical deterioration of productive facilities and do not include the depreciation of hand tools and similar equipment which is not amortized in current tax-accounting practice. The capital consumption allowance, which totaled over $206 billion in the United States in 1981, is subtracted from the gross national product in order to give a more accurate measure (the net national product) of a country's economic growth. Historical data on capital consumption allowances are published annually in U.S. Department of Commerce, *Survey of Current Business,* national income number (July issue).

capital expenditure (capital investment)   The amount of money spent for a fixed asset, such as a plant, a piece of machinery, or a truck. Business capital expenditures constitute a key factor in a nation's economic activity.

Historically, capital expenditures in the United States have fluctuated widely. The low rate of U.S. economic growth in the 1970s has been blamed on the low rate of capital expenditure, which approximated less than 7% of the gross national product during that period, whereas in earlier and later periods of prosperity it ran as high as 10% or more. For further discussion of capital expenditure and its relationship to the nation's economy, see Dexter M. Keezer and Associates, *New Forces in American Business,* McGraw-Hill, New York, 1959.

capital formation   The net addition to total capital stock in a given period. It represents the addition of new capital stock to existing stock after subtracting depreciation, damage, and other physical deterioration of the existing capital stock. This is the accounting procedure used by individual business firms, but nations often include human knowledge as well as fixed capital in their accounts. Capital formation is important because capital is the basis of future production. Moreover, gross investment fluctuates greatly from year to year and is thus a prime ingredient of minor business cycles. See Thomas F. Dernburg and Duncan M. McDougall, *Macroeconomics,* McGraw-Hill, New York, 1976; Simon Kuznets, *Capital in The American Economy,* National Bureau of Economic Research, Princeton University Press, Princeton, N.J., 1961; Eli Shapiro and William L. White (eds.), *Capital for Productivity and Jobs,* Prentice-Hall, Englewood Cliffs, N.J., 1977.

capital gains tax   A tax on that portion of personal income earned through the sale of such capital items as stocks, bonds, and real estate. The capital gain is measured by the difference between the acquisition price and the final sale price of the capital item. If the asset is held for more than six months, the income from its sale is classified as a long-term capital gain and is subject to special taxation by the federal government and most state governments. The maximum rate is 25% for federal taxation of long-term capital gains. Much controversy has arisen over whether or not capital gains should be taxed and whether they should receive special tax treatment. Since appreciation on capital items is accumulated over several years, the employment of a progressive tax rate on capital gains may result in overtaxation at the time when the gain is realized. It is also argued that high taxation of capital gains distorts the stock market and investment decisions, since sales are discouraged as capital values rise. In periods of rising prices, a capital gain may merely represent an increase in the price of a capital item and not an increase in the value. Those who favor capital gains taxation argue that capital gains represent unearned increments in income and should be included in income taxation. If capital gains were not subject to taxation, individuals with large incomes would convert substantial parts of their funds into investments on which the return would be in the form of capital gains rather than dividends or ordinary income. Thus, unless capital gains are taxed, they provide a loophole for avoiding personal income taxation. For additional information, see Joseph A. Pechman, *Federal Tax Policy,* 3d ed., Brookings Institution, Washington, D.C., 1977.

capital goods Economic goods used in the production of other goods. They include factory buildings, machinery, locomotives, trucks, and tractors. Land and money are not usually considered capital goods. In the United States during the period 1959–1978 the share of business' expenditures devoted to machinery and equipment was more than 70%; that devoted to plants and other capital construction, less than 30%. For further information, see Simon Kuznets, *Capital in the American Economy,* Princeton University Press, Princeton, N.J., 1961; for statistics on business' expenditures for capital goods, see U.S. Department of Commerce, *Annual Surveys of Expenditures for New Plants and Equipment; Annual Surveys of Business' Plans for New Plants and Equipment,* McGraw-Hill Department of Economics, New York.

capital-intensive industry An industry that uses large amounts of capital equipment in relation to its labor force or its output. The capital intensity of an industry can be measured by either capital-labor or capital-output ratios. Examples of industries with high ratios are petroleum, primary metals, chemicals, and paper; those with low ratios are the apparel, leather, and furniture industries. In general, capital-intensive industries predominate in the world's more highly developed nations; in developing countries they are generally found in export industries. Such industries imply efficient production methods and a high output per worker, which, in turn, indicate high real incomes and standards of living. For this reason, less highly developed nations stress the need for capital accumulation, which they consider the path to higher output and wealth. For a discussion of how capital intensity is measured and how it is related to investment theory, see Gardner Ackley, *Macroeconomics: Theory and Policy,* Macmillan, New York, 1978.

capitalism *See* **free-enterprise system.**

capitalized value The term applied to a technique used to determine the present value of an asset that promises to produce income in the future. To calculate the present value, the total future income expected must be discounted, that is, offset against the cost (as measured by the current interest rate) of carrying the asset until the income has actually been realized. For example, if the current rate of interest is 9%, the present discounted value of an asset that will yield $1,000 per year is about $910. If the asset promises a stream of income (for example, prospects for $1,000 annual rental income from a house for the next ten years), its capitalized value is calculated by adding together the present discounted values of the income in each year. The general formula for this calculation is

$$\frac{I}{(1 + r)^t}$$

where *I* is the annual income, *r* is the current rate of interest, and *t* is the number of years involved. In this manner, an investor confronted with a choice of properties can determine which alternative is the most remunerative, though the formula tells nothing about the relative risks involved.

capital markets Financial markets involved with long-term investment and saving. Common stock, bonds, and debentures are all associated with the capital market. The federal government issues long-term securities through either the direct obligation of the Treasury or through various government agencies or corporations. The long-term securities of the government are notes and bonds, with maturities typically ranging from two years to as long as thirty years. They are generally highly regarded by investors since they are risk-free. However, the climate of high inflation and high short- and long-term interest rates threatened to destroy the long-term capital market in the early 1980s as a strong priority was placed by investors on liquid assets. In this climate the thrift institutions are especially vulnerable because they are suffering from both an earnings and a cash-flow standpoint. For additional information, see Board of Governors of the Federal Reserve System, *The Flow of Funds in the United States,* 1955.

capital-output ratio (capital coefficient) The ratio between the book value (net of depreciation) of plant and equipment and the gross value of output. It is a measure of capacity utilization and the capital intensity of an industry. In economic theory, the capital-output ratio is the amount of capital necessary to produce an additional unit of output. Capital-output coefficients vary tremendously from industry to industry. Lumber, nonferrous metal products, iron and steel, paper and allied products, and petroleum have high capital-output coefficients, while apparel, tobacco, leather, and furniture and fixtures have low coefficients.

capital stock (issued stock) The aggregate equity or ownership in a corporation. Capital stock is that part of authorized stock which has been issued and is still outstanding, as opposed to treasury stock, which comprises those shares of stock that were issued but were bought back by the corporation. It also represents the permanently invested capital of a corporation. Capital stock can be classified into two broad groups, common stock and preferred stock. The owners of the corporation hold certificates which indicate how many shares of the corporation's capital stock they own and what rights and privileges they have. For further information, see Jules I. Bogen (ed.), *Financial Handbook,* 4th ed., Ronald, New York, 1968; J. Fred Weston and Eugene F. Brigham, *Essentials of Managerial Finance,* 5th ed., Holt, Rinehart and Winston, New York, 1979.

cartel An association of independent industrial enterprises producing similar goods that is formed to secure a monopoly in a specific market. In current usage, the term cartel refers to the monopolization of world markets, as opposed to trusts, syndicates, and the like, which are monopolies in more restricted markets. Membership in such associations is usually voluntary, although it may be required by law or by competitive pressures in some instances, and the members maintain their separate identities and financial independence. The distinguishing characteristic of a cartel is that the agreement invariably requires substitution of common policies for independent policies of pricing and production. Cartels are classified into four major categories: (1) associations which attempt to control the conditions of sale; (2) associations which attempt to fix prices; (3) associations which attempt to allocate productive activities, sales territories, and customers among their members; and (4) associations which attempt to award a fixed share of the business to each member. Associations can punish their members by revoking licenses granted under patents and held in a common pool; by imposing fines against money held in deposit; and by withholding payments from equalization pools, profit pools, sales receipt pools, or other funds over which they exert control. They can compel outsiders to join by threatening to put them out of business, by underselling them, or by cutting off their sources of supplies. Oil Producing Export Countries (OPEC) is the most prominent and long-lasting cartel. Cartels are generally held to be illegal under U.S. antitrust laws, but the Webb-Pomerene Act exempts from prosecution associations entered into solely for the purposes of promoting export trade on the theory that members of such associations should be able to compete on equal terms with cartel members of other countries. See R. E. Caves and M. E. Porter, "From Entry Barriers to Mobility Barriers," *Quarterly Journal of Economics,* vol. 91, no. 2, May 1977, pp. 241–261.

cash In an accounting sense, any type of money, including both currency and demand deposits. For example, the cash entry on the asset side of a firm's balance sheet covers currency on hand and bank demand deposits. In general usage, however, cash sometimes refers to currency alone, as when there is a choice of paying by check or by cash, that is, in bills or coins.

cash basis A method of accounting in which income is considered earned when it is received, and expenses are recorded when they are paid. This method differs from the accrual basis of accounting, in which revenues and expenses are allocated to the periods in which they are applicable regardless of when the actual cash is received or paid out. Only corporations selling services are permitted to use the cash basis in preparing their income tax returns. All corporations in which inventories are an income-determining factor (this provision includes all merchandising and manufacturing firms) must use the accrual basis. Most firms, and almost all large ones, use the accrual basis in preparing their financial statements. For further information, see Walter B. Meigs and Robert F. Meigs, *Accounting: The Basis for Business Decisions,* McGraw-Hill, New York, 1980.

cash budget   A method of budgeting federal expenditures and receipts which includes the transactions in a number of government trust-fund accounts. It is less comprehensive than the unified budget but more comprehensive than the administrative budget, which was the traditional method of federal budgeting until 1969 and which includes all funds for which the government considers itself the sole owner. The cash budget was devised as a method of including all government accounts, such as those used to finance social security, highway, and housing programs, for which the government does not consider itself the full owner. Since it shows more precisely what is happening to tax collections and how federal funds are being distributed, it is a better measure of the extent of government fiscal operations in the economy than the administrative budget.

cash flow   The sum of profits and depreciation allowances. (Instead of profits, many economists use retained earnings, which are profits after taxes and after deductions for dividend payments.) Gross cash flow is composed of total profits plus depreciation; net cash flow, of retained earnings plus depreciation. Thus, cash flow represents the total funds that corporations generate internally for investment in the modernization and expansion of plants and equipment and for working capital. The growth of depreciation allowances over the years has made them a much more important part of cash flow than retained earnings. Both gross and net cash flow are important tools of financial and economic analysis. For a more detailed explanation of the use of cash flow, see J. Fred Weston and Eugene F. Brigham, *Essentials of Managerial Finance,* 5th ed., Holt, Rinehart and Winston, New York, 1979.

caveat emptor   A Latin phrase meaning "Let the buyer beware."

caveat venditor   A Latin phrase meaning "Let the seller beware."

central bank   The most important bank in a country, usually possessing official standing in the government. It regulates the banking system and the supply of money and credit to help promote the public goals of economic growth and high employment with a minimum of inflation. The central bank of England is the Bank of England, that of France is the Banque de France, and that of the Federal Republic of Germany is the Deutsch Bundesbank. The U.S. central bank is the Federal Reserve System, created by act of Congress and placed in operation in 1913. Its tasks are clearly and succinctly set forth in its publication, *The Federal Reserve System: Purposes and Functions,* and statistics pertaining to the System's operations and banks under its aegis are published monthly in the *Federal Reserve Bulletin.*

central-limit theorem   The sum of *n* random, independent variables having finite variances will tend to be normally distributed as the number of variables approaches infinity regardless of the manner in which the individual variables are distributed. It is through this theorem that the normal distribution, which occurs frequently in observations of natural and social phenomena, acquires its central importance in the theories of probability and sampling. For additional information, see Gerhard Tintner and Charles B. Millham, *Mathematics and Statistics for Economists,* Holt, Rinehart and Winston, New York, 1970.

certificate of deposit   A certificate for money deposited in a commercial bank for a specified period of time and earning a specified rate of return. The use of certificates has grown rapidly in the United States since 1961, when they were introduced to attract time money, especially that of domestic corporations. Until that time, large banks had rarely accepted interest-bearing time deposits from domestic firms. The certificate of deposit, commonly called a CD, is a negotiable instrument and has a secondary market for the sale of outstanding issues. CDs thus compete for idle funds with treasury bills, commercial paper, and other short-term money instruments. For a detailed discussion of certificates of deposit, see Lawrence S. Ritter and William L. Silber, *Principles of Money, Banking and Financial Markets,* 3d rev. ed., Basic Books, New York, 1980.

ceteris paribus   A Latin phrase meaning "all other things remaining the same" or "all relevant factors being equal." The term is used in the analysis of a variety of economic phenomena. For example, in price theory the analysis of a price change is often carried on under *certeris paribus* assumptions. Giving a declining demand schedule for a particular consumer good, a reduction in the price of this good will cause a larger quantity to be purchased *ceteris paribus,* meaning that this will be the result if consumer incomes and tastes remain unchanged and the prices of other goods and services also are unchanged.

chain banking   The control and operation of three or more independently incorporated banks by one or more individuals. The control is usually exercised by stock ownership or interlocking directorates, but it can take other forms. Usually, such chains are centered at one or a few key banks which are larger and more important than the others in the chain. Chain banking differs from branch banking, which is a form of multiple-office banking in which the bank is a single legal entity and merely operates more than one banking office. It also differs from group banking, in which three or more banks are controlled by a holding company. Usually a looser and less formal arrangement than group banking, chain banking offers the advantage of coordinating the resources and policies of the chain members. In the United States, chain banking is now significant in only a few middlewestern states where branch banking is prohibited by law, and its general importance in the banking system is declining.

chain index An index number whose value at any given point in time is related to a base in the immediately preceding time period rather than to a fixed base period in the more distant past. The individual index numbers thus constructed may then be linked together (link relatives) in attempting to make comparisons between nonconsecutive periods. The chain index is accurate in measuring changes over relatively short time periods. Its accuracy decreases as the time period between two chain-index numbers that are being compared is extended. A modified form of the chain index is used in deriving the implicit deflator of the U.S. gross national product. For additional information, see Leonard J. Kazmier, *Statistical Analysis for Business and Economics,* McGraw-Hill, New York, 1978.

cheap money *See* **easy money.**

checkless society Most money transfers in the United States occur by checks, which are instruments in writing directing a bank to pay funds to a named person or organization. The process of sending checks and returning them to their makers creates great expense and gives rise to varying amounts of funds which have been collected by some parties but not yet deducted from the accounts of the payers. Such problems, among others, could be eliminated by electronic transfer of funds from one person's account to another's instantaneously or within a very short time interval. In theory, such systems can speed payments and lower costs. Users, however, have found the cumbersome checking system provides advantages, such as the ability to pay bills with no money in an account, and then arrange for the money to be in the account by the time the check is presented for payment. In addition, many people like their canceled checks as permanent proof of payment, and the IRS places great stress on taxpayers showing payment by check in tax audits. As a result, payments systems based on electronic transfer of funds have usually met with a poor reception, and electronic funds transfer (EFT) has not progressed very far in the United States, although efforts to implement it are continuing. In the meantime, the magnetic ink character-recognition system used on checks allows them to be processed by machinery, and thus reduces costs compared with hand treatment of checks at every step of the process. See *Executive Report of the Monetary and Payments System,* Planning Committee, American Bankers Association, Washington, D.C., 1971; R. Long and L. Fenner, *An Electronic Network for Interbank Payment Communications: A Design Study,* Bank Administration Institute, Park Ridge, Ill., 1969.

Chicago school The name given to a group of economists adhering to a neoliberal economic philosophy who teach at the University of Chicago. Among them are Henry C. Simons, F. A. von Hayek, Frank Knight, Milton Friedman, and George J. Stigler. All have strong faith in competition and free markets as a means of allocating resources in the economy, although they do not agree on the exact nature of the institutional framework that should be used to achieve their goals. In addition, the followers of the Chicago school are generally considered to believe that the behavior of the economy can be explained better by changes in the money supply than by other variables, although this view has been enunciated principally by one member of the Chicago school. Not all professors at the University of Chicago embrace the neoliberal philosophy. For views of individuals associated with the Chicago school, see F. A. von Hayek, *The Road to Serfdom,* University of Chicago Press, Chicago, 1944; Henry C. Simons, *Economic Policy for a Free Society,* University of Chicago Press, Chicago, 1948; Milton Friedman, *Capitalism and Freedom,* University of Chicago Press, Chicago, 1962. For a discussion of the ideas and policy implications of the Chicago school, see Warren J. Samuels (ed.), *The Chicago School of Political Economy,* Michigan State University, East Lansing, Mich., 1976.

chronic unemployment Unemployment lasting for at least six months as a result of factors other than seasonal slackness in a particular industry or routine job changing and similar causes. A common measure of chronic unemployment is the statistical series of the U.S. Department of Labor covering long-term unemployment. Among frequently cited causes of chronic unemployment are structural changes in the economy that render particular skills obsolete; inadequate education for suitable jobs; increasing automation that displaces unskilled and semiskilled workers in a variety of jobs; and an unsatisfactory rate of growth for the economy as a whole, resulting in relatively low demand for the services offered by particular groups of workers. For a discussion of chronic unemployment, see *The Rise of Chronic Unemployment,* National Planning Association, Planning Pamphlet 113, Washington, D.C., 1961.

circular flow The continual circular movement of money and goods in the economy. The concept of the circular flow of income is a simplification which attempts to illustrate the flow of money and goods from households to business enterprises and back to households. As resource owners, individuals sell their resources to businesses; as consumers, they spend the income received from this sale to buy goods and services. Businesses buy resources from households and produce finished products, which are sold to the consuming households for money, which is then used to pay for resource costs. Resources and finished goods flow in one direction, and money income and expenditures in the other direction. In the resource markets, the businesses are on the demand side of the market while households are on the supply side. In the product market, these positions are reversed, the households demanding goods and the businesses supplying them. A number of problems arise from the use of this simple circular-flow model. It ignores transactions occurring within the business and household sectors; it assumes that households spend all their income, so that flows of income and expenditures are constant; and it does not explain the determination of resource and product prices but assumes that they are already given. For further information, see Walter W. Haines, *Money, Prices and Policy,* 2d ed., McGraw-Hill, New York, 1966.

classical liberalism (nineteenth-century liberalism)   An economic philosophy that is characterized by strong faith in the general beneficence of markets largely unfettered by governmental or other restraints. An assumption of classical liberalism is that human wants are best satisfied and productive resources most efficiently employed when goods and services are sold in competitive markets. The social ethics emphasized are the freedom and the self-reliance of the individual. The political framework implied consists of the supremacy of the rule of law and a minimum role for the government in the economy, although the philosophy explicitly recognizes the need for public works projects, defense, and other governmental operations. Classical liberalism emphasizes economic freedom, namely, the right to engage in any occupation without restriction or to produce any good or service. There is a strong presumption that if all individuals seek their own self-interests, the results will be the promotion of social welfare and the creation of economic harmony. The theory developed in England in the late 1700s and early 1800s. Adam Smith, Jeremy Bentham, and John Stuart Mill were among the leaders of classical liberalism. They favored free trade, competition, the gold standard, some public works, relief to the indigent, and work laws protecting women and children. The U.S. version of classical liberalism became known as social Darwinism, or the survival of the fittest in the rough-and-tumble of the free market. Herbert Spencer, a British writer who had greater influence in the United States than in England, proposed a form of laissez faire that would now be regarded as radical. He favored extreme individualism and even opposed sanitary laws and compulsory free education. For further information, see Overton Taylor, *Economics and Liberalism,* Harvard University Press, Cambridge, Mass., 1955; James M. Buchanan and Richard E. Wagner, *Democracy in Deficit,* Academic Press, New York, 1977

classical school   A late eighteenth- and early nineteenth-century school of political economists who believed that economies function better under free private initiative and vigorous competition than under government control. The school's founder was Adam Smith, and its leaders were David Ricardo, Nassau W. Senior, John Stuart Mill, and Jean Baptiste Say. The classical theory was based on the notion that the production, consumption, and distribution of wealth are determined by economic laws. The classicists considered that the power of competition alone determined prices, wages, profits, and rent. They were opposed to relief for the poor because it promoted instability, but they believed that the government should undertake some type of investment projects which would prove useful to the nation as a whole. Classical theory and analysis were spelled out in relatively clear and systematic statements of common-sensible notions about economics. The school had an intuitive grasp of the important elements and relationships in the development of the real economy, although it was unable to express precisely all the political, social, and economic implications. The main differences between the classical school and the neoclassical school, which evolved later, were the emphasis of the latter on mathematical economics and its stress on the analysis of the psychological background of consumer demands, decisions, and actions. For further discussion of the classical school and classicists, see Thomas Sowell, *Classical Economics Reconsidered,* Princeton University Press, Princeton, N.J., 1974; for theories of the classicists, see Adam Smith, *The Wealth of Nations,* Random House, New York, 1937; David Ricardo, *The Principles of Political Economy and Taxation,* Irwin, Homewood, Ill., 1963.

clearinghouse   An association of banks in a given area, the representatives of which meet daily to exchange checks drawn on each other. Each participating bank, by settling simultaneously the claims against it and its claims against the other members of the clearinghouse, reduces to a net balance the amount that it must settle. This settlement is a single payment that was originally made in cash, later in clearinghouse loan certificates, and now, in most cases, through entries in the books of the respective Federal Reserve banks (or, in smaller centers, in drafts on correspondent banks). In most cities, clearinghouse associations also exchange drafts on large local business firms, state and county warrants, and a variety of noncash items as well as drafts originating in interbank transactions and payments to or by the Federal Reserve Bank. Nonbank institutions that habitually have frequent and large payments to make to each other—airlines that accept each other's tickets, railroads that use each other's freight cars, etc.—organize clearinghouses of their own to reduce the necessity of settling each transaction individually. For a more explicit explanation of bank clearings, see *Information Regarding the Operation of the New York Clearing House,* The New York Clearing House, New York, 1962.

clearing union   An association of international banking institutions (usually the central banks of various countries) that operates as an international clearinghouse by offsetting a nation's balance-of-payments deficits with one country against its balance-of-payments surpluses with another, leaving only each nation's net surplus or deficit with its trading partners as a group for settlement. No international clearing union has ever existed on a worldwide scale; the nearest thing to it was the London Clearing House, which operated before 1931, when most of the world's major banking institutions held deposits in correspondent banks in London, effected payments to each other through these accounts, and settled their balances in sterling credits or gold. In 1943, John Maynard Keynes suggested a worldwide clearing union that would involve not only clearings but the settlement of net balances with credits financed in "bancor," a proposed international currency under the jurisdiction of an international authority. His suggestion was not accepted at the Bretton

Woods Conference of 1944, which agreed instead on the establishment of the International Monetary Fund. The essence of Keynes' plan has reappeared in the European Payments Union, which came into existence in 1950 after the operation of more limited clearing schemes among the participants of the European Recovery Program in 1948 and 1949. The purpose of all clearing unions is to facilitate multilateral trade and payments, giving each participant the opportunity to concentrate on one trading partner for its imports even when its exports go mostly to another one and reducing to a minimum the size of the necessary settlements, whether in gold or in international credits. For a thorough discussion of postwar clearing arrangements, see Robert Triffin, *Europe and the Money Muddle,* Yale University Press, New Haven, Conn., 1957.

closed economy   The economy of an isolated area. In a closed economy, no person has any business or trade relationships with anyone outside the area. The term closed economy usually refers to an economy in which no imports, exports, or factor movements are permitted across boundaries.

closed-end investment company   An investment company that has a fixed capital structure. Unlike an open-end investment company (mutual fund), whose capital structure is almost constantly changing as people buy and redeem shares, a closed-end investment company raises capital as ordinary corporations do; that is, it sells common and preferred stocks to the public and sometimes floats bonds and borrows from banks. Once issued, these securities are traded in the same manner as other securities; many of the large companies are listed on the New York Stock Exchange, while others are traded in the over-the-counter market. Price is determined by supply and demand, which is obviously related to the net asset value of the fund per share of stock outstanding. (Net asset value equals assets minus liabilities divided by the number of shares outstanding.) Price rarely exactly equals net asset value, being either higher (premium) or lower (discount), depending on the market's appraisal of the stock. Closed-end investment companies can be classified by investment objectives. Common-stock funds, as their name suggests, invest primarily in common stocks, although they reserve the right to hold cash, bonds, or other securities of the defensive type if the market is weak. Some common-stock funds specialize in certain kinds of equity securities, such as growth stocks, blue chips, electronics companies, or chemical companies, while others diversify their holdings. Balanced funds invest in common and preferred stocks and bonds and generally try to keep the proportions of each type of security that they hold close to stated policies. Because balanced funds diversify not only the companies they hold, but also the type of security, they are more conservative than common-stock funds. Finally, fully managed funds are those that invest at the discretion of the managers. They do not have stated investment objectives like those of common-stock and balanced funds. See *Fact Book,* Investment Company Institute, New York, periodically; *Annual Reports,* U.S. Securities and Exchange Commission; Linda Snyder, "The Closed End Funds May Be Opening Up," *Fortune,* February 1978, p. 137.

Cobb-Douglas production function   A physical relationship between output and various inputs in the form $Y = kL^aC^{(1-a)}$, where Y represents national output, L is the quantity of labor input, C is the quantity of capital employed, and k and a are positive constants (and $a < 1$). This production function is linear and homogeneous of degree 1, implying constant returns to scale. Furthermore, if each of the factors is paid according to its marginal product, it can be shown that this production function will yield relative shares of wages and return to capital which are independent of the variables Y, L, and C. The relative share of wages in total output will be a, the exponent of L, while the relative share of the return to capital will be $1-a$, the exponent of C. Both relative shares are constant for all variations of the ratio of capital to labor. The Cobb-Douglas production function was proposed as an empirical hypothesis to explain the relative constancy of the share of wages in the national income of the United States since the early 1900s. So far, statistical evidence has not contradicted this production function. For additional information about the function and an empirical test of it, see Paul H. Douglas, *The Theory of Wages,* Macmillan, New York, 1934, chaps. 5–9; James M. Henderson and Richard E. Quandt, *Microeconomic Theory: A Mathematical Approach,* 3d ed., McGraw-Hill, New York, 1980.

cobweb theorem   A theory which attempts to explain the regularly recurring cycles observed in the production and prices of some commodities. Although many economists had attempted to explain cyclical movements, it was not until 1930 that H. Schultze of the United States, J. Tinbergen of the Netherlands, and U. Ricci of Italy, working independently, presented the theory in three separate articles. N. Kaldor first suggested the name cobweb theorem because the pattern traced by the price movements resembles a cobweb. Classical economic theory assumed that production and prices, if disturbed from equilibrium, would tend to return automatically to equilibrium. The cobweb theorem demonstrates that on classical assumptions of pure competition under static conditions, prices and production, if disturbed, do not necessarily return to equilibrium. The assumptions on which the theorem is based are (1) pure competition, in which each producer assumes that present prices will continue and that his or her production plans will not affect the market (once plans for production are made, they cannot be changed until the next time period); (2) the establishment of price by available supply (price is completely a function of the preceding period's supply); and (3) the perishability of the commodity produced. These assumptions suggest that the theorem has been used mainly in analyzing agricultural commodities. The accompanying three figures show three cases of the cobweb in action. In each

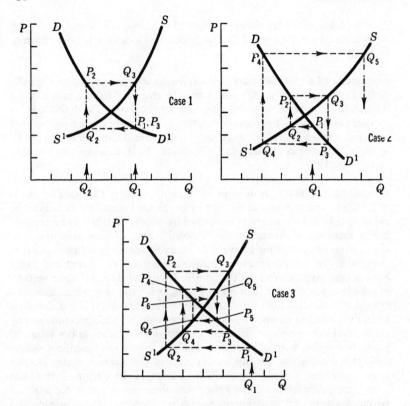

case, the first period's price (P_1) is established by supply Q_1; producers use this price to determine their output in period 2. This output Q_2, determines the price for period 2, which is P_2. The output for period 3, Q_3, is determined by the price of period 2, P_2, etc. The elasticity of demand equals the elasticity of supply in case 1; this leads to constantly and regularly fluctuating prices and outputs. Case 2, in which the elasticity of supply is greater than the elasticity of demand, yields a diverging cobweb and eventually a change in elasticities; if this change did not occur, chaos would result. The elasticity of supply in case 3 is lower than that of demand, leading to a converging cobweb and eventually to an equilibrium price and output. A complete statement of the theorem is given in M. Ezekiel, "The Cobweb Theorem," *Quarterly Journal of Economics,* Cambridge, Mass., February 1938, reprinted in American Economic Association, *Readings in Business Cycle Theory,* McGraw-Hill, New York, 1951; for a criticism of the theory, see Norman S. Buchanan, "A Reconsideration of the Cobweb Theorem," *Journal of Political Economy,* Chicago, February 1939, reprinted in R. Clemence (ed.), *Readings in Economic*

Analysis, Addison-Wesley, Reading, Mass., 1950; Donald S. Watson and Mary A. Holman, *Price Theory and Its Uses,* 4th ed., Houghton Mifflin, Boston, 1976.

coefficient of determination In correlation analysis, the squared coefficient of correlation (r^2 or R^2) which may be corrected to take into account the number of observations and constants involved in the analysis. It is interpreted as the ratio of explained variation of the dependent variable to total variation. For additional information, see Gerhard Tintner and Charles B. Millham, *Mathematics and Statistics for Economists,* Holt, Rinehart and Winston, New York, 1970.

coincident indicator A measure of economic activity that usually moves in the same direction and at the same time as total economic activity. The use of statistical indicators was developed by Wesley Mitchell and Arthur F. Burns, members of the staff of the National Bureau of Economic Research, and Warren Persons of the Harvard Economic Society, to indicate historical changes in the general course of business. Geoffrey H. Moore and Julius Shiskin, also staff members of the bureau, have carried the indicator method of business-cycle analysis forward to a point at which many economists consider that coincident indicators provide the basis for determining the dates when the general economy reaches peaks or troughs. Other economists merely use the peaks or troughs of either the gross national product or the industrial production index, both of which are included among the coincident indicators, as indications of the top and bottom of the business cycle. *Business Conditions Digest,* a report of the U.S. Bureau of the Census, lists fifteen coincident indicators and divides them into three major groups for analysis: (1) employment and unemployment, (2) production, and (3) income and trade. For the development and analysis of coincident indicators, see Geoffrey H. Moore (ed.), *Business Cycle Indicators,* Princeton University Press, Princeton, N.J., 1961, vol. 1. See also J. Shiskin, "Business Cycle Indicators: The Known and the Unknown," in *Business Cycle Developments,* U.S. Department of Commerce, Washington, D.C., September 1963.

collective bargaining Negotiations between employees' representatives (usually labor union functionaries) and employers for the purpose of establishing mutually acceptable terms to govern conditions of employment. Collective bargaining covers topics ranging from the obviously important, such as wage rates, hours of work, hiring, and layoff procedures, to the seemingly trivial, such as rest time or time allowed employees for washing and changing clothes at the end of a workday. The terms ultimately arrived at are included in a collective bargaining agreement, or contract, which is binding on both employees and employer. There are now more than 100,000 such agreements in force in the United States, some governing a single facet of a plant operation, others a firm's entire operations, and some applying to entire industries, such as the giant steel industry. Although collective bargaining has long existed in some form, it owes its vigorous growth since the 1930s to the passage of legislation explicitly permitting workers to organize for purposes of collective bargaining (Norris-La Guardia Act of 1932) and, later, of federal statutes making it illegal for an employer to refuse to bargain in good faith with employees' representatives (National Labor Relations Act of 1935—the Wagner Act). More recently, 1947, the Labor-Management Relations Act (Taft-Hartley Act) imposed some restrictions on the scope of collective bargaining. Numerous criticisms of the collective bargaining process have arisen. A frequent one has been the argument that the parties directly involved, industry and labor, tend to ignore the interest of the general public in arriving at their agreements. For further discussion, see Lloyd G. Reynolds, *Labor Economics and Labor Relations,* 7th ed., Prentice-Hall, Englewood Cliffs, N.J., 1978; Edwin F. Beal, E. D. Wickersham and P. K. Kienast, *The Practice of Collective Bargaining,* 5th ed., Irwin, Homewood, Ill., 1976.

command-directed economy   A mode of economic organization in which the three key economic problems—what goods will be produced, how they will be produced, and who will receive them once they have been produced—are solved by the central government or ruler. The U.S.S.R. and the People's Republic of China are examples of nations with command-directed economies. Even in these countries, however, some economic decisions are made by private citizens in response to prices rather than by the government. In the United States, less drastic elements of command are found, such as taxes that preempt a part of private income for public purposes. See Robert H. Heilbroner, *The Making of an Economic Society,* Prentice-Hall, Englewood Cliffs, N.J., 1962.

commerce   Business activity concerned with the buying, selling, and transportation of goods and services. Commerce, as opposed to industry, usually refers to the trade of large quantities of goods. It may take place between different firms, communities, or countries. In the United States, intrastate commerce is trade carried on entirely within the borders of a single state, whereas interstate commerce refers to trade between different states and is subject to control by Congress. International commerce refers to any trade between businesses in different countries.

commercial bank   A financial institution which for the most part makes short-term commercial and industrial loans. It has the power to create and destroy money, within limits, through the use of loans and demand deposits. Commercial banks lend money by creating demand deposits and retire loans by canceling demand deposits. In addition, they carry on functions duplicated by other financial institutions, such as holding time deposits, making loans (including business, mortgage, and consumer short- and long-term loans), operating trust departments, offering safe-deposit boxes, and so forth. Commercial banks may be chartered by federal or state governments. For further information, see Lester V. Chandler and Stephen M. Goldfeld, *The Economics of Money and Banking,* 7th ed., Harper & Row, New York, 1977; for statistics on the number, classes, and forms of assets and liabilities of commercial banks, see *Federal Reserve Bulletin,* Washington, D.C., monthly.

commercial credit company (sales finance company)   A firm engaged in the business of buying installment contracts and accounts receivables from other businesses, especially retailers. Since commercial credit companies are substantial borrowers from banks in order to finance their operations, their discount rate (about 18%) is much higher than the rate that they pay for bank loans. Such companies enable retailers and other business firms to do a large volume of credit or installment sales without tying up their own capital in unpaid balances on goods sold. See J. Fred Weston and Eugene F. Brigham, *Essentials of Managerial Finance,* Holt, Rinehart and Winston, New York, 1979.

commercial and industrial loans   Loans made to various types of business firms, including companies engaged in manufacturing, mining, wholesale and retail trade, transportation services, public utilities, and construction contractors. The volume of commercial and industrial lending is used by economists and financial analysts as one indicator of business plans for future investment in new plant and equipment and in inventories—i.e., in business expansion, a key driving force in the economy. Data on commercial and industrial loan activity of large commercial banks are reported weekly by the Federal Reserve Board. Such information includes the volume of outstanding loans and the net change in loan volume, both classified by industry.

commercial paper   Unsecured promissory notes of well-known business concerns having the highest credit ratings. Except for large finance companies, which place their paper directly with investors, corporations usually sell to commercial-paper houses (dealers), which resell the paper to investors, chiefly commercial banks. Commercial paper is generally written in amounts ranging from $5,000 to $1,000,000 or more (notes of less than $50,000 are not common), with maturities of thirty days to nine months; however, most paper carries an original maturity of less than ninety days. Interest at the prevailing rate and a commission of about 0.25% of the principal amount of the note are deducted in advance by the dealer. As a rule, the interest rate on commercial paper is less than that on an ordinary bank loan. Moreover, commercial paper has a certain prestige value because only the largest and most creditworthy corporations can issue it. Its major disadvantage is that it does not allow the extension of the loan. Although commercial banks are prohibited from issuing commercial paper, bank holding companies may, and have, been quite active in this area. The amount of commercial paper outstanding and the prevailing interest rate on commercial paper are published in *Federal Reserve Bulletin,* Washington, D.C., monthly; for further information, see Lawrence S. Ritter and William L. Silber, *Principles of Money, Banking, and Financial Markets,* 3d rev. ed., Basic Books, New York, 1980.

commodity A good that is available for sale. Commodities may be characterized by such qualities as function, size, shape, and grade. The concept of a commodity is basic in economic theory, and is used in conjunction with such market characteristics as supply, demand, and price. For certain types of commodities—those whose markets are widespread and which can be classified, according to various characteristics, into homogeneous groupings—commodities exchanges have been organized. These exchanges serve to facilitate trading of these commodities, both within an individual country and internationally. These exchanges also allow for trading to take place without actual delivery of the goods; trading can be conducted on either a spot, or current, basis, or on the basis of future delivery. A major function of commodities exchanges is to allow for price hedging, and to ensure the availability of goods when needed. Speculation in commodities prices is also prevalent where much trading is being done on the commodities exchanges. Commodities which are traded on exchanges include various metals, such as copper, gold, and silver; food items, such as beef, pork, wheat, corn, and frozen orange juice; and the expanding area of trading in financial futures, which is actually trading on interest-rate expectations. For further information, see B. A. Goss and B. A. Hamey, *The Economics of Futures Trading: Readings Selected, Edited, and Introduced,* Wiley, New York, 1978.

commodity exchange An organized association of traders who buy and sell contracts for immediate or future delivery of certain commodities. The commodities are not brought to the exchange; only the promises of immediate delivery, called spots, and the promises of future delivery, futures, are traded. The commodity exchange offers a continuous, stable market on which spots and futures may always be bought and sold. The great bulk of the transactions consists of the trading of futures, with relatively little spot trading. The commodity exchange, through an affiliated clearinghouse, also guarantees that the merchandise traded in the exchange will be delivered at the agreed time and that full payment will be made. The continuous existence of a stable and liquid market also facilitates the formal financing of commodity production. In the United States, the main commodity exchanges exist for wheat, corn, other grains, cotton, sugar, and coffee. For further information on the significance and workings of commodity exchanges, see B. A. Goss and B. A. Hamey, *The Economics of Futures Trading: Readings Selected, Edited and Introduced,* Wiley, New York, 1978.

commodity stabilization agreement A pact concerning the production and trade of a certain commodity that is made between a group of producer and consumer nations. Stabilization measures are usually undertaken to reduce the widely fluctuating prices and volumes of some internationally traded goods (primary goods in particular) whose instability is an important cause of inefficiency in the international economy, especially for developing countries. There are two basic kinds of commodity agreements, the buffer-stock type and the production-market control type. In a buffer-stock agreement, the participating nations attempt to produce a stable flow of a good by establishing an intergovernmental agency to buy the surplus of the good when the price falls below a certain point, store it while the price is normal, and sell it when a shortage causes the price to rise above a fixed point. Buffer-stock schemes involve a number of difficulties, especially problems of storage and the setting of buying and selling prices. The second approach, the production-market control type of agreement, entails restriction programs and marketing-quota systems. It sometimes involves an upper price, at which exporting nations agree to sell a specified amount of the good, and a lower price, at which the importing nations agree to buy a specified amount, with a free market operating between these prices. In other cases, it may incorporate a rigid system of export and import quotas and prices governing trade. The freezing of production involved in the production-market control type of agreement may lead to serious misallocation and maladjustment in the economic system. Commodity agreements among nations are similar to cartels in that they are associations of producers who try to control production. Unlike private cartels, they give the consumer nations a voice in supply and price policies, and they seek to avoid the mere restriction of output and bolstering of prices without removing the basic causes of disequilibrium. The major intergovernmental commodity stabilization agreements effected since World War II have been the International Wheat Agreement and the International Sugar Agreement. For additional information, see John Pincus, *Trade, Aid and Development,* McGraw-Hill, New York, 1967, pp. 233–294.

common stock The capital stock of a corporation, which gives the holder an unlimited interest in the corporation's earnings and assets after prior claims have been met. Common stock represents the holder's equity or ownership in the corporation. Common stockholders have certain fundamental legal rights, including preemptive rights; the right, in most cases, to vote for the board of directors, who actually manage the company; the right to transfer any or all shares of stock owned; and the right to receive dividends when they are declared by the board of directors. For monthly information concerning new issues of common stocks, see *Federal Reserve Bulletin,* Washington, D.C.; for technical explanations, see Jules I. Bogen (ed.), *Financial Handbook,* 4th ed., Ronald, New York, 1968; J. Fred Weston and Eugene F. Brigham, *Essentials of Managerial Finance,* 5th ed., Holt, Rinehart and Winston, New York, 1979.

communism According to Marxists, the highest and inevitable stage in social development in the historical sequence of slavery, feudalism, capitalism, socialism, and communism. The term is defined not only as the public ownership of productive resources but also as the "withering away" of central governmental authority. Marxists argue that all human relationships are affected by the stage through which society is passing; therefore, personal relationships will be different, and better, under communism, which will eliminate all social problems. Because these relationships are determined largely by economic factors, Marxists call themselves materialists, and the successive stages of development are called dialectical materialism, meaning that a new stage (synthesis) is reached as a result of the impact of new forces (antithesis) on the original stage (thesis). It is argued that earlier stages of development pass out of existence through internal strains (contradictions) and that communism is brought about by the growing awareness of wage earners (the proletariat) of their political role, leading them to form and support Communist parties. In practice, Communist parties often have been imposed by military force on societies weakened by war. Although Communist parties control the U.S.S.R., the People's Republic of China, and certain countries in eastern Europe, these countries are considered to be passing through a period of socialist development and not to have reached the stage of communism. Despite the original insistence that communism would come about only after society had passed through a capitalist stage of development, Communists have seized power only in predominantly agricultural societies. Today, despite an equally strong insistence on the "scientific" nature of communism, Communist practice is essentially pragmatic, relying on military force and rapid technological and industrial growth to demonstrate Communist superiority over other forms of economic practice. For further discussion, see Karl Marx and Friedrich Engels, *The Communist Manifesto,* Henry Regnery, Chicago, 1954; Zbigniew K. Brzezinski, *Ideology and Power in Soviet Politics,* Praeger, New York, 1967; Fernando Claudin, *The Communist Movement,* Monthly Review Press, New York, 1977.

comparative advantage The special ability of a country to provide one product or service relatively more cheaply than other products or services. This concept is generally used in international trade theory, although it also applies to cost comparisons among firms in an industry and among individual workers. It explains why a country capable of providing a wide range of goods and services at a lower cost than any other country should concentrate on selling that product or service for which its cost advantage is greatest and leave the production of other goods, in which it has a positive but lesser cost advantage, to other countries. The idea of comparative advantage was first formulated by David Ricardo, an English economist. In his model of a two-country, two-commodity world, Ricardo showed that Portugal was better off if it concentrated on producing wine (at a cost of 80 hours of labor per unit, compared with England's 120 hours of labor) instead of expending any of its resources on the production of textiles, in which Portugal had a cost advantage of 90 hours of labor per unit to England's 100. In this example, a unit of domestic wine would, in the absence of international trade, exchange for only eight-ninths of a unit of textiles in Portugal instead of as much as one and one-fifth units of English textiles if the wine were shipped to England in trade. The converse would also be true. The example and its variants explain why producers with an absolute advantage in a number of goods are still best advised to concentrate on producing that good in which their advantage is greatest. For a discussion of the principle of comparative advantage, see David Ricardo, *Principles of Political Economy and Taxation,* Everyman's Library, New York, 1917, chap. 7; see also Mark Blaug, *Economic Theory in Retrospect,* 3d ed., Cambridge University Press, New York, 1978, chaps. 4 and 6.

comparative statics The comparison of different positions of static equilibrium of the economy. Comparative statics analysis disregards the delays involved in economic changes and is not concerned with the process through which the economy moves from one equilibrium point to another. Instead, it traces the variables from one static equilibrium situation to another, concentrating on the final location of the equilibrium rather than on the transition. In the model first introduced by John Maynard Keynes, comparative statics analysis is used in the determination of national income. A model of this type cannot handle dynamic problems, such as those connected with the movement between equilibrium and stages of change over time, but it can be used to determine the final equilibrium point of national income under a set of given static conditions.

compensating balance The minimum percentage (usually from 10 to 20%) of a line of credit that a bank's customer is expected to keep on deposit at all times. Thus, if a manufacturer has a line of credit of $1 illion, it might be expected to keep 20% of that amount, or $200,000, on deposit. Since most firms require large working balances, this restriction is normally not particularly significant, and the bank may never make the requirement explicit if the customer keeps the correct amount in a checking account. There was, however, a growing tendency during the 1950s for firms to use their deposits more intensively. As a result, many bankers were forced to remind their customers of compensating balances. If a prospective borrower is not a regular customer of a bank, the compensating-reserve requirement may induce the borrower to become a regular customer, since it is required to keep a certain portion of borrowings on deposit. The portion kept on deposit can be used as a normal working balance. Compensating-balance requirements are considerably more common among large banks than among small ones and among large borrowers than among small borrowers. Balance requirements change considerably during business cycles. They may be high when money is tight and low when credit is easy. One result of compensating balances is to make effective bank interest rates higher than conventional statistical measures indicate. In addition, the fluctuation of effective rates is greater over the course of the business cycle than is indicated by the fluctuation of nominal rates.

compensation of employees   Income received as remuneration for work. It includes wages and salaries paid to employees including executive salaries and bonuses, commissions, payments in kind, incentive payments, and tips in a given time period irrespective of when they were earned. It also includes supplements to wages and salaries, such as employer contributions for social insurance and employer payments for private pension, health, and welfare funds. Compensation of employees accounts for about 70 to 75% of national income. For a detailed discussion of the concept, coverage, and sources of data, see U.S. Department of Commerce, *National Income Supplement*, 1954; see also Richard Ruggles and Nancy D. Ruggles, *National Income Accounts and Income Analysis*, 2d ed., McGraw-Hill, New York, 1956; for quarterly and annual data, see U.S. Department of Commerce, *Survey of Current Business*, monthly.

compensatory fiscal policy   The management of government finance to compensate for fluctuations in national income and employment. Compensatory fiscal policy, which combines deficit and surplus financing, attempts to achieve a high level of employment by maintaining a high level of national income. It uses taxation and spending to produce the desired balance. To maintain the desired level of income during a business decline, any decrease in private spending or investment must be balanced by a government policy of either increasing government spending (raising total government purchases from private business) or reducing taxes (increasing the income of consumers, business, or both). To maintain the desired level of income during a period of overexpansion and inflation, government policy would comprise a reduction in federal spending, a possible increase in taxes, or both steps. If such government action is timely and the amounts involved are large enough, substantial fluctuations in national income and employment may be avoided. Generally, private consumption is relatively stable in the short run, while private investment is relatively volatile. Thus, compensatory fiscal policy is primarily an attempt to counterbalance changes in private investment. For further information, see W. L. Smith and John M. Culbertson (eds.), *Public Finance and Stabilization Policy*, Elsevier, Amsterdam, 1974; Herbert Stein, *The Fiscal Revolution in America*, University of Chicago Press, Chicago, 1969.

competition   The condition prevailing in a market in which rival sellers try to increase their profits at one another's expense. In economic theory, the varieties of competition range from perfect competition, in which numerous firms produce or sell identical goods or services, to oligopoly, in which few large sellers with substantial influence in the market vie with one another for the available business. Early economists envisioned perfect competition as the most effective assurance that consumers would be provided with goods and services at the lowest possible prices. In practice, however, perfect competition is virtually unknown in major industries. Most large industries are dominated by relatively few firms, and competition frequently prevails between substitute goods or services rather than between identical goods or services. In the United States, since the late nineteenth century the federal government has played an active role in attempting to preserve and encourage some measure of competition in major industries. Antitrust laws, such as the Sherman Antitrust Act and the Clayton Antitrust Act, are cornerstones of the government's activities in this area. See Edward H. Chamberlin, *The Theory of Monopolistic Competition,* Harvard University Press, Cambridge, Mass., 1931; Joan Robinson, *The Economics of Imperfect Competition,* 2d ed., St. Martin's Press, New York, 1969; Lester G. Telser, *Economic Theory and the Core,* University of Chicago Press, Chicago, 1978.

competition, imperfect (monopolistic competition)   The market situation that exists when there are many sellers and buyers of a product but each seller has a product with some feature that distinguishes it from other goods, either in fact or in the minds of purchasers. As a result, there are combined features of pure competition and of monopoly in the same firm. The monopolistically competitive firm produces slightly less than a purely competitive firm would, but in the long run it will not earn the excess profits associated with monopoly. Edward H. Chamberlin and Joan Robinson developed the theory independently at about the same time in the 1930s, and it is widely cited as the prevailing condition in retail trade. See Edward H. Chamberlin, *The Theory of Monopolistic Competition,* Harvard University Press, Cambridge, Mass., 1931; Joan Robinson, *The Economics of Imperfect Competition,* 2d ed., St. Martin's Press, New York, 1969; D. S. Watson and Mary A. Holman, *Price Theory and Its Uses,* 4th ed., Houghton Mifflin, Boston, 1976.

competition, perfect   The condition prevailing in a market in which, in addition to the conditions prevailing under pure competition (large numbers of sellers, identical products, unrestricted entry of new sellers), there are (1) perfect knowledge among buyers and sellers of existing market conditions; (2) complete interindustry mobility of productive factors, enabling new entrants to set up selling operations; and (3) no differences among firms in the cost of transporting their products to buyers. This is a refinement of theoretically pure competition. Economic theory says that, under conditions of perfect competition, the consumer is assured of the widest availability of goods at the lowest possible price level. In the real world, however, examples of perfect competition are rare. See Edward H. Chamberlin, *The Theory of Monopolistic Competition,* Harvard University Press, Cambridge, Mass., 1931; Joan Robinson, *The Economics of Imperfect Competition,* 2d ed., St. Martin's Press, New York, 1969.

competition, pure The condition prevailing in a market in which (1) there are a large number of sellers, (2) the goods or services sold are identical, and (3) additional sellers are free to enter the market. Under these circumstances, no single seller is able to affect significantly the price of the product being sold or the quantity offered for sale. Each seller sells at the established market price. Only under purely (or perfectly) competitive conditions, economic theory says, is the consumer assured the widest availability of goods at the lowest possible price level. In the real world, however, examples of purely competitive markets are scarce. With the possible exception of agricultural products, no major industry in the United States meets the criteria of pure competition. John Kenneth Galbraith maintains, however, that certain countervailing powers have developed in the United States between large sellers and buyers that provide the economy with many of the benefits associated with theoretically pure competition. See Edward H. Chamberlin, *The Theory of Monopolistic Competition,* Harvard University Press, Cambridge, Mass., 1931; Joan Robinson, *The Economics of Imperfect Competition,* 2d ed., St. Martin's Press, New York, 1969.

competition, workable The adaptation of businesses to their markets in a way which gives rise to reasonably satisfactory market performance. A satisfactory market performance would include average profit margins which were just large enough to pay for a normal return on investment plus a risk reward, an efficient scale of operation for the producing firms without inefficient, small-scale producers and chronic excess capacity, and a reasonable degree of product quality. Workable competition does not require the standardization of commodities, equally informed firms, equal advantages for all firms, complete independence of action, frictionless movement of resources, free entry, or many of the other requirements of perfect competition. Rather, an attempt is made to prevent the deliberate reduction of output and survival of inefficient firms. Although complete flexibility or optimum use of resources is not achieved under workable competition, the system is an attempt to develop a market structure which offers access to genuine alternatives and protects weaker firms against domination by stronger ones. Workable competition is a less nearly perfect market situation than pure competition, but it is a much more realistic goal for public policy. For further information, see John M. Clark, "Toward a Concept of Workable Competition," *American Economic Review,* vol. 30, no. 2, June 1940, pp. 241–256; Joe Bain, "Workable Competition in Oligopoly," *American Economic Review,* vol. 40, no. 2, May 1950, pp. 35–47.

complementary goods Products or commodities so related that a change in the consumption of one will be accompanied by a similar change in the consumption of the other. Thus if the price of tea declines, its consumption would be expected to increase, which in turn will induce an upward shift in the demand for lemons. The degree of this relationship may be measured by the coefficient of cross elasticity, which in this example relates the change in the quantity of lemons purchased to the change in the price of tea. The formula for this coefficient is

$$CE = \frac{\text{percent change of } Q_1}{\text{percent change of } P_2}$$

where Q_1 is the quantity of commodity 1 and P_2 is the price of commodity 2. (When the prices of one commodity and the quantities of the other commodity move in opposite directions, the sign of the coefficient is minus.) If the goods are substitutes (the prices of one commodity and the quantities of the other move in the same direction), the sign of the coefficient is plus. Independent goods have a zero coefficient of cross elasticity because no relationship exists. See John R. Hicks, *Value and Capital*, 2d ed., Oxford University Press, New York, 1946; Donald S. Watson and Mary A. Holman, *Price Theory and Its Uses*, 4th ed., Houghton Mifflin, Boston, 1976.

complete system of equations   In econometrics, a model or set of equations that includes all equations involved in determining a given economic sector or system. The model is complete if it can be solved for all its endogenous variables. A complete system makes unbiased estimates of parameters possible. For additional information, see Lawrence R. Klein, *An Introduction to Econometrics*, Greenwood, Westport, Conn., 1977.

concentration ratio   The percentage of total business in a given industry that is handled by a specified number of the largest firms. This ratio is a relative index, showing to what extent the ownership or control of an industry is concentrated in the hands of a relatively small number of firms. There is no standard way of measuring the degree of industrial concentration, and a number of different indices have been used. Generally, the concentration ratio has been expressed as the percentage of business assets, production, sales, employment, or profits accounted for by the three to eight largest firms. Concentration refers to both the number and the size distribution of the producers within a given industry. Thus, a market which may be said to be more highly concentrated in the first sense may be relatively less concentrated in the second sense. This ambiguity in the measures of concentration may develop because the standard measures pertain to only the few largest units of a group and do not show whether the firms are dominated by a single firm or whether they share approximately equal market power. Another problem in the use of concentration measures is that these measures do not show the existence of possible competition on the other side of the market: countervailing power. For further information, see Betty Bock and Jack Farkas, *Concentration and Productivity*, The Conference Board, Studies in Business Policy, no. 103, New York, 1969; F. M. Scherer, *Industrial Market Structure and Economic Performance*, Rand, Chicago, 1980.

confluence A situation encountered in regression analysis in which there are linear relations between the independent variables or in which errors of observation introduce linear relations in the independent variables. Multicollinearity and underidentification are two special cases of confluence. For example, when multicollinearity appears, one cannot separate the effects of two or more independent variables because they happen to move together. Where confluence exists, it results in the indeterminacy of the coefficients of a regression equation. The technique known as bunch-map analysis was developed by Frisch in 1934 in an effort to cope with the problems of confluence. For additional information see Lawrence R. Klein, *An Introduction to Econometrics,* Greenwood, Westport, Conn., 1977.

conglomerate A diversified corporation that has grown through mergers that are neither horizontal nor vertical. Conglomerate mergers are classified into three types: product-extension, market-extension, and pure conglomerate mergers. There are those who hold that proliferation of conglomerates is leading to the death of competition, while others argue that the conglomerate is making new forms of competition possible. During the 1969–1970 recession, conglomerates appeared to have lost some of their earlier glamour in the stock market. For additional information, see Betty Bock, "The Conglomerate and the Hippogriff," *The Conference Board Record,* National Industrial Conference Board, New York, February 1972; Keith V. Smith and J. Fred Weston, "Further Evaluation of Conglomerate Performance," *Journal of Business Research,* vol. 5, March 1977, pp. 5–14.

conjugate In mathematics, a term describing two quantities, curves, etc., that present themselves simultaneously and are interchangeable in the enunciation of properties. For example, *conjugate samples* are two samples consecutively drawn from the same time span and are such that the disturbances that brought about corresponding observations have the same absolute value in the two samples. The two samples form a *conjugate set.* For additional information, see Lawrence R. Klein, *An Introduction to Econometrics,* Greenwood, Westport, Conn., 1977.

conservatism An approach to economics and politics which generally favors the *status quo* and resists change. Conservatism views society and its body of institutions as a phenomenon that has developed over a period of time and cannot arbitrarily be changed. It is wary of broad solutions based on abstract reasoning and places greater reliance on experience and gradual change. Conservatism holds the individual and freedom of the individual as its supreme value. The individual is encouraged to exercise individuality, creativity, and self-reliance. Thus, the free enterprise system of free markets, competition, and decentralization of power is basic to economic conservatism. The conservative wishes to limit the role of government, especially the central government, to a few necessary spheres. According to the conservative view, the government should not undertake any program which could be undertaken equally well by private enterprise. Government spending should be kept as low as possible, and the traditional rule of the balanced budget should be upheld. Furthermore, wages, prices, and interest rates should be completely free from government influence. For a fuller exposition of the doctrines of economic conservatism, see Milton Friedman, *Capitalism and Freedom*, The University of Chicago Press, Chicago, 1962.

consolidated statement   The financial reports (statement of financial position, and statement of income and retained earnings) for two or more corporations, eliminating intercorporate debts and profits, and showing minority stockholders' interests. See C. H. Griffin, T. H. Williams, and K. D. Larson, *Advanced Accounting*, Irwin, Homewood, Ill., 1971; for consolidation in the context of generally accepted accounting principles, see Martin A. Miller, *Miller's Comprehensive GAAP Guide*, Harcourt Brace, New York, 1980.

consolidation   A union of two or more companies into a new company. The new corporation takes over the assets and customers of the constituent companies, and the constituent companies are then dissolved. For example, if company A is formed to take over companies X, Y, and Z, only company A remains in existence after the consolidation. Strictly a statutory procedure, consolidation differs from a merger, in which one of the constituent companies remains while the other companies are legally dissolved. Despite this legal difference between a merger and consolidation, the economic consequences of both are the same, permitting operations to be combined under centralized control. See J. Fred Weston and Eugene F. Brigham, *Essentials of Managerial Finance*, 5th ed., Holt, Rinehart and Winston, New York, 1979.

conspicuous consumption   Consumption intended chiefly as an ostentatious display of wealth. Thorstein Veblen, who introduced the concept, maintained that conspicuous consumption exists among all classes of society, even the poorest, who, in their own modest way, attempt to outshine their neighbors by purchasing superior goods even though these are beyond their means. Among the wealthy, costly entertainment, such as fancy balls, were, Veblen maintained, a favored means of carrying out conspicuous consumption. To determine whether a particular outlay fell under the heading of conspicuous consumption, the question was "whether, aside from acquired tastes and from the canons of usage and conventional decency, its result is a net gain in comfort or in the fullness of life." Rigidly applied, Veblen's standard would label as conspicuous consumption the overwhelming majority of consumer expenditures in most industrial nations. See Thorstein Veblen, *The Theory of the Leisure Class*, Random House, New York, 1934, chap. 4.

constant-dollar values (real-dollar values)   A series of dollar values, such as gross national product, personal income, sales, or profits, from which the effect of changes in the purchasing power of the dollar has been removed. The resulting series is in real terms and thus indirectly measures physical volume. The process of converting current-dollar values into constant-dollar values is generally called deflating. Different deflators may be used to adjust different sets of data to constant dollars. Among them are the U.S. Department of Commerce's implicit price deflator, which roughly measures the general price level of the whole economy and is used to deflate gross national product to constant-dollar terms; the U.S. Bureau of Labor Statistics' producer price index of industrial commodities, which is used to deflate industrial sales; and the U.S. Bureau of Labor Statistics' consumer price index, which is used to deflate consumer income and consumer purchases of goods and services. Usually, dollar figures are expressed in terms of dollars of some selected year, such as 1960, 1970, or 1980, or a set of years, such as the average for 1957, 1958, and 1959 or the average for 1976, 1977, and 1978. For deflating techniques, see John E. Freund and Frank J. Williams, *Elementary Business Statistics,* 3d ed., Prentice-Hall, Englewood Cliffs, N.J., 1978.

constant returns, theory of   *See* **returns to scale.**

consumer credit   An arrangement that enables consumers to buy goods and services immediately and pay for them later. Consumer credit is essentially short-term debt. It includes both installment credit, which is scheduled to be repaid in two or more payments; and noninstallment credit, such as single-payment loans, charge accounts, credit cards, and credit extended by hospitals, physicians, and utilities. It does not include home mortgages, which are long-term loans. In U.S. history, consumer credit has existed since the Pilgrims booked passage on the *Mayflower* and paid for it on the installment plan. In the United States, about two-thirds of all cars and about one-half of all television sets, furniture, washing machines, and outboard motorboats are bought on time. For an account of consumer credit practices, see Thomas A. Durkin and Gregory E. Elliehausen, *1977 Consumer Credit Survey,* Federal Reserve Board, Washington, D.C., 1978; for monthly data, see *Federal Reserve Bulletin,* Washington, D.C.

consumer finance company (personal finance company)   A financial institution which specializes in small and personal loans. In the United States, state laws limit the amount of a single loan to $300 or $500 in most cases and specify the amount of interest that can be charged, usually about 2 to 3% per month on the unpaid balance. As high as these interest rates are, they are low in comparison with the loan-shark rates that prevailed before state regulation of these businesses.

consumer goods   Manufactured products used primarily by individuals and families. Consumer goods are generally classified into two major categories according to the degree of durability: (1) durables, such as passenger cars and appliances; and (2) nondurables, such as food, clothing, and tobacco. In the United States, sales of consumer goods totaled nearly $1 trillion in 1981, with durables accounting for about $235 billion, and nondurables for $750 billion. For historical statistics and methods of estimating consumer goods in the national accounts, see U.S. Department of Commerce, *U.S. Income and Output: A Supplement to the Survey of Current Business;* for the latest quarterly estimates, U.S. Department of Commerce, *Survey of Current Business.*

consumer price index   A monthly measure, compiled by U.S. Bureau of Labor Statistics, of changes in the prices of goods and services consumed by urban families and individuals. The index is based on about 125,000 monthly quotations of prices, rents, and property tax rates collected from about 65,000 sources. The items range from food to automobiles and from rent to haircuts, normally purchased by urban wage earners and clerical consumers representing both families and single persons. It does not include items that are brought primarily by suburban and rural families or by lower- and upper-income families. The relative importance given individual items in the index is based on periodic surveys of consumer expenditures. Current prices are expressed as a percentage of average prices during 1967. Although the consumer price index is sometimes incorrectly called the cost-of-living index, it fails to measure the cost of living. This is partly because (1) quality changes are not measured precisely, and (2) there are delays in including new goods and services. The monthly index is prepared for the nation as a whole, for each of seventeen large metropolitan areas, for individual items, and for commodity and service groupings. All data are published in U.S. Department of Labor *Monthly Labor Review;* for a detailed critique of concepts and problems, see *The Price Statistics of the Federal Government,* National Bureau of Economic Research, New York, 1961.

consumer sovereignty   The dominant role of the consumer in determining the types and quantities of goods produced by an economic system. The principle of consumer sovereignty is a key factor in the organization of production in a free economy. Each consumer purchase is actually the casting of "dollar votes," by which consumers register their desires in terms of goods and services. The casting of dollar votes by consumers is translated directly into business profits, the motivating factor in production, so that changes in demand result in corresponding changes in production patterns. As consumer demand for certain goods increases, production of those goods is increased to take advantage of the new potentialities for profit. Many economists believe that consumer sovereignty is limited by such factors as lack of knowledge about products and by monopoly. For further information, see George Katona, *The Powerful Consumer,* McGraw-Hill, New York, 1960; Richard H. Leftwich, *The Price System and Resource Allocation,* 6th ed., Dryden Press, Hinsdale, Ill., 1976.

consumer's surplus   The difference between the price that a consumer pays for a good or a service and the amount that the consumer would be willing to pay rather than to do without the purchase. The concept of the consumer's surplus was introduced formally into value theory by Alfred Marshall, who held that it serves as a measure of the satisfaction that a consumer receives from a purchase, above and beyond the sacrifices made to acquire the purchase as measured by its price. For Marshall's statement, see Alfred Marshall, *Principles of Economics,* 8th ed., Macmillan, New York, 1948, book III, chap. 6; see also E. Mishan, *Elements of Cost-Benefit Analysis,* Allen and Unwin, Winchester, Mass., 1971, chaps. 5–7.

consumer theory   The abstraction of consumer behavior patterns based on analysis of consumer activity. Originally, consumer theory was concerned solely with the way consumers allocated a specified income among a set of purchased goods and services; now consumer theory has broadened to include concern with how consumers divide income between spending and saving, the role consumers play in supply of labor services to the market, and the way in which consumers divide their time between the marketplace, home production and consumption, and leisure time. Standard consumer theory is represented by Marshallian demand analysis—the demand function indicates the amount that consumers are willing to purchase at a given price—and indifference function analysis developed by Hicks and Slutsky, which attempts to determine how consumers will allocate a fixed budget among various purchasable commodities. Modern economics is concerned with aggregate movements in consumer spending or saving relative to income. The so-called consumption function is the relationship between consumer income and consumer spending. Friedman's permanent income hypothesis treats consumption decisions as being based on a longer-run concept of income. The life-cycle model developed by Modigliani, Ando, and Brumberg, which attempts to deal normatively with the way in which consumers dispose of their income over time, maintains that wealth (including future earnings) plays a crucial role in consumption decisions. Another related approach relies on analysis of the effect of waves of optimism and pessimism on consumer spending and saving decisions. A different development in consumer theory concerns analysis of the supply side of consumer choices and of the way in which consumers allocate their time between various types of consumption and production activities. For additional information, see Thomas F. Juster, "Consumer Theory," in D. Greenwald (ed.), *Encyclopedia of Economics,* McGraw-Hill, New York, 1982.

consumption function   A function relating the level of consumption expenditures to the level of national income. The basis of the formulation introduced by John Maynard Keynes was that real consumption expenditures are a stable function of real income. Keynes felt that the marginal propensity to consume (the percentage of an addition to income which is spent for consumption) is positive but less than unity, that the marginal propensity to consume is less than the average propensity to consume and that it falls as the level of income rises. Empirical studies seem to confirm the stable relationship of consumption to the level of income, the value of the marginal propensity to consume being about 0.75 in the United States. There is, however, little evidence that the marginal propensity declines with rising income even though it has been found to be lower than the average propensity to consume. It has also been determined that the longer the time period considered, the steeper the consumption function becomes (the higher the marginal propensity to consume). This fact indicates that the consumption function may be related not so closely to current income as to some measure of long-run income or wealth. It has also been proposed that differences in consumption behavior may be due to differences in relative income (income to which one is accustomed) rather than to the level of absolute income. For further information, see J. M. Keynes, *The General Theory of Employment, Interest, and Money,* Harcourt Brace, New York, 1936, chaps. 8, 10; Milton Friedman, *A Theory of the Consumption Function,* National Bureau of Economic Research, New York, 1955; Michael R. Darby, "The Consumer Expenditure Function," in *Explorations in Economic Research,* no. 4, National Bureau of Economic Research, New York, Winter–Spring, 1977–1978, pp. 645–674.

consumption tax   A levy on consumer goods. The base of a consumption tax levied on the buyers or sellers of products is the amount or value of goods bought or sold. Not all consumption taxes are levied originally on consumers, but those that are levied on manufacturers and distributors can be shifted forward by including the amount of the tax in the price of the consumer good, so that the consumer bears the final`burden. The amount of the tax for each individual varies with the level of that individual's expenditures. The most common forms of consumption taxes are the retail sales tax, the turnover tax, taxes on the production, sale, and use of particular goods (taxes on business gross receipts, use taxes, and excise taxes), and import duties. Although consumption taxes are considered to be regressive, placing a larger burden on the poor than on the rich, they offer the advantages of stable revenues (since consumption is usually more stable than income), relatively low cost of collection, ability to produce revenue immediately, and utility in regulating consumption (e.g., consumption of luxuries). The regressive nature of such consumption taxes as the sales tax can be reduced by exempting certain necessities, such as food. For additional information, see Harold Groves, *Federal Tax Treatment of the Family,* Greenwood, Westport, Conn., 1977.

contestable market   A market in which entry is absolutely free and exit is absolutely costless. The entrant firm suffers no disadvantage in terms of production techniques or product quality relative to firms already in the market. It is a requirement of contestability that there be no cost discrimination against entrants. Any firm can leave the market without impediment, and in the process of departure can recoup any costs incurred in the entry process. The most distinctive aspect of a contestable market is its vulnerability to hit-and-run entry. Thus even a transient profit opportunity need not be neglected by a potential entrant firm, for it can enter and, before prices change, collect its gains and depart without cost should the business climate become hostile. Contestability is a broader ideal than perfect competition. Perfectly contestable markets do not populate the real world any more than perfectly competitive markets do. But perfect contestability, as a broader ideal, provides a standard for policy that is far more flexible and widely applicable than perfect competition. In a perfectly contestable marketplace the invisible hand holds sway. The theory of contestability permits reexamination of the domain of the invisible hand and contributes to the theory of oligopoly. Contestability theory departs from competition theory, which implicitly takes industry structure to be determined exogenously in a totally unspecified way. Instead, contestability theory analyzes the determination of industry structure endogenously, that is, simultaneously with other variables that are more traditionally treated in the theory of the firm and industry, such as prices and outputs. For further information, see William J. Baumol, "Contestable Markets: An Uprising in the Theory of Industrial Structure," *American Economic Review,* vol. 12, no. 1, March 1982, pp. 1–15; William J. Baumol, John C. Panzar, and Robert D. Willig, *Contestable Markets and the Theory of Industry Structure,* Harcourt Brace, New York, 1982.

contract authorization   A financial grant by the Congress of the United States, empowering federal agencies to incur obligations, usually for construction projects which will take a considerable time to complete, before appropriations have been made to cover them. Most authorizations are enacted for a one- or two-year period; if they are not obligated during that time, they usually expire. Before money may be disbursed to pay a federal obligation incurred under authorization, an appropriation of funds is necessary. For details of the process by which the federal government reaches decisions on expenditures, see Peter O. Steiner, "Public Expenditure Budgeting," in *The Economics of Public Finance, Studies of Government Finance,* Brookings Institution, Washington, D.C. 1974; see also Murray L. Weidenbaum, "The Federal Government Spending Process," in U.S. Joint Economic Committee, *Federal Expenditure Policy for Economic Growth and Stability,* Washington, D.C., 1957.

contract curve   The locus of optimal points in a trading situation with one buyer and one seller. The contract curve is derived with the help of the Edgeworth box, introduced by the English economist F. Y. Edgeworth. In the situation analyzed by the contract curve, there is one seller (the input supplier) and one buyer (the input purchaser). First, an indifference map between money and X (the quality of input sold) is drawn for each of the

Buyer's Indifference Map   **Seller's Indifference Map**

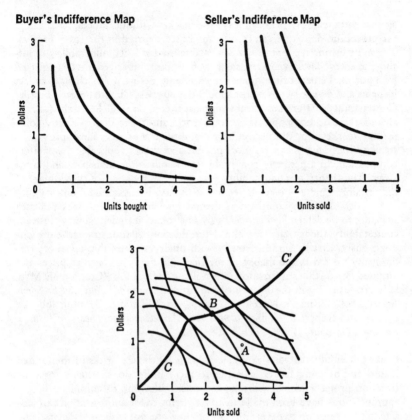

two individuals (see the accompanying figure). The two indifference maps are combined by rotating one (the seller's) by 180° and joining the ends of the axes (see figure). The length of the vertical axis (money) is determined by the buyer's money supply; the length of the horizontal axis (output sold), by the productive capacity of the seller. Every point in the box can be interpreted as a trade of a certain number of dollars (e.g., 1 at point A) for a certain number of input units (e.g., 3 at point A). Whatever input does not remain in the hands of the seller after the trade has been completed must have gone to the buyer; whatever money the buyer does not have after the trade must be in the hands of the seller. The contract curve (CC') is the locus of all points of tangency between the buyer's and the seller's indifference curves. For every trading point not on the contract curve, there exists a point on the curve which is mutually advantageous to both buyer and seller. For example, if the trade first agreed on by both buyer and seller is represented by point A, they could not move to point B and both be better off. Thus, the actual trading point should finally be located somewhere along the contract curve (the actual location along the curve is indeterminate); otherwise, it would be to the advantage of both buyer and seller to renegotiate the deal and move to a point on the curve where no further mutually advantageous renegotiation would be possible. For a fuller explanation of the contract curve, see William Baumol, *Economic Theory and Operations Analysis,* 4th ed., Prentice-Hall, Englewood Cliffs, N.J., 1977; F. Y. Edgeworth, *Mathematical Psychics,* Kelley, New York, 1881, pp. 17ff.

contraction A widespread decline in economic activity. The term covers both depressions and recessions. A contraction begins after the peak in economic activity has been attained and continues until the trough has been reached. Contractions vary widely in the degree and duration of the decline. Between 1854 and 1980 there were twenty-seven contractions in the United States; the shortest (1980) lasted three months, and the longest (1873–1879) sixty-five months. The 1929–1933 contraction lasted forty-five months. For more detailed information on contractions, see Geoffrey H. Moore (ed.), *Business Cycle Indicators,* Princeton University Press, Princeton, N.J., 1961.

conversion The exchange of one security for another. The term usually applies to the exchange of preferred stock for common stock or of bonds or debentures (unsecured bonds) for common or preferred stock. All convertible securities are restricted by the terms of conversion, which are contained in the certificate of incorporation in the case of stocks and in the indenture in the case of bonds. The terms of conversion stipulate the kind of security which the bondholder or stockholder can convert to, the conversion rate, and the period during which the holder is allowed to exchange the securities. For example, a holder of a debenture worth $1,000 may be allowed to convert it into fifty shares of common stock of the same corporation at $20 per share at any time during a ten-year period. As long as the market prices of the debenture and the stock are at $1,000 and $20, respectively, it makes little difference which security is held (except for any difference between dividend and interest yields). Generally, when the price of the common stock increases, the price of the convertible debenture also rises. See J. Fred Weston and Eugene F. Brigham, *Essentials of Managerial Finance,* 5th ed., Holt, Rinehart and Winston, New York, 1979.

convertible debenture A certificate issued by a corporation as evidence of debt that can be converted at the option of the holder into other securities (usually common stock, but sometimes preferred stock) of the same corporation. Each debenture can be converted into a specified number of shares of stock at a stipulated price for a certain period. There are two advantages to convertible debentures for the issuing corporation: (1) The conversion privilege makes the debentures more attractive to investors and tends to reduce interest costs. (2) The debentures facilitate the extinction of debt because debt declines and equity (stock) increases as holders convert their debentures. The major disadvantage is discrimination against the company's stockholders, whose equity is diluted as the holders of debentures convert them. At all times during the conversion period, there is a price relationship between the debenture and the stock. It is based on the conversion price, the number of shares into which each debenture can be converted, and the value that the market puts on the conversion privilege. For example, a $1,000 debenture that can be converted into fifty shares of common stock at $20 per share will normally trade in the market at a price higher than $1,000 because of the conversion privilege. Moreover, the price of the convertible debenture will change as the price of the stock changes because of the conversion feature. Convertible debentures appeal to investors because they yield a fixed income (interest) without limiting the holder's participation in the growth of the company; if the company grows, the price of the common stock will increase. Speculators favor convertible debentures because the law allows them to borrow more money to purchase and carry debentures than common or preferred stocks, thus giving them more leverage. See J. Fred Weston and Eugene F. Brigham, *Essentials of Managerial Finance*, 5th ed., Holt, Rinehart and Winston, New York, 1979.

corporate income tax   A tax levied on the earnings of corporations. It was first instituted on the federal level in the United States in 1901. Since 1936, when it became progressive, the tax has applied to undistributed net income as well as to income distributed as dividends. In 1980 the corporate income tax was reduced from 48 to 46%. The tax is regarded as a companion measure to the personal income tax, constituting an extension of that tax to corporate income, but it differs from the latter in several important respects. The corporate income tax does not provide for a minimum exemption to cover the cost of equity capital. The rate of the tax depends on the size of the corporation's total income rather than on the net income of its owners, and the dividends distributed by the corporation are taxed twice, once as corporate earnings and again as shareholders' dividend income. Many experts believe that this double taxation of distributed corporate profits, without regard for the individual shareholder's ability to pay the tax, is the most objectionable part of the corporate tax structure. For further information on the federal corporate income tax, see Joseph A. Pechman, *Federal Tax Policy,* 3d ed., Brookings Institution, Washington, D.C., 1977.

corporation, business   A voluntary organization of persons, either actual individuals or legal entities, legally bound together to form a business enterprise. Industrial corporations became significant in the United States after the Civil War, when it was necessary to raise large amounts of capital for reconstruction. About 25% of U.S. businesses are now in the corporate form, and corporations clearly dominate the economy. The advantages of the corporate form of business enterprise are as follows: (1) It is by far the most effective form of business organization for the raising of capital funds. (2) It has limited liability. The owners (stockholders) risk only what they paid for the stock; their personal assets are not at stake if the corporation goes bankrupt. Creditors can sue the corporation as a legal person but not the owners of that corporation as individuals. (3) As a legal entity, the corporation has a perpetual life independent of its owners or of its individual officials. Proprietorships and partnerships, on the other hand, are subject to sudden and unpredictable demise. (4) Because of its size, the corporation can secure more specialized and more efficient management than can proprietorships and partnerships and can take full advantage of any gains to be had from large-scale production. (5) Incorporation may provide tax advantage when net profits are sizable. The maximum tax rate of 46% on a corporation is preferable to the maximum personal income tax rate of 50%. There are also disadvantages to the corporate form: (1) The corporation is difficult to form because of legal complications and expense in obtaining a corporate charter from the state. (2) Corporate operations are limited to those enumerated in the charter, thus making the corporation seem less flexible than other forms in its business activities. (This shortcoming is, however, more apparent than real.) (3) Whereas in the sole proprietorship and partnership forms, the persons who own the real and financial assets of the firm also manage and control these assets, corporate ownership is widely scattered among relatively small owners. Thus, real control is likely to rest not with those who own a majority of the stock but rather with the management (the board of directors). (4) Corporate income paid out as dividends to stockholders is taxed twice, once as part of corporate profits and again as part of the stockholders' personal incomes. See Lyman A. Keith and Carlo E. Gubellini, *Introduction to Business Enterprise,* 4th ed., McGraw-Hill, New York, 1975.

correlation   The statistical technique which relates a dependent economic variable to one or more independent variables over a period of time in order to determine how close the relationship between the variables is. This technique may be used for business forecasting. When more than one independent variable is used, the relationship is called a multiple correlation. Thus, a forecaster may relate disposable personal income and time, in units of a year, to consumer expenditures to derive a mathematical formula which will predict the future level of consumer spending. A single business or industry can use similar relationships to predict its own sales. Gross national product, disposable income, and industrial production are commonly used as the independent variables. For information concerning correlation methodology, see Karl A. Fox and Tej K. Kaul, *Intermediate Economic Statistics,* Krieger, Melbourne, Fla., 1980.

correlogram   The graph of the serial correlation of order k as ordinate against k as abscissa; a chart technique that may help to identify the type of econometric model to which a given time series conforms. In the nonstochastic case, if a trendless or detrended time series is cyclical (or periodic), its nature can be determined by the unaided eye observing a faithful pattern. In the stochastic case, if a series oscillates (is neither random nor periodic), the true pattern may be obscured by superimposed random effects. A strictly periodic time series has a periodic correlogram. In contrast, the correlogram of a moving average of random terms reveals no fixed periodicity. The larger the random element in a time series, the less reliable that time series' correlogram is. The term correlogram was coined by Wold in 1938, but the technique was used earlier by Yule. For additional information, see Karl A. Fox and Tej K. Kaul, *Intermediate Economic Statistics,* Krieger, Melbourne, Fla., 1980.

cost In economics, the value of the factors of production used by a firm in producing or distributing goods and services or engaging in both activities. The cost of a factor unit to the firm equals the maximum amount which the factor could earn in alternative employment. For this reason, the term alternative cost, or opportunity cost, is used in economic theory instead of cost alone. A firm's costs include expenditures, or outlay costs, which are the ordinary business expenses; and nonexpenditures, or implicit costs, which are not paid out by the firm, but which accrue directly to the firm itself or to its owners. Implicit costs arise when factors and money capital are owned by the firm. For additional details on the role of cost in economics, see George J. Stigler, *The Theory of Price,* rev. ed., Macmillan, New York, 1952; for a discussion of the types of costs relevant to decision making, see Milton H. Spencer, *Managerial Economics,* Irwin, Homewood, Ill., 1968, pp. 213–221.

cost-benefit analysis Any systematic, quantitative appraisal of a public project to determine whether the benefits of the project justify the costs. The cost-benefit analysis is an aid to decision makers. Described as applied welfare economics, the cost-benefit analysis is comprised of five steps: (1) identification of all the effects of the project—such as changes in output levels, prices, income, environment, (2) quantitative estimation, in units, of these effects, (3) development of a monetary value of these effects, (4) aggregation of all effects in each time period and over all time periods through an approach to discounting future costs and benefits, and (5) determination of how sensitive the results of the study are to changes in the values of the variables and parameters and to changes in the probability of these occurrences. In 1844, Jules Dupuit, a French engineer, developed the concept of consumers' surplus, the cornerstone of cost-benefit analysis. The U.S. Flood Control Act of 1936, the benefits of which were to be greater than the cost, stimulated work in theory and application of cost-benefit analysis in water resources. Cost-benefit analysis was later employed in defense analysis and, since the 1960s, in all areas of public expenditures. Capital-budgeting analysis in the private sector is equivalent to cost-benefit analysis in the public sector. Critics of cost-benefit analysis point out that it is not possible to reduce everything to the common denominator of money and that economic substitutes for the political process are insidious. Proponents admit that criticisms are justified, but they ask what the alternative is. For further discussion, see E. J. Mishan, *Cost Benefit Analysis*, Praeger, New York, 1976; Peter G. Sassone and W. A. Schaffer, *Cost-Benefit Analysis: A Handbook*, Academic Press, New York, 1978.

cost depletion   *See* depletion allowance.

cost of living   The amount of money needed to buy goods and services to provide a given standard of living. Throughout the world, there are various standards of living, ranging from the subsistence level to the luxury level. The term cost of living is sometimes incorrectly used to describe a consumer price index, which measures price changes of a fixed list of goods and services in which the quantities and qualities remain constant over a period of time. For differences between a cost-of-living index and a consumer price index, see *Government Price Statistics, Hearings before the Subcommittee on Economic Statistics of the U.S. Joint Economic Committee,* Jan. 24, 1961, Washington, D.C., 1961; see also Stephen D. Braithwait, "The Substitution Bias of the Laspeyres Price Index: An Analysis Using Estimated Cost-of-Living Indexes," *American Economic Review,* March 1980, pp. 64–77.

cost-plus-percentage-fee contract   A contract which provides that the contractor will be paid for all the costs necessary to perform the work of the contract, plus a fee specified as a definite percentage of the total cost of the work. The cost-plus-percentage-fee form is often used in construction contracts. With such a contract, the owner does not know in advance what the work will finally cost, but construction can begin at an early date, and the job can soon be completed. Under a cost-plus-percentage-fee contract, however, the owner must exercise a greater degree of control over the contractor than would be necessary under a cost-plus-fixed-fee contract. The contractor obviously has an incentive to increase total costs, since the contractor's fee, which is based on a percentage, increases as the costs of the operations increase.

countercyclical action   A governmental effort to combat the cyclical instability of the private enterprise system. Such action can take many countercyclical forms, including fiscal policy, monetary policy, and transfer payments. The basic aim of all such actions is to eliminate the effects of the periodic fluctuations on the national economy and to stabilize national income and production.

countervailing duty   An import tax levied on a commodity on which exporters have been paid a subsidy or an export bounty. The main purpose of a countervailing duty is to offset the special advantage of subsidized exports, placing them on an equal footing with other imports and with domestic products. The amount of the countervailing duty usually equals the amount of the subsidy. The use of the countervailing duty is a method of counteracting subsidized dumping operations by foreign countries.

countervailing power   The term applied to the forces that arise in an economy to offset some of the bargaining power enjoyed by large buyers and sellers in the marketplace. Countervailing power thus acts as a substitute for some of the forces normally expected in a competitive economy. Among the countervailing powers that have evolved in the United States are, on the one hand, powerful labor unions, which influence the prices that large corporations must pay for an important natural resource, labor; and, on the other hand, large retail chains (such as Sears, Roebuck and Company or A&P), which through their purchasing policies can influence the prices that large manufacturing firms receive for their products. The theory of countervailing power is advanced by John Kenneth Galbraith in *American Capitalism: The Theory of Countervailing Power,* Houghton Mifflin, Boston, 1952; for a criticism of Galbraith's theory, see George J. Stigler, "The Economist Plays with Blocs," Papers and Proceedings, 66th annual meeting of the American Economic Association, *American Economic Review,* vol. 44, no. 2, May 1954.

covariance   The first product moment of two variates about their mean values. The econometric formulation measures the degree of intercorrelation between the independent variables in multiple correlation analysis. For additional information, see Karl A. Fox and Tej K. Kaul, *Intermediate Economic Statistics,* Krieger, Melbourne, Fla., 1980.

craft union   A labor union that limits its membership to a particular craft or skilled trade. It was in this form that trade unionism first made its appearance in the United States. Most modern craft unions, however, have broadened their jurisdiction to include occupations and skills not closely related to the originally designated craft. Thus, the International Association of Machinists, a craft union, has brought production workers in the aircraft industry into its union and, in effect, has become an industrial union. In most craft unions, the local has a geographical jurisdiction, that is, the members of a craft in a given city or county. The craft basis of a local is often finer than that of its national union. Thus, the bricklayers, masons, and plasterers, all members of the same national union, have separate locals in most U.S. cities. Despite the long-run trend toward the narrowing of pay differentials among occupations in the economy as a whole, some unions of highly paid craftspeople have been successful in limiting the narrowing of differentials in their industries. When several crafts are represented in one craft union, the highest-paid crafts often dominate the internal politics of the union. See Gordon F. Bloom and Herbert R. Northrup, *Economics of Labor Relations,* 5th ed., Irwin, Homewood, Ill., 1977.

Cramer's rule A rule for solving multivariate, simultaneous linear equations. It is based on the fact that all terms in simultaneous equations, except coefficients of regression, are known numbers. The coefficients of regression may be solved for by using Cramer's rule: the ratio of two determinants that yield each unknown value. The determinants are always square, and their numerical values can be determined. For a detailed set of instructions, consult Karl A. Fox and Tej K. Kaul, *Intermediate Economic Statistics*, Krieger, Melbourne, Fla., 1980.

crawling peg (sliding peg) A technique for allowing exchange rates to drift slowly and steadily by weekly, monthly, or quarterly alterations up to a maximum annual rate of 2 to 3%, either automatically or with deliberate guidance. This type of limited exchange-rate flexibility is thought to be small enough to discourage speculation in foreign-exchange markets. It would also provide relative stability for international trade and payments and sufficient scope for long-run exchange-rate adjustments. Some economists believe this technique would be appropriate for offsetting differences in the rate at which different countries' cost levels are rising, but they have doubts that it would discourage speculation. For additional information, see Paul A. Samuelson, *Economics*, 9th ed., McGraw-Hill, New York, 1973, pp. 653–654.

credit An exchange of goods or services for a promise of future payment. Credit is necessary in a dynamic economy because of the time that elapses between the production of a good and its ultimate sale and consumption. Credit bridges this gap. About 90% of the sales made by manufacturers and wholesalers and 30% of the retail sales involve the use of credit. Credit in manufacturing industries is called business credit, and credit extended by retail stores is called consumer credit. A common form of credit used in business is the open, or book, account, in which the seller keeps a record of the credit extended to the buyer and bills the buyer when payment is due. Written business credit instruments include promissory notes, trade acceptances, and letters of credit. Consumer credit, which facilitates the immediate purchase of goods and services, usually takes the form of charge accounts, installment accounts, and personal loans. The risk in extending credit is the possibility that future payment by the buyer will not be made. For additional details, see the Hunt Commission, *The Report of the President's Commission on Financial Structure and Regulation*, Washington, D.C., 1971.

credit control Regulation of the flow of new credit into the economy, either to curb inflationary pressures or to help stimulate economic activity. Several different levers are available for this regulation: (1) The Federal Reserve System can raise or reduce the rediscount rate, which is the price that commercial banks must pay for borrowing from the central bank. (2) It can engage in open-market operations in the government securities market to absorb or increase the supply of idle funds. (3) It can raise or lower the level of reserves that commercial banks must keep immobile. (4) With congressional authorization, it can set limits on the credit terms offered in loans on securities, mortgages, and consumer credit. The first three of these levers limit or augment the volume of funds available to the commercial banking system for credit expansion. They also have an indirect impact on the price (interest rate) charged for new credit, and they influence indirectly the size and quality of the new loans that can be made by the banks. Only the specific controls on securities, mortgages, and consumer credit can be called direct rationing. Some observers believe that the fiscal policies of the U.S. Treasury Department also represent a form of credit control, in that they may add to or relieve the strain on capital markets. See *The Federal Reserve System, Purposes and Functions,* Board of Governors of the Federal Reserve System, Washington, D.C., 1974.

credit crunch   A stage in the business cycle at the end of an expansion, characterized by high interest rates and restrictions on the availability of bank credit. A credit crunch occurs when the demand for credit outruns the supply of credit and the central bank is unwilling to expand the money supply to accommodate these demands. Credit crunches usually contribute to a slowdown in economic activity, and a recession follows shortly thereafter.

credit rating   The evaluation of an individual's or business firm's creditworthiness, or ability and willingness to repay a loan. Credit ratings are made to assist potential lenders in determining the probable risk associated with lending money to an individual or business firm. Credit ratings of business firms, and of securities of state and local governments, are made by the large credit-rating services: Dun & Bradstreet and Standard & Poor's. Particularly difficult to determine are the ratings of privately held businesses, which are not required to make public their financial statements. Other credit-rating firms provide credit information on individuals, through a collection of information on their payments of loans, credit card balances, etc. These firms include TRW Credit Data, Trans Union, and CBI. Legislation has been passed that allows individuals to obtain the information about themselves that is on file with these consumer credit information services to check their accuracy. Credit ratings are not infallible guides to, or guarantees of, loan repayments. However, those firms and individuals with higher credit ratings will generally be able to secure larger amounts of financing, and at lower interest rates, than those with less favorable credit ratings.

cross elasticity   A measure of the influence of the price of one good on the demand for another. The cross elasticity of demand for good X in terms of the price of good Y is the percentage change in the quantity bought of X divided by the percentage change in the price of Y, assuming that consumer tastes, money incomes, and all other prices are constant. The cross elasticity measures the degree of relationship between the two goods; the higher the cross elasticity between X and Y, the greater the interdependence between them. If a fall in the price of Y causes the demand for good X to rise (e.g., a fall in the price of tennis rackets causes a greater number of tennis balls to be demanded), the cross elasticity of demand is negative (since the numerator and denominator have different algebraic signs), and the two goods—tennis balls and tennis rackets—are complementary goods. A decline in the price of one of the complementary goods, by stimulating an increased use of the good, will raise the marginal utility of the other good and thus increase the quantity of the second good that is bought. If, however, a reduction in the price of Y causes the demand for X to fall (e.g., a fall in the price of coffee causes the demand for tea to fall), then the cross elasticity of demand between coffee and tea is positive, and the two goods are rival commodities, or substitute goods. The fall in the price of one good, by stimulating an increased use of the good, lowers the marginal utility of the other good and thus decreases the quantity of the second good that is bought. Cross elasticity is a pure measure of complementarity and the ability of goods to be substituted only if the commodities in question account for a very small proportion of the total budget, so that the income effect of the price change can be ignored. For further information, see George J. Stigler, *The Theory of Price,* 3d ed., Macmillan, New York, 1966.

cross-sectional analysis   The analysis of variation arising from interindividual differences with respect to one or more characteristics at a given point in time or during a short time interval—for example, the analysis of family budgets showing expenditures in combination with information on income and a variety of demographic characteristics. The involved information is usually collected according to a rigorous sample design that is based on probability calculations and is intended to produce a sample that is representative of some universe. For additional information, see Karl A. Fox and Tej K. Kaul, *Intermediate Economic Statistics,* Krieger, Melbourne, Fla., 1980; G. S. Maddala, "The Use of Variance Components Models in Pooling Cross-Section and Time Series Data," *Econometrica,* no. 138, 1971, pp. 341–358.

currency   The tangible, circulating portion of a nation's money supply, composed of bank notes, government notes, and coins. The term is sometimes used to refer to paper money only. Currency constitutes about 23% of the U.S. money supply, narrowly defined; paper money alone accounts for about 20%. The rest of the money supply is in the form of demand deposits or checking accounts. Currency alone is legal tender in the United States. It is used chiefly for retail purchases and the payment of wages. The currency of the United States consists of Federal Reserve notes and treasury notes and coins. This currency is put into circulation when the Federal Reserve banks supply vault cash to commercial banks. The latter, in turn, need it for their customers and pay for it by drawing on their reserve on deposit at the Federal Reserve banks. See Lawrence S. Ritter and William L. Silber, *Principles of*

Money, Banking and Financial Markets, 3d rev. ed., Basic Books, New York, 1980; for monthly data on the total amounts of currency in circulation, see *Federal Reserve Bulletin,* Washington, D.C.; for data on weekly changes in the amount of currency in circulation, see Federal Reserve Bank of New York, *Monthly Review.*

currency convertibility   The privilege extended to a holder of a nation's currency to exchange holdings, at the rate of exchange, for the currency of another nation for any purpose. Under a condition of full currency convertibility, any holder of any national currency is guaranteed unrestricted currency exchange privileges even in times of balance-of-payments deficits. The major advantage of currency convertibility is that it permits consumers or producers to transact their business in the markets most satisfactory to themselves. Consumers, for example, can purchase goods or services in a foreign market when those available in the home market are unsatisfactory and pay for them in their national currency, which the seller abroad may, in turn, exchange for an equivalent value of the seller's national currency. Currency convertibility is thus an essential element in the workings of international economic competition. Because of inadequate holdings of foreign currencies, a nation may be forced to suspend currency convertibility. Some nations have used such suspensions as a discriminatory weapon for political or other purposes. The International Monetary Fund attempts to prevent the involuntary rupture of currency convertibility by lending sufficient funds in appropriate national currencies to nations faced with a sudden rise in the demand for foreign currency. For a fuller discussion of the question, see Gottfried Haberler, *Currency Convertibility,* American Enterprise Association, Washington, D.C., 1954.

currency school   A school of economic thought that was prominent in England in the first half of the nineteenth century. At that time there was a public debate on the proper role of the Bank of England in the issuance of currency and the currency needs of the economy. The railroad boom and the subsequent panic of 1837 led to a controversy between the currency school and the banking school. The former advocated a regulated supply of money, letting it vary as a purely metallic currency so that it responded automatically to any inflow or outflow of gold. The Bank of England leaned toward this view and followed the rule of maintaining a constant ratio of security holdings, loans, investments, and discounted paper to total liabilities. In contrast, members of the banking school denied that it was possible to overissue convertible-currency paper, inasmuch as "the needs of trade" automatically regulated the volume of issued notes. They argued that there was no need for statutory control of the currency, provided convertibility was maintained. Underlying the debate was the definition of money supply. The currency school insisted that only bank notes and coin were money. Therefore, bank lending policies did not need to be regulated, and if the monetary system could be tied directly to gold, all monetary problems would be avoided. For further information, see L. Robbins, *Robert Torrens and the Evolution of Classical Economics,* Macmillan, London, 1958; T. Humphrey, "The Quantity Theory of Money: Its Historical Evolution and Role in Policy Debates," *Economic Review,* no. 60, May–June 1974, pp. 2–19.

current account, balance-of-payments   Entries in the balance-of-payments account which summarize all international current account transactions. These include exports and imports of goods and services by individuals and government. Thus, current account transactions cover both visible items (merchandise) and invisible items (services). Among the invisible items are shipping and air transportation, travel expenditures, interest and dividends on investments, private and governmental gifts, and miscellaneous services. For additional information, see International Monetary Fund, *Balance of Payments Manual,* Washington, D.C., January 1981.

customs duty   *See* **tariff.**

customs union   An agreement between countries to abolish all tariffs between the members of the union and to adopt a uniform tariff vis-à-vis other nations. The agreement may refer not only to import and export duties, but also to any charges or quotas tending to restrict trade. Thus, in order to be able to sell to a larger market, individual countries surrender their right to protect domestic industry from other members of the union through the traditional devices of trade restriction. The term customs union may refer to one group of products (iron and steel, for example) or to complete economic integration, such as now exists in the European Economic Community. A customs union differs from a free-trade area, which does not include a uniform external tariff, each country maintaining autonomy in its relations with third countries. In general, the higher the barriers removed, the greater will be the expansion of trade; the lower the external trade barriers, the less diversion there will be. Domestic producers tend to resist tariff reductions that threaten to increase total imports, but they are much more amenable to tariff reductions which merely shift the source of imports from one outside supplier to another foreign supplier within the preferential area. A classic work in this field is Jacob Viner, *The Customs Union Issue,* Carnegie Endowment for International Peace, New York, 1950.

cyclical unemployment   Unemployment that results from the depression period of the business cycle. Its immediate cause is a lack of demand for labor due to the downward swing in the economy. Cyclical unemployment is hard to predict, since it is irregular in occurrence and variable in duration and intensity. In the United States, it has varied in severity from 6% of the labor force in the 1949–1950, 1953–1954, and 1969–1970 recessions to 25% in 1934, and in length from one year in the 1957–1958 recession to the twelve years of depression from 1930 to 1941. Cyclical unemployment affects different industries and workers in different ways. The capital goods industries are usually the most susceptible, since the demand for their goods fluctuates widely with the swings in the business cycle. The burden of cyclical unemployment is concentrated in low-paid, unskilled workers, especially in recessions of short duration. To reduce cyclical unemployment, it is necessary to attack the basic cause and to smooth out the fluctuations in the business cycle. For further information, see Gordon F. Bloom and Herbert R. Northrup, *Economics of Labor Relations,* 4th ed., Irwin, Homewood, Ill., 1977.

data bank   A collection of organized, usually computer-readable data, textual and/or numerical, put in by an administrator and withdrawn by a relatively large number of independent users. The primary purpose of data banks is the maintenance and easy dissemination of information. Textual data banks consist of bibliographies, abstracts, indexes, or other reference material. Numerical or statistical data banks may contain company statistics, cross-sectional data, microdata, macroeconomic time series, or any variation and combination of these. Machine-readable microdata banks consist of microdata files which are usually organized in a cross-sectional manner—they contain a number of items of information about each unit at one point in time or over one period of time. Time-series data banks contain historical time series at all levels of aggregation. Some advantages of time-series data banks are that they eliminate duplication of effort, users do not have to collect data from various sources as they are updated, they do not have to keep track of revisions, and they need not computerize the data for use in analyses, models, simulations, or other processes. Disadvantages of data banks are that users have little control over the accuracy of the data and have to depend on explanatory information provided by the data bank. For a general discussion, see Ralph L. Bosco (ed.), *Data Bases, Computers and the Social Sciences,* Wiley-Interscience, New York, 1970. For a discussion of one data bank, see Charlotte Boschan, "The NBER Time Series Data Bank," *Annals of Economic and Social Measurement,* National Bureau of Economic Research, New York, April 1972.

dear money *See* **tight money.**

debenture A bond which is not protected by a specific lien or mortgage on property. Debentures (debts), which are issued by corporations, are promises to pay a specific amount of money (principal) at a specified date or periodically over the course of the loan, during which time interest is paid at a fixed rate on specified dates. The distinction between a debenture and a note of a corporation is that the debenture, like a bond, is issued under an indenture or deed of trust. Since the safety of a bond or debenture depends ultimately on the earning power of the issuing corporation, a bond is more secure than a debenture (because of the lien) only if the bonds and debentures of the same corporation are compared. Debentures were not issued in the United States until after the Civil War, and they became an important type of security only after 1900. Three types of corporations issue debentures: (1) service corporations that have a small proportion of their assets in tangible form, which means that they have little property that can be mortgaged; (2) large, blue-chip companies that enjoy high credit ratings and do not need to mortgage property to entice the investor; and (3) corporations that have mortgaged all their available assets. See J. Fred Weston and Eugene F. Brigham, *Essentials of Managerial Finance,* 5th ed., Holt, Rinehart and Winston, New York, 1959.

debt limit A legislative provision placing a ceiling on the amount of debt that may be outstanding at any one time. The term is usually used in public finance, in which it refers to debt limitations placed on federal, state, and local governments. The purpose of such debt limitations is to restrict current governmental expenditures to a limited amount in excess of current revenue collections. States impose debt limits on local governments, while state debt itself is usually limited by state constitutions. The federal government operates under limitations imposed by section 21 of the the Second Liberty Bond Act, passed in 1917 and amended many times. Most state governments have debt limits calculated in dollar amounts, but a few have limits calculated as a percentage of the valuation of property within the state. Debt limits for local governments are most frequently stated as percentages of property valuation. For further information on the federal debt limit, see John F. Due and Ann F. Friedlaender, *Government Finance,* 6th ed., Irwin, Homewood, Ill., 1977.

debt management A term applied to the operations of the U.S. Treasury Department which determine the composition and nature of the national debt. Debt management consists primarily of the manipulation of three aspects of outstanding debt: the level of interest rates, the pattern of ownership of debt, and the maturity schedule. Both the financing of new government debt and the replacement of maturing debt with new securities are included. A government debt-management policy may have a number of different objectives,

including the minimizing of the interest burden of the debt, stabilization of
the business cycle, gradual reduction of the debt, and support of general
growth policies. Since the public debt is a reliable and controllable part of
the liquidity base of the economy, its management can have an important
impact on economic conditions. The most significant role of debt-management policy is in the area of stabilization, in which the nature of the maturity
of the debt is the most important factor. The shorter the maturity of an issue,
the more liquid it is, since it can be turned into cash more easily. Thus, by
varying the length of the maturities of the national debt, the Treasury can
exercise some control over the liquidity base of the economy. For example,
during a period of excessive expansionary forces, the Treasury could increase
its use of long-term securities and reduce outstanding short-term bills, thus
tightening conditions in the capital market and slowing down the inflationary
forces. Similarly, in times of recession, a Treasury shift toward shorter-term
issues adds liquidity to the economy and stimulates recovery. For additional
information, see Richard A. Musgrave and Peggy B. Musgrave, *Public Finance
in Theory and Practice,* McGraw-Hill, New York, 1976.

decision making   The whole range of activities involved in establishing a
corporate or governmental policy or an effective means of executing an existing policy, including the collection of facts needed to make judgments on
a specific proposal and the analysis of alternative means of achieving a desired
goal. The introduction of mathematical techniques, such as linear programming, and the availability of electronic computers and other innovations have
tended to formalize decision-making procedures and to put them on a more
scientific footing. In general, however, these advances have provided means
of determining more clearly the consequences of alternative courses of action,
and the final choice of appropriate corporate policies remains with the business executive. See Paul C. Nystrom, B. L. T. Hedberg, and William Star-
buck, "Intersecting Processes as Organizational Designs," in Ralph H. Kilmann,
Louis Pondy, and Dennis P. Slevin (eds.), *The Management of Organization
Design,* vol. 1, Elsevier, New York, 1976, pp. 209–230.

decreasing returns, theory of   *See* **returns to scale.**

dedicating of revenues   *See* **earmarking of taxes.**

deductive method   A method of analyzing an economic problem which
works from the general to the particular, starting with a premise accepted as
true and arriving at a conclusion based on this premise. It is an alternative to
the inductive method. Lacking much important data that would serve as a
basis for scientific generalizations, the early economic thinkers, particularly
members of the classical school, adopted the deductive method. Critics of
this method considered that its use led to abstraction, extreme conclusions,
and beliefs at variance with reality. They argued that use of the deductive

method produced an abstract economic thinker who reached conclusions that were formally true but could not be applied in practice. Overemphasis on deduction results in fixed assumptions which, taken as premises, prove unsound in dealing with evolving social and economic conditions. For additional history, explanation, and examples, see William Fellner, *Modern Economic Analysis,* McGraw-Hill, New York, 1960, chap. 1.

defense expenditures Money spent by federal government agencies to provide for national security. In the United States, these expenditures cover military and civilian personnel, procurement, maintenance, research and development, military construction, civil defense, military assistance to allies, atomic energy, and defense-related activities. U.S. defense expenditures amount to 75% of total federal expenditures and to about 9% of the dollar value of national output. The high level of defense spending contributes to budget deficits and to an unfavorable balance of payments. Progress in military technology is so rapid that the rate of obsolescence is extremely high, and replacement with new equipment is very expensive. For details of defense expenditures see U.S. Office of Management and Budget, *The Budget of the United States Government.*

defensive stock Common stock whose earnings are only slightly dependent on changing economic conditions. For this reason, defensive stocks, as the term suggests, are better able to withstand selling pressure in declining markets and, in this sense, are safer securities to hold when economic conditions are less than buoyant. Price movements of defensive stocks are generally less volatile than the equity securities of growth or cyclical companies. Most analysts would consider that the common stock of utilities and food companies, for example, fall into the defensive stock category. For further information, see Jerome B. Cohen, Edward Zinbarg, and Arthur Zeikel, *Investment Analysis and Portfolio Management,* rev. ed., Dow Jones–Irwin, Homewood, Ill., 1973, pp. 17–19.

deficit financing A practice by a government of spending more money than it receives in revenue. In the United States, deficit financing has been the rule rather than the exception since the early 1930s. The practice is still highly controversial, however, some observers arguing that expenditures and revenues should balance every year, while others contend that they need never balance. According to surveys of economists working both in business and in universities, the majority of them seem to think that the most prudent policy is to have expenditures and revenues balance over the span of the business cycle. For an analysis of developments in the 1960s, see Herbert Stein, *The Fiscal Revolution in America,* University of Chicago Press, Chicago, 1969. For deficit financing in 1982, see "The Built-in Deficit," *Business Week,* Aug. 16, 1982, pp. 84–93.

deflation   A fall in the general price level associated with a contraction of the supply of money and credit. A drop in prices, usually accompanied by declining levels of output and increasing unemployment, is associated with the downturn stage of the business cycle. Although not all economists agree on the exact cause of a deflation, it is generally believed that a spiraling contraction in the volume of bank credit and a deficiency in total spending are important factors in causing a fall in the price level. Most prices fall in a deflation, but not all prices fall evenly. Since the earnings of fixed-income groups probably fall less than those of other groups, they stand to gain from a deflation. This remains true, however, only if they can retain their sources of income. The threat of unemployment during such periods is so great that all gains are precarious, and few groups actually gain during a deflation and depression. For this reason, modern governments have undertaken various contracyclical programs to try to reduce the force of the deflationary spiral. These policies include government deficit spending for public works, relief expenditures, and easy-money programs. For a fuller discussion of deflation, see Gottfried Haberler, *Prosperity and Depression,* League of Nations, Geneva, 1939.

deflationary gap   A descriptive term for the deficiency between actual investment and savings. In a full-employment economy, it is the value of demand for goods and services below that which can be produced under full employment. For example, national income in the United States at the full-employment level totals $3 trillion, but consumers and investors spend only $2.3 trillion. This means that there is a $700-billion gap. Through the multiplier principle, the $700-billion gap could develop into an even larger drop in income. On the other hand, by use of this principle much less than a $700-billion increase in investment would bring the economy to full employment. For a brief explanation of the deflationary gap and its relation to the theory of income determination, see Paul A. Samuelson, *Economics,* 9th ed., McGraw-Hill, New York, 1973, pp. 240–241.

degressive tax   A progressive tax which increases at a decreasing rate. A degressive tax is progressive, since the tax rate increases as the size of the tax base increases, but for each additional increase in the size of the base, the increase in the tax rate is lower. In practice, most income tax schedules are degressive, since as the rates increase, they apply to wider and wider income brackets until all income above a certain amount is taxed at a constant (proportional) rate. For additional details on types of taxes, see Harold Groves, *Financing Government,* 6th ed., Holt, Rinehart and Winston, New York, 1964.

demand   The desire, ability, and willingness of an individual to purchase a good or service. Desire by itself is not equivalent to demand: the consumer must also have the funds or the ability to obtain funds in order to convert the desire into demand. The demand of a buyer for a certain good is a schedule of the quantities of that good which the individual would buy at possible alternative prices at a given moment in time. The demand schedule, or the listing of quantities that would be bought at different prices, can be shown graphically by means of the demand curve. The term demand refers to the entire schedule of possibilities and not only to one point on the schedule. It is an instantaneous concept, expressing the relationship of price and the quantity that is desired to be bought, all other factors being constant. By adding the quantities demanded by each consumer at the various possible prices, the schedule of demand for all consumers, or the market demand, can be derived. A fundamental characteristic of individual and market demand is that as the price rises, the quantity demanded falls, and as price falls, the corresponding quantity demanded rises. This inverse relationship between the price of a good and the quantity demanded is known as the law of demand and is represented graphically by the downward slope of the demand curve. The reasons for this inverse relationship are as follows: (1) The lowering of prices brings new buyers into the market. (2) Each reduction in price may induce each of the good's consumers to make additional purchases, since an attempt is made to substitute the good for other goods as its price falls in relation to those of other goods. (3) As the price falls, real income rises, so that the individual's consumption of all goods rises proportionately. The basic determinants of the level of market demand are the tastes and preferences of the consumers, consumers' money incomes, the prices of other related goods (substitute goods), consumer expectations with respect to future prices and income, and the number of consumers in the market. Any change in these factors results in a change in demand or a shifting of the entire demand curve. This change should not be confused with a change in the quantity demanded, which merely describes the movement from one point to another along a given demand curve. For further information, see George J. Stigler, *The Theory of Price,* 3d ed., Macmillan, New York, 1966; Donald S. Watson, "Demand," in D. Greenwald (ed.), *Encyclopedia of Economics,* McGraw-Hill, New York, 1982, pp. 231–234.

demand deposit (checkbook money)   A bank deposit which can be withdrawn by the depositor without previous notice to the bank. Demand deposits do not earn interest, as do time deposits, but they can be withdrawn by check and therefore possess many of the liquid characteristics of circulating currency. For this reason, demand deposits are sometimes called checkbook money and are counted as part of the total money supply. Demand deposits can be classified into two categories: primary deposits, which arise from a deposit of cash in a bank account; and derived deposits, which are created by the bank through the making of loans. It is through the creation of derived demand deposits that banks are able to increase the money supply to meet the needs of business. For additional details, see Lawrence S. Ritter and William L. Silber, *Principles of Money, Banking and Financial Markets*, 3d rev. ed., Basic Books, New York, 1980; for monthly data on demand deposits, see *Federal Reserve Bulletin*, Washington, D.C.

demand schedule   *See* **demand.**

demographics and economics   The population of a nation—its size, growth rate, and age composition—significantly affects the nation's economic well-being. When abrupt changes in the fertility rates occur, they have far-reaching economic implications. For example, a sharp rise in the level of births over a decade will eventually mean a much bigger labor force and, most likely, an increase in the rate of economic growth. Because of medical advances which have increased longevity, in most nations of the world an increasing proportion of the population consists of relatively older and economically dependent individuals. See Wilbur J. Cohen and Charles F. Westhoff, *Demographic Dynamics in America,* Free Press, New York, 1977.

demonstration effect   The impact on an individual of seeing a larger variety of goods, or superior goods, influencing the individual to increase expenditures to buy these goods even though the individual's income has not changed. According to James S. Duesenberry, the demonstration effect amends the Keynesian theory of the consumption function, which has postulated that a family's consumption expenditures are related only to the level of its income. Consumers who have a chance to inspect goods that are better than the ones that they had been buying may raise their expenditures even though their incomes have not changed or refuse to reduce their expenditures even when their incomes decline. Ragnar Nurkse extended this theory to the international level when he suggested that the aggregate consumption functions of different countries might be similarly interrelated, especially through extended communications and trade, which bring the people of one nation into contact with the different and perhaps superior goods of another nation and induce them to change their consumption habits. For example, worldwide distribution of consumer magazines with all the advertising they contain may stimulate the demands of families in India to levels far above those to which they have been accustomed, thereby creating problems of inadequate savings and severe balance-of-payments deficits. See James S. Duesenberry, *Income, Savings, and the Theory of Consumer Behavior,* Harvard University Press, Cambridge, Mass., 1949; Ragnar Nurkse, *Patterns of Trade and Development,* Oxford University Press, New York, 1961.

depletion   A decrease in the value of land or other natural resources due to the extraction of minerals or other natural wealth. Depletion resembles depreciation in that both are reductions in the value of fixed assets. Whereas depreciation is a reduction in the quality and usefulness of an asset because of physical deterioration, depletion is the reduction of the physical quantities of a fixed asset. Although both the passage of time and use cause depreciation, in almost all cases depletion is not affected by the passage of time but only by the removal of the asset for use. Depletion occurs in such natural resources, or wasting assets as they are sometimes known, as mines, oil wells, and timber, which are constantly being removed and sold, so that the proportion of the asset remaining declines from period to period. The depletion for a given period is usually determined by multiplying the unit depletion charge (the total cost of the asset divided by the estimated number of resource units, such as barrels of oil, that it will produce in its lifetime) by the number of units produced in the period.

depletion allowance A tax allowance extended to the owners of exhaustible natural resources. The return from the sale of natural resources partly represents a return on the owner's investment in resource property. If the income from these sales were taxed, this would be, in effect, a tax on the return to capital, or a capital levy. The primary purpose of a depletion allowance is to prevent the imposition of a capital levy on the owners of natural resources. In addition, it encourages the investment of risk capital in the development of unused resources. The depletion allowance permits owners to deduct from their incomes part of the cost of the investment in natural resources as the property becomes exhausted or depleted. There are two methods of computing depletion allowance, cost depletion and percentage depletion. Under the cost-depletion method, the value of the depletion deduction is calculated by dividing the number of resource units (e.g., barrels of oil) by the total number of units present at the beginning of the accounting period and multiplying this figure by the total value of the resources, so that the deduction represents the value of the depleted resources. Under the percentage-depletion method, a specified percentage of the gross income from the property is deductible. For additional information, see Joseph A. Pechman, *Federal Tax Policy*, 3d ed., Brookings Institution, Washington, D.C., 1977, pp. 151–153.

deposit turnover The ratio of bank debits to bank deposits. This ratio is used as (1) a fairly accurate indicator of the total velocity of money, since commercial bank deposits account for 77% of the nation's money and (2) a business-cycle indicator, since fluctuations in the rate of turnover of bank deposits generally coincide with fluctuations of the business cycle. For a discussion of the usefulness of statistics on bank debt in economic analysis, see George Garvy, *Debits and Clearings Statistics and Their Use*, Board of Governors of Federal Reserve System, Washington, D.C., 1959; for monthly statistics on the ratio of debits to deposits, see *Federal Reserve Bulletin*, Washington, D.C.

depreciation A reduction in the value of fixed assets. The most important causes of depreciation are wear and tear (loss of value caused by the use of an asset), the effect of the elements (i.e., decay or corrosion), and gradual obsolescence, which makes it unprofitable to continue using some assets until they have been fully exhausted. The annual amount of depreciation of an asset depends on its original purchase price, its estimated useful life, and its estimated salvage value. A number of different methods of figuring the amount of depreciation have been developed. Using the simple straight-line method, which considers depreciation a function of time, the annual depreciation cost is calculated by dividing the cost of the asset (original minus salvage cost) equally over its entire life. When the life of a fixed asset is a function of activity (use) rather than of time, industry employs the production method, in which depreciation is charged to periods in proportion to the use (generally expressed in terms of hours of operation or units produced) which has been made of the asset. There are also a number of decreasing-charge methods, such as the diminishing-value method and the sum-of-the-digits method, which allocate higher depreciation costs to the beginning years of the operation of an asset and lower depreciation costs to the later years. These methods assign the greatest depreciation loss to the earlier years of the asset's life, when the greatest decrease in resale value normally occurs. Such accelerated-depreciation methods can be used in accordance with the tax laws to reduce the overall cost of new capital investment. For additional details, see George Terborgh, *Inflation and the Taxation of Business Income,* Machinery and Allied Products Institute, Washington, D.C., 1976.

depreciation reserve   A valuation-reserve account used to record depreciation charges. The use of the word reserve does not mean that a fund of cash has been set aside; rather, the word is employed to stand for a valuation reserve, in which credits are made to show the reduced valuation of an asset. The depreciation reserve is shown on the asset side of the balance sheet as a deduction from its corresponding fixed-asset account. As the asset depreciates, periodic additions are made to the reserve for depreciation, thus reducing the stated valuation of the asset. Because of the common misinterpretation of the term reserve, terms such as allowance for depreciation and accumulated depreciation are coming into use. For additional details, see Harold Bierman, Jr., and Allan R. Drebin, *Managerial Accounting,* 3d ed., Dryden Press, Hinsdale, Ill., 1978.

depressed area (distressed area)   A locality that is not participating in a nation's overall economic growth and, as a result, has an exceptional amount of unemployed resources, particularly unemployed workers. A depressed area may be the result of a variety of developments. In some cases, changes in consumer demand have sharply reduced the market for the products that an area has specialized in producing. Among other possible causes are the exhaustion of the natural resources on which an area's economy has been dependent, the loss of an area's markets to competitive products imported from abroad, and the migration of established industries to other localities. Prime examples of depressed areas are the coal mining towns of Pennsylvania and West Virginia, whose economic decline is the result of the widespread adoption of new energy sources, particularly gas and oil, in markets long served by coal. Other examples are New England milling towns that have seen their economic viability affected by the migration of textile mills to other areas in the United States and by competition from imported products. To help overcome the economic difficulties of depressed areas, Congress in 1961 enacted the Area Redevelopment Act, which includes provisions designed to encourage new business investment in such areas and to assist unemployed workers to develop new skills in order to improve their chances of employment. For further discussion of the problems of depressed areas, see *The Rise of Chronic Unemployment,* National Planning Association, Planning Pamphlet 113, Washington, D.C., 1961; for current statistics on depressed areas, see U.S. Department of Labor, Employment and Training Administration, *Area Trends in Employment and Unemployment,* monthly.

depression   A protracted period in which business activity is far below normal and the pessimism of business and consumers is great. It is characterized by a sharp curtailment of production, little capital investment, a contraction of credit, falling prices, mass unemployment and low employment, and a very high rate of business failures. The two longest depressions in U.S. history were those of 1873–1879 (65 months) and 1929–1933 (45 months). One of the key problems of modern times is the prevention of severe depressions. The reason for the great concern in the United States about severe depressions is that these represent a grave threat to the democratic way of life in both political and economic terms. For a measurement of the length and depth of depressions, see Geoffrey H. Moore (ed.), *Business Cycle Indicators,* Princeton University Press, Princeton, N.J., 1961.

depth interview   *See* qualitative interview.

Deregulation and Monetary Control Act of 1980   An act signed into law March 31, 1980, that substantially changed the financial structure of the United States. In general, it has provided for greatly increased competition between commercial banks and thrift institutions, and has vastly increased the similarities between the types of services the two can offer. On the other hand, the act imposes obligations on thrift institutions that they were not formerly subject to, such as the holding of reserves that Federal Reserve member banks always were required to hold. The act is divided into nine parts, with provisions summarized very briefly as follows: (1) All depository institutions will hold reserves against transaction deposits, with Federal Reserve services available at a fee, and the discount window available to all institutions holding reserves. (2) There will be a phaseout over a six-year period of all deposit interest-rate ceilings. (3) All depository institutions may offer negotiable order of withdrawal (NOW) accounts except to business customers. (4) Thrift institutions are given increased loan and trust powers. (5) State usury laws are preempted in a wide variety of circumstances. (6) Truth-in-lending laws are simplified. (7) The powers of the comptroller of the currency over national banks are increased. (8) Financial regulations must be reviewed periodically to ensure clarity and simplicity. (9) Foreign acquisition of U.S. financial organizations is hampered. For a detailed discussion of the provisions of the act, refer to "The Deregulation and Monetary Control Act of 1980," *Voice of the Federal Reserve Bank of Dallas*, September 1980, pp. 1–4. For a discussion of the effect of the law on the economy, see "America's New Financial Structure," *Business Week*, Nov. 17, 1980, pp. 138–144.

derived demand   The demand for a factor of production that results from the demand for a final good which it helps produce. The shape of the demand curve for a factor of production, steel, is derived from the demand curve of the final product, automobiles, for which it is used. If we assume profit maximization by the steel producer, the demand curve for steel is its marginal-revenue curve. This demonstrates the fallacy of advocating a rise in steel prices because the price of automobiles is high. The principle of derived demand shows that such a price rise is not a solution, since the demand for steel is derived from the demand for automobiles. A higher price for steel would raise profits for steel companies in the short run, but the price of automobiles might also rise, and the demand for both automobiles and steel would therefore decline. See J. R. Hicks, *Value and Capital*, Oxford University Press, New York, 1947.

devaluation   The lowering of the value of a nation's currency relative to gold or to the currency of other countries. Devaluation usually occurs when a country is having serious balance-of-payment difficulties, that is, when the relative prices of its goods and services are such that the value of its imports far exceeds the value of the goods and services that it exports. Devaluation of the currency, providing other countries do not follow suit, helps increase a country's physical exports and decrease its physical imports. For example, the United States, faced with a sizable trade deficit in 1971, devalued the dollar by 7.88% at the end of that year through increasing the price of gold 8.57%, from $35 to $38 per ounce. At the same time, the British and French kept their price per ounce of gold at the previous levels. Thus the dollar depreciated in relation to the pound and the franc: $100 would buy 38.38 pounds or 511.6 francs, as compared with 41.67 pounds or 555.4 francs prior to the devaluation. The outcome of the devaluation would be an increase of American exports to Britain and France and a reduction of American imports. For further information, see Lawrence S. Ritter and William L. Silber, *Principles of Money, Banking, and Financial Markets*, 3d rev. ed., Basic Books, New York, 1980.

developing nation   A nation whose people are beginning to utilize available resources in order to bring about a sustained increase in per capita production of goods and services. In general, a developing nation is a country that is capable of greater substantial improvements in its income level and is in the process of achieving these improvements. For additional information on economic development, see C. P. Kindleberger and Bruce Herrick, *International Economics,* 3d ed., McGraw-Hill, New York, 1977.

difference equation   An equation that involves a variable y and the first differences of the same variable. A first difference is the value obtained by subtracting an observation $y(x)$ from the value following it in a series $y(x + 1)$. Autoregressive, linear difference equations are useful in the econometric analysis of business cycles. For additional information, see Gerhard Tintner and Charles B. Millham, *Mathematics and Statistics for Economists,* Holt, Rinehart and Winston, New York, 1970.

diffusion index   A statistical device used to summarize in one figure the proportion of a group of series that has increased in a given time interval. The index gives the percentage expanding: if a greater number of series is rising than is declining, the index will be above 50; if fewer are rising than are declining, it will be below 50. A common form of this index is the ratio of stocks whose prices have risen in a day to the total number of stocks traded on the New York Stock Exchange. A more complex form consists of the diffusion indices of business indicators. For a more detailed explanation of diffusion indices, see Geoffrey H. Moore (ed.), *Business Cycle Indicators,* Princeton University Press, Princeton, N.J., 1961.

digital computer   A computer that processes information in digital form, using the familiar arabic numbers from 0 through 9. Electronic digital computers usually use binary notation (various combinations of 0 and 1) or decimal notation and solve problems at high speeds by repeated use of the conventional arithmetic processes of addition, subtraction, multiplication, and division. In addition to speed, the digital computer offers the further advantage of a very high degree of accuracy that is limited only by the number of digits that any individual computer can manipulate. For further elementary discussions of digital computers and their use, see Jeremy Berstein, *The Analytical Engine,* Random House, New York, 1964; Andrew G. Favret, *Introduction to Digital Computer Applications,* Reinhold, New York, 1965.

dilution of earnings   The reduction in a firm's common-stock earnings per share (EPS) that results from some action taken by the firm. For instance, if a company uses common stock to finance a capital investment and that project turns out to be less profitable than the firm's existing investments, EPS will decline and earnings will be diluted. Dilution of earnings also occurs when a company pays a high price for an acquisition. Specifically, if the acquired firm has a higher price-earnings ratio than the acquiring company, the EPS of the latter will decrease following completion of the acquisition, other things remaining equal. The notion of dilution is also applied to corporations with convertible securities or warrants outstanding. These firms are required to report EPS in two ways: first, the actual earnings available to common stockholders divided by the number of shares outstanding; second, fully diluted EPS, which assumes that all convertibles have been converted and all warrants exercised, when computing EPS. For further information, see John J. Hampton, *Financial Decision Making, Concepts, Problems & Cases*, 2d ed., Reston, Reston, Va., 1979.

diminishing returns, law of (law of variable proportions)   The economic principle which states that successive additions of quantities of variable factors of production to other fixed factors of production will result in diminishing marginal productivity, at least after some point. Thus, successive additions of capital to a fixed quantity of labor will result in an increase in output, but subsequently the marginal output and then the average production associated with the variable factor will begin to drop. The fixed factor decreases in proportion to the variable factor, so that each unit of the variable factor has a diminishing quantity of the fixed factor to work with. Anne Robert Jacques Turgot, influenced by the physiocrats' system, provided a clear statement of this law in the eighteenth century. Under the influence of David Ricardo, statements of the law were prevalent among classical economists in the early nineteenth century. For further discussion, see Donald S. Watson and Mary A. Holman, *Price Theory and Its Uses*, 4th ed., Houghton Mifflin, Boston, 1976.

direct cost   A cost which can be consistently identified with a specific unit of output. Direct, or variable, costs consist of two types: (1) direct materials, or supplies which can be connected directly with an individual product; and (2) direct labor, which is that proportion of wages and salaries that can be identified with a specific product. As a rule, all materials and supplies which are related specifically to the product are classified as direct materials. Thus, the raw materials used in a given production process are classified as direct-cost items, whereas the cost of lighting facilities for an area in which a number of goods are being produced is considered an indirect cost. Labor which changes the form of materials in the productive process is usually called direct, or productive, labor. Thus, the wages of machine operators and welders are examples of direct-labor costs, whereas the wages of supervisors and maintenance workers are examples of indirect-labor costs. There is, however, wide leeway in deciding whether a given material or job can be identified with a specific product. This is especially true for labor. For further information, see James R. McGuigan and R. Charles Moyer, *Managerial Economics*, 2d ed., West, St. Paul, Minn., 1979.

direct investment Investment by U.S. business firms or individuals in overseas business operations over which the investor has a considerable measure of control. Direct investment differs somewhat from portfolio investment, which includes holdings intended primarily for their income yields. Much U.S. direct investment takes the form of investment in overseas subsidiaries of U.S. business firms. For a discussion of direct investment and the flow of international capital in general, see Stephen H. Hymer, *The International Operations of National Firms: A Study of Direct Foreign Investment,* MIT Press, Cambridge, Mass., 1976; for data on U.S. overseas investment, see U.S. Department of Commerce, *U.S. Business Investment in Foreign Countries: A Supplement to the Survey of Current Business,* 1960; for annual data on U.S. holdings abroad, see U.S. Department of Commerce, *Survey of Current Business.*

direct labor Labor expended directly on the actual production of a firm's finished goods or services. It is thus directly identifiable with product costs. For example, employees who work on a product with tools or operate machines in the production process are considered to constitute direct labor. Direct labor is distinguishable from indirect labor, which includes those activities that are not applied specifically to the production of goods or services but are applicable to production activities in general. Sometimes the distinction between direct and indirect labor becomes difficult to draw, as in the case when fully automatic machinery is used and the worker becomes, in effect, a machine tender. For additional details, see James R. McGuigan and R. Charles Moyer, *Managerial Economics,* 2d ed., West, St. Paul, Minn., 1979.

direct tax A tax that cannot be shifted from the original payer to the ultimate consumer of the good or service taxed. Poll taxes, property taxes, and income taxes are generally considered direct taxes, although many economists believe that it is possible to pass on property taxes and certain income taxes, especially those levied on corporate incomes. The concept is important in the United States largely because the Constitution expressly provides that direct taxes "shall be apportioned among the several states . . . according to their respective numbers." Since the Constitution does not define the concept, however, the definition has been left to the courts. The constitutionality of the federal income tax was first questioned during the Civil War, when the U.S. Supreme Court held that the federal income tax was not a direct tax and was therefore legal; this decision was reversed in 1894, and the legality of the federal income tax was not finally established until 1913, when passage of the Sixteenth Amendment permitted the collection of an income tax without apportionment among the states. See John F. Due and Ann F. Friedlaender, *Government Finance,* 6th ed., Irwin, Homewood, Ill., 1977.

dirty float When a nation purports to be allowing international forces of supply and demand to influence the price of its currency, but is in reality intervening in the market. The contrast is a clean float in which only unimpeded world supply-and-demand forces influence the price of a nation's currency. In the 1950s and 1960s, many nations' currencies were pegged, or held in a rigid price relationship to other nations' currencies. This is only possible if a nation has the ability to either buy or sell its own currency in unlimited quantity. In the face of the substantial supply-and-demand imbalances, few countries found it possible to peg their currencies. Therefore, they permitted their currencies to change price in response to supply-and-demand forces—or to float. See Isaiah Frank, Charles Pearson, and James Reidel, "The Implications of Managed Floating Exchange Rates for U.S. Trade Policy," Monograph 1979-1, New York University, Graduate School of Business Administration, New York, 1979; Nicholas Carlozzi, "Pegs and Floats: The Changing Face of the Foreign Exchange Market," *Business Review*, May–June 1980, pp. 13–21. See also Miltiades Chacholiades, *International Monetary Theory and Policy*, McGraw-Hill, New York, 1978.

discontinuous hypotheses   In econometrics, hypotheses that lead to "yes" or "no" solutions to assumed relationships. For example, where there is interdependence between two variables (or several variables), it is possible to determine which variable is the causal factor. For additional information, see Lawrence R. Klein, *An Introduction to Econometrics*, Greenwood, Westport, Conn., 1977.

discounted-cash-flow method   A method of measuring the return on capital invested. The value of a project is expressed as an interest rate at which the project's total future earnings, discounted from the time that they occur to the present, equal the original investment. It is more precise than most of the other methods used to measure return on capital invested because it recognizes the effect of the time value of money. It may be used to determine whether a given project is acceptable or unacceptable by comparing each project's rate of return with the company's standard. For additional information, see J. Fred Weston and Eugene F. Brigham, *Essentials of Managerial Finance*, 5th ed., Holt, Rinehart and Winston, New York, 1979.

discount rate (rediscount rate)   The interest that a commercial bank pays when it borrows from a Federal Reserve bank, using a government bond or other eligible paper as security. The discount rate is one of the tools of monetary policy; when Federal Reserve authorities are trying to prevent inflation, they raise the discount rate. The opposite course is followed when business is lagging, although lowering the discount rate may be less effective in stimulating loans and investments if banks already possess ample reserves which they could lend. Over the years, the discount rate has ranged from 16%, in 1980, to $\frac{1}{2}$%, during World War II. Rates are set by the regional Federal Reserve banks with approval of the Board of Governors of the Federal Reserve System. The current levels of discount rates are given in *Federal Reserve*

Bulletin, Washington, D.C.; their use is discussed in *Purposes and Functions of the Federal Reserve System,* Board of Governors of the Federal Reserve System, Washington, D.C., 1974.

discrimination economics   Discrimination is usually equated with the unequal economic positions typically observed among demographic groups within an economy. Discrimination based on race, sex, and ethnic differences is of prime concern. Demand-oriented theories of discrimination consider the possibility that firms or nonminority workers express preference with regard to new workers and coworkers. Such attitudinal patterns result in minority workers being relegated to the least desirable jobs—if any—at the lowest possible wages. Supply-oriented theories indicate that differences in economic positions are more a societal phenomenon than a phenomenon of business or labor relations. Institutions within society, such as marriage, the division of labor within the home, and the educational system, help to create group differences in labor-market expectations. See Gary S. Becker, *The Economics of Discrimination,* 2d ed., University of Chicago Press, Chicago, 1971.

disguised unemployment   The employment of persons in jobs which do not make use of their full capacity or in occupations in which their productivity (output per worker-hour) is lower than it would be if they were working at other jobs. In recessions, a downgrading of skilled workers to semiskilled jobs and of semiskilled workers to unskilled jobs indicates that the employed are not always used effectively. Disguised unemployment is high even in prosperous times in service industries where workers earn relatively low wages and have a relatively low output per worker-hour. It is also relatively important in underdeveloped areas where job opportunities for highly educated and skilled persons are limited. For additional details, see Lloyd G. Reynolds, *Labor Economics and Labor Relations,* 7th ed., Prentice-Hall, Englewood Cliffs, N.J., 1978.

disinflation   The process of retarding the rate of price inflation. In the U.S. economy, some rate of inflation is expected to occur each year. Economists now generally claim that a rate of inflation of about 5% per year would be acceptable and would not cause a great problem to the economy. But when the general rate of price increase goes much beyond this level, as has been true since the mid-1960s, many problems of income distribution emerge, especially for those on fixed incomes. State and municipal governments also face tremendous obstacles in meeting their financial obligations when inflation is galloping. A number of proposals have been advanced for disinflating the economy from the cost-push price spiral we have been experiencing. These range from "jawboning" (or mild reproach by government) to complete wage and price controls. The wage-price guideposts of the Kennedy-Johnson years were an attempt to hold price increases to the rate of increase in output per worker-hour. The guideposts were unsuccessful in holding down wage demands, which soared in the late 1960s and into the 1970s. The Nixon administration attempted to disinflate by making direct attacks on wage demands and price increases which it considered to be excessive and extremely inflationary.

disintermediation The removal of funds from interest-bearing time accounts in savings institutions and commercial banks for the purpose of reinvesting the funds at higher rates in market instruments. This process occurs when rates on market instruments—for example, corporate bonds—are substantially higher than the rates being paid by financial intermediaries. Time accounts in financial institutions generally carry a maximum interest-rate ceiling set by state law regulatory bodies. When the demand for money becomes extremely heavy relative to the supply, corporations can compete in the marketplace by offering much higher yields than financial institutions, which are subject to state interest-rate ceilings. The process of disintermediation generally continues until the supply of funds becomes more plentiful and/or the demand for funds slackens. Then yields on market instruments decline, and putting funds in savings institutions becomes more attractive. A 6% yield in time deposits would probably be more attractive than a 6% corporate bond because the risk is somewhat less, since banks' funds are insured by the federal government. Disintermediation generally causes major problems for housing construction, since savings and loan associations, mutual savings banks, and life insurance companies are the major source of mortgage loans for housing construction in the United States. When disintermediation takes place, funds for housing shrink. A heavy demand for new housing cannot be met at such times, and housing shortages grow more severe. Four significant episodes of disintermediation occurred in the United States in the period 1965–1980. The term disintermediation was coined in 1966 when the first of these episodes occurred. The others occurred in 1969–1970, 1973–1974, and 1979–1980. For example, between 1972 and 1974, a cut of over 50% in the net savings inflows of savings and loan associations and mutual savings banks, paying low interest rates, resulted as the public sought higher interest rates from nonmortgage outlets for the diverted funds, primarily treasury bills and notes. For additional information, see Lawrence S. Ritter and William L. Silber, *Principles of Money, Banking and Financial Markets*, 3d rev. ed., Basic Books, New York, 1980.

disposable personal income The income that individuals retain after they have deducted personal taxes—including income taxes, estate and gift taxes, personal property taxes, poll taxes, and automobile use taxes—and have paid to government other noncommercial fees, such as state college tuition, traffic fines, and public hospital fees. It is the concept closest to what is commonly known as take-home pay. It is the amount which individuals can use either to make personal outlays or to save. Considered the single most important determinant of consumption expenditures, U.S. disposable personal income since World War II has grown far more steadily than any other measure of economic activity. After adjustment for changes in population and prices, disposable income is frequently used to measure changes in the nation's standard of living. Monthly data are published in U.S. Department of Commerce, *Survey of Current Business.*

dissaving   The expenditure of more than one's income, either from past savings or from loans. The subtraction of total dissaving from gross saving gives net saving, the figure used in national income statistics. Studies of empirical data made during the 1940s and 1950s showed that dissaving was not directly related to income but to other factors. For example, George Garvy explained that dissaving occurred in relatively the same proportion of spending units in all income classes except the very highest. According to Garvy, dissaving seemed to depend on such factors as high unexpected expenses, unemployment or retirement of the head of the spending unit, purchases of consumer durable goods, or a recent decline in income. See George Garvy, "The Role of Dissaving in Economic Analysis," *Journal of Political Economy,* October 1948; see also George Katona, *The Powerful Consumer,* McGraw-Hill, New York, 1960.

distressed area   *See* **depressed area.**

distributed lag   In econometrics, the problem that arises when the full response to some form of economic stimulus or change spans several established data reporting periods—specifically, the pattern of response in affected areas immediately after the stimulus and in subsequent periods until the stimulus is no longer a factor generating change. For example, the pattern of changes in private business capital expenditures immediately after liberalization of rules governing depreciation charges for tax purposes and in subsequent data-reporting periods would represent a distributed lag. For additional information, see Karl A. Fox and Tej K. Kaul, *Intermediate Economic Statistics,* Krieger, Melbourne, Fla., 1980.

disutility   The ability of a good or service to cause discomfort, inconvenience, or pain. It is the opposite of utility. Whereas short periods of exposure to the sun may feel good and provide the skin with a pleasant color, too great an amount of exposure will cause pain and skin damage. Thus, each added increment of exposure beyond a certain point provides disutility rather than utility. In classical economic theory, it was believed that the utility of the wage when a given volume of labor is employed is equal to the marginal disutility of the amount of employment. Disutility of labor is understood to mean any reason that would cause a worker not to accept a job at a certain wage which was under the worker's minimum utility. Thus, the wage serves to overcome the disutility of working. As wages increase, their marginal utility is no longer high enough to overcome the disutility of the additional work required. For further information, see W. Stanley Jevons, *The Theory of Political Economy,* 5th ed., Kelley and Millman, New York, 1957, chap. 3.

diversification   The participation by a single firm in the production or sale of widely divergent kinds of goods and services. In diversifying its output, a firm seeks to avoid the sharp changes in revenue that might accompany the fluctuations of business in a single market or in closely related markets. To stabilize revenues, a firm with substantial income from the production of consumer durable goods, which tend to undergo sharp fluctuations, might choose to diversify its operations by undertaking the production of food products, whose sales tend to grow at a fairly regular, albeit moderate, pace as population increases. See Milton Leontiades, *Strategies for Diversification and Change,* Little, Brown, Boston, 1980.

dividend   A payment, usually in cash, that a corporation makes to its stockholders. It represents the stockholders' share of that part of the profits of the business which the board of directors decides to distribute. In some cases, to maintain a consistent record of dividend payments, a corporation will pay a dividend even though a loss was incurred in its last accounting period. Preferred stockholders receive a fixed amount of dollars in dividends, provided that the company earns enough to pay them and the board of directors declares the dividend. They must, however, be paid their dividends before the common stockholders are paid. The amount of the dividend declared on a common stock is determined mainly by the company's earnings and the portion of its earnings that the company retains to finance expansion, modernization, and operations. The total amount of dividends paid by corporations is published in U.S. Department of Commerce, *Survey of Current Business;* for individual companies, see their annual reports; for further information on dividends, see J. Fred Weston and Eugene F. Brigham, *Essentials of Managerial Finance,* 5th ed., Holt, Rinehart and Winston, New York, 1979.

division of labor   A method of production in which each worker specializes in some aspect or step of the production process. Division of labor is characteristic of a modern industrial economy; it increases a nation's productivity. In a chronological division of labor, one worker carries out one step in production, a second worker does another part, and a third then adds a share, until the finished product emerges. The advantages of specialization have been recognized since the late eighteenth century. They include the greater skill acquired in specialization, the avoidance of wasted time in shifting from one task to another, and the employment of persons best suited to particular types of work. For Adam Smith's classic example of the division of labor, see *The Wealth of Nations,* Random House, New York, 1937, pp. 7–8; for further information, see Armen A. Alchian and William R. Allen, *University Economics,* 3d ed., Wadsworth, New York, 1971.

Doolittle method A computational technique used in solving a set of simultaneous, symmetrical linear equations. Similar methods were worked out by both Gauss and Doolittle. The technique enables the statistician immediately to detect arithmetic errors made while solving simultaneous equations. Its use is recommended whenever more than two variables are involved in computations. The same technique can be extended to include computation of the standard errors of partial regression coefficients. For additional information, see Lawrence R. Klein, *An Introduction to Econometrics,* Greenwood, Westport, Conn., 1977.

doomsday model One of several computer-based models that illustrate the interrelation between economic activity and environmental quality. One of the first models was presented in *Limits to Growth,* a book published by the Club of Rome in 1970. It claimed to substantiate that if humanity did not move rapidly to control pollution and recycle resources, it was doomed to extinction within 150 years. The analysis was widely criticized because it extrapolated from a few years of data to a forecast of many years, and because it failed to allow for substitution among resources. Later versions of the model have sought to correct these errors. One of these is the limits-to-growth model, which is based on work by Jay Forrester at the Massachusetts Institute of Technology. More recent work in this area was done for the federal government and published as the *Global 2000 Report.* Related work has been done on the economics of exhaustible resources. These models show the behavior of resource price and production for the life of the resource reserve. See Gerald O. Barney (ed.), *Global 2000 Report to the President of the US: Entering the 21st Century,* 3 vols., Pergamon, Elmsford, N.Y., 1980.

double taxation The application of two distinct taxes to the same tax base. Double taxation may occur because the same base is assessed twice by the same tax jurisdiction or because it is assessed by two competing tax jurisdictions. A common case of the first kind of double taxation in the United States is the taxation of dividends, in which a corporate income tax is levied against all corporation profits and a personal income tax is then levied against the same profits distributed as dividends to stockholders. Double taxation of the second kind often arises through the imposition of taxes on the same base by different levels of government, as in the case of federal and state taxation of personal incomes and inheritances. Another example of the second kind is territorial multiple taxation, in which the same levels of government in several different areas all claim jurisdiction in taxing the same base. The double taxation of the property owner who owns property in one state and resides in another is a common instance of this type. Cases of double taxation in which all sources of income are treated equally, such as that of federal and state income taxes, result not in inequality but only in higher taxes, since the actual burden of this double taxation is the same as if one tax equal in amount to the other two taxes were imposed. Inequality does arise when double taxation treats income received from different sources in a discriminatory manner, as is the case in the taxation of dividends. For further information, see John F. Due and Ann F. Friedlaender, *Government Finance*, 6th ed., Irwin, Homewood, Ill., 1977.

Dow-Jones averages Four stock price averages computed and published by Dow Jones & Co., publishers of the *Wall Street Journal*. They comprise the Dow-Jones industrial average of thirty industrial stocks, the oldest and most popular average; an average of twenty transportation stocks; an average of fifteen utility stocks; and a composite average of these sixty-five stocks. All stocks in the Dow-Jones averages are listed on the New York Stock Exchange. Originally, the Dow-Jones averages represented the average (arithmetic-mean) price of a share of stock in the group. As stock splits, the substitution of issues in the averages, and other factors occurred, however, a formula was devised to compensate for these changes. Although the Dow-Jones averages no longer represent the actual average prices of the stocks in the groups, they still represent the levels and changes in the stock prices reasonably well. Hourly Dow-Jones averages are published in each edition of the *Wall Street Journal*. Many other newspapers publish the high, low, and closing Dow-Jones averages each day. For further information and criticism, see Frank G. Zarb and Gabriel T. Kerekes, *The Stock Market Handbook*, Dow Jones–Irwin, Homewood, Ill., 1970.

Dow theory A theory that purports to predict future stock price movements solely on the basis of the past actions of the Dow-Jones industrial and railroad averages. Originally promulgated by Charles H. Dow, founder of the Dow-Jones financial news service (publishers of the *Wall Street Journal*), as a technique of forecasting business activity, the Dow theory was refined and formulated by William P. Hamilton, who succeeded Dow as editor of the *Wall Street Journal*. The basic rationale of the Dow theory, as of all technical analyses of the stock market or of individual stocks, is that past price and volume movements of the averages or of individual stocks discount everything except acts of God; that is, the careful interpretation of these patterns gives the best picture of the supply and demand for stocks, or for a given stock, because the combined actions of all investors are reflected. The Dow theory is based on three basic stock-market movements: (1) the primary trend, which is either a long-term upward (bull) or downward (bear) trend in prices; (2) the secondary trend, which is a short-term upward trend in a primary bear market or a short-term downward trend in the primary bull market; and (3) the day-to-day price fluctuations in the stock market. The most important of these movements is the primary trend. Dow theorists claim that, through study of the averages, they can determine when the primary trend changes. Critics argue that when the Dow theory confirms a basic change in the long-term trend of stock prices, it is frequently too late, or that the theory does not predict future movements at all. For a pro-Dow theory analysis, see Robert J. Edwards and John Magee, *Technical Analysis of Stock Trends,* John Magee, Springfield, Mass., 1958; for a more critical analysis of the theory, see George L. Leffler and L. C. Farwell, *The Stock Market,* Ronald, New York, 1963.

dummy variable   A constructed variable used as a means of including factors that are not naturally quantifiable in an econometric model. It may assume two and only two values (usually 1 and 0) used to represent the presence of a factor and its opposite or its absence. For example, an economic model builder, knowing or suspecting that a worker's sex influences income levels, may introduce a dummy variable in which the number 1 is paired with data for male workers and 0 is paired with data for female workers in a single-equation model. Dummy variables that assume values of 1 and 0 can be used like any other numerical variables in correlations. The dummy variable may also represent a composite of many factors, such as those associated with "wartime" in contrast to "peacetime." An alternative to the use of dummy variables is that of splitting the sample into two parts for the purposes of analysis. For additional information, see Lawrence R. Klein, *An Introduction to Econometrics,* Greenwood, Westport, Conn., 1977.

dumping   The sale of a product in another country for less than in the home market in order to gain an advantage in competition with other foreign suppliers. The General Agreement on Tariffs and Trade, which almost all the world's major trading nations have signed, prohibits the practice and provides for a defense against it through higher tariffs. Charges of dumping are difficult to prove, however, and this is especially true when the exporter's government shares the blame because it offers an export subsidy or facilitates the export through foreign aid or discriminatory currency arrangements. Whereas an individual firm dumps its product abroad mostly for competitive reasons, a government may have political reasons or a balance-of-payments incentive to encourage such sales, making prosecution all the more difficult. In the United States, the Anti-dumping Act of 1921 gives the Tariff Commission power to recommend retaliatory action when it finds that foreign goods are being dumped in the country. The theoretical aspects of dumping are discussed in Gottfried Haberler, *The Theory of International Trade,* Macmillan, New York, 1936; see also Mordechai E. Kreinen, *International Economics: A Policy Approach,* Harcourt Brace, New York, 1975. For examples of dumping, see Irving B. Kravis and Robert E. Lipsey, *Price Competitiveness in World Trade,* National Bureau of Economic Research, New York, 1971.

duopoly   A market structure in which there are only two sellers of a commodity. The important feature of duopoly is that each firm generally must consider the other firm's reaction to any changes that it may make in price or output. Since there are only two competing firms, their interdependence is great. There is a strong tendency for duopolists to reach a tacit agreement to set a common price, limit output, or divide markets. In actual practice, genuine duopolies are rare. The air-brake industry is one example of the existence of only two manufacturers of a commodity in the United States, Westinghouse Air Brake and New York Air Brake. For many years, two companies, Texas Gulf Sulphur and Freeport Sulphur Company, produced about 90% of all the sulphur sold in the United States. For further information, see James M. Henderson and Richard E. Quandt, *Microeconomic Theory: A Mathematical Approach,* 3d ed., McGraw-Hill, New York, 1980.

durable good A piece of equipment, for either consumers or producers, that in normal use is likely to last longer than three years. Consumer durable goods include automobiles, appliances, furniture, jewelry, and books. Producer durable goods include a wide range of machinery and equipment. Buildings, roads, airports, etc., are excluded. In 1981 expenditures for consumer durables in the United States totaled more than $235 billion; expenditures for producer durable goods, more than $186 billion. The purchase of many durable goods is postponable, and in periods of declining earnings both consumers and producers tend to put off buying new durables and continue to use existing equipment. As a result, spending for durable goods fluctuates widely. During the 1960–1961 recession the rate of durable-goods spending in the United States declined from $74 billion to $63 billion. Quarterly data on durable-goods expenditures appear in U.S. Department of Commerce, *Survey of Current Business.*

Durbin-Watson statistic A measure d that tests for the presence (or absence) of autocorrelation in least-squares relationships. It is computed by dividing the sum of the squared first differences of residuals by the sum of the squared residuals. Exact significance levels for d are not available, but Durbin and Watson have tabulated lower and upper bounds for various values of n (the number of paired observations) and k (the number of explanatory variables). If the derived statistic d falls below the lower limit d_L, autocorrelation is present. If it falls above the upper limit d_U, the residual is random. And if it falls between the upper and lower limits, the test is inconclusive. For additional information, see J. Durbin and G. S. Watson, "Testing for Serial Correlation in Least Squares Regression," parts I and II, *Biometrica,* 1950 and 1951.

dynamics The study of movement and change in economic systems. In contrast to static analysis, dynamics is concerned mainly with the changes in given conditions over time and the dynamic processes of adjustment and not with the determinants of equilibrium. The dynamic emphasis is achieved by introducing the element of time, so that the values of the economic variables at a given instant depend partly on their values at past moments of time. Economic processes are traced over a time path made up of a sequence of periods with the use of appropriate time lags. An economic model is characterized as dynamic if at least one observable variable in the equations has values taken at various points of time or at least one equation contains a function of time, such as trend or seasonal fluctuations. Complex problems in economics, especially when they involve movement toward a constantly changing equilibrium, may be analyzed by dynamics. For example, economic dynamic analysis has played an essential role in studies of economic growth. For further information, see T. C. Koopmans (ed.), *Statistical Inference in Dynamic Economic Models,* Wiley, New York, 1950; William J. Baumol, *Economic Dynamics,* 3d ed., Macmillan, New York, 1970; Michael R. Darby, *Intermediate Economics,* McGraw-Hill, New York, 1979.

E

earmarking of taxes (dedicating of revenues) The practice of designating specific revenues for the financing of specific public services or projects. Generally, it refers to a single tax source, for example, a state tax on gasoline for a single public project, such as the building and maintenance of roads. In the overall U.S. tax system, earmarking is relatively important; it is particularly important at the local government level, at which such special projects as schools claim a preponderant share of tax revenues. A state of Montana study of 50 states indicated that 23% of the state collections in fiscal year 1979 were earmarked. For additional information, see *Earmarked State Taxes,* Tax Foundation, Washington, D.C., 1983; James M. Buchanan, *The Economics of Earmarked Taxes,* Brookings Institution, Washington, D.C., 1963.

easy money (cheap money) The term used to designate a condition in which a combination of relatively low interest rates and great credit availability exists. When the term is used, it means that interest rates are lower than they were earlier, that many qualified borrowers who previously were denied loans are now granted them, and that capital is somewhat easier to raise. Since the term indicates a relative condition, no specific interest rate or degree of credit availability signals easy money. In the United States, the Federal Reserve System can help create easy-money conditions by providing commercial banks with free reserves (reserves above those that they are legally required to hold minus their borrowings from the Federal Reserve), thereby making it easier for them to extend loans. Even if the Federal Reserve System supplies banks with as much as $1.6 billion in free reserves (a sign of ample lending ability in the post-World War II period), however, banks may not respond immediately with more liberal lending policies. One reason may be that banks believe that they have already extended too great a volume of loans in relation to their capital. Moreover, even during easy-money periods no single individual or organization can borrow indefinitely without encountering increased resistance from lenders. For further information, see James M. Buchanan and Marilyn R. Flowers, *The Public Finances,* 4th ed., Irwin, Homewood, Ill., 1975.

econometrics The branch of economics which expresses economic theories in mathematical terms in order to verify them by statistical methods. It is concerned with the empirical measurement of economic relations that are expressible in mathematical form. Econometrics seeks to measure the impact of one economic variable on another in order to be able to predict future events or advise the choice for economic policy to produce desired results. Economic theory can supply qualitative information concerning an economic problem, but it is the task of econometrics to provide the quantitative content for these qualitative statements. Econometrics can be divided into four major divisions: specification, estimation, verification, and prediction. Specification is the process of building a mathematical model of an economic theory, i.e., of expressing the economic theory in mathematical terms. Through estimation, the parameters of the equation are filled in. Then, by verification, certain criteria of success are used to accept or reject the economic theory under investigation. Finally, through prediction, the model can be rearranged and fed new data about autonomous variables, and their effect on the endogenous variable can be predicted. The ability of the econometric model to make accurate predictions is a crucial test of the theoretical relationships that the model expresses. The use of econometrics has been confined largely to problems of the type included in partial-equilibrium theory and in the theory of income and employment. In partial-equilibrium theory, an estimation of the functions of supply and demand, a forecast of price in a single market, and an estimation of cost curves are included. In income theory, forecasts of consumer demand at various levels of income and estimations of the demand for money have been made. Attempts at large-scale econometric models of a whole economy have not been entirely successful. For further information, see Lawrence R. Klein, *An Introduction to Econometrics,* Greenwood, Westport, Conn., 1976.

economic determinism *See* **economic interpretation of history.**

economic efficiency The use of resources in the most efficient manner. Economic efficiency is concerned with the utilization of scarce resources employed in turning out products and with the resulting output itself. An economy is considered 100% efficient if it is producing at 100% of capacity, employing all methods of production and resources as effectively as present technology allows. An economy that has achieved full employment has attained economic efficiency, but full employment has not necessarily been reached when all workers are employed. Workers harvesting wheat by hand or using a horse-drawn plow may have jobs, but in terms of economic efficiency they are unemployed. In these cases, the workers are underemployed; they are doing a job, but not efficiently. If they were replaced by more efficient production methods, output could still be maintained at the same level. Unutilized resources, both human and capital, mean waste and inefficiency. For a study of particular aspects of the problem of economic efficiency, see Armen A. Alchian and William R. Allen, *University Economics,* Wadsworth, New York, 1971.

economic growth   An increase in a nations's or an area's capacity to produce goods and services coupled with an increase in production of these goods and services. Usually, economic growth is measured by the annual rate of increase in a nation's gross national product, as adjusted for price changes. A better measure, however, is the increase in the real gross national product per capita; in some underdeveloped countries yearly gains in output are surpassed by gains in population, leaving the average person with a lowered standard of living. Even when population changes are taken into account, however, growth rates do not always accurately measure changes in the standard of living. U.S. workers, for instance, have gained about thirty hours of additional leisure per week since 1900, but the value of this commodity, the freedom from work, is nowhere included in U.S. growth rates. Comparative growth rates are usually deceptive. One reason is that, because of business fluctuations, output does not rise smoothly and evenly from one year to another. As a result, by a careful selection of beginning and terminal years, it is possible to make economic growth over a period of time appear either bad or good in relation to another period. Comparisons of international growth rates are even more complicated because of differences in national income definitions and accounting methods. Moreover, in some cases statistics may be used deceptively for propaganda purposes. Annual growth rates for some major industrialized countries since 1960 are as follows: Federal Republic of Germany, 3.8%; Italy, 4.2%; Japan, 8%; United Kingdom, 2.3%; and U.S.S.R., 5.5%. These may be compared with a U.S. growth rate of about 3.5% in the same period. Current growth rates for foreign countries may be computed from the national income figures reported in Statistical Office of the United Nations, *Monthly Bulletin of Statistics,* New York; see also Simon Kuznets, *Modern Economic Growth: Rate, Structure, and Spread,* Yale University Press, New Haven, Conn., 1966.

economic indicator   A statistical series that has been found to represent fairly accurately changes in business conditions. There are three major groups of economic indicators that demonstrate a consistent relationship to the timing of general business fluctuations: (1) Leading indicators, such as new orders and profits, usually rise and fall in advance of turns in general business activity. (2) Coincident indicators, such as the unemployment rate and bank debits, generally rise and fall with the changes in overall business activity. (3) Lagging indicators, such as capital expenditures and consumer installment debt, usually move up or down after general business activity has altered its course. Although economic indicators constitute a valuable tool in forecasting business conditions, they are not infallible, and relationships among the indicators and business activity on the whole do not always hold fast. Hence, changes in key indicators cannot automatically be taken as evidence of impending changes in general business conditions. For a fuller discussion of the indicators, see Geoffrey H. Moore (ed.), *Business Cycle Indicators,* Princeton University Press, Princeton, N.J., vol. 1.; for current indicator data, see U.S. Bureau of the Census, *Business Cycle Developments,* monthly.

economic interpretation of history (economic determinism; materialistic concept of history) The thesis, advanced by Karl Marx in *A Contribution of the Critique of Political Economy* (1859), that the events of any historical epoch are determined by the economic institutions prevailing at the time rather than by the wishes and will of the individuals of the period; in short, that the manner in which people make their living practically dictates their worldly outlook and actions. In Marx's words, "The mode of production in material life determines the general character of the social, political and spiritual process of life. It is not the consciousness of men that determines their existence, but, on the contrary, their social existence that determines their consciousness." To Marx, the systems of production and distribution of goods in any society established the society's class structure. In order to change undesirable features of an existing class structure, it was necessary to alter the means of production and the distribution of wealth. There is a close relationship between Marx's interpretation of history and his thesis of class struggle, which held that antagonisms between social classes are the driving forces in history. These two doctrines provide the basis for the Communists' firm belief in inevitable success for their economic system. Scholars have criticized Marx's insistence on the overriding importance of economic organization in history. See Joseph A. Schumpeter, *Capitalism, Socialism, and Democracy,* Harper & Row, New York, 1950, chap. 11; William Fellner, *Modern Economic Analysis,* McGraw-Hill, New York, 1960, pp. 125–127.

economic law A generalization concerning the relationship between various economic phenomena, such as that between price and total sales. The most important purpose of an economic law is to permit prediction, and prediction, in turn, permits control over phenomena. Economic laws are generalizations, containing no precise quantitative results. Thus, they are stated in ordinal terms, such as *increasing* and *greater than,* rather than in cardinal terms, such as *increase by 20%*. An example of an economic law is the law of variable proportions, which holds that if the quantity of one productive service is increased while the quantities of other services are held constant, the resulting increments of product will decrease after a certain point. See George J. Stigler, *The Theory of Price*, 3d ed., Macmillan, New York, 1966.

economic model   A mathematical statement of economic theory. An economic model is a method of analysis which presents an oversimplified picture of the real world. The situation in the real world is composed of a bewildering variety of major and minor variables, and unless the less important factors are eliminated, rigorous analysis is either hopelessly complicated or impossible. By making certain assumptions, many minor elements can be eliminated and a model can be set up. The model permits analysis of the specific situation defined by the assumptions. Economic models themselves can be set out in equation form with diagrams or with words. A complete mathematical model must have as many equations as there are unknowns. For further information, see Lawrence R. Klein, *An Introduction to Econometrics*, Greenwood, Westport, Conn., 1977.

economic planning   Governmental direction of the economy. There are two types of modern economic planning. One is the partial economic planning that has evolved under the private enterprise system, and the other is total control, or overall planning, by communist and socialist governments. Under a partial economic planning system, government direction may be applied through economic policy that is designed to smooth economic fluctuations experienced in a free enterprise economy. It may take the form of actions to offset a recession, the institution of public works projects to provide employment, the reduction of taxes to increase purchasing power, or the lowering of interest rates to encourage investment. Governmental policies to prevent inflation and to encourage economic growth are also examples of limited economic planning. Total economic planning implies the determination by a supreme governmental authority of the quality, kind, and quantity of goods to be produced by a nation. Although economic planning is quite broad in scope, it always involves some specific forecasts of the results of economic operations. For further information see C. R. Blitzer, P. B. Clark, and L. Taylor (eds.), *Economy-Wide Models and Development Planning*, Oxford University Press, London, 1975.

economics   The social study of the production, distribution, and consumption of wealth. With the expansion of the tools used by modern economists in their analyses and the discarding of out-of-date theories, economics is becoming more a science and less an art. Despite this trend, however, economists still interpret the same economic data differently. Like scientific research, economics can be divided into two major categories, basic economics and applied economics. Basic economics is the study of economic principles, which for the most part is carried out by academic economists, while applied economics puts the basic principles to work in developing economic programs and policies, with economic progress as the overall goal.

economic theory   The study of relationships in the economy. Its purpose is to analyze and explain the behavior of the various economic elements. The relationships established by economic analyses, which are called economic principles, may be analytical generalizations, following logically from certain assumptions, or empirical statements, defining a relationship between observed data. The body of economic theory can be divided into two broad categories, positive theory and welfare theory. Positive theory is an attempt to analyze the operation of the economy without considering the desirability of its results in terms of ultimate goals. Its major subdivisions are price and distribution theory, which is concerned with the behavior of individuals and firms and with the determination of the prices, output, and distribution of goods, and national income theory, which focuses on the level of national income and employment. Welfare theory is concerned primarily with an evaluation of the economic system in terms of ethical goals which are not themselves derived from economic analysis. For further information, see Kenneth E. Boulding, *Economic Analysis,* 4th ed., Harper & Row, New York, 1966; William Baumol, *Economic Theory and Operations Analysis,* 4th ed., Prentice-Hall, Englewood Cliffs, N.J., 1977.

economic trend   *See* **secular trend.**

economies of mass production   *See* **benefits of large-scale production.**

economies of scale   *See* **benefits of large-scale production.**

economist   An individual with a knowledge of economic theory who can apply the theory to the real world. An economist must, therefore, understand the behavior of consumers and business people. Economists' problems generally concern numerical magnitudes which vary from time to time, from place to place, and from case to case.

effective interest rate   The true rate of interest paid on an installment loan. The problem of effective interest rates arises in the case of consumer loans, in which the principal is paid back in periodic installments. The rate of interest quoted by the lender on consumer installment loans is usually the simple nominal rate of interest; e.g., on $120 borrowed for a year, with an interest charge of $6, repayable in twelve monthly installments of $10, the nominal rate of interest is 5% per annum. This is not the effective rate of interest, or that actually paid by the borrower, however, since the credit in use is reduced as each payment is made. Thus, in the example given above, $120 is not borrowed for twelve months; rather, $10 is borrowed for one month, $10 is borrowed for two months, etc. The effective rate of interest must be calculated only on the basis of the unpaid balance and not on the total amount of the original loan. The effective rate, which is about twice as high as the nominal rate, can be calculated according to the following formula:

$$\text{Effective rate} = \frac{\begin{array}{c}2 \times (\text{nominal rate of interest}) \\ \times (\text{number of payments})\end{array}}{\text{number of payments plus } 1}$$

Thus, in the example given above, the effective rate of interest would not be 5%, but rather 2(0.05)(12)/13, or 9.23%. Another convenient method for calculating the annual effective rate of interest is as follows:

$$\text{Effective rate} = \frac{\begin{array}{c}2 \times (\text{number of payments in one year}) \\ \times (\text{total amount of finance charges})\end{array}}{\begin{array}{c}(\text{original unpaid balance}) \\ \times (\text{number of payments plus } 1)\end{array}}$$

For additional information, see Robert W. Johnson, *Methods of Stating Consumer Finance Charges*, Columbia University, Graduate School of Business, New York, 1961.

efficiency In statistics and econometrics, an estimating criterion or objective evaluation of the relative merits of possible estimators (parameters) attributed to Fisher. Thus if c_1 and c_2 are two estimators from a sample of observations, the one with the smaller variance is the more efficient. Efficiency implies also sufficiency, i.e., that no other estimator from the same sample can add to information about the parameter. For additional information, see Lawrence R. Klein, *An Introduction to Econometrics*, Greenwood, Westport, Conn., 1977.

elastic demand The percentage change induced in one factor of demand divided by a given percentage change in the factor that caused the change. For example, if the price of a commodity is raised, purchasers tend to reduce their buying rate. The relationship between price and purchasing rate, which is known as the elasticity of demand, expresses the percentage change in the buying rate divided by the percentage change in price. The concept of elasticity for a given point on a line or curve is simple, but in practice elasticities may have to be calculated over given finite ranges of price and quality changes. In such cases, there is a great difference if the percentage change is computed from the beginning of the change, from the midpoint of the change, or from the end of the change. To illustrate the difference in percentage change in quantities, let us assume that the amount of wheat purchased per day changes from 1,000 bushels to 1,200 bushels. The change, therefore, is 200 bushels, and the percentage change (200 divided by 1,000) is 20%. If we move from 1,200 bushels to 1,000 bushels, the change is the same, 200 bushels, but the percentage change (decrease) is only 16.67% (200 divided by 1,200). One formula designed to eliminate this asymmetry is as follows, with Q_1 representing the initial purchase rate, Q_2 the second purchase rate, and similarly for prices:

$$\text{Elasticity of demand} = \frac{(Q_2 - Q_1)\,(P_1 + P_2)}{(P_1 - P_2)\,(Q_1 + Q_2)}$$

The elasticity concept is extremely useful because it applies independently of the units in which prices and quantities are measured. The concept may be used to express the relationship between any two variables, such as price and amount supplied or income and purchase rate. The rudiments of the concept are treated in Paul A. Samuelson, *Economics*, 9th ed., McGraw-Hill, New York, 1973; for a more advanced treatment, see George J. Stigler, *The Theory of Price*, 3d ed., Macmillan, New York, 1966; for the mathematics of the topic, see James M. Henderson and Richard E. Quandt, *Microeconomic Theory: A Mathematical Approach*, 3d ed., McGraw-Hill, New York, 1980.

elasticity The relative response of one variable to a small percentage change in another variable. The general formula for elasticity is

$$\frac{\Delta y/y}{\Delta x/x} \qquad \text{which can be written} \qquad \frac{dy}{dx} \cdot \frac{x}{y}$$

if the changes are extremely small. The concept of elasticity is dimensionless; that is, it is totally independent of units of measurement. This allows one to compare, for example, the price elasticity of demand for land with that of automobiles, ball-point pens, or any other good or service. Perhaps the most common specific examples of the concept of elasticity are price elasticity of demand $(q/q)/(\Delta P/P)$ and income elasticity of demand $(\Delta q/q)/(\Delta y/y)$, where q is quantity demanded, p is price, and y is disposable income. For additional information, see George Stigler, *Theory of Price*, 3d ed., Macmillan, New York, 1966; Jack Hirshleifer, *Price Theory and Applications*, Prentice-Hall, Englewood Cliffs, N.J., 1976, chap. 5.

elasticity coefficient Many problems in economics involve relationships between one factor and another. If the percentage change in one factor is related to the percentage change in the other, the units in which the items are measured become irrelevant, and one percentage divided by the other will yield a pure signed number. For example, it is well known that the purchase rate of a commodity or service tends to decline as the price rises, and elasticity of demand is defined as the percentage change in the purchase rate divided by the causative factor, the percentage change in the price. Since price and purchase rate move in opposite directions, the number will have a negative sign, although descriptive material concerning the elasticity of demand often neglects the sign because it is understood to be negative. The percentage response of price may be greater than, the same as, or less than the percentage change in price (see *elastic demand* and *inelastic demand*). The elasticity concept may be applied to any pair of relevant statistics, such as income and purchase rate. Unfortunately, the question of calculating the correct percentage changes is often troublesome. Strictly speaking, the elasticity coefficient applies to an infinitesimally small point on a function, but the calculation of percentage changes is necessarily over some finite distance. If the distance appears to be relatively small, the distinction is sometimes ignored. If the distance is deemed to be of some significance, an arc-elasticity coefficient may be calculated. This procedure calculates an elasticity at the midpoint of a straight-line segment connecting the initial and terminal points of the function. The arc elasticity is calculated as follows:

$$\text{Arc elasticity} = \frac{(Q_2 - Q_1)\ (P_2 + P_1)}{(Q_2 + Q_1)\ (P_2 - P_1)}$$

where the subscripts 1 and 2 indicate the initial and terminal periods, respectively. If the exact formula of the demand function is known, as it often will be in empirical estimation of demand functions, calculus may be used to yield a more precise measure of elasticity at a point:

$$\text{Elasticity} = \frac{dq}{dp}\frac{p}{q}$$

The above formula will be seen to be the slope of the function at the point, multiplied by the quotient of the price (independent variable) over the purchase rate (the dependent variable). A general description of elasticity calculations will be found in D. S. Watson and Mary A. Holman, *Price Theory and Its Uses,* 4th ed., Houghton Mifflin, Boston, 1976, and the mathematical applications will be found in the Mathematical Notes to the various sections of the work.

elasticity of substitution   A measure of the ease with which one input can be substituted for another input when responding to a change in the ratio of the prices of the inputs. For instance, given a production function, suppose that the ratio of the return to capital to wages declined 1%, making labor relatively more expensive than capital. If the ratio of the amount of capital input to labor input used increases more than 1%, the elasticity of substitution is elastic, which implies that it is relatively easy to substitute capital for labor. Formally the elasticity of substitution is defined as follows:

$$\frac{\Delta(K/L)\ (K/L)}{\Delta(MP_K/MP_L)/(MP_K/MP_L)}$$

where K is capital input, MP_K is marginal product of capital, L is labor input, and MP_L is marginal product of labor. Originally introduced by J. R. Hicks in 1932, the concept of the elasticity of substitution has played an important role in economic theory, particularly production and growth theory. The Cobb-Douglas production function, which is frequently used in economic growth models, has an elasticity of substitution equal to 1. Unitary elasticity of substitution means that the relative shares of income going to capital and labor remain unchanged even if the ratio of the prices of these inputs changes. For additional information, see J. R. Hicks, *The Theory of Wages,* Macmillan, New York, 1932; Joan Robinson, *The Economics of Imperfect Competition,* 2d ed., St. Martin's Press, New York, 1969.

elastic money supply The situation occurring in a monetary system in which the volume of currency in circulation can be varied to meet different needs. In the United States, for example, the amount of currency needed by the public increases on such holidays as July 4, Labor Day, and Christmas. The demand for currency varies for different days of the week, and in agricultural regions the need is heavy at harvest time. There is also a long-term aspect of monetary growth: a rising level of business requires a greater amount of currency. The Federal Reserve System was established in 1914 to provide the United States with an elastic currency supply, which had not been available under earlier banking systems. It provides elasticity by increasing bank reserves at times when currency is in greatest demand. Technically, the term elastic money supply is erroneous, because elasticity refers to the conversion of checking accounts into currency and vice versa. Normally, money is considered to be the sum of currency and demand deposits (except for demand deposits owned by banks). The seasonal pattern of the demand for currency is discussed in detail in *The Federal Reserve System: Purposes and Functions,* Board of Governors of the Federal Reserve System, Washington, D.C., 1964; John J. Klein, *Money and the Economy,* Harcourt Brace, New York, 1978.

elastic supply A measure of a relative responsiveness of a producer in supplying quantities of a good when the market price of the good changes. When a producer is responsive to price changes, supply is elastic; when the producer is relatively insensitive to price changes, supply is inelastic. The elasticity of supply is measured by the elasticity coefficient E_s:

$$E_s = \frac{\text{percentage change in quantity supplied}}{\text{percentage change in price}}$$

The main determinant of the elasticity of supply is the time during which a producer must respond to a given change in the price of a product. A given change in price will have a greater effect on the quantity supplied over the long run. A supply schedule is perfectly elastic if an unlimited amount is offered at all prices and perfectly inelastic if the quantity supplied is the same regardless of price. Supply elasticity is considered less useful as an economic concept than demand elasticity because the latter provides some indication of what is happening to the producer's revenue. For additional information, see George J. Stigler, *The Theory of Price,* 3d ed., Macmillan, New York, 1966;

Donald S. Watson and Mary A. Holman, *Price Theory and Its Uses,* 4th ed., Houghton Mifflin, Boston, 1976.

employment   The state of being employed. According to the concept of the U.S. Department of Labor, all persons who work for pay or profit or for fifteen hours or more without pay in a family business or farm are employed. Total employment is measured each month by the U.S. Bureau of the Census for the department. During the week containing the twelfth of the month, census interviewers visit 50,000 households in 449 different areas, asking questions designed to learn who was employed and who was unemployed during the survey week. The Bureau of Labor Statistics compiles from payroll data civilian employment figures for all nonagricultural establishments. Its figures exclude proprietors, self-employed persons, and domestic servants. For additional information, see Gordon F. Bloom and Herbert R. Northrup, *Economics of Labor Relations,* 8th ed., Irwin, Homewood, Ill., 1977.

Employment Act of 1946   An act of Congress which placed the official responsibility for promoting stable prosperity in the hands of the federal government. An essential objective of the act is the maximum utilization of available resources, which means a low unemployment rate and a high rate of utilization of industrial facilities. The act created little new authority for the management of the national economic program, but it did establish additional machinery to achieve a better understanding and focusing of attention on the important problems of the economy. It required that the President make an annual economic report to Congress on current economic trends and prospects and recommend a program designed to promote high levels of employment, production, and purchasing power. The Employment Act also established the Council of Economic Advisers and a Joint Committee on the Economic Report. For further information, see "The Employment Act in the Economic Thinking of Our Times: A Symposium," *American Economic Review,* May 1957.

endogenous variables   In econometrics, any economic time series that influences a set of economic relationships that is being studied and is also itself influenced by changes in the same relationship—hence, a variable that is determined within the system itself. For example, private wage payments, consumption, savings, investment, and profit are generally treated as endogenous variables in studies of a nation's aggregate economic activity. For additional information, see Lawrence R. Klein, *An Introduction to Econometrics,* Greenwood, Westport, Conn., 1977.

Engel's law   The law which states that, as a family's income increases, a smaller and smaller proportion of the income is spent for food. It was named for Ernst Engel, a nineteenth-century German administrator and statistician who was the first to call attention to the different proportions of income spent for various categories of goods and services by different income groups in Saxony. More recently, it has become clear that the other basic necessities of life, such as clothing and housing, similarly claim a declining share of a family's growing income. Thus, higher-income groups spend relatively and absolutely larger sums for luxury goods and services than do lower-income groups. Among modern offshoots of Engel's law is the concept of optional consumption, which states that a considerable proportion of consumer expenditures in relatively wealthy nations is devoted to goods and services not essential to physical well-being and that the consumer consequently has the option of spending or refraining from spending money for these items. A related concept is that of discretionary income, a measure of the share of consumer income that remains after consumers have made essential purchases and hence can be used for luxuries and less pressing expenditures. For a discussion of Engel's law, see Joseph A. Schumpeter, *History of Economic Analysis,* Oxford University Press, New York, 1954, p. 961.

entrepreneurial ability One of the four factors of production, entrepreneurial ability is the most difficult to define, quantify, and identify. In recent decades, discussion of the entrepreneur as a specific factor of production has diminished because entrepreneurs are closely associated with the owner-managed firm and not with the modern corporation. Marshall was one of the earliest economists to consider entrepreneurial ability specifically as a factor of production and as the residual income recipient. The concept of the entrepreneur as an innovator was developed primarily by Schumpeter, while Kaldor emphasized the managerial role and Knight stressed the risk-bearing function. See R. B. Ekelund and R. F. Hebert, *A History of Economic Theory and Methods,* McGraw-Hill, New York, 1975.

equilibrium The state of an economic system in which all forces for change are balanced, so that the net tendency to change is zero. An economic system is considered to be in equilibrium when all the significant variables show no change over a period of time. For example, at an equilibrium price for a given good, the buyers in the market are just willing to purchase the entire amount of the good which the sellers are willing to offer. The equilibrium price is the only one at which both buyers and sellers will be satisfied, so that while given supply-and-demand conditions remain unchanged, the price remains the same. The concept of equilibrium is used in economics not only as a description of a final set of conditions but also as an indication of the direction in which economic variables are headed. Often, the external conditions defining the equilibrium position are constantly changing, so that equilibrium is never attained. It is still useful to know the direction in which the economic variables are changing, however, whether or not they are expected to reach the equilibrium value. There are two general types of economic equilibriums, stable and unstable. In a stable equilibrium, any movement away from the equilibrium level automatically generates forces tending to bring the variables

back to the equilibrium level. On the other hand, any movement away from
an unstable equilibrium generates forces tending to move the variables even
farther away from the equilibrium level, even though at the equilibrium
position itself there is no set pressure for change. For example, when the
slope of the supply curve for a given good is steeper than the slope of its
demand curve, a stable-equilibrium position is determined, whereas if the
slope of the supply curve is less steep than that of the demand curve, an
unstable equilibrium results. For additional details, see Frank Knight, *On the
History and Method of Economics,* University of Chicago Press, Chicago, 1956,
chap. 8; W. Hildenbrand and A. Kirman, *Introduction to Equilibrium Analysis,*
North-Holland, Amsterdam, 1976.

equity   The excess of a firm's assets over its liabilities. In a proprietorship
or partnership, equity is the claim or stake of the owner or owners. In a
corporation, it is measured by the capital stock and surplus. For further information, see J. Fred Weston and Eugene F. Brigham, *Essentials of Managerial
Finance,* 5th ed., Holt, Rinehart and Winston, New York, 1979.

equity capital   The total investment in a business by all its owners. Investors supply equity capital to a corporation when they buy newly issued shares
of its stock. They are not promised a fixed rate of interest but participate in
the profits. Firms can raise additional money by accepting a greater amount
of equity capital and by admitting the persons who furnish it into the enterprise as stockholders or owners. Equity capital is usually associated with the
development of a new business and with business expansion. For further
information, see J. Fred Weston and Eugene F. Brigham, *Essentials of Managerial Finance,* 5th ed., Holt, Rinehart and Winston, New York, 1979.

error term   The error term in an econometric model is a special variable
(usually designated by u) to allow for the facts that economic theory is necessarily incomplete, that the analyst may not have specified the correct relationship, and that some variables affecting the model have almost certainly
been omitted. The error term can be included as an additive, multiplicative,
or exponential factor. It is always assumed to be a random real variable, and
it can be either discrete or continuous. The error term is never observed, but
its existence is established by the known imperfections of econometric technique. After estimates of a model's parameters (for example, the familiar $\hat{a}$
and $\hat{b}$ of a linear equation) have been derived, it is possible to compute residuals $\hat{u}$ as estimates of the error u. For additional information, see Lawrence
R. Klein, *An Introduction to Econometrics,* Greenwood, Westport, Conn., 1977.

escalator clause   A contractual provision in the financial terms of an
agreement that requires the payment of automatic increases or decreases in
the event of certain price changes. One of the most familiar forms of the

escalator clause is that found in wage agreements, in which the clause provides for adjustments in wage rates on the basis of increases or decreases in consumer prices. The path-making agreement was between General Motors and the United Auto Workers in 1948. In periods of relative price stability, escalator clauses lose some of their attraction for labor unions, but in periods of inflation interest increases. Interest in escalator clauses rose tremendously in the late 1960s and 1970s with the inflationary wave. A typical clause provides for a 1-cent hourly wage change for a half-point change in the U.S. Bureau of Labor Statistics' consumer price index. There is always a specified floor to the downward movement of wage escalators. Other price and cost indices, such as the Bureau of Labor Statistics' wholesale price index and *Engineering News-Record*'s construction cost index, are used in escalation agreements to adjust costs of plant and equipment. For a discussion of escalator clauses in labor contracts, see U.S. Department of Labor, *Prices, Escalation and Economic Stability,* Washington, D.C., 1971, chap. 3; U.S. Department of Labor, *Escalation and the CPI: Information for Users,* Washington, D.C., 1978.

escape clause   A provision in U.S. trade agreements that enables the United States to terminate or modify a specific trade concession if the concession threatens serious injury to a domestic industry. First suggested by President Franklin D. Roosevelt in 1934, it became applicable to agreements concluded under the National Trade Agreements Act by means of an executive order of February 1947 and was written into the act in 1948. The Trade Agreements Extension Act of 1951 made the inclusion of an escape clause in all new trade agreements a statutory requirement. Recommendations to the President for use of the escape clause originate in the U.S. International Trade Commission, which, at its own motion or at the request of an interested party, is required to investigate whether a proposed or actual tariff reduction has injured or is likely to injure an American industry. The commission has recommended action for only one-fourth of the relief applicants, and the President has followed its recommendations only about one-half of the time. Where tariffs have been reinstated, the imports affected have been of little economic significance to the United States. Escape-clause action does not give a U.S. industry indefinite protection, because a review of each case of tariff relief is required two years after the granting of relief and in each year thereafter. Although many factors are used to determine injury to an industry, production trends and profit levels are used most often. Since 1955 injury to one product of a multiproduct industry is considered acceptable as serious injury, although previously injury was applicable only to the overall operations of an industry. See I. B. Kravis, "The Trade Agreement Escape Clause," *American Economic Review,* vol. 44, no. 3, June 1954, pp. 319–338; C. P. Kindleberger and P. H. Lindert, *International Economics,* Irwin, Homewood, Ill., 1978.

estate tax A levy on the entire estate left by a decedent. Whereas an inheritance tax is based on the amount of the estate received by each beneficiary, the estate tax is levied on the value of the entire estate before it has been divided. The estate tax is simpler and more productive than the inheritance tax, because it avoids the sometimes difficult task of determining the value of each beneficiary's share. On the other hand, the inheritance tax is considered to be more equitable than the estate tax, because it is more closely linked to the heirs' ability to pay. There is often little or no difference between the effects of estate and inheritance taxes, since in most cases the estate is passed on to the surviving spouse. The estate tax is usually based on a steeply progressive rate schedule, so that it involves a sizable redistribution of wealth. Avoidance of estate taxes is attempted principally through gifts and the creation of limited interests in an estate. For additional details, see Richard A. Musgrave and Peggy B. Musgrave, *Public Finance in Theory and Practice*, 2d ed., McGraw-Hill, New York, 1976.

Euler's theorem The propositon that, if a production function involves constant returns to scale, the sum of the marginal products will equal the total product. Euler's theorem played an important role in the development of the marginal-productivty theory of distribution. The theorem involves the partial differentiation of homogeneous equations. It states that if $f(x, y)$ is homogeneous to degree n, then

$$x\frac{\partial f}{\partial x} + y\frac{\partial f}{\partial y} = nf(x, y)$$

To prove the theorem, let $P = f(L, C)$ be the production function involving labor (L) and capital (C) for a given good. Since it is assumed that the production has constant returns to scale, the production function is linearly homogeneous, and Euler's theorem can be applied, with $n = 1$, as follows:

$$L\frac{\partial f}{\partial L} + C\frac{\partial f}{\partial C} = f(L, C) = P$$

Since $\partial f/\partial L$ and $\partial f/\partial C$ are the marginal products of a single unit of labor and capital, respectively, the equation states that the marginal product of labor $\partial f/\partial L$, multiplied by the number of laborers L, plus the marginal product of capital $\partial f/\partial C$, multiplied by the number of capital units C, equals the total product P. For additional details, see James M. Henderson and Richard E. Quandt, *Microeconomic Theory*, 3d ed., McGraw-Hill, New York, 1980; see also Joan Robinson, "Euler's Theorem and the Problem of Distribution," *Economic Journal*, vol. 44, September 1934, pp. 398–414.

Eurodollars Dollar deposits with U.S. banks that are acquired by foreigners and are redeposited in banks outside the United States, mainly in Europe.

The trading center for Eurodollars is London, where merchant bankers lend these dollars to local or foreign banks or to commercial borrowers. This form of financing is playing an increasingly important role in world trade, providing the nucleus of a trade international money market. In theory, a typical Eurodollar transaction works as follows: A West German commercial bank with a surplus of marks may exchange them with the West German central bank for dollars, which the central bank has accumulated because of the persistent surplus in the German balance of payments. The German bank then puts its newly acquired dollars to work in London at an interest rate of 8 or 10%. The London banker relends the dollars, perhaps to a Japanese banker at 12 or 14%, and the Japanese can now finance imports calling for payment in dollars. The Eurodollar market provides incentives for both borrowers and lenders. Short-term holders of dollars can put their money to work at interest rates above those available in New York, and short-term borrowers generally can obtain credit at rates below those in the United States and abroad. See Herber V. Prochnow (ed.), *The Eurodollar,* Rand McNally, Chicago, 1970; Geoffrey Bell, *The Eurodollar Market and the International Financial Sector,* Halsted Press, New York, 1974.

ex ante   A Latin phrase meaning "beforehand" and "as applied." In business-cycle theory, it refers to quantities of investment, savings, or consumption defined in terms of action planned at the beginning of the period in question. It alludes to the anticipations, calculations, and plans driving the dynamic economic machinery forward. Recognition of the time period under discussion is important in dynamic economic theory. In this context, the concepts of ex ante and ex post were originated by Gunnar Myrdal in his discussion of monetary theory. Myrdal pointed out that there is an important distinction between prospective (ex ante) and retrospective (ex post) methods of calculating economic quantities. The ex ante method is based on discounted anticipations or forecasts of expected profitability, which is a decisive element in business decisions. For further discussion, see Gunnar Myrdal, *Monetary Equilibrium,* William Hodges, London, 1939.

excess reserves   The surplus of cash and deposits owned by commercial member banks of the Federal Reserve System over what they are legally required to hold at reserve banks or in their own vaults. The excess-reserve position of a bank is an indication of its ability to invest in government bonds or to make loans to customers. Therefore, if the Federal Reserve System is trying to stimulate business in periods of economic sluggishness, it buys government bonds from private sellers, thus increasing bank reserves; it takes the opposite course when inflation is a problem. At any given time, however, reserves do not give a complete picture of the potential of commercial-bank lending, since commercial banks can borrow at the local Federal Reserve bank to obtain reserves. A better indication of the banking system's lending potential consists of free reserves, that is, excess reserves minus borrowing at the reserve banks. The concept of excess reserves is theoretically applicable to banks that are not members of the Federal Reserve System, but since reserve rules in each state differ, no statistics are available on a current basis for nonmembers' excess reserves. The dollar volume of free and excess reserves is reported monthly in *Federal Reserve Bulletin*, Washington, D.C.; for additional information see Lawrence S. Ritter and William L. Silber, *Principles of Money, Banking and Financial Markets*, 3d rev. ed., Basic Books, New York, 1980.

exchange control   A system of governmental regulation of foreign exchange. Under this system, all purchases and sales of foreign exchange are handled by the government, which allocates or rations the supply of foreign currencies to its citizens. In this way, a country facing balance-of-payment difficulties may restrict imports to the amount earned through the accumulation of foreign exchange by its nationals. The government can force a balance-of-payments equilibrium on the nation by restricting imports to the value of exports. Exchange control can also be used to discriminate against importers so that only desired goods are imported. For example, in order to encourage imports of more essential goods, foreign exchange may be denied for the importation of luxury or nonessential goods. For further information, see Armen A. Alchian and William R. Allen, *University Economics*, 3d ed., Wadsworth, New York, 1971.

excise tax   A levy imposed on the sale of a particular commodity. An excise tax is usually levied on the manufacturers of consumer goods, but it can be shifted to the consumers of the product by including the amount of the tax in the selling price. The tax is frequently paid by the purchase of tax stamps, which must be affixed to the product before it enters distribution channels. In the United States, excise taxes are part of both federal and state taxation systems. Commodities subject to excise taxation usually are widely consumed, have a relatively inelastic demand, and generally are not among the necessities of life. Among the more common excise taxes are those levied on cigarettes, alcohol, and gasoline. Excise taxes may be specific, amounting to a fixed sum per unit of the product (e.g., 5 cents per pound of tobacco), or they may be ad valorem, amounting to a fixed percentage of the selling price of the product (e.g., 4% of the selling price). Although excise taxes are considered regressive, placing a larger burden on the poor than on the rich, they offer the advantages of stable revenues, a low cost of collection, and the ability to produce revenue immediately. They also can be used to regulate consumption (e.g., of luxuries). For additional details, see Joseph A. Pechman, *Federal Tax Policy*, 3d ed., Brookings Institution, Washington, D.C., 1977.

exogenous variable   In econometrics, any economic time series that influences a set of economic relationships that is being studied but is not itself influenced by changes in those relationships—hence, a variable that is determined outside the system. For example, export statistics are usually considered an exogeneous variable in a study of a nation's aggregate economic activity. For additional information, see Lawrence R. Klein, *An Introduction to Econometrics,* Greenwood, Westport, Conn., 1977.

expansion, business-cycle   The phase of the business cycle during which general business activity is rising from the trough to the next peak. The amplitude of expansion may be expected to show a high degree of consistency with the rate of growth during the previous expansion. Expansion rates are usually higher when the expansion follows a severe contraction than when it follows a mild contraction. The severity of the previous recession also affects the length of time required to return from the trough to the prerecession level of business activity. Moreover, there is a tendency toward slower growth after the initial expansion. For a detailed discussion of expansion in the business cycle, see Geoffrey H. Moore (ed.), *Business Cycle Indicators,* Princeton University Press, Princeton, N.J., 1961, vol. I.

expectations   What people do is influenced not only by events that occurred in the past but also by expectations regarding events that have yet to occur. While economists recognize the importance of expectations about future events in conditioning present behavior, economic analysis is not characterized by serious attempts to measure expectations or to incorporate expectations into empirical work. One method of incorporating expectational phenomena into economic thinking is to treat behavior as adaptive to the differences between expected and realized events. The most popular current theory dealing with expectational phenomena is the rational expectations theory, which assumes that people make guesses about the future on the basis of the best information available to them at the time they must make a decision. For additional information, see F. Thomas Juster and L. D. Taylor, "Towards a Theory of Saving Behavior," *American Economic Review,* vol. 65, no. 2, May 1975, pp. 203–209.

expected value   The mean value of single observations drawn from a finite or infinite universe in repeated sampling. It has been described as a statistical or combinatorial concept in contrast to the arithmetic mean, an algebraic concept. The expected value is not necessarily the most frequently encountered value, and it need not be a possible value. For additional information, see Lawrence R. Klein, *An Introduction to Econometrics,* Greenwood, Westport, Conn., 1977.

export   A good or commodity that is shipped from one country or area to another in the conduct of foreign trade. The country that ships the goods is the exporter. For further information, see Charles P. Kindleberger and P. H.

Lindert, *International Economics,* 6th ed., Irwin, Homewood, Ill., 1978; John Hein, "United States Exports in World Markets," *The Conference Board Information Bulletin,* Conference Board, New York, December 1978.

ex post   A Latin phrase meaning "afterward" and "as applied." In business-cycle theory, it refers to quantities of investment, savings, or consumption defined in terms of measurement made at the end of the period in question. Thus, it refers to realized investment, savings, or consumption. Recognition of the time period under discussion is important in dynamic economic theory. In this context, the concepts of ex post and ex ante were originated by Gunnar Myrdal in his discussion of monetary theory. Myrdal pointed out that there is an important distinction between retrospective (ex post) and prospective (ex ante) methods of calculating economic quantities. The ex post method is based on actual bookkeeping results and represents past experience. Ex post profitability is used only indirectly as evidence of the possibility of future profitability. For further discussion, see Gunnar Myrdal, *Monetary Equilibrium,* William Hodges, London, 1939.

externalities (spillovers or neighborhood effects)   The discrepancies between private and social costs or private and social benefits. The key aspect of externalities is interdependence without compensation. Some individual or firm benefits without paying, or causes others to have higher costs without compensation. Consumption externalities exist when someone gains or loses utility from another person's activity. For instance, neighbor A enjoys neighbor B's well-kept lawn, which means that social benefits exceed the private benefits to B and that A gains external economies. On the other hand, if A envies B's higher living standard, A suffers an external diseconomy, since costs exceed private costs. In production, if one firm's activities—e.g., training a labor force—benefit other firms (when workers change jobs and do not have to be retrained), external economies exist. Conversely, and prevalent today, if one firm's activities—pollution, for example—cost other firms and society more than is recorded on the firm's private accounting statements, external diseconomies exist. The concept of externalities is important for economic theory and policy. In the former case, the existence of externalities makes it impossible to reach a Pareto optimum unless external economies are exactly offset by external diseconomies. In the latter case, the existence of externalities provides a strong argument for government intervention in the private economy. See A. C. Pigou, *The Economics of Welfare,* Macmillan, New York, 1932; Hugh Macauley and Bruce Yandle, *Environmental Use and the Market,* Lexington Books, Lexington, Mass., 1977; E. J. Mishan, "The Postwar Literature on Externalities: An Interpretive Essay," *Journal of Economic Literature,* vol. 9, no. 1, March 1971.

extraneous estimates (a priori estimates)   Estimates of parameters that do not emerge in final form from computations but instead involve the use of related economic information not obtained from the available sample of data being studied. For example, a priori information can be used to overcome barriers caused by multicollinearity in multiple correlation. For additional information, see Karl A. Fox and Tej K. Kaul, *Intermediate Economic Statistics*, Krieger, Melbourne, Fla., 1980.

F

factor cost   A term used in connection with the valuation of net national product in measuring what it costs to produce the output of a nation in terms of the payments to the factors of production employed, and with the valuation of national income in measuring the income which the factors of production are paid for their services. Factor-cost valuation contrasts with market-price valuation, which measures output and/or income in terms of the prices paid for goods and services on the market. Factor-cost valuation represents a measure of the resources used. But it can be misleading as a measure of resource utilization because the payments made to the factors of production are only equal to factor costs under conditions of competitive equilibrium. See Richard Ruggles and Nancy D. Ruggles, *National Income Accounts and Income Analysis*, 2d ed., McGraw-Hill, New York, 1956.

factoring   A type of business finance in which financial specialists called factors take responsibility for collection and the credit of their clients. Let us assume that an apparel manufacturer annually sells $100,000 worth of merchandise to various department stores, which are allowed sixty days to pay their accounts. The manufacturer transfers these accounts to a factor who accepts the responsibility for making collections and absorbs any credit losses. The factor pays the manufacturer $75,000 and retains about 25% of the total amount to cover various charges, which include the factoring commission of about 5% and the interest on the money advanced, normally computed at 20% per annum on the basis of the daily net debit balance. Factoring differs from other types of accounts receivables financing in two essential respects. First, the factor assumes the seller's credit functions, including credit investigation and record keeping. Second, the factor buys the receivables outright, that is, without recourse to the seller for credit losses. See Lawrence D. Schall and Charles W. Haley, *Introduction to Financial Management,* McGraw-Hill, New York, 1980.

factor of production An economic resource which goes into the production of a good. The three major productive factors are property resources, including land; capital; and human resources, or labor. Land includes all natural resources: land itself, mineral deposits, forests, etc. Capital includes all human-made aids to production, such as buildings, machinery, and transportation facilities. Labor includes all the human physical and mental talents employed in producing goods. Entrepreneurial ability is often considered a fourth factor of production; it includes the organization of the other three factors for productive purposes, innovation, and the bearing of the risks of the business operation. Since all economic resources are relatively scarce and limited in supply, they all receive some type of income for their services. Income for the use of land is rent, income for use of capital in interest, and the income of labor is wages. Income for entrepreneurial ability is profits. For further information, see William Fellner, *Modern Economic Analysis,* McGraw-Hill, New York, 1960; Donald S. Watson and Mary A. Holman, *Price Theory and Its Uses,* 4th ed., Houghton Mifflin, Boston, 1976; C. E. Ferguson, *The Neoclassical Theory of Production and Distribution,* Cambridge University Press, Cambridge, 1975.

family A statistical concept that attempts to measure the number of households composed of individuals related by blood, marriage, or adoption and residing together. All such persons are considered members of one family. The average family size in the United States is about 3.3 persons. In March 1980, there were 61 million families in the United States, or about 10 million more than in 1970. The number and characteristics of families are used to determine market potentials for consumer durable goods, such as passenger cars and house furnishings. For definitions, historical statistics, and forecasts of the number of families in the U.S. population, see U.S. Bureau of the Census, *Current Population Reports: Population Characteristics,* ser. P-20.

fascism A totalitarian, collectivistic system of government in which central control is exercised over all economic, political, and social activities. A complete rejection of liberal democracy, fascism represents a return to an authoritarian system of power elites. It is based on an exaggerated nationalism which entirely eliminates individualism and regards the state as the highest expression of the will of the group. The state is ruled by an elite, headed by a leader whose will is supreme and whose power is based on the control of an organized system of terror and propaganda. All economic activities are subservient to national ends, which are determined by the ruling elite. Private ownership of production is maintained, but extreme restrictions are imposed on private economic freedoms. Decisions on production, investment, prices, and wages are all subject to arbitrary government control. There is no concentrated program for progressive economic development; instead, the economic system is subordinated to the political and military ends of the state. Fascism is similar to communism, in that both are totalitarian systems that accept the principle of terror and submerge the individual, but fascism relies on the private ownership of industry, whereas communism abandons private ownership. Fascism denies the equality of individuals and emphasizes class and racial distinctions, whereas communism pursues absolute equality and the elimination of all elites. Moreover, in a fascist system the state is regarded as a necessary and permanent form of control, whereas Communists see the totalitarian state as only a temporary phase which will eventually disappear. Fascism arose in Italy after World War I under the leadership of Benito Mussolini and was later adopted in Germany in the similar form of national socialism (Nazism). For additional information, see Walter Laqueur (ed.), *Fascism: A Reader's Guide,* University of California Press, Berkeley, 1976.

featherbedding A term applied to union rules or practices designed to increase artificially the number of persons employed. Unions can attempt to regulate the number of workers employed in a crew, such as dock workers on the waterfront or musicians in an orchestra, or they can require the employment of unnecessary workers, such as the use of two operators for each projection machine in a motion picture theater or a stoker on a diesel-powered locomotive. See Neil W. Chamberlain et al., *Sourcebook on Labor,* 3d ed., McGraw-Hill, New York, 1979.

federal budget: national-income-account basis (federal sector account) A measure of the direct impact of federal fiscal activity on the current flow of income and output in the United States. The federal sector account, like the federal cash budget, is more comprehensive than the federal administrative budget, for it includes most trust-fund transactions. Differing from both the administrative and the cash budgets, it records only receipts and expenditures which directly affect the flows of current income and output. The federal budget on the national-income-account basis records the purchase of goods and services when delivery is made, whereas the other two budgets generally count expenditures at the time of payment. Moreover, the federal sector account records some business tax receipts, particularly corporate income taxes, as they accrue, whereas in the administrative and cash budgets business tax receipts are counted as they are collected. For additional details on the size and description of the federal budget on the national-income-account basis, see *Special Analyses, the Budget of the United States Government Fiscal Year 1981,* Washington, D.C., 1980.

federal debt subject to limitation *See* administrative budget.

federal funds market   An informal market for the trading of reserves among member banks of the Federal Reserve System. A bank with deposits at the regional Federal Reserve bank in excess of its legal requirements can sell (lend) some of these deposits (in multiples of $1,000,000), usually for one day at a time, to another bank that is deficient in reserves. The money lent by one bank to another is called federal funds because it is legally in the hands of the Federal Reserve System and is merely transferred from the account of one commercial bank to that of another. Most large New York City banks have officers who act as federal funds brokers for correspondent banks in other large cities and purchase and sell reserves for their own banks. In addition to the major banks, one commercial finance house in New York City acts as a broker for federal funds, mainly for banks that do not trade in the market regularly. The net effect of trading reserves among banks is to enable each bank to hold only the legal minimum in non-interest-earning reserves. Normally, the interest rate on federal funds does not rise above the Federal Reserve discount rate, since a bank can borrow from the Federal Reserve System at the low rate rather than from private sources at the high rate. However, in periods of tight credit some banks pay a premium in order to avoid facing Federal Reserve lending officers. The System takes no part in the federal funds market other than to transfer reserves on its books as dictated by the bank that owns them. The federal funds market becomes more active in tight-money periods, but no instruments of monetary policy are brought to bear in this market. For further information, see Lawrence S. Ritter and William L. Silber, *Principles of Money, Banking and Financial Markets* 3d rev. ed., Basic Books, New York, 1980.

federal funds, receipts, and outlays   *See* **administrative budget.**

Federal Reserve note   Currency in denominations of $1 and more that is issued by the Federal Reserve System. Federal Reserve notes are direct obligations of the federal government. The Federal Reserve System limits the amount of notes in circulation in relation to the goods available for purchase. The Federal Reserve note differs from the now-unimportant Federal Reserve bank note, which is being withdrawn from circulation. The latter had to be secured dollar for dollar by U.S. bonds. For monthly statistics on the amount of Federal Reserve notes in circulation, see *Federal Reserve Bulletin,* Washington, D.C.

final goods and services   Goods and services which are purchased for final use or consumption and not for resale or for further processing or manufacturing. In order to eliminate double counting, only the value of final goods and services is included in the national income and product accounts. The following example shows that if all the transactions involved in the selling of a suit of clothing were included in the U.S. national accounts, the estimate of the national product would be affected by double counting (in this case, quintuple counting). Wool comes from a sheep rancher, who sells it for $20 to a wool processor. The processor, in turn, sells the processed wool for $30 to a suit manufacturer, who, in turn, sells the suit to a wholesaler for $50. The wholesaler sells the suit for $70 to a retail store which sells it to a consumer for $80. Thus, the final value of $80 is included in the U.S. national income accounts and not the $250 total of the five values. Clearly, the level of the gross national product could be increased by merely increasing the number and frequency of intermediate transactions, but this procedure would not give much information about the actual output of goods and services in the nation. For a detailed definition, see Richard Ruggles and Nancy D. Ruggles, *National Income Accounts and Income Analysis*, 2d ed., McGraw-Hill, New York, 1956; for a criticism of the concept, see National Bureau of Economic Research, *A Critique of the U.S. Income and Product Accounts*, Studies in Income and Wealth, vol. XXII, Princeton University Press, Princeton, N.J., 1958.

financial institutions   Private or governmental organizations which serve the purpose of accumulating funds from savers and channeling them to individuals, households, and businesses needing credit. The smooth flow of funds from savers to investors is essential to the growth of the economy. Financial institutions are composed of deposit-type institutions—bank and nonbank—contractual savings institutions, investment-type institutions, personal and business finance companies, government and quasi-government agencies, and miscellaneous lenders. The deposit-type financial institutions account for more than half of all assets held by financial institutions. For additional information, see Charles N. Henning, William Pigott, and Robert H. Scott, *Financial Markets and the Economy*, Prentice-Hall, Englewood Cliffs, N.J., 1978.

financial intermediary   A financial institution that receives funds from savers and lends them to borrowers. In a broad sense, the term financial intermediary is applicable to all financial institutions, including commercial banks, mutual savings banks, savings and loan associations, insurance companies, finance companies, pension trusts, and investment trusts. In a narrower sense, however, it excludes commercial banks. Financial intermediaries in this narrow sense constitute a large and growing part of the U.S. financial system. For further information, see Charles N. Henning, William Pigott, and Robert H. Scott, *Financial Markets and the Economy*, Prentice-Hall, Englewood Cliffs, N.J., 1978.

firm   A business unit producing goods and services. It consists of capital facilities and other resources combined under entrepreneurial control for the purpose of making a profit. The firm buys labor and other resource materials, transforms these materials through a productive process, adding value, and sells the goods or services in another market. The firm is distinguished from other social organizations, such as households and government, by its relatively great emphasis on profit seeking. Ownership and control of the firm may take various forms, such as proprietorship, partnership, and corporation. For additional details, see L. A. Keith and C. E. Gubellini, *Introduction to Business Enterprise,* 4th ed., McGraw-Hill, New York, 1975.

firm theory In microeconomic theory, the firm is modeled as an economic unit that employs inputs—capital and labor—to produce a good or a service which is sold to consumers or, in some cases, to other producers. The process by which the firm transforms inputs into outputs is represented analytically by a production function which typically allows for the substitution of inputs. Thus there are many combinations of inputs that will produce a given output. For each level of output, the total cost function shows what the cost of producing that output will be when the inputs are chosen in an optimal manner. If the firm chooses output levels to maximize profits, and if the firm is a price taker in the output market, then the amount the firm will supply at any given output price can be determined using the total cost function. The relationship between output price and quantity supplied by the firm is the supply schedule for the firm. However, the presence of externalities and entry into and exit from the industry by various firms complicates the method of deriving the industry supply schedule. For additional information, see John P. Gould and C. E. Ferguson, *Microeconomic Theory,* 5th ed., Irwin, Homewood, Ill., 1980.

fiscal dividend The money available for discretionary use by the President and the Congress to expand existing federal programs, to create new ones, to reduce federal taxes, or to hold as a surplus for economic stabilization purposes. The revenue-raising power of the federal tax system produces a built-in average increase of about $10 billion a year in federal revenues. Unless it is offset by such fiscal dividends as tax cuts or expanded federal programs, this increase in revenues will act as a fiscal drag, siphoning off too much from the private economy and thus checking expansion. This was part of the basic philosophy of the New Economics of the 1960s. See Walter Heller, *New Dimensions of Political Economy,* Harvard University Press, Cambridge, Mass., 1966, chap. 11; for a specific projection of the budget and fiscal dividend, see Charles L. Schultze et al., *Setting National Priorities: The 1972 Budget,* Brookings Institution, Washington, D.C., 1971, chap. 17.

fiscal drag The retarding effects on economic activity produced when automatic growth in federal revenues siphons off increasing amounts of funds from the private sector. Growth of the national economy brings forth an increase in federal revenues each year. In times of severe inflation, an approate course for fiscal policy might be to allow the increment to become absorbed into a government surplus, thus slowing down inflation. But when economic activity is slack, the New Economics of the 1960s held that the added revenues received by government should be turned back to the private sector in the form of fiscal dividends. These dividends could take a number of forms, including tax cuts, increased government spending, and revenue sharing with state and municipal governments. See Walter Heller, *New Dimensions of Political Economy,* Harvard University Press, Cambridge, Mass., 1966; Herbert Stein, *The Fiscal Revolution in America,* University of Chicago Press, Chicago, 1969.

fiscal policy   The use of a government's spending and revenue-producing activities to achieve specific objectives. In the United States since the 1940s, the objectives of the federal government's fiscal policy have been largely the achievement of full employment with price stability. To realize these objectives, the government may alter its decisions on the amount and source of its revenues. When the government taxes to a greater extent than it spends, it causes a net reduction in the flow of income, thereby reducing aggregate demand. When it spends a greater amount of money than it receives in taxes, it stimulates the flow of national income and aggregate demand. Fiscal policy uses budget deficits or surpluses to regulate economic stability and growth. Some tools of fiscal policy work automatically, without specific action by the President or Congress. The progressive income tax, for example, is a built-in stabilizer that tends to reduce the government's revenue collections when personal and business incomes are declining and hence helps offset the cutbacks in consumer and business spending that accompany such declines. During business expansions, on the other hand, federal tax collections tend to rise fairly rapidly and hence tend to reduce inflationary pressures. In postwar business declines, Congress has legislated emergency spending measures, such as temporary increases in public works expenditures, as additional means of offsetting cutbacks in private spending and preventing unemployment. See T. F. Dernburg and D. M. McDougall, *Macroeconomics,* 5th ed, McGraw-Hill, New York, 1976, chaps. 5 and 18.

fixed asset   An asset of a relatively permanent nature, such as land, buildings, and machinery. A fixed asset is used in the regular operation of a business and cannot be sold for cash without disrupting normal operations. Usually, any asset with a life greater than one year is classified as fixed. Most fixed assets except land have a limited life, and their cost is distributed over their productive life by permitting periodic depreciation. For further information, see Harold Bierman, Jr., and Allan R. Drebin, *Managerial Accounting,* 3d ed., Dryden Press, Hinsdale, Ill., 1978.

fixed cost A cost which does not vary with changes in a firm's output over the short run. Fixed costs, or overhead, would remain even if there were no output, since they are associated with the existence and maintenance of the firm's facilities. Rent, interest payments, depreciation of plants and equipment, property taxes, and the salaries of top management are commonly classed as fixed costs. Such costs are fixed because they cannot be avoided; the firm has no choice with respect to them. While these costs are fixed in the short run, in the long run there are no fixed costs, since the firm can change its scale of operations as well as its products. For further information, see George J. Stigler, *The Theory of Price,* 3d ed., Macmillan, New York, 1966.

fixed input A productive resource employed by a firm in set amounts. Generally, the term fixed input refers to a factor whose quantity is invariable over the short run, such as land, buildings, and machinery. The longer the time period considered, the less clear is the dividing line between fixed and variable inputs. Over the long run, no inputs are fixed, since a firm can vary the scale of its operations as well as its output.

flat-rate income tax A single-rate tax on an income base broader than that of current law. The idea of broadening the tax base, closing loopholes, or repealing tax expenditures is not new. It is the core of a school of thought about tax policy that used to be called tax reform. Base broadening can yield substantial benefits of efficiency, simplicity, and fairness. Broadening the tax base by repealing the tax preference for various previously favored types of income and expenditures would help solve economic inefficiency problems, and is often described as the ultimate simplification of the income tax since it could trim the size and radically alter the complexity of the tax returns. Fairness suggests that all income be taxed in the same way. But some persons who are not abusers of the current system—for example, homeowners, who claim deductions for interest and mortgages—would find the elimination of the preferences unfair. If deductions and exclusions were removed from the tax law and all forms of income were added to the tax base, many opportunities for manipulating taxes would be cut off. Using a flat tax rate, say 19%, would permit reducing some marginal tax rates only at the expense of raising others. Unquestionably it would mean raising lower-income people's marginal tax rate and lowering that of high-income taxpayers. Taxing all income at a flat rate would simplify the income tax since it would eliminate some of the tax forms, simplify others, and eliminate the need for the various tax-rate schedules. Although the flat rate may seem fairer to some people, in practice it would redistribute a significant share of the tax burden from upper-income to middle-income and possibly even lower-income families. Some tax experts believe that the benefits of broadening the tax base can be achieved through a measured approach without repealing every deduction and exclusion. They also suggest that the tax-rate schedule under a broad-base system could be lower than it is now for most taxpayers without being flat. For additional information, see P. Brimelow, "One tax bracket? The flat rate levy has gained widespread support," *Barrons,* Dow-Jones, New York, August 3, 1981, p. 11; Joint Economic Committee of the U.S. Congress, *Hearings on Flat Tax Rate,* July 27, 1982.

flexible price   A price that is not rigid. It can move downward to as great an extent as it can move upward. For the most part, flexible prices are limited to the prices for agricultural products and other basic raw materials, especially those purchased on organized exchanges, but they also apply to a few manufactured products of which the dominant cost component is a flexibly priced material. For example, leather is a flexibly priced item because its dominant cost component is the price paid for hides. Among other flexibly priced products are those, such as apparel, in which a large number of sellers actively compete in market areas in which the particular prices are determined. See Gardiner C. Means, *Administrative Inflation and Pricing Policy,* Anderson Kramer Associates, Washington, D.C., 1959.

flexible tariff   A duty on foreign-made products which can be raised or lowered quickly. In the United States, the President can order a flexible-tariff program without the ratification of Congress. Introduced into the U.S. tariff system in 1922, the first flexible-tariff law empowered the President to raise by 50% the duty levied on any and all products of a country found to be discriminating against U.S. exports. This flexibility to raise tariffs, both for the purpose of preventing discrimination and for the protection of U.S. industries, has since been included in all tariff agreements. The first authorization for downward tariff flexibility was included in the Reciprocal Trade Agreements Act of 1934, which permitted the President to lower existing duties by 50%. This downward flexibility has also been included in all subsequent tariff acts. For further information, see Harry G. Johnson, *Aspects of the Theory of Tariffs,* Harvard University Press, Cambridge, Mass., 1971.

float   The amount of money outstanding at any specific time in checks which have been used but not collected. The float arises from the time differential between the crediting and collection of payments. If, for example, the Federal Reserve Bank of New York credits a New York City member bank on its reserve account for a check drawn on a California bank in advance of the actual collection of the check, total reserve balances temporarily increase, since the New York bank has been given a credit while the California bank has not yet been charged. This type of credit extension is necessary because of the huge task of check collection and the large volume of checks that are handled each year. Instead of keeping track of each check and crediting the proper account only at the time of collection, the reserve banks grant credit according to a specified time schedule, based primarily on the location of a drawee bank in relation to its Federal Reserve bank office. Under present time schedules, credit is granted in two business days for checks drawn on banks in areas where no Federal Reserve banks or branches are located, even if it takes three days to make the collection. The inability of the system to make the collection within a specific time schedule is due to the impossibility of meeting time requirements even though no unusual delays have occurred, to bad weather, and to strikes or similar factors which delay the delivery or payment of checks. Figures for the float appear in the Federal Reserve report and are published weekly in most national newspapers. See John J. Klein, *Money and the Economy,* Harcourt Brace, New York, 1978.

floating exchange rate   A technique to allow exchange rates in a single country and for a certain time period to float freely in order for the currency to find its own level in a free market. This method of flexibility was chosen by West Germany and the Netherlands in May 1971 outside the Articles of Agreement of the International Monetary Fund. This device anticipates exchange-rate adjustments and thus prevents a long period of speculation. For additional information, see Paul A. Samuelson, *Economics,* 9th ed., McGraw-Hill Book Company, New York, 1973.

flow-of-funds analysis (money-flow analysis)   A method of social accounting which focuses attention on the sources and uses of funds not only for goods and services, but also for instruments of ownership and debt. Since the expenditures of one economic unit are the receipts of others and every financial liability is someone else's asset, the flow-of-funds analysis is used to give an overall picture of financial relationships between the various sectors of the economy, tracing the use made by the various sectors of their savings and the sources of investors' funds. The flow-of-funds analysis is more comprehensive than the national product accounts, since it includes transactions of existing capital assets, borrowing, etc. It also shows how the savings of one sector is used to finance the investment of another sector. The major sectors used in the flow-of-funds accounting system are consumers, corporations, nonfarm and noncorporate businesses, farms, the federal government, state and local governments, commercial banks, savings banks, insurance companies, and other investors, and the rest of the world. A generalized framework for the composition of a flow-of-funds summary is shown in the table on page 140. The flow-of-funds approach is useful in analyzing the effect that different monetary policies have on the general functioning of the economy. For quarterly figures on the flow-of-funds account in the United States see *Federal Reserve Bulletin,* Washington, D.C.; see also Morris Copeland, *A Study of Moneyflows in the U.S.,* National Bureau of Economic Research, New

York, 1952; *Introduction to Flow of Funds,* Board of Governors of the Federal Reserve System, Washington, D.C., 1975.

Funds raised	Funds supplied
Mortgages	Financial intermediaries:
Corporate bonds	Life insurance companies
Corporate stocks	Other insurance companies
U.S. government securities	Private pension funds
Federal agency securities	State and local retirement funds
State and local government securities	Savings and loan associations
Short-term credit:	Mutual savings banks
Business credit	Credit unions
Consumer credit	Money market funds
Security credit	Investment funds
Foreign loans	Banking system
Other loans	Business
Total short-term credit	Government
	Foreign
	Households (residual)
Total =	Total

foreign exchange All monetary instruments which give residents of one country a financial claim on another country. The use of foreign exchange is a country's principal means of settling its transactions with other countries. Thus, a country's demand for foreign exchange depends on the amount of goods that it wants to import, while the supply of foreign exchange available to it depends on the amount of goods that it can export. When a nation imports a greater amount of goods than it exports, so that foreign-exchange expenditures exceed foreign-exchange receipts, the nation has a balance-of-payments deficit, which it must finance from reserves of foreign exchange accumulated in the past. The balancing out of the supply and demand for foreign exchange occurs in the foreign-exchange markets. The most common forms of foreign exchange are foreign currencies and gold. Since August 15, 1971, the buying and selling of gold in transactions with foreign central banks has been suspended. Thus foreign central banks acquiring dollars are not able to convert them into gold or any other monetary reserve asset. For additional information see Fritz Machlup, "The Theory of Foreign Exchanges," in Howard S. Ellis and Lloyd A. Metzler, *Readings in the Theory of International Trade,* McGraw-Hill, New York, 1959, chap. 5; R. M. Levich, "On the Efficiency of Markets for Foreign Exchange," in R. Dornbusch and J. A. Frenkel (eds.), *International Economic Policy: Theory and Evidence,* Johns Hopkins University Press, Baltimore, Md., 1979.

foreign-exchange rate   The price of a foreign nation's unit of money in terms of that of another nation. Thus on a given day, in U.S. dollars the Japanese yen may be worth $0.003, the English pound $1.95, and the French franc $0.195. A knowledge of foreign-exchange rates helps Americans buy some foreign goods directly, since dollars can easily be converted into the proper currencies and payment be made. For example, if an American wishes to purchase an English automobile the price of which is £1,000, $1,950 is required to buy the necessary pounds to purchase the car. There are two types of exchange rates, the freely fluctuating rate based on supply and demand and the stable exchange rate based on government adherence to the gold standard. A free exchange rate is determined by the freely competitive forces of supply and demand; in the case of the United States, the demand is composed of the desires of the nationals of the particular country to import U.S. goods, while the supply of dollars is determined by the desires of Americans for the goods of the other country. Under a stable exchange rate, the government offers to buy gold at a fixed price and to sell gold at about the same price. By fixing each currency in terms of gold, each currency is then in a fixed exchange rate with every other one. For further information, see R. M. Levich, "On the Efficiency of Markets for Foreign Exchange," in R. Dornbusch and J. A. Frenkel (eds.), *International Economic Policy: Theory and Evidence,* Johns Hopkins University Press, Baltimore, Md., 1979.

foreign trade   The exchange of goods and services of all types between different countries. Business firms in industrial countries sell machinery and equipment to developing countries, which, in turn, sell raw materials to firms in industrial countries. The growth of international trade has been greatly helped by modern techniques of transportation and communications. These relatively new developments have brought countries closer together than they have ever been in the past and have made the conduct of trade much easier. More up-to-date and complete international economic information has made the buyer and the seller more knowledgeable regarding available products and markets. For further information, see C. P. Kinderberger and P. H. Lindert, *International Economics,* Irwin, Homewood, Ill., 1978.

Fourier analysis   A technique for analyzing periodic movements in composite time series—hence, a form of harmonic analysis. It treats the variable under study as the sum of a series of sine and cosine terms where the unknown periods of component series are not necessarily identical. Variances of deviations from a fitted Fourier series provide estimates of the variance of the error term. For additional information, see Lawrence R. Klein, *An Introduction to Econometrics,* Greenwood, Westport, Conn., 1977.

fractional-reserve banking   A system in which banks hold less than 100% of their depositors' money idle. Usually, the government specifies that not less than a certain percentage (20%, for example) of total deposits must be held in reserve as cash in the bank or placed on deposit with the government. Since all banks want to earn as much money as possible, they lend and invest the portion of deposits that they are not legally required to hold idle. Thus, the banking system creates money, because demand deposits (checking-account balances) are money, and the bank lends a major proportion of its deposits, which are subsequently deposited at another bank in the system and thus are counted as money again. If the reserve ratio is 20%, the banking system may create $400 of additional deposits for each new deposit of $100. Only a banking system with a reserve ratio of less than 100% can create money, and the ability to do so has been criticized on two major counts. First, it is often said that no special group in the economy should have the power to create money to earn interest. Second, it is often observed that banks extend their loans greatly during booms, thereby promoting inflation, and contract their loans sharply when business slackens, thus deepening recessions. For additional details, see Harold Barger, *Money, Banking and Public Policy*, Rand McNally, Chicago, 1962.

free banking   A liberalization of the granting of bank charters. Until the early nineteenth century, bank charters in the United States were granted only by special legislative acts. Often political corruption was involved in securing charters, and the monopoly power which the chartered banks enjoyed was sometimes abused. In 1838, in an attempt to reform this system, New York adopted the first free-banking law, which was based on the principle that banking should not be the privilege of the few but, like other businesses, be open to all. Under the free-banking law, any individual or group of individuals who met a few minimum requirements could receive a state charter for a bank. To safeguard the public, the law required that the bank's note issues could be secured only by depositing with the state approved bonds or mortgages equal in value to the note issue. The New York law was copied by many states. However, while the New York system worked relatively efficiently the application of free banking in other states led to the introduction of unsound banks, since the authorities granted charters too liberally, and deposit requirements to back issues of notes were sometimes very lenient. In the west, the practice of free banking degenerated into wildcat banking. Issue requirements were gradually tightened, however, and in 1863 Congress adopted the National Bank Act, patterned after the provisions of the New York Free Banking Act. For additional details, see Herman E. Krooss (ed.), *Documentary History of Banking and Currency in the United States,* Chelsea House, New York, 1980.

freedom of entry   The ease with which new sellers may enter a market. The term refers to the advantages which established firms in an industry have over new entrants. Barriers to entry, factors which make it hard for additional firms to enter the market, may arise for a number of reasons. There may be economies of large scale which place the new, small-scale firms at a cost disadvantage; the buyers of the industry's goods may have preferences for the products of the established firms; or certain firms may have absolute cost advantages, such as patent rights and ownership of essential raw materials. When freedom of entry is restricted, established firms are able to raise their selling prices above the minimal competitive costs without attracting new firms into the industry. Strong barriers to entry give rise to industries characterized by an oligopolistic market structure; weaker barriers permit a greater number of firms, often resulting in monopolistic competition. One statistical measure of freedom of entry into an industry is the degree to which established firms can raise their prices above minimal average costs without attracting new firms. A very high barrier exists if prices can be raised by 10% or more, a substantial barrier exists if they can be raised by 5 to 8%, and a moderate barrier exists if they can be raised by 3 or 4%. In the United States, entry into agriculture, wholesale and retail distribution, construction, and service industries is easy, whereas entry into the finance industry is of medium difficulty, and entry into public utilities, such as transportation and communications, is very difficult. Freedom of entry into manufacturing industries is mixed. Barriers to entry in the automobile, cigarette, and liquor industries are very high; in steel, copper, and petroleum, they are substantial; and in rubber tire manufacturing, meat packing, and cement, they are low. For additional information, see Richard Caves, *American Industry: Structure, Conduct, Performance*, 4th ed., Prentice-Hall, Englewood Cliffs, N.J., 1977.

free enterprise system (capitalism)   An economic system characterized by private ownership and initiative. Basic to a free enterprise, or capitalist, system is the concept of private property, the right of ownership and use of wealth to earn income. From private property comes the institution of private enterprise or production by privately owned businesses. Firms are free to hire, produce, and price as they see fit. Furthermore, there is private initiative to carry on production. The motive for this private initiative is the desire of the owners of business firms to earn profits. Because of private ownership and initiative, a free enterprise system is characterized by the very large number of decisions reached independently by producers and consumers. The function of controlling the economy and coordinating the many independent decisions is achieved through the operation of a free-price system. The force of competition is expected to be an important factor in assuring the smooth and efficient functioning of the price system. Finally, a free enterprise system implies a relative absence of governmental control of the economy. Governmental activity is limited to a few spheres, such as national defense and police protection, but in questions of production and pricing the government is expected to take a laissez faire position and exert little or no control. For further information, see Michael Kalecki, *Selected Essays on the Dynamics of the Capitalist Economy, 1933–1970*, Cambridge University Press, London, 1971.

freely flexible exchange rates   Rates of foreign exchange which would be determined by the supply-and-demand mechanism, not by the balance of international payments. Thus all exchange rates would be determined in the free market, avoiding all official interventions. Under this system gold would be completely demonetized and a nation would be free to do anything it desired domestically, allowing the exchange rate to adjust to economic conditions. Flexible exchange rates can make the effects of inflation and price rigidities less intolerable. For additional information, see Paul A. Samuelson, *Economics,* 9th ed., McGraw-Hill, New York, 1973, pp. 647–650, 724–726.

free reserves   The margin by which excess reserves exceed borrowings at Federal Reserve banks. They are a better indicator of the banking system's ability to expand loans and investments than excess reserves. Manipulation of the net free-reserve position of member banks is an indication of the monetary policy which the Federal Reserve wishes to pursue. If the policy is one of aggressive ease, the Federal Reserve pumps reserves into the banking system with the intention of stimulating sluggish business activity. Free reserves act as high-power money, each dollar being capable of supporting more than a dollar's worth of loans and investments. Thus, with an average legal reserve requirement of 15%, the banking system may expand its loans and investments by as much as six and two-thirds times per dollar of free reserves. On the other hand, to halt a business upswing that is exerting inflationary pressures, it adopts a policy of aggressive tightness, contracting free reserves by the appropriate methods. The net free-reserve position of the banking system is published weekly in the Federal Reserve reports and appears in the Friday newspapers. For additional information, see Beryl W. Sprinkel, *Money and Markets,* Irwin, Homewood, Ill., 1971, pp. 85–93; Lawrence S. Ritter and William L. Silber, *Principles of Money, Banking and Financial Markets,* 3d rev. ed., Basic Books, New York, 1980.

free trade   A situation in which there are no restrictions on the international exchange of goods. In such a situation, there would be no import duties, quotas and import licenses, import embargoes, exchange controls, government-purchasing preferences, subsidies to domestic producers, compulsory marks of origin, copyright and trademark enforcement, excessive valuations, unnecessary inconvenience in clearing customs, dumping duties, and escape clauses. In a free-trade economy, each country would be free to specialize in those products in which it had a comparative advantage, i.e., a relatively plentiful supply of the necessary resources of production. The prices at which goods would be traded would be determined by the reciprocal demand schedules of the respective countries involved, which, in turn, would be determined by the price structures existing in these countries. Rates of exchange would be determined by the demand and supply for the various currencies, which, in turn, would depend on the demand for goods purchasable with these currencies. Each country would specialize in the goods which it produced most efficiently, so that the production of all goods in the economy as a whole would be maximized and goods would be plentiful and inexpensive. On balance, academic economists favor a freer trade than now exists among the industrial nations of the world, but they would not demand the utopian state of complete free trade, since they would support some restrictions for the protection of health and welfare, the furthering of national security, and, possibly, the economic development of underdeveloped countries. See C. P. Kindleberger and P. H. Lindert, *International Economics,* Irwin, Homewood, Ill., 1978.

frequency distribution A statistical method of condensing large masses of economic data by arranging them into various classes. This simple classification makes analyses of the data much easier. For further information on the organization of data into frequency distribution tables, see John E. Freund and Frank J. Williams, *Elementary Business Statistics,* 3d ed., Prentice-Hall, Englewood Cliffs, N.J., 1978.

frictional unemployment Temporary unemployment caused by functional imperfections in the labor market. It arises because of the dynamic structure of the U.S. economic system, in which changing consumer tastes cause old jobs to disappear and new jobs to replace them. Frictional unemployment is due to the time required in changing jobs, and its magnitude depends on the structural difficulty encountered in getting the unemployed worker and the job together. The main structural difficulties in finding a new job are lack of information about work opportunities and inability to reach the job. Frictional unemployment is also associated with the freedom of workers to seek new jobs and to change jobs at will, since such voluntary work changes also require the time to find new employment. Since frictional unemployment is noncyclical and is only indirectly connected with the state of the national economy, it cannot be reduced merely by increasing public spending. It can, however, be decreased by increasing labor mobility and information about employment opportunities so that the time required for job hunting can be reduced. For further information, see Lloyd G. Reynolds, *Labor Economics and Labor Relations,* 7th ed., Prentice-Hall, Englewood Cliffs, N.J., 1978.

fringe benefit Any nonwage benefits or payment received by workers in addition to their wages, for example, supplemental unemployment benefits, pensions, travel pay, vacation and holiday pay, and health insurance. Fringe benefits include benefits provided by law, those introduced unilaterally by employers, and those obtained by unions through collective bargaining. Although fringe benefits antedate World War II, it was the war that stimulated their growth because wages were frozen. In 1981 fringe benefits totaled more than $300 billion in the United States, as compared with $140 billion a decade earlier. Fringe benefits have accounted for a greatly increasing percentage of worker income and labor costs, particularly in firms in which unions are active, although they have also been popular with employers, who realize that some fringe benefits (those that accumulate over the period of the worker's service and cannot be transferred to another firm) reduce the costs of labor turnover. For the economy at large, however, diminished labor mobility may impede efficiency and a smooth adjustment to changing conditions. Another incentive to fringe benefits is the high level of income taxes, since some of the benefits are either not taxed at all or taxed at a preferential rate. For a more detailed discussion, see Lloyd G. Reynolds, *Labor Economics and Labor Relations,* 7th ed., Prentice-Hall, Englewood Cliffs, N.J., 1978; William C. Greenough and Francis P. King, *Pension Plans and Public Policy,* Columbia University Press, New York, 1976.

full employment A state of the economy in which all persons who want to work can find employment without much difficulty at prevailing rates of pay. Some unemployment, both voluntary and involuntary, is not incompatible with full employment, since allowances must be made for frictional and seasonal factors which are always present to some degree. In the United States, a figure of 5½% is generally taken as the normal rate of such temporary unemployment, and this figure is thus also considered the maximum permissible unemployment level for a full-employment situation. The achievement and maintenance of full employment constitute an important factor in economic growth. Also important is the raising of the standard of living, since total demand must increase at a rate equal to the expansion of the economy's productive capacity if maximum growth is to be realized. Periods of less than full employment depress investment and capital accumulation and thus hamper future growth. The U.S. government set full employment as a major goal with the introduction of the New Deal, relying on the use of monetary and fiscal policy to achieve this aim, but it was not until passage of the Employment Act of 1946 that detailed objectives were formalized. For further information on full employment, see Sir William Beveridge, *Full Employment in a Free Society,* Norton, New York, 1945; Neil W. Chamberlain et al., *Sourcebook on Labor,* 3d rev. ed., McGraw-Hill, New York, 1979.

full-employment budget A budget concept which indicates for any point in time what the budget position would be if the economy were operating at full employment (96% of the civilian labor force) given actual federal expenditure programs and tax rates. The concept was originally developed by the Committee for Economic Development in 1947. Under this system there is no effort to raise taxes or cut federal expenditures in order to offset deficits caused by the shortfall in revenues that is due to economic slack. The absolute level of the full-employment budget does not tell much about its impact on the economy. Instead, it is the change in the full-employment surplus or deficit as measured on the national-income-account basis that indicates whether a proposed new budget is likely to be expansive, neutral, or depressing. For more detail, see Herbert Stein, *The Fiscal Revolution in Amer-*

ica, University of Chicago Press, Chicago, 1969, chap. 9; see also Joseph A. Pechman, *Federal Tax Policy,* 3d ed., Brookings Institution, Washington, D.C., 1977.

full-employment output *See* **potential gross national product.**

full faith and credit bond A municipal bond that is a general obligation of the state or local government that issued it. Full faith and credit means that payment of interest and principal is secured by the issuing of government's power to tax real property and other items.

functional finance A system in which the federal government's fiscal policy not only would concern itself with raising or borrowing enough money to meet expenses, but also would consider the state of the national economy: the level of income and employment, price stability, and a satisfactory rate of economic growth. The proponents of functional finance would suggest a deficit in the federal budget in times of lagging economic activity whether or not higher government expenditures were then needed; they might also suggest a budget surplus to withdraw liquid funds from the public in times of inflationary pressures. Furthermore, they would countenance the printing of additional amounts of money, without raising taxes or the federal debt, in periods when the government needed greater funds but could not raise them from the public. In short, they would advocate much greater flexibility for both the tools and the objectives of governmental fiscal policy. Their position has been attacked by those who believe that such flexibility is ill-advised when no clear standards of behavior have been set up and no policy goals have been defined. For varying views of functional finance, see Abba P. Lerner, *Functional Finance and the Federal Debt,* reprinted in Arthur Smithies and J. Keith Butters (eds.), *Readings in Fiscal Policy,* Irwin, Homewood, Ill., 1955; for the argument that the concept of functional finance ignores the banking system and the scope of monetary policy, see Lawrence S. Ritter, "Functional Finance and the Banking System," *American Journal of Economics and Sociology,* July 1956; John G. Ranlett, *Money and Banking: An Introduction to Analysis and Policy,* 3d ed., Wiley, New York, 1977.

funded debt The long-term indebtedness of a corporation or a government, generally in the form of long-term, interest-bearing bonds. Payment on this type of debt is generally due more than one year after the debt has been incurred. In public finance, funded debt usually refers to the debt incurred from the sale of long-term securities whose proceeds have been used to retire one or more issues of short-term bills. For more detailed information, see J. Fred Weston and Eugene F. Brigham, *Essentials of Managerial Finance,* 5th ed., Holt, Rinehart and Winston, New York, 1979.

futures market A market in which contracts for the future delivery of commodities or foreign exchange are bought and sold. The commodities themselves are not brought to the futures market; it is only the promises of future delivery, commonly called futures, that are traded. The futures market for a commodity is often incorporated in an organized commodity exchange, which offers a continuous and stable market on which the futures may always be bought and sold. The primary service of the futures market lies in its provision of a means of insurance against the risk of adverse price fluctuations between the time of the production of the commodity and its final utilization. This insurance function is carried out by hedging, or taking an opposite position on the futures market from that held in the spot market. A commodity market without a futures market usually does not have a large enough number of risk-bearing dealers and a sufficient amount of risk capital to carry out this hedging function adequately. The continuous existence of a stable and liquid futures market also makes the formal financing of commodities much easier. For further information on the operation of the futures market, see B. A. Goss and B. A. Yamey, *The Economics of Futures Trading: Readings Selected, Edited and Introduced,* Wiley, New York, 1978.

game theory The mathematical analysis of principles of decision making in situations involving two or more players with conflicting problems. John von Neumann said that a game of strategy consists of a series of events each of which may have a finite number of distinct results; the results of some events are determined by chance, and the results of others by the free decision of players. For each event it is known which player is to make the decision and how much that player knows about the results of the earlier events at the time of the decision. Until the late 1950s, the work of developing and extending game theory was done by mathematicians. During the 1960s, an increasing number of economists became interested in reformulating problems of market structure and competition in game theory terms, and by the late 1970s, this was one of the most active fields of economic research. See

Lester G. Telser, *Economic Theory and the Core,* University of Chicago Press, Chicago, 1978.

Gauss-Markoff theorem The variance of an unbiased linear estimate of a population parameter is minimized when the estimator is obtained by the method of least squares. This theorem can be expanded to include the simultaneous estimation of several parameters or their linear functions. It is subject to the conditions that the function to be estimated be linear in the unknown parameters and that the errors or deviations (actual minus calculated) be independent random variables. For additional information, see Gerhard Tintner and Charles B. Millham, *Mathematics and Statistics for Economists,* Holt, Rinehart and Winston, New York, 1970.

General Agreement on Tariffs and Trade (GATT) An international code of tariffs and trade rules, signed in 1947 by twenty-three countries, including the United States. It became effective on January 1, 1948. The agreement was the culmination of an American-led drive for freer trade after World War II. GATT was originally intended to be a temporary provision to handle tariff and trade questions along multilateral lines until the charter of the International Trade Organization (ITO) was established, but in 1950 the U.S. Senate rejected the ITO charter and GATT became effective. Since then, it has been renewed and amended many times. GATT is dedicated to three basic principles: (1) equal, nondiscriminatory treatment for all trading nations, (2) reduction of tariffs by negotiations, and (3) elimination of import quotas. GATT has eliminated and negotiated reductions in binding tariffs, quantitative restrictions, and discriminations, permitting the freer movement of international trade. About 55,000 tariff concessions were involved in the first three major rounds of tariff reductions concluded in the agreement. On August 15, 1971, the Nixon administration unilaterally set a 10% surcharge on imported goods other than those items covered by quotas, thus setting a barrier to trade and voiding the intent of GATT. The surcharge was revoked on November 13, 1971. For further information, see J. H. Jackson, *World Trade and the law of GATT,* Bobbs-Merrill, Indianapolis, 1969.

general-equilibrium theory That part of economic theory concerned with the structure of prices and output of the economy as a whole. Developed by Leon Walras at the end of the nineteenth century, general-equilibrium theory takes into account the interrelationship of prices and outputs of goods and resources in different markets. Once resource supply schedules, consumer preferences, and production functions have been given, general-equilibrium theory can demonstrate mathematically that resources and commodity prices can adjust themselves to levels which are mutually consistent with each other. Thus, any given set of basic determinants defines a unique stable equilibrium state for the economy as a whole. Any shift in the determinants affecting one good may have widespread repercussions on the equilibrium prices and outputs of the other goods. Although general-equilibrium analysis is very useful as a theoretical tool for stressing the interdependence of the various sectors of the economic system, it is essentially static and thus of limited value in studying trends in economic development. Furthermore, the tremendous complexity of the economic system makes it very hard to use general-equilibrium theory to determine the actual equilibrium values for the real world. For a fuller discussion of general-equilibrium analysis, see Leon Walras, *Elements of Pure Economics*, W. Jaffé (trans.), Irwin, Homewood, Ill., 1954; G. Debreu, *Theory of Value: An Axiomatic Analysis of Economic Equilibrium*, Wiley, New York, 1959; K. J. Arrow and F. H. Hahn, *General Competitive Analysis*, Holden-Day, San Francisco, 1971.

general obligation bond *See* full faith and credit bond.

general sales tax *See* turnover tax.

gift tax A levy on the value of donated property. It is paid by the donor. The gift tax was first used in the United States in 1924 as a supplement to estate and inheritance taxes, which were avoided by giving away property before death. Except for specified exemptions, all gifts are taxable at progressive rates, and the rate on gifts made in a single year is based on the cumulative sum of all gifts made during the donor's lifetime. There is a cumulative lifetime exemption of $30,000 and, in addition, a yearly exemption of $3,000 per recipient. Gift taxes constitute only a minor part of federal and state revenues and are not levied at the local level. See Joseph A. Pechman, *Federal Tax Policy*, 3d ed., Brookings Institution, Washington, D.C., 1977; for statistics on federal revenues from death and gift taxes (combined), see U.S. Internal Revenue Service, *Statistics of Income, Estate and Gift Tax Returns Filed during Calendar Year* . . . ; for statistics on state revenues, see U.S. Department of Commerce, *Compendium of State Government Finances.*

Gini coefficient A measure that shows how close a given distribution of income is to absolute equality or inequality. Named for Corrado Gini, the Gini coefficient is a ratio of the area between the 45° line and the Lorenz curve and the area of the entire triangle. As the coefficient approaches zero, the distribution of income approaches absolute equality. Conversely, as the coefficient approaches 1, the distribution of income approaches absolute inequality. The Gini coefficient can be used to determine the impact of a change in taxes on income distribution. For example, if a given tax change would decrease the Gini coefficient, that tax would be progressive in its overall effects since it would lead to an income distribution closer to absolute equality. See Richard A. Musgrave and Peggy B. Musgrave, *Public Finance in Theory and Practice*, McGraw-Hill, New York, 1975.

gold exchange standard An elaboration of the pure gold standard under which some countries keep their monetary reserves in currency other than gold that is convertible into gold at a fixed rate of exchange. The gold exchange standard owes its existence to the facts that requirements for reserves to back rising national money supplies outstripped the rate of gold production and that convertible foreign currencies were the next-best reserve available. Before 1931 the world's major reserve currency was the British pound sterling, and the gold exchange standard collapsed when this currency was devalued by 18%. After World War II, the U.S. dollar, one of the few convertible currencies of the time, became the most popular reserve currency. With the spread of convertibility in succeeding years, it was joined by British sterling, Belgian francs, Swiss francs, Deutsche marks, and others. The major prerequisite for a reserve currency is a stable rate of exchange, a requirement which may, however, limit the freedom of currency's issuing authorities to tailor their monetary policy to domestic requirements. For example, interest rates in the United States may have to be kept higher than the domestic situation warrants to forestall excessive liquidation of foreigners' dollar holdings and a run on the dollar. Since August 15, 1971, the buying and selling of gold in transactions with foreign central banks has been suspended. Thus foreign central banks acquiring dollars are not able to convert them into gold or any other monetary reserve asset. For a critical analysis of the gold exchange standard, see Robert Triffin, *Gold and the Dollar Crisis: The Future of Convertibility,* Yale University Press, New Haven, Conn., 1960; for the history of the gold exchange standard in the interwar period, see *International Currency Experience,* League of Nations, Geneva, 1944. For additional information, see Eli Shapiro, Ezra Solomon, and William L. White, *Money and Banking,* 5th ed., Holt, Rinehart and Winston, New York, 1968, pp. 615–619; Arthur I. Bloomfield, *Monetary Policy under the International Gold Standard,* Arno, New York, 1978.

gold points Rates of exchange at which, under the gold standard, the import or export of gold became profitable. The gold points have not operated in the United States since 1933, when the gold standard was abandoned and it became illegal for private citizens to buy or sell gold. Under the gold standard, an exchange rate (e.g., the dollar price of pounds sterling) could not rise above a certain point, because if it had done so, U.S. importers, instead of buying pounds for dollars, could buy gold at the Treasury. They could then export the gold to England and sell it for pounds, paying fewer dollars than it would have cost them on the regular exchange market. The upper rate at which the supply of pounds became perfectly elastic was called the upper gold point or gold export point. It was the ceiling price for pounds in terms of dollars, the point at which the importers found it cheaper to buy gold and export it in payment for their imports than to buy foreign exchange directly. The reverse situation worked in the same way. The rate at which the demand for pounds became perfectly inelastic was called the lower gold

Gold Points

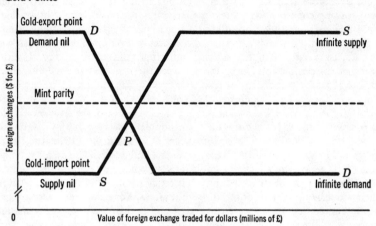

point or the import point for pounds. It was the lowest price at which pounds would sell in terms of dollars, since gold could always be imported at a lower rate. The distance between the export and import points depended on the costs of shipping the gold and the interest charges on the value of the gold while it was in transit. Any increase in transportation costs increased the spread of the gold points, while any decrease in the interest charges narrowed the gap between the gold points. The operation of the gold points under the gold standard provided a high degree of exchange stability, since the range in which the exchange rate could fluctuate was limited. For additional details, see Fritz Machlup, "The Theory of Foreign Exchanges," in Howard S. Ellis and Lloyd A. Metzler (eds.), *Readings in the Theory of International Trade*, McGraw-Hill, New York, 1949; Arthur I. Bloomfield, *Monetary Policy under the International Gold Standard*, Arno, New York, 1978.

gold standard   A monetary standard under which the basic unit of currency is a fixed quantity of gold and the currency is freely convertible at home or abroad into the fixed amount of gold per unit of currency. Whenever the gold value of the monetary unit of a country is divorced from the market value of gold in free world markets, the country is not on a true gold standard. Advantages of the gold standard include simplicity, public confidence, automatic operation requiring little political management, an international character, and stability of value. The basis of the gold standard is the fact that the value of a monetary unit is tied to the value of gold by fixing the gold price. Inasmuch as gold is a commodity in the world market, it has a world value, and the gold standard therefore gives a world value to the monetary unit itself. When the gold standard was predominant, the market for gold was simply the market for gold-standard currencies. The task of a central bank was to keep the value of the monetary unit in the international market as near as possible to par with other gold-standard currencies. Any failure would mean a gain or loss of gold, which was liable to be both larger and more sudden than any movement to and from internal circulation. These international movements were the main consideration in settling the amount of gold reserves. When currency demands outstripped the supply of gold for reserves, however, the gold exchange standard was developed. In using the gold standard, it is essential to guard against exhaustion of the reserve of gold. See Donald N. McCloskey and Richard Zecker, "How the Gold Standard Worked, 1880–1913," in J. A. Frenkel and H. G. Johnson (eds.), *The Monetary Approach to the Balance of Payments,* University of Toronto Press, Toronto, 1976, pp. 351–385.

government expenditure Spending by federal, state, and local governments. In 1980 the manifold governments of the United States spent nearly $535 billion in terms of the gross national product, the federal government accounting for about $200 billion, and state and local governments for about $335 billion. Total U.S. expenditures by governments have increased over the years (exclusive of war years), so that by 1980 they accounted for about 20% of the gross national product, whereas in 1929 they accounted for only 8%. Most federal expenditures go for national defense, with national security accounting for about 66% of federal spending. Natural resources, agriculture and agricultural services, social security, welfare and health, and commerce and housing are the other major areas of federal government expenditures. Among state and local government expenditures, education is the largest item. For statistics on government expenditures in gross national product form, see U.S. Department of Commerce, *Survey of Current Business: National Income Supplement;* for statistics on government budget bases, see *The Budget of the United States Government* for fiscal years, Washington, D.C.

government regulation of business The setting or maintenance by the government of legal conditions required for a private enterprise system to function fairly, safely, and efficiently. Implementation of this idea usually involves creation of a public authority to establish rules of conduct for the businesses in a given industry or for all industry. The increasing economic impact of regulation has given rise to calls for regulatory reform and even deregulation. Estimates of total regulatory costs, direct and indirect, vary widely, but Murray L. Weidenbaum held that regulating costs for the American economy in 1979 totaled $102.7 billion, the greatest proportion of which was in compliance costs to U.S. industry. Proponents of regulation hold that industry cannot function in a legal vacuum and that business competition requires antitrust statutes and other rules of fair play. Proponents of deregulation argue that excessive regulation has added to inflationary pressures and has jeopardized American competitiveness in world markets. For additional information, see Dudley F. Pegrum, *Public Regulation of Business,* Irwin,

Homewood, Ill., 1959; Yale Brozen, "Government Regulation of Business," address made at a meeting of the National Association of Manufacturers, Washington, D.C., March 29, 1979.

government sector *See* **public sector.**

graduated payment mortgages *See* **mortgages, nontraditional.**

grant-in-aid A payment by a central government to assist smaller governmental units. In the United States, for example, the federal government makes grants to both state and local governments (but primarily to the states), and the states make grants to municipalities, counties, school districts, and other governmental units. The common characteristic of all grants-in-aid is that the larger governmental units provide financial assistance without supplanting the smaller units that actually provide the public service. Grants-in-aid have been used primarily to achieve specific objectives rather than to offer general financial assistance. Such objectives have included the building of roads, lunches for schoolchildren, old-age assistance, and cancer research. In 1929, federal grants amounted to less than 2% of total state spending; by 1980 they had grown to 22%. During the same year, state grants accounted for about 36% of local government spending. Grants are lauded primarily because they serve as an effective device for cooperative government and stimulate state and local governments to launch and expand services for which these governments should have responsibility. They are sometimes criticized because they lessen the democratic dispersal of political power and add to the cost of public services by placing two levels of administration on a single program. For a detailed discussion of grants-in-aid, their uses, advantages, and disadvantages, see Kenneth E. Boulding and Thomas F. Wilson (eds.), *Redistribution through the Financial System: The Grants Economics of Money and Credit,* Praeger, New York, 1978.

grants economics The field of economic inquiry which identifies the size and traces the leverage of grant elements as they interface with exchange elements in all kinds of economic processes. Any transaction deviating from the norm of exchanging equal values contains grant elements. Beyond the clearly visible, explicit grant such as a gift or unilateral transfer, there exists a vast array of implicit grants in the private, as well as public, sections of the economy. A recurrent theme among proponents of grants economics is that it is a major instrument by which people hope to change the world for the better. Much of the initial work in grants economics has dealt with the issues of the urbanized economy, income distribution and redistribution, the tax expenditure structure, externalities in the environment, and intrafamily and intergenerational granting. Stretching over several disciplines—economics, psychology, sociology, anthropology, and political science—it stresses the economic importance of the family, an institution neglected in exchange economics. For additional information, see Kenneth E. Boulding, *The Economy of Love and Fear: A Preface to Grants Economics,* Wadsworth, Belmont, Calif., 1975; Martin Pfaff (ed.), *Grants and Exchange,* North-Holland, Amsterdam, 1976.

great depression   The longest and most severe period of economic depression ever experienced by the United States. It began with a collapse of stock prices in October 1929 and did not end until the United States entered World War II in 1941. On March 6, 1933, President Franklin D. Roosevelt was forced to declare a bank holiday to forestall a complete collapse of the banking system. In early 1933, at the lowest point of the depression, national income had dropped by almost one-half, capital investment had declined to the point where net investment was negative, and one out of every three people in the labor force was unemployed. The great depression marked the coming of an age of the United States as a mature industrial economy. The events of that period demonstrated the need for changes in the economic structure. The New Deal introduced some of those changes in response to the pressures at the time and began a process of economic reform which was to continue for the next four decades or so. The experience of the great depression serves as a continual reminder of the potential instability of the market economy in the United States, a memory which spurs a continued search for economic stability. For additional information, see Lester V. Chandler, *America's Greatest Depression, 1929–1941,* Harper & Row, New York, 1970.

Gresham's law   A law usually stated simply as follows: "Bad money drives out good." It was named for Sir Thomas Gresham, a sixteenth-century English financier, merchant, and adviser to Queen Elizabeth I. Gresham pointed out to the queen that because of the debasement of English coin by her predecessor, England's foreign trade, which was being financed by coins of cheaper metallic content, was suffering while the valuable metals were being hoarded and kept out of circulation. Gresham's law also holds that when metals of differing value are endowed with equal powers of legal tender, the cheaper metal will become the chief circulating medium, while more costly metals are hoarded or exported and hence disappear from circulation. The principles embodied in Gresham's law remain an important part of economic theory and practice. They enter, for example, into foreigners' decisions to accept gold as opposed to dollars in payment for goods imported by the United States. For a full discussion of Gresham's law and its implications, see Irving Fisher, *The Purchasing Power of Money,* Macmillan, New York, 1912, chap. 7; for a discussion of Gresham's law and American monetary history, see Charles R. Whittlesey, Arthur M. Freedman, and Edward S. Herman, *Money and Banking: Analysis and Policy,* Macmillan, New York, 1968, pp. 31–40.

gross cash flow   *See* cash flow.

gross income tax   *See* **turnover tax.**

gross national product (GNP)   The most comprehensive measure of a nation's total output of goods and services. In the United States, the GNP represents the dollar value in current prices of all goods and services produced for sale plus the estimated value of certain imputed outputs, that is, goods and services that are neither bought nor sold. The rental value of owner-occupied dwellings and the value of farm products consumed on the farm are the most important imputed outputs included; the services of homemakers are among the most important nonmarket values excluded. The GNP includes only final goods and services; for example, a pair of shoes that costs the manufacturer $2.50, the retailer $4.50, and the consumer $6 adds to the GNP only $6, the amount of the final sale, and not $13, the sum of all the transactions. The GNP may be calculated by adding either all expenditures on currently produced goods and services or all incomes earned in producing these goods and services. Calculated from the expenditure side, it is the sum of (1) consumption expenditures by both individuals and nonprofit organizations, plus certain imputed values; (2) business investment in equipment, inventories, and new construction (residential as well as business construction is counted as an investment); (3) federal, state, and local government purchases of goods and services; and (4) the sale of goods and services abroad minus purchases from abroad. From the income side, the GNP is the sum of all wages, interest, and profits before taxes and depreciation earned in the current production of goods and services. The GNP is a key measure of the overall performance of the economy and a gauge of the health of important sectors. Historically, the U.S. gross national product has fluctuated to a much smaller extent than measures of industrial activity. For a detailed discussion of the concept, coverage, and sources of data, see U.S. Department of Commerce, *National Income Supplement,* 1954; see also Richard Ruggles and Nancy D. Ruggles, *National Income Accounts and Income Analysis,* 2d ed., McGraw-Hill, New York, 1956; for quarterly and annual data, adjusted for price changes as well as in current dollars, see U.S. Department of Commerce, *Survey of Current Business,* monthly.

gross national product gap   The gap between the economy's output of goods and services and its potential output at full employment without inflation. The magnitude of the gap is imprecise, and there have been arguments among economists about the possibility of measuring potential GNP at all. Without an estimate of potential GNP, the gap cannot be estimated. At the end of 1961, the Council of Economic Advisers attempted to measure the gap, and found that it was $32 billion (in 1960 prices) for the year 1960. The council used mid-1955, when a 4% unemployment rate was prevalent, as the bench mark and a growth rate of 3.5% to measure potential GNP. In refuting the notion of a gap or the size of the gap, Arthur F. Burns showed that the gap could be $20 billion, or even −$2 billion, if the second quarter of 1957 and the second quarter of 1947 were used as respective bench marks (an unemployment rate of about 4% was prevalent at both times). Arthur M. Okun has estimated the GNP gap by measuring the extent to which output is depressed by unemployment in excess of 4%, a relationship that can be expressed as follows: "On the average, each extra percentage point in the unemployment rate above 4% has been associated with an approximate 3% decrease in real GNP." For further discussion of the GNP gap, see Arthur M. Okun, "Potential Gross National Product," in D. Greenwald (ed.), *Encyclopedia of Economics,* McGraw-Hill, New York, 1982.

gross private domestic investment   Expenditures by private businesses and individuals for new buildings, machinery, vehicles, and inventories. Gross private domestic investment includes all agricultural and business spending on new plants and equipment, all new private housing and construction, and the net change in privately held inventories. As calculated by the U.S. Department of Commerce, it also includes a small amount of outlays for equipment and construction that some firms carry on their books as current expenditures rather than as investment (for example, jigs and dies used in the automobile industry). It is the most comprehensive measure of nongovernmental investment. The term gross indicates that no allowance is made for depreciation or for the retirement of existing plants and equipment. Gross private domestic investment differs from capital formation, which is gross investment minus the loss of value that plants and equipment suffer in use. The use of the concept in economic analysis is described in Richard Ruggles and Nancy D. Ruggles, *National Income Accounts and Income Analysis,* 2d ed., McGraw-Hill, New York, 1956; for a detailed explanation of technical concepts, see U.S. Department of Commerce, *Survey of Current Business: National Income Supplement,* 1954; for recent quarterly data, see U.S. Department of Commerce, *Survey of Current Business,* monthly.

gross private fixed investment   Expenditures by private businesses and individuals for new buildings, machinery, and vehicles. It is a measure of additions and replacements of private capital brought about through purchases of durable equipment and structures for business and residential purposes. This is a major component of the gross national product and has accounted for about 15% of U.S. GNP over the past decade. It does not take account of that portion of the stock of capital used up in the course of producing the current period's output. There is no direct measure of net private fixed investment. For a detailed discussion of the concept, coverage, and sources of data, see U.S. Department of Commerce, *National Income Supplement,* 1954; see also Richard Ruggles and Nancy D. Ruggles, *National Income Accounts and Income Analysis,* 2d ed., McGraw-Hill, New York, 1956; for quarterly and annual data, see U.S. Department of Commerce, *Survey of Current Business,* monthly.

gross profits   *See* **profits.**

group banking An arrangement whereby two or more separately incorporated banks are brought under the control of a single corporation known as a holding company. The holding company may have as its principal business the control of banks, or it may itself be a bank or business trust. For further information on this type of banking, see Dudley G. Luckett, *Money and Banking,* 2d rev. ed., McGraw-Hill, New York, 1980.

guaranteed annual wage A type of wage payment that would assure minimum earnings for employees over a year. In most guaranteed annual wage plans, employees with a degree of seniority (usually one to three years of steady employment) are assured a specified number of hours or weeks of work each year. If work is not available, the company must provide the employees with income to supplement unemployment benefits. By means of such programs, labor unions hope to stabilize employment throughout the year, eliminating the seasonal ups and downs of some industries. The agreement made between the Ford Motor Company and the UAW-CIO in June 1955 is the best-known guaranteed annual wage plan, although many plans antedated it. For a history and discussion of guaranteed annual wage plans, see A. D. H. Kaplan, *The Guarantee of Annual Wages,* Brookings Institution, Washington, D.C., 1947.

guidelines for noninflationary wage increases *See* annual improvement factor.

Haavelmo's proposition When the two variables in a two-equation economic model are both influenced by a third variable (as, for example, consumption and income are influenced by investment), any assumption of an exact linear relationship is likely to be wrong and unrealistic, even in the simplest cases where one of the equations is an identity. A least-squares solution to the model tends to result in an overstatement of the slope (b) and an understatement of the intercept (a). This problem can usually be overcome by the use of a simultaneous-equation-estimation technique. For additional information, see Trygve Haavelmo, "The Statistical Implications of a System of Simultaneous Equations," *Econometrica*, vol. 11, January 1943, pp. 1–12; Karl A. Fox and Tej K. Kaul, *Intermediate Economic Statistics,* Krieger, Melbourne, Fla., 1980.

hard currency   A national currency that is freely convertible into gold or into the currencies of other countries. A nation allows its currency to become freely convertible when it has no fear of depreciation that might force devaluation. Convertibility develops when the currency's official exchange rate as set by the government either values correctly or undervalues the currency and when the currency is relatively stable, so that the nation need not consider quick changes in its value. Hard currency therefore differs from soft currency, which is regulated by exchange controls and is thus not freely convertible. Nations are willing to export a greater amount of goods to a country paying in hard currency than to a country paying in soft currency, because hard currency can be exchanged for their own currency. Hard currencies thus serve as international currency. See C. P. Kindleberger and P. H. Lindert, *International Economics,* Irwin, Homewood, Ill., 1978.

hard loan   A foreign loan repayable in a hard currency, usually U.S. dollars. This type of loan typically has a high interest rate. Hard loans are difficult to repay, because countries receiving them usually have soft currencies which are not freely convertible into dollars and therefore must obtain most of their dollars through trade. The theory behind the extension of foreign aid in the form of hard loans is that the difficulty of repayment makes the receiving country use the money more wisely than if the aid took the form of a grant. Nevertheless, the difficulty involved in accumulating dollars means that some of the countries most in need of foreign aid are unable to receive much money through hard loans. In an attempt to arrive at a compromise between hard loans and grants, soft loans (loans repayable in the receiving countries' own soft currency) formerly were made. Soft loans proved unsatisfactory, however, and most lending agencies now make foreign loans repayable in dollars. See C. P. Kindleberger and P. H. Lindert, *International Economics,* Irwin, Homewood, Ill., 1978.

Heckscher-Ohlin theory in international trade   A theory stating that a country will tend to export the commodity that uses more of the factor of production that is relatively more abundant in that country. It assumes that countries have different quantities of the various factors of production—land, labor, capital—but identical production functions. For additional information, see M. Blaug, *Economic Theory in Retrospect,* 3d ed., Cambridge University Press, New York, 1978.

hedging A technique of buying and selling that minimizes the risk of loss due to price fluctuations. It is commonly used by commodity dealers and by a variety of manufacturers, including flour millers, shortening processors, and textile producers. The technique can best be explained by example. Grain-storage operators who make their profit through the storage and distribution of grain rather than through speculation buy corn at current market prices (spot prices) but do not ordinarily resell it until some months later, when prices may be lower. In order to protect themselves against such price declines, these dealers can hedge their purchases. At the same time that they purchase corn in the spot market, they sell an equal amount in the futures market—that is, they contract to deliver an equivalent amount of corn at a later date for a price that is set now. If prices fall, the dealers lose on their corn inventories but gain an equal sum on their futures sales because the corn called for in the contract can be purchased at a lower price. If prices rise, the dealers lose on their futures sales but gain on their inventories. In either case, they also ensure themselves against loss by price declines, although they also relinquish the possibility of gain through rising prices. And the dealers are then free to devote all their attention to the provision of their particular services, the storage and distribution of corn. Hedging is also used to a considerable extent in the foreign-exchange market. For a discussion of hedging in the commodity markets, its advantages, and its limitations, see B. A. Goss and B. A. Yamey, *The Economics of Futures Trading: Readings, Selected, Edited and Introduced,* Wiley, New York, 1978; for a discussion of hedging in the foreign-exchange markets, see Imanuel Wexler, *Fundamentals of International Economics,* Random House, New York, 1968, pp. 130–134.

hidden tax An indirect tax which is paid by consumers without their knowledge. Certain taxes, such as import duties, some excise taxes, and taxes on the gross income of businesses, are classified as hidden because they often can be shifted to the consumer by increasing the price of the goods sold and because the consumer often does not know how much of the price is due to the tax. In fact, the consumer may not even be aware of the existence of the tax that caused an increase in price. Thus, the excise tax on gasoline, which has received wide publicity, cannot be considered a hidden tax, whereas a duty on imported petroleum can be so classified.

historical school A school of economic thought which advocated a departure from the abstract, deductive approach of the classical economists toward a more inductive historical study of economic systems. Its major leaders were primarily Germans of the mid-nineteenth century, among them Wilhelm Roscher, Bruno Hildebrand, and Gustav Schmoller. The historical school developed because the classical and neoclassical approaches were considered too theoretical, too atomistic, and too materialistic. Greater emphasis was placed on dynamic elements and on the history and the observation of actual economic institutions and phenomena as the basis for economic analysis. Members of the historical school argued that the earlier writers had underestimated nonmaterialistic human motivations and neglected activities which people follow as members of groups rather than as single individuals. For this reason, they placed great emphasis on nationalism. They also stressed the continuous evolution of economic societies and the constantly changing nature of economic and social institutions. For further information, see Joseph A. Schumpeter, *History of Economic Analysis*, Oxford University Press, New York, 1954; Eric Roll, *A History of Economic Thought*, 4th ed., Faber, London, 1973, Chap. 7.

historic stage   Any of the various stages of society which, according to Karl Marx, were based on a distinct pattern of property ownership. Marx advanced an economic interpretation of history for which the economic relationships of each period were the main factor in controlling all human motivations and activity. In his view, the historical progression of society is basically an evolution of the techniques, methods, and organization of production. Every stage of social organization, with the exception of the final stage of communism, generates forces within itself which eventually overthrow it, according to the mechanism of the dialectic: thesis, antithesis, and synthesis. An institution or a given state of society, called the thesis, becomes overdeveloped and gives way to something opposed, called the antithesis. The antithesis expands, but eventually it also becomes unstable and collapses into a third, more moderate form, the synthesis. The synthesis is adequate for a while, but soon it, too, is ready to collapse and start the cycle over again. The driving force in this constant evolution of social organization is the class struggle between the bourgeois class, which owns the means of production, and the proletarian class, which does not. According to Marx, the first historical stage was the common ownership of land by primitive peoples. As production increased, division of labor arose, and the distribution of material shares became increasingly unequal. Finally, the institution of private property emerged, and with it the stage of chattel slavery. In time, chattel slavery brought about its antithesis, the stage of empire. Growing empires eventually led to increasing decentralization and to the next stage, feudalism. Feudalism, in turn, caused the growth of towns and industry and the accumulation of capital, ushering in the stage of full-fledged capitalism. In Marx's opinion, the inadequacies of capitalism would result in the proletarian revolution and the achievement of the final stage, pure communism. For further information, see Karl Marx, *Capital*, Charles Kerr, Chicago, 1906; Paul M. Sweezy, *The Theory of Capitalist Development*, Oxford University Press, New York, 1942.

hoarding   The accumulation of money or goods in excess of immediate needs. Reasons for hoarding include fear of a future shortage and expectation of a future rise in the price of the goods or in the money hoarded. In monetary theory, hoarding is considered to be any part of savings which is not used for investment. Thus, hoarding is a leakage in the income stream, taking money out of circulation and reducing total income. The larger the proportion of income hoarded in the form of money, the more slowly money turns over. The velocity of money in circulation varies inversely with the rate of hoarding.

holding company A corporation that owns the majority of stock or securities of one or more other corporations for purposes of control rather than investment. A corporation which exists only for this purpose is a pure holding company. One which also carries on a business of its own is called a mixed holding company or a holding-operating company. A holding company can acquire a subsidiary either by purchasing the stock of an existing corporation or by forming a new corporation and retaining all or a controlling share of the stock of the new corporation. The advantages of forming a holding company are as follows: (1) The company is a legally simpler and less expensive way of acquiring control over another corporation than consolidation, merger, or purchase of assets. (2) The parent company retains the goodwill and reputation of the subsidiary without necessarily becoming responsible for its liabilities. (3) A corporation can gain legal advantages by purchasing or forming a subsidiary that is incorporated in states or countries that have laws directed against corporations from other states or countries. There are also a number of disadvantages to the formation of a holding company: (1) The relations between a holding company and its subsidiaries can become so complex that they result in inefficiency. (2) Taxes imposed because of the maintenance of separate subsidiaries often are greater than if the companies were united. (3) A holding company may encounter legal difficulties because of the laws specifically regulating holding companies. See Herman Daems, *The Holding Company and Corporate Control*, Kluwer Boston, Hingham, Mass., 1978.

horizontal integration The situation existing in a firm whose products or services are competitive with each other. The term also applies to the expansion of a firm into the production of new products that are competitive with older ones. Horizontal integration may be the result of a merger of competing firms in the same market, or involve expansion of a firm from its original base to a wider area, as in the case in the growth of retail chains. The advantages of horizontal integration stem primarily from economies of large-scale management, large-scale buying from suppliers, and large-scale distribution. Horizontal integration may result in a monopoly in a particular market. For additional details, see Frederick M. Scherer, *Industrial Market Structure and Economic Performance*, Rand-McNally, Chicago, 1971.

horizontal labor mobility *See* **labor mobility.**

hot money   A term used to describe speculative and flight movements of capital which are generally motivated by the anticipation of a change in exchange rates, a desire to escape losses associated with war, high taxation, capital levies, internal economic difficulties, or inflation. These movements accentuate instability because they aggravate balance-of-payments difficulties rather than moderate them. This is so because hot money leaves countries with balance-of-payment deficits and goes to countries with surpluses. For an examination of movements of hot money in postwar international economics, see Arthur I. Bloomfield, *Speculative and Flight Movements in Postwar International Finance*, Princeton University Press, Princeton, N.J., 1954.

hourly earnings, average   Average pay per hour worked. Average hourly earnings are computed by dividing the total wages of an industry or economy by the number of worker-hours worked. They include sick pay and holiday and vacation pay and are computed before deductions for taxes and social security. Thus, statistics on hourly earnings reflect changes in basic hourly rates and also take account of pay for overtime and late-shift work at premium rates. Average hourly earnings should not be confused with wage rates, which represent the basic rate for a given unit of work. National, state, and industry data are published in U.S. Bureau of Labor Statistics, *Employment and Earnings*.

household formation   The net annual increase in the number of households. Estimates of future household formation are used to forecast the demand for new homes as well as the sales potential for many types of consumer durable goods. Forward estimates of this statistical series prepared by the U.S. Bureau of the Census have not, however, proved particularly useful because of the wide range of the projections. In the Bureau's interim report for 1995, for example, the range of estimates for total households in that year runs from 97.2 million under one set of assumptions to 107.5 million under another set. For projections of household formation to 1995, see U.S. Bureau of the Census, *Current Population Reports: Population Characteristics,* ser. P-25.

housing start   The commencement of construction of a new residential unit designed for housekeeping, usually counted when excavation for the foundation has begun. Representatives of the Bureau of the Census, the compiling agency for housing statistics in the United States, do not actually go out and count all the new holes in the ground; instead, they estimate the number of starts on the basis of the building permits issued each month for housing units, as adjusted for the time lags which occur between the issuance of the permit and the actual start of construction. The Bureau does, however, undertake surveys to ascertain the pattern of these time lags and the number of construction projects that are canceled after permits have been issued.

Monthly data on housing-start statistics may be found in U.S. Department of Commerce, *Construction Reports: Housing Starts.*

human capital The investment in the education and skills of a nation's population. The development of human capital is one of the most distinctive features of the U.S. economic system. The growth of human capital, particularly investment in education, is one of the largest sources of past and future economic growth. According to some authorities, the gains in human capital have made greater contributions to the growth of the United States than the growth of its physical plants and equipment. For further information on the contribution of human capital to growth, see Gary S. Becker, *Human Capital,* Columbia University Press, New York, 1964; Theodore W. Schultz, "Education and Economic Growth," in N. B. Henry (ed.), *Social Forces Influencing American Education,* University of Chicago Press, Chicago, 1968.

identification In simplest form, the problem of distinguishing, for example, between a supply function and a demand function when a single set of paired prices and quantities, for a single time interval, is available for analysis. Usually such limited data do not permit a good estimate of either function. When two endogenous or logically dependent variables appear in a single equation, there is one equation with which to determine the values of two variables. Thus, in general, the identification problem arises in systems of stochastic equations where it is not possible to estimate all parameters without bias, no matter how extensive the information and even when the number of equations is equal to the number of endogenous variables. Haavelmo generalized the problem of identification and developed the method of reduced forms for solving it in many instances. The problem also gave rise to the limited-information–maximum-likelihood method, two- and three-stage least-squares techniques, and *k*-class estimators. For additional information, see Karl A. Fox and Tej K. Kaul, *Intermediate Economic Statistics,* Krieger, Melbourne, Fla., 1980.

identity equation In econometrics, the regression of a variable upon itself; hence, $y = 0 + 1.0y$. Thus the term identity is used here in a restricted sense and should not be confused with the term identity used in a purely algebraic sense and meaning identical equations. For additional information, see Karl A. Fox and Tej K. Kaul, *Intermediate Economic Statistics*, Krieger, Melbourne, Fla., 1980.

implicit price deflator The price index that is usually associated with the gross national product and its components. The reason the index is implicit is due to the way it is constructed. Price indexes, based on Laspeyres formulas, are used to deflate in the greatest detail possible the various spending series that make up GNP. The result is spending in constant dollars. These constant-dollar spending series are then added up to form GNP in constant dollars. When that total is divided into nominal GNP, an implicit measure of the price index is obtained that will exactly reconcile the current and constant-dollar GNP figures. The implicit price index is not a fixed weighted index of prices. Its movements do not reflect price changes alone, but the composite of change in prices and changes in quantity when measured between periods other than the base period. Thus it has not been a totally satisfactory measure of pure price change for use and analysis of GNP. The implicit deflator has been available quarterly since 1946 from the Bureau of Economic Analysis of the Commerce Department. For further information, see Department of Economic and Social Affairs, *Guidelines on Principles of a System of Price and Quantity Statistics*, Statistical Papers, ser. M, no. 59, United Nations, New York, 1977.

import A good or commodity that is received from a foreign country or area in the conduct of foreign trade. The country that receives the good is the importer. In the United States, imports have usually been considerably lower than exports, so that the United States has enjoyed a trade surplus. For example, imports averaged $4 billion less than exports in the years 1955 to 1970. However, imports in 1971 were higher than exports, so that 1971 was the first year in which the United States experienced a trade deficit. This was one of the reasons for the devaluation of the dollar at the end of that year. For further information, see C. P. Kindleberger and P. H. Lindert, *International Economics*, 6th ed., Irwin, Homewood, Ill., 1978.

import duty A tax on goods imported. Most nations now levy some import tariffs. There are two main purposes of import duties, protection and revenue. In the United States, import tariffs are not considered important as a method of raising federal revenues, but in smaller countries in which imports account for a sizable share of the national product, revenue import tariffs may be significant. In the free world, many protective import tariffs are being reduced or eliminated. For an analysis of the effects of import duties, see

C. P. Kindleberger and P. H. Lindert, *International Economics,* 6th ed., Irwin, Homewood, Ill., 1978.

imputed income Income that is not in money form, such as free food or lodging received in exchange for services performed, food produced and consumed on the same farm, and the services of a house in which the owner lives rent-free. The U.S. Department of Commerce estimates the market value of imputed income and includes it in the national income accounts. Some countries include other items, such as the income that housewives would receive if they did their housework for hire. Other forms of income—e.g., the psychic income derived from living in a particularly pleasant spot or from doing particularly pleasant work despite a somewhat lesser wage—are never imputed numerically even though they resemble the imputed incomes that are estimated. For a thorough discussion of the problems and procedures of the Department of Commerce in imputing income, see U.S. Department of Commerce, *Survey of Current Business: National Income Supplement,* 1954.

imputed interest Interest that is considered a cost even though no cash outlay is ever made and the interest never appears on the financial records of the business. The investment of capital in a business raises the question of whether or not to charge interest on the capital and count it as a manufacturing overhead charge. The belief is that this capital has an opportunity alternative cost which is called imputed interest; that is, if the capital had not been invested in the business, it would have provided the firm with some other income. This income creates an opportunity cost, resulting in an imputed-interest charge. Although very few firms enter imputed interest in their accounts, many use it in the solution of problems of alternative choice.

income The gain derived from capital or labor or from both combined. Because of the broad interpretations of income made by economists, it is difficult to draw lines between the various income classifications. This difficulty has led many economic writers to urge a more precise use of the concept of income. Generally, income is applied to a family of concepts all of which are related in some way to wealth and value. Such categories as personal income, business income, gross income, net income, national income, and taxable income are used. For further information, see Stanley Lebergott, *The American Economy: Income, Wealth and Want,* Princeton University Press, Princeton, N.J., 1975.

income distribution The manner in which personal income is distributed among the various income classes in a nation. Generally, inequality in income is attributable to differences in (1) educational and training opportunities; (2) native ability; (3) property ownership; (4) ability to exert market power; and

Distribution of Family Income in Constant 1980 Dollars

	1960	1970	1980
Number of families	45,539,000	52,227,000	60,309,000
Median income	$15,637	$20,939	$21,023
Income distribution			
Under $2,500	4.6%	2.1%	2.1%
$2,500–4,999	6.8	4.0	4.1
$5,000–7,499	7.8	5.6	6.2
$7,500–9,999	8.3	6.1	6.5
$10,000–12,499	11.9	6.9	7.3
$12,500–14,999	8.3	6.7	6.9
$15,000–19,999	22.8	19.7	14.0
$20,000–24,999	10.6	11.3	13.7
$25,000–34,999	18.9	22.7	19.8
$35,000–49,999	★	9.3	12.8
$50,000 and over	★	5.5	6.7

Source: U.S. Bureau of the Census.
★ Detailed income data above $25,000 were not tabulated for 1960. In that year, 18.9% of all families had incomes of $25,000 or more.

(5) such arbitrary factors as illness, accident, and other misfortunes. It is believed that the distribution of personal income in the United States is tending toward greater equality and that the upper-income groups are losing ground to the rest of the income classes. Arthur F. Burns characterized this development as a revolution. Studies by the National Bureau of Economic Research and the U.S. Bureau of the Census seem to indicate that a revolution in income distribution has taken place. Since 1929 the share of income of the upper 5% of income receivers has decreased from about one-third of total income to about one-fourth. Part of the explanation for this trend can be found in the progressive tax system and the development of welfare policies. For the historical development of income-distribution theory, see John Bates Clark, *The Distribution of Wealth,* Macmillan, New York, 1899; see also A. B. Atkinson, *The Economics of Inequality,* Clarendon Press, Oxford, 1975.

income effect   A term used in demand analysis to indicate the increase or decrease in the amount of a good that is purchased because of a price-induced change in the purchasing power of a fixed income. When the price of a commodity declines, the income effect enables a person to buy more of this or other commodities with a given income. The opposite occurs when the price rises. By using indifference curves, it is possible to separate the income effect from the so-called substitution effect, in which the demand for a price-reduced good rises as it is substituted for other goods whose prices have remained constant. See George J. Stigler, *Theory of Price,* 3d ed., Macmillan, New York, 1966; Donald S. Watson and Mary A. Holman, *Price Theory and Its Uses,* 4th ed., Houghton Mifflin, Boston, 1976.

incomes policy Any attempt by a government to affect the level of money incomes or prices, usually in an effort to slow down or reduce the rate of price inflation. Great Britain, following the Netherlands and Sweden, tried to develop an incomes policy in the 1960s that would make full employment and price stability compatible. Incomes policies can take various forms. Wage-price guideposts are one type. During the Kennedy administration norms were established for "noninflationary" price and wage increases. These norms were based on the average increase in productivity during the period 1945–1960. The guideposts called for an average increase in prices and wages of 3.2% per year, the long-term rate of productivity gain. Jawboning, or government pressure in specific wage or price situations, is another form of incomes policy. Wage-price control, where the government sets and enforces criteria for wages and prices throughout the economy, is a third type of incomes policy, employed in the United States during World War II and the last phase of the Vietnam War. In recent years, as inflation had worked its way through our economy, many public leaders called for wage and price controls, as a solution to the wage-price spiral. Others opposed such controls, claiming that controls would distort the supply-and-demand mechanism of a market economy and lead to extreme shortages of some goods and services and large surpluses of others. However, wages and prices were frozen in August 1971, and after the freeze was lifted, wages and prices were controlled. For additional information, see Daniel Quinn Mills, *Government, Labor and Inflation: Wage Stabilization in the United States,* University of Chicago Press, Chicago, 1975.

income tax A tax levied on individual and corporate incomes. The basic purpose of the tax is to finance governmental operations. The base of the U.S. income tax is net income, which is calculated by subtracting the amount of specific items from gross income of a given period (generally one year). Gross income is defined as all accretion to wealth plus any increase in net worth during the period. From this total are subtracted income not taxable (e.g., interest from state and municipal bonds), credits (e.g., credits for the taxpayer and dependents), and other deductions. These deductions can take the form of business and professional expenses or of certain personal expenses (e.g., contributions to charity and specified medical expenses). Once the tax base of net income has been determined, the tax is calculated by applying graduated rates to the income brackets. The progressive nature of both personal and corporate income taxes is based on the ability-to-pay principle of taxation, whereby a larger tax burden is placed on individuals or firms whose capacity to pay the tax is greater. The first federal income tax in the United States appeared temporarily during the Civil War. Reenacted in 1894, it was declared unconstitutional by the Supreme Court, and not until the passage of the Sixteenth Amendment in 1913 did the United States have a permanent income tax. In 1980, federal receipts from individual income taxes totaled about $244 billion, and receipts from corporate income taxes nearly $65 billion. These two income taxes provided the bulk of federal revenues, together accounting for about 85% of all federal receipts in 1980. Many states have turned to income taxation as a source of revenue, and some municipalities have also adopted taxation of income in one form or another. For further information, see John F. Due and Ann F. Friedlaender, *Government Finance,* 6th ed., Irwin, Homewood, Ill., 1977.

increasing costs Increases in the average costs of unit production that take place as the volume of output rises. In any type of business, because of the operation of the law of diminishing returns, increasing output (in the short run) leads eventually to increasing costs. A plant is designed for a certain level of efficient output. When production increases beyond that level, average costs rise because of such factors as overcrowding, the use of obsolete equipment, and the overuse of machinery. While the concept of increasing average costs is a short-run phenomenon, an increasing-cost industry is one in which the long-run cost schedules of individual firms rise as the number of firms in the industry increases and the total output of the industry rises. Such long-run increasing-cost conditions result from external diseconomies of large-scale production. Usually, the diseconomies are due to increases in factor prices as a larger number of factors is employed by the industry. Increasing-cost industries are most likely to be those which use a large portion of a resource, the supply of which cannot be increased very easily. For example, wheat farming is an increasing-cost industry. As wheat production rises, the demand for wheat-growing land increases, and thus the rental and sale prices for all wheat land rise. Long-run increasing costs may also be due to a reduced efficiency that occurs as output increases. For example, the greater the number of oil wells in a certain area, the more costly it is for each well to pump up the oil because of the reduced pressure in each well. For further information, see Robert W. Clower and John F. Due, *Microeconomics,* Irwin, Homewood, Ill., 1972.

indexation The tying of deferred payments to the value of a price index. Important examples of indexation are cost-of-living adjustment (COLA) clauses in labor contracts, indexed bonds (the linkage of interest and/or principal payments to the price level), and the automatic adjustment of tax brackets and of social security benefits for inflation. In practice, indexation has been most widespread in countries experiencing high rates of inflation. Indexation has been supported by Marshall, Jevons, Keynes, Friedman, and Tobin, who have generally argued that indexation is an efficient method of removing inflation risk from long-term contracts. However, international experience shows that indexation arrangements are at best clumsy instruments for dealing with inflation. Fellner argued that indexation is of little help in reducing the inflationary rate, since the rate of price increase has to be reduced in the first place to get the beneficial effects of the indexation. For additional information, see Herbert Giersch et al., *Essays on Inflation and Indexation*, American Enterprise Institute, Washington, D.C., 1974.

index number A measure of the relative changes occurring in a series of values compared with a base period. The base period usually equals 100, and any changes from it represent percentages. For example, if an index of machinery prices with the year 1967 = 100 as a base rises to 110, the price of machinery has increased by 10% since 1967. Comparisons are usually made over periods of time, but indices may also be used for comparisons between places or categories. For example, an index of consumption expenditures in Philadelphia and San Francisco could be computed in relation to an index in New York, or an index of the relative efficiency of the voltage output of different machines in different types of generating equipment could be calculated. By use of an index number, large or unwieldy business data, such as sales in thousands of dollars or costs in dollars and cents, are reduced to a form in which they can be more readily used and more easily understood. An Italian, Giovanni R. Carli, is generally credited with inventing index numbers. For a detailed explanation of index-number construction, theory, and practice, see R. G. D. Allen, *Index Numbers in Theory and Practice*, Aldine, Chicago, 1975.

indifference curve A graphic curve which represents the various combinations of two goods that will yield the consumer the same total satisfaction. For example, a household may receive the same satisfaction from consuming 4 pounds of steak and 3 pounds of chicken as from consuming 5 pounds of steak and 1 pound of chicken. By assuming that the two commodities can be substituted for each other, it is possible to draw an indifference schedule that contains all of the possible combinations of the commodities which will yield the same satisfaction. When the schedule is plotted on a graph, with one commodity along the vertical axis and another along the horizontal axis, the curve which connects the points is called an indifference curve. The curve tells nothing about the absolute level of satisfaction, but only that each point represents a combination that is equal to any other combination in total satisfaction. For each level of total satisfaction, there is another indifference curve. Most indifference curves slope downward to the right, indicating that as more of one good is added, less of the other good is required to maintain the level of satisfaction. The slope of the curve is the marginal rate of substitution between the two commodities: the amount of one commodity necessary to replace one unit of the other commodity while maintaining the same level of satisfaction. Because of the diminishing rate of marginal substitution, indifference curves are usually convex to the point of origin; that is, as additional units of one commodity are added, progressively less of the other commodity will be necessary to replace units of the first commodity to maintain the same level of satisfaction. For further information, see John R. Hicks, *Value and Capital,* 2d ed., Oxford University Press, New York, 1946; Donald S. Watson and Mary A. Holman, *Price Theory and Its Uses,* 4th ed., Houghton Mifflin, Boston, 1976.

indirect cost Any cost which cannot be consistently identified with a specific product unit. Indirect costs, which include all fixed costs, are joint in nature and can be apportioned to different products only by a rough approximation. They are related to the quantity of output only in an indirect way, if at all. As a whole, indirect costs are often called burden, overhead, or indirect manufacturing expense. Such factors as the wages of supervisors, power, maintenance, and taxes are classified as indirect costs.

indirect tax A tax that can be shifted from the original payer to the ultimate consumer of the good or service taxed. Sales taxes, excise taxes, and import duties are generally regarded as indirect taxes, although some economists believe that sales and excise taxes, or some part of such taxes, are actually borne by the factors of production.

individual retirement accounts Retirement income programs for workers who lack private pension plans that qualify for tax advantages. Any employed person who is not an active participant in a government retirement plan, a tax-exempt organization retirement plan, or an employer's tax-qualified retirement plan is eligible to establish an individual retirement account (IRA). The first tax law providing for IRAs was contained in the Employee Retirement Income Security Act of 1974. There have since been several revisions to the regulation. As revised in 1981, the law now provides that any employed person may pay up to $2,000 or 15% of annual earned income into an IRA; federal income taxes on the money deposited and on the earnings of accumulated funds will be deferred until the money is withdrawn when the account holder reaches the age of $59\frac{1}{2}$ years. In general, the income of retired persons is lower than it was while they were working, and their income tax bracket is also lower. In addition to regular IRAs, there are two other types: Rollover IRAs may be established by someone who is changing jobs or for some other reason receiving a distribution from an employer's qualified pension plan. Spousal IRAs can be established for an unemployed spouse by a spouse who is eligible for regular IRA participation. Although the broad provisions of the law establishing IRAs appear very simple, the regulation is, in fact, quite complex and subject to ongoing interpretations. Anyone contemplating starting an IRA account should become completely familiar with the tax regulations involved since there are stiff penalties for violations. Furthermore, IRAs are not appropriate saving vehicles for all wage earners. For example, no one who cannot withstand the reduction in disposable income involved should consider an IRA. Most wage earners should seek the advice and assistance of an attorney, a tax accountant, or an investment counselor to determine their IRA qualifications and to obtain assistance in making intelligent decisions about an IRA. For further information, see L. L. Unthank and Harry M. Behrendt, *What You Should Know about Individual Retirement Accounts,* Dow Jones–Irwin, Homewood, Ill., 1978; Bureau of Consumer Protection, *Plain Talk about IRAs,* Federal Trade Commission (available from the Bureau of Consumer Protection, Distribution Branch, Room 270, Washington, D.C. 20580); Internal Revenue Service, *Tax Information on Individual Retirement Arrangements,* Publication 590, and *Tax Information on Self Employed Individual Retirement Plans,* Publication 560, both available at Internal Revenue Service offices.

indivisibility   The qualification that certain factors of production (the work force and equipment) cannot be divided into smaller units. For example, a single big machine is indivisible in that it cannot be divided in half and produce half its maximum output at half its previous costs. It can, however, operate at 50% of its capacity, although unit costs are then higher than when it operates at 90% of capacity. Indivisibility is a prime factor in producing economies of large-scale production. Indivisible factors can be most efficiently employed when output is large; they work less efficiently at lower production levels because they cannot be divided into smaller units. For the relation of indivisibility to cost, see James R. McGuigan and R. Charles Moyer, *Managerial Economics,* 2d ed., West, St. Paul, Minn., 1979.

induced investment   Investment that occurs in response to actual or anticipated increases in outlays for specific existing products or throughout an economy. Among the causes of induced investment are income gains and population growth, which result in a greater demand for goods and services. In general, therefore, induced investment is an expenditure for additional equipment in order to produce greater quantities of a given good or service. Autonomous investment, in contrast, occurs independently of rising economic activity, as a result, for example, of the introduction of new products or processes. Through the additional economic activity that it produces, autonomous investment in a given industry may generate induced investment in the economy generally. In economic theory, the acceleration thesis holds that there is a fixed relationship between income or output changes and the investment that they induce. In fact, however, such a rigid relationship has not been confirmed. For a classical statement of the acceleration thesis, see John M. Clark, "Business Acceleration and the Law of Demand: The Technical Factor in Economic Cycles", reprinted in *Readings in Business Cycle Theory,* McGraw-Hill, New York, 1944; for a more recent discussion of induced investment, see Gardner Ackley, *Macroeconomics and Theory and Policy,* Macmillan, New York, 1978.

induced variable In statistics and econometrics, a variable that depends wholly on economic factors. Its movement can be predicted from correlation relationships with business activity. An induced variable changes freely in structure over the short run. Consumption expenditures for soft goods and for services are generally considered induced variables.

inductive method A method of analyzing an economic problem. An alternative to the deductive method, the inductive method proceeds from the particular to the general, stressing the observation of facts from the empirical world as the basis for its generalizations. Induction bases its conclusions on the collection and observation of many particular and illustrative cases in actual life. Thus, it stresses variation and allows for a changeable theory. The major fault of the inductive method is that its use makes it impossible to reach a degree of finality in economic thinking. The system is always open to new observations that might yield a different conclusion. The validity of a system depends on the observable facts used in making the generalizations. For additional history, explanation, and examples, see William Fellner, *Modern Economic Analysis,* McGraw-Hill, New York, 1960, chap. 2.

industrial migration The movement of industries from one region to another within a country. The basis for the migration of individual industries may be found in the demand for the firm's product, in the supply of resources which it needs, or in wage differentials or tax benefits. In the early history of the United States, manufacturing plants were located as close as possible to sources of raw materials, since transportation was slow and expensive. Transportation is now much less of a problem, however, and the importance of raw materials has therefore declined. For this reason, the consumer market exerts a much stronger influence on plant location, and the areas of fastest population growth are becoming the areas of fastest industrial development. In the United States, this trend has meant that industries have migrated from east to west and from north to south. For example, a major portion of New England's textile industry moved southward to North and South Carolina, while its shoe industry moved westward to St. Louis, Missouri. Similarly, a significant share of Pittsburgh's steel industry moved to the south and the west. For additional information, see David M. Smith, *Industrial Location: An Economic Geographical Analysis,* 2d ed., Wiley, New York, 1981.

industrial production index A measure of the physical output of U.S. manufacturing, mining, and utility industries compiled monthly by the Board of Governors of the Federal Reserve System. Covering about 35% of the total U.S. output of goods and services, the index includes a representative group of products, ranging from pig iron and cotton yarn to machine tools and electricity. It excludes agriculture, construction, and service industries. The relative importance assigned to individual products is based on quantity and value data determined from recent government censuses. Manufacturing accounts for 87.95% of the index, mineral production for 6.36%, and utilities for 5.69%. Current output is expressed as a percentage of annual production levels during 1967. Historically, the industrial production index has fluctuated to a greater extent than most other measures of economic activity. In addition to the total index, indices are prepared for individual items, product classes, industries, and industry groups. All indices are published monthly in *Business Indexes*, Board of Governors of the Federal Reserve System, Washington, D.C.; for detailed information, see *Industrial Production*, Board of Governors of the Federal Reserve System, Washington, D.C., February 1976; for industrial production data of other countries, see Statistical Office of the United Nations, *Monthly Bulletin of Statistics*, New York.

industrial revenue bond   A revenue bond that state and local governments and authorities issue to finance plant construction and the purchase of equipment. The plant and equipment are then leased to a private corporation. The rent paid by the corporation is structured to cover interest, principal, and all other costs of debt service. Because interest payments on industrial revenue bonds are exempted from federal income taxes, the interest rates they carry are invariably lower than the rate a corporation would have to pay if it directly issued bonds to finance plant and equipment. State and local governments originally created this security to attract industry to their areas, and succeeded because of the savings in interest cost that it represents for corporations. For further information, see David Darst, *The Complete Bond Book—A Guide to All Types of Fixed Income Securities*, McGraw-Hill, New York, 1975; Robert Lamb and Stephen P. Rappaport, *Municipal Bonds—The Comprehensive Review of Tax-Exempt Securities and Public Finance*, McGraw-Hill, New York, 1980.

industrial union   A labor union which represents all the workers, skilled and unskilled, in a plant, industry, or group of industries. The industrial union evolved as a consequence of the development of mass production, since skilled and unskilled workers worked together in large production plants. Many traditional craft unions have become industrialized in certain industries without abandoning their craft ties in others. An outstanding example is the Machinists Union, which is, in effect, an industrial union in the aircraft industry. Pure industrial unions which limit themselves to one identifiable industry are rare. Virtually all industrial unions function in more than one industry, and often the concept of industry is not precise. The industrial union differs from the semi-industrial union and the multi-industry union. The International Ladies Garment Workers, a semi-industrial union, does not typically cover maintenance employees. The United Automobile Workers, a multi-industry union, has members in the automobile, aircraft, and farm-implement industries. Industrial unions often adopt a policy of reducing relative price differentials among occupations, principally by bargaining for across-the-board wage increases. See Gordon F. Bloom and Herbert R. Northrup, *Economics of Labor Relations,* 8th ed., Irwin, Homewood, Ill., 1978.

industry   A group of businesses that produce and/or sell the same, or similar, types of goods or services. An industry may be characterized by many types of measurements, such as level of concentration; durability of the commodity produced; market structure; levels of capital investment, advertising, or research and development spending; and geographical distribution of producers and customers. Companies are classified as industries by various government agencies, including the Commerce Department, the Federal Reserve Board, and the Securities and Exchange Commission. A particular firm or plant may be placed under different classifications depending on the purpose of the classification. Industry determinations and classifications are particularly important in antitrust considerations, yet classification of conglomerate firms has been a particular problem.

inelastic demand (inelasticity)   A term used to describe a proportionately smaller change in the purchase rate of a good than the proportional change in price that caused the change in amount bought. When the demand for a product is inelastic, a relatively large price change is necessary to cause a relatively small increase in purchases. To calculate the elasticity of demand, the percentage change in buying rate (the quantity bought per period of time) is divided by the percentage change in price. Theoretically, the numerical value of the elasticity can vary from zero to infinity, and the sign of the number is negative, denoting the fact that price and quantity move in opposite directions. When the number is less than 1, demand is said to be inelastic; when it is exactly 1, demand is called unitary; and when elasticity is greater than 1, it is simply called elastic. The accompanying table summarizes the relationship between various elasticities and the behavior of total receipts (price times purchase rate):

	Elastic demand (-1 or more)	Unitary demand (-1)	Inelastic demand (less than -1, e.g., $-\frac{1}{2}$)
Price falls	Receipts rise	Receipts unchanged	Receipts fall
Price rises	Receipts fall	Receipts unchanged	Receipts rise

For further information, see Donald S. Watson and Mary A. Holman, *Price Theory and Its Uses,* 4th ed., Houghton Mifflin, Boston, 1976.

inelastic supply   The relative insensitiveness of a producer to supply a good when the market price of the good changes. A supply schedule is perfectly inelastic when the quantity supplied by the producer remains the same regardless of price. It is perfectly elastic if an unlimited quantity is offered by the producer at all prices. For further information, see George J. Stigler, *Theory of Price,* 3d ed., Macmillan, New York, 1966.

infant industry An undeveloped industry which may not be able to weather the initial period of experimentation and financial stress because of strong foreign competition. In the *Report of Manufacturers,* Alexander Hamilton stated that such industries should be protected by tariffs until they had a chance to grow out of the infantile stage. It was believed that, given such a grace period, they could be expected to develop economies of scale and technological efficiency so that prices would be reduced and they would be more competitive with foreign industries. Essentially, the argument says, "We can produce it cheaper if you give us the chance." See C. P. Kindleberger and P. H. Lindert, *International Economics,* Irwin, Homewood, Ill., 1978.

inflation A persistent upward movement in the general price level. It results in a decline of purchasing power. According to most economists, inflation does not occur until price increases average more than 3.5% per year for a sustained period. However, in the eight years from 1974 to 1981, prices rose at an annual rate of more than 8%. Price increases of less than 3.5% per year need not cause concern for the U.S. economic system, although an increase of 2.5% per year over a decade would reduce the purchasing power of a dollar by about 25 cents. Price inflation is most likely to occur when demand increases while the labor supply is tight and industrial capacity is fully utilized, when increases in wage rates are out of step with gains in productivity, when sources of supply dry up, or when the money supply rises faster than output increases. The greater part of inflation in U.S. history is associated with wars or their aftermath. Some economists use the term inflation to designate the forces or pressures that cause a general increase in prices rather than the increase itself. For a comprehensive discussion of inflation, see James Tobin, "Inflation," in D. Greenwald (ed.), *Encyclopedia of Economics,* McGraw-Hill, New York, 1982.

inflationary gap A term used to describe the excess of investment over savings in a full-employment economy. The inflationary gap is the value of excess demand for goods and services over the goods and services that can be produced with full employment. For example, the demand for goods and services in the United States totals $3 trillion, but actual output at full employment is $2.7 trillion. The $300-billion excess in purchasing power can result only in price increases because only through price changes can national income increase above the maximum full-employment output level. The upward movement in price continues as long as there is an inflationary gap, that is, while demand is greater than supply. For an explanation of the inflationary gap, see Gardner Ackley, *Macroeconomics: Theory and Policy,* Macmillan, New York, 1978.

inflation, cost-push A rise in prices believed to occur because wages increase to a greater extent than productivity. Frequently cited examples of cost-push inflation are the U.S. inflationary periods 1957–1958 and 1969–1971, when prices rose while economic activity declined well below capacity operations. Employers frequently take the view that cost-push inflation is spurred by strong labor unions that force wage increases. Union leaders, on the other hand, charge large corporations with raising prices independently of increases in costs. A U.S. economist, Harold G. Moulton, provides an argument for the cost-push theory based on the view that sellers' prices are determined by their costs and that wage costs are the most important factor in total costs. The Chicago school of economists, led by Milton Friedman, is opposed to the cost-push theory. Adhering to the quantity theory of money as the basic reason for inflation, this group argues that there is no conclusive evidence that prices behave differently than they probably would behave if strong labor unions and administered prices were not in existence. Many U.S. economists believe that during an inflationary period some cost-push, some demand-pull, and some structural inflation take place at the same time. For a comprehensive discussion of cost-push inflation, see Paul A. Samuelson, *Economics,* 11th ed., McGraw-Hill, New York, 1980, pp. 768–771, 774–777.

inflation, demand-pull A rise in prices believed to occur because consumers and investors with rising incomes increase their wants and compete for a relatively limited supply of available goods. Goods are in short supply either because resources (labor and industrial capacity) are being fully utilized or because production cannot be increased on very short notice. When purchasing power exceeds the total value of capacity output, the excess can cause a rise in the price level in an unregulated economy. The example of demand-pull inflation usually cited for the United States is the inflationary period 1955–1956. Most U.S. economists believe that during a period of inflation some demand-pull, some cost-push, and some structural inflation take place at the same time. For a comprehensive discussion of demand-pull inflation, see Paul A. Samuelson, *Economics,* 11th ed., McGraw-Hill, New York, 1980, pp. 769–770, 774–777.

inflation, structural A rise in prices believed to be caused by excess demand for the output of particular industries even when overall economic demand is not excessive. Initially, prices and wages increase because of pressures in specific sectors of the economy. As a result, general inflation occurs because the floor under prices and wages in those sectors in which demand has not kept pace tends to be inflexible. For example, in the 1950s the demand for services and the prices of services and wages of service workers rose substantially while there was a relative decline in the demand for consumer durable goods and capital goods. Wages of workers in the consumer-durable-goods industries and capital goods industries rose, however, while prices did not decline significantly, resulting in general inflation. Most U.S. economists believe that during an inflationary period some structural, some demand-pull, and some cost-push inflation take place at the same time. For a comprehensive discussion of structural inflation, see Charles L. Schultze, "Recent Inflation in the United States," Study Paper 1, a report prepared in connection with the study of *Employment, Growth and Price Levels*, U.S. Joint Economic Committee, Sept. 21, 1959.

infrastructure (social overhead capital) The foundation underlying a nation's economy (transportation and communications systems, power facilities, and other public services) upon which the degree of economic activity (industry, trade, etc.) depends. It may include such intangible assets as the population's educational level and social attitudes, industrial skills, and administrative experience. The better and more complete a nation's infrastructure, the better and more effectively its economic activity can be carried on. Because of its essential nature, the infrastructure is discussed most often in connection with the economic development of underdeveloped nations. The building up of a country's infrastructure, which generally involves projects with a high initial cost and a very long payoff period, is frequently carried out either by the government or with its aid. Private investment alone cannot finance such development. Most underdeveloped countries are well aware of the importance of social overhead capital, but some economists warn that the building of the infrastructure can be overemphasized and that perhaps, after a minimum amount of infrastructure has been constructed, investment funds could be better utilized in productive activities. See Walter W. Rostow, *The Stages of Economic Growth: A Non-Communist Manifesto*, Harvard University Press, Cambridge, Mass., 1960; Charles P. Kindleberger and Bruce Herrick, *Economic Development*, 3d ed., McGraw-Hill, New York, 1977.

inheritance tax A tax on individuals who receive property upon the death of a benefactor. It differs from an estate tax, which is levied on the deceased's estate before the estate is divided among the heirs. Inheritance tax rates are generally progressive, and they also increase as the relationship of the heir to the decedent grows more remote. There are usually fairly high exemptions to the tax. The main theoretical justification for an inheritance tax is the ability-to-pay principle. It is reasoned that a bequest of property creates an ability on the part of the heir to contribute to the support of the government. Another argument in favor of the tax is that it can help prevent the formation of a permanent moneyed group that can live on property handed down from one generation to another. See Boris Bittker, *Federal Income, Estate and Gift Taxation*, 3d ed., Little, Brown, Boston, 1964.

initial claim for unemployment insurance An application made for the first time for unemployment insurance benefits. The initial claim may be the first claim in a benefit year or the first claim at the beginning of a second or additional unemployment period in the same benefit year. The initial claim establishes the first date for any insured unemployment, but it does not guarantee that any benefit payment will be made, since some claimants may not meet eligibility requirements. The initial-claims series is a significant indicator of overall business activity, which the National Bureau of Economic Research classifies as one of its thirty leading indicators. A rise in initial claims takes place when gains in business activity begin to slow down, and a decline occurs when business prospects appear bright. The statistical series is compiled by the Employment and Training Administration and released weekly in *Unemployment Insurance Claims,* U.S. Government Printing Office, Washington, D.C.

innovation   The introduction of something new—either new goods and services or new ways of producing them. Innovation differs from invention in one essential respect; an invention is the discovery of something new, whereas an innovation is the actual introduction or application of something new. Usually a means of increasing productivity or of providing a superior product, innovation has long been recognized as a vital ingredient of economic growth. Joseph A. Schumpeter, a twentieth-century U.S. economist who cited the economic impact of the railroads and electric power, called innovation ". . . the outstanding fact in the history of capitalist societies." The hope of increasing profits or of maintaining them in the face of competition is an important incentive for business innovations. Major innovations often lead to large capital investment in new plants and equipment, thus providing an important stimulant to economic activity. Among the more dramatic innovations in the United States in the mid-twentieth century have been jet airliners, nuclear-powered electric-generating stations, and automated automobile plants. Other examples are transistors, the packaging of soft drinks in cans, credit cards, and wash-and-wear fabrics. For a classical discussion of the impact of innovations on the level of business activity, see Joseph A. Schumpeter, *Business Cycles,* 2 vols., McGraw-Hill, New York, 1939; see also Edwin Mansfield, *The Economics of Technology and Change,* Norton, New York, 1968.

input   Any good or service that a firm uses to produce an output. It could be land, labor, materials, capital goods, or management skills.

input-output analysis (interindustry analysis)   A systematic method of analyzing in great detail the interrelationships between an industry's or an economy's output of goods and services and the volume of goods and services needed to achieve a given volume of production. For example, the steel industry, in increasing its output of steel ingots, needs additional quantities of coal, iron ore, flatcars, electricity, and many other items. To satisfy the additional demands from the steel industry, coal and iron-ore mines, railroad-equipment makers, and electric-generating stations similarly need additional quantities of the goods and services that they consume in turning out their final products. Input-output analysis is usually conducted with the aid of a numerical grid showing in detail the interrelationships among industries along vertical and horizontal axes. An illustrative input-output table is shown on page 181. United States economists agree that the introduction of the input-output technique has greatly aided the historical analysis of the economy's performance. Some, however, doubt its usefulness as a means of predicting future interindustry requirements. For further discussion, see A. Brady and A. P. Carter (eds.), *Input-Output Techniques,* North-Holland, Amsterdam, 1972; Wassily Leontief, *The Structure of the American Economy,* Harvard University Press, Cambridge, Mass., 1951, a pioneering work in the field; updated statistics for input-output work are provided by the U.S. Department of Commerce in the monthly *Survey of Current Business.*

installment credit Credit granted in which repayment, including interest charges, is made by regular payments at specified intervals. The origin of installment credit is uncertain, but it is believed that it began in the United States in a New York City furniture store in the mid-nineteenth century. The rapid growth of installment credit did not take place until after World War I. For a long time, installment credit was used by only relatively poor people, but subsequently all income classes came to use it as a convenient means of making purchases although it is a relatively expensive type of credit. Installment credit is also used in the business field for the purchase of industrial machinery and equipment as well as for goods and services. Automobile purchases constitute the largest single item of installment credit. For further information, see Roger W. Babson, *The Folly of Investment Buying,* Arno, New York, 1976.

institutional economics A school of economic thought that holds that most economic activities are determined by institutions which are largely psychological and are composed of customs and existing economic arrangements. The leader of this school was Thorstein Veblen. Institutionalists used the elements of economic theory as tools for measuring and modifying the economic institutions which they studied. According to this school of thought, competition was an important feature of economic behavior, but it was competition for property and power rather than competition in the marketplace. According to the institutionalists, the classicists erred in basing economic behavior largely on rational motives instead of instincts and customs. For further discussion of institutional economics and institutionalists, see Joseph Dorfman et al., *Institutional Economics: Veblen, Commons and Mitchell Reconsidered,* University of California Press, Berkeley, 1963; Allan G. Gruchy, *Contemporary Economic Thought,* Macmillan, New York, 1972.

instrumental variable In econometrics, a predetermined variable that is used to derive consistent estimators of the parameters of a system of equations. A predetermined variable is one whose values are known at any point

Illustrative Input-Output Table (in Billions of Dollars)

Sellers \ Buyers	Intermediate sales					GNP components							Total
	Agriculture	Industry	Trade and transportation	Services	Total intermediate	Personal consumption	Fixed investment	Change in inventory	Exports	Imports	Government	Final demand	
1. Agriculture	...	76	...	4	80	20	0	-3	10	-8	1	20	100
2. Industry	8	150	30	45	233	313	110	12	50	-48	30	467	700
3. Trade and transportation	1	15	3	5	24	249	10	...	2	-5	20	276	300
4. Services	2	50	10	20	82	276	5	...	30	-33	40	318	400
5. Total intermediate (= 1 + 2 + 3 + 4)	11	291	43	74	...	858	125	9	92	-94	91	1081	1221
6. Labor income	66	260	170	200	...	...	...	...	...	...	140	140	
7. Capital income	20	130	70	106	...	...	...	...	...	...			
8. Indirect taxes	3	19	17	20	...	...	...	...	...	...			
9. Total value added (6 + 7 + 8)	89	409	257	326	1081	...	...	...	...	...	140	140	1221
10. Total (5 + 9)	100	700	300	400	...	858	125	9	92	-94	231	1221	1221

in time; hence it may be an exogenous variable or a lagged endogenous variable. Use of an instrumental variable may be applied to incomplete systems, and it is efficient in relation to a complete set of equations in the sense that only a limited portion of information is employed. The instrumental variable is one of several limited-information methods for estimating an exactly identified or overidentified equation. For additional information, see Lawrence R. Klein, *An Introduction to Econometrics,* Greenwood, Westport, Conn., 1977.

integer programming A mathematical technique designed to choose the "best" course of action from among various alternatives. Integer programming is similar to linear programming, the chief distinction between the two methods being that integer programming requires that the answer consist only of integers, that is, whole numbers. Integer programming can be a useful tool in those situations where inputs or outputs are indivisible. For example, suppose a firm were trying to determine the optimum number of trucks to acquire. Because you cannot buy a fractional part of a truck, nor can you hire, say, three-quarters of a driver, the optimum answers must be whole numbers, and integer programming might be helpful. For additional information, see William J. Baumol, *Economic Theory and Operations Research,* 4th ed., Prentice-Hall, Englewood Cliffs, N.J., 1977.

interest The price paid for the use of money over a period of time. Individuals, businesses and governments buy the use of money. Businesses pay interest for the use of money to purchase capital goods because they can increase production and productivity through the introduction of new plants and new machines. Individuals pay interest for the use of money because they wish to make purchases of goods and services in excess of their current income. Governments pay interest for the use of money because their expenditures usually exceed their receipts. According to the loanable-funds theory of interest, the price of money equals the price paid for the use of loanable funds. The intersection of the supply and demand curves of loanable funds designates the rate of interest. In medieval canon law, interest was prohibited because money was considered barren, that is, incapable of producing goods and services. For further information, see J. M. Keynes, *The General Theory of Employment, Interest, and Money,* Harcourt Brace, New York, 1936; Irving Fisher, *The Theory of Interest,* Kelley and Millman, New York, 1965; John J. Klein, *Money and the Economy,* Harcourt Brace, New York, 1978.; Sidney Homer *A History of Interest Rates,* 2d ed., Rutgers University Press, New Brunswick, N.J., 1977.

interest equalization tax A U.S. tax on foreign securities purchased by U.S. citizens. This type of restrictive government action was taken in the 1960s to prevent capital outflows in the interest of maintaining a strong dollar. From 1964 to 1974 the interest equalization tax prohibited the sale in the

United States of debt securities issued by foreign borrowers other than Canadian provinces and international institutions such as the World Bank. This restriction was one of the principal reasons for the rapid development of the Eurodollar and Eurobond markets. Without this capital control, foreign borrowers would have carried out more financing in U.S. markets. For additional information, see Robert Soloman, *The International Monetary System, 1945–76*, Harper & Row, New York, 1977.

interindustry analysis   *See* **input-output analysis.**

intermediate goods   Goods that enter into the production of other goods. In the manufacturing process, goods and materials pass through various states of production, frequently requiring transfer from one plant to another or sale by one firm to another. For example, a steel ingot made in a blast furnace may be processed into a steel sheet in a rolling mill and then into an automobile chassis at a stamping mill before being made into a car at an assembly plant. In this case, the steel ingot, the steel sheet, and the chassis are intermediate goods even though each may be the final good of a particular plant or firm. According to the analysis of Eugen von Böhm-Bawerk, it is normal for a mature economy to devote most of its resources to the production of intermediate goods. In principle, the value of intermediate goods does not enter into the calculation of the gross national product, which counts only the value of the final product (in the example cited above, the automobile) that embodies the intermediate goods. Since some intermediate goods, such as flour that a bakery buys, can also be final goods (if a consumer buys flour), national income statistics class as intermediate goods only those products which another firm buys and charges off as a current cost during a particular accounting period. This means that capital goods, an integral factor in roundabout production, are counted in the gross national product because they are depreciated over a long period of time. For a detailed definition, see Richard Ruggles and Nancy D. Ruggles, *National Income Accounts and Income Analysis*, McGraw-Hill Book Company, New York, 1956; for a criticism of the concept, see Conference on Research in Income and Wealth, *A Critique of the United States Income and Product Accounts*, Studies in Income and Wealth, vol. XXII, Princeton University Press, Princeton, N.J., 1958; for a discussion of the relationship between production of intermediate goods and mature and less advanced economics, see Eugen von Böhm-Bawerk, *Capital and Interest*, Libertarian Press, South Holland, Ill., 1959.

international commodity agreement   A pact between the countries exporting and importing a particular commodity that specifies, sometimes in fixed amounts and sometimes in ranges of maximum to minimum, the volume and price at which the commodity shall be traded while the agreement is in force. International commodity agreements seek to replace individual, uncoordinated national policies that have frequently led to international price wars and to chaos in the commodity markets, but they generally have encountered problems because of the enormous difficulty of accurately forecasting demand, supply, and trading channels. For example, the International Wheat Agreement of 1949 suffered from unexpected price rises after the outbreak of the Korean conflict, and the International Sugar Agreement of 1958 disintegrated with the severing of commercial relations between Cuba, the world's major exporter of sugar, and the United States, its principal customer. Droughts, currency devaluations, and many other developments can render international commodity agreements useless and even detrimental to their signatories. Economists generally oppose commodity pacts because they rigidify the structure of commodity trade instead of allowing flexible adjustments to changing conditions. On the other hand, commodity producers, who hope for stable export prices for their product, commodity importers, whose domestic producers press for protection against increasing foreign competition, and internationally oriented agencies, which seek to promote not only economic but also social and political stability in underdeveloped countries, remain firm advocates of such agreements. For a theoretical discussion of their effects by a panel of experts, see *Trends in International Trade*, General Agreement on Tariffs and Trade, Geneva, October 1958; see also UN Department of Economic and Social Affairs, *International Compensation for Fluctuations in Commodity Trade*, New York, 1961.

invention   The active combination of presently known elements into a new form. The term is closely associated with discovery, since discoveries often lead to invention and since the process is often reversed. For example, the invention of the steam engine led to the discovery of the theories that led, in turn, to the development of thermodynamics, while the discovery that liquids expand and contract when temperature changes led to the invention of the thermometer. Many believe that the important inventions which contributed to the technical and social changes in western Europe and the United States during and after the industrial revolution were momentous. These innovations provided the seeds of capitalism, thus increasing production and opening ever-widening markets. The leading inventions of this period took place in the textile trades, metallurgy, and chemistry. For further information, see Richard R. Nelson (ed.), *The Rate and Direction of Inventive Activity: Economic and Social Factors*, National Bureau of Economic Research, Princeton University Press, Princeton, N.J., 1962.

inventory   The supply of various goods kept on hand by a firm in order to meet needs promptly as they arise and thus assure uninterrupted operation of the business. In manufacturing, for example, inventories include not only finished products awaiting shipment to selling outlets, but also raw materials, nuts and bolts, paper and pencils, and countless other major and minor items required for the production and distribution of the products. Occasionally, because of sudden changes in demand or unanticipated changes in output,

excessive inventories accumulate, and deliberate efforts are then made to reduce new purchases until the excessive supplies have been eliminated. When
widespread, such inventory-cutting endeavors have been a chief ingredient
of U.S. business recessions since World War II. Because inventories are a
costly form of investment, firms strive to keep them at the lowest level
consistent with good business practice, and sophisticated techniques, such as
linear programming and operations research, have been developed for achieving that goal. Detailed data on business inventories are published regularly
in U.S. Department of Commerce, *Survey of Current Business;* see also Moses
Abramowitz, *Inventories and Business Cycles,* Princeton University Press,
Princeton, N.J., 1950.

inventory change   The increase or decrease in the level of total business
inventories in a given period. As a form of business investment, inventory
change, like investment in new plants and equipment, can have a sharp impact
on a nation's economic activity. Since World War II, inventory changes have
played a major role in business fluctuations in the United States, and in four
postwar recessions (1953–1954, 1957–1958, 1960–1961, and 1969–1970) declines in the gross national product and industrial production were largely
the result of inventory reductions. Inventory changes are included in the
calculation of the gross national product in annual-rate terms. Quarterly data
on inventory changes as a segment of gross private domestic investment may
be found in *Economic Indicators,* prepared monthly by the Council of Economic
Advisers for the U.S. Joint Economic Committee; for details of calculations
on inventory change, see U.S. Department of Commerce, *Survey of Current
Business: National Income Supplement,* 1954; for a discussion of inventories and
their role in business fluctuations, see Moses Abramowitz, *Inventories and
Business Cycles,* Princeton University Press, Princeton, N.J., 1950.

inventory-sales ratio   The ratio between a company's or an industry's
stock of goods and its sales or shipments in a given period. One objective of
inventory control is to maintain inventory-sales ratios at the lowest level
possible under existing business conditions. The rapid introduction of effective inventory control in the late 1950s permitted many U.S. firms to reduce
permanently the inventories required to service their customers. As a result,
inventory-sales ratios in many industries have tended to decline, although
short-term fluctuations still occur. Inventory-sales ratios are a useful forecasting tool. Relatively sharp increases in the ratios suggest that inventories
are growing at a faster pace than an industry's sales; hence, it may be necessary
to cut back production in the immediate future. A declining inventory-sales
ratio, on the other hand, indicates that sales are growing in relation to an
industry's inventory of goods; hence, it may be necessary to increase production in the immediate future to meet customers' demands. Current data
on inventory-sales ratios are printed in U.S. Department of Commerce, *Survey of Current Business,* monthly.

inventory-valuation adjustment A measure of the profit or loss which takes place as a result of increases or decreases in prices affecting the values of inventories held by corporations. Total business profits include profits or losses made on inventory as well as profits from operations. Since corporations generally value the materials that they consume in production at the original cost and not at the cost of replacement, profits tend to be overstated when the costs of materials are rising and understated when their costs are falling. The inventory-valuation adjustment is used by the U.S. Department of Commerce in its computations of national income to correct the overstatement or understatement of profits. For a detailed discussion of the inventory-valuation adjustment, see U.S. Department of Commerce, *Survey of Current Business: National Income Supplement,* 1954.

inverted economic series A series of key business-cycle indicators which conform negatively to the business cycle; that is, they decline when general business activity rises and rise when general business activity declines. Examples of negatively conforming indicators are the unemployment rate, initial claims for unemployment insurance, and liabilities of business failures. A rise in one of these series indicates deterioration in business activity, and a decline indicates improvement. In business-cycle analysis, it is convenient to invert these indicators so that their behavior may be compared more easily with that of the other indicators. Depending on the type of analysis to be made, there are several methods of inverting indicators. Two of the simplest: (1) invert the scale in graphic presentation, that is, show numbers of the scale in increasing magnitude from top to bottom; and (2) take period-to-period percentage changes in the actual data and invert the signs, that is, show declines as positive (+) and rises as negative (−) changes. For further discussion on inverted series, see Geoffrey H. Moore (ed.), *Business Cycle Indicators,* Princeton University Press, Princeton, N.J., 1961, vol. I.

invested capital (capital structure) The sum of bonds and owner-contributed capital (stock accounts and surplus) in a corporation. Thus, invested capital is the total of a corporation's net worth and its long-term debt. The rate of return on invested capital is an important measure of the profitability of a corporation. For further information, see J. Fred Weston and Eugene F. Brigham, *Essentials of Managerial Finance,* 5th ed., Holt, Rinehart and Winston, New York, 1979.

investment bank *See* investment banking.

investment banking The marketing of new corporate securities. The investment-banking firm purchases large blocks of new corporate issues of stocks and bonds and resells them in smaller amounts to individual or institutional investors. The investment bank acts as the intermediary between the issuer of securities and the investing public, facilitating the flow of available savings into investment. Most investment banking takes the form of the purchase, or underwriting, of entire new issues of securities. Since the capital involved in such underwriting is often so large that no one investment bank can handle it alone, it is common practice for several firms to form a purchasing syndicate to buy and distribute the securities jointly. The purchase group assures the issuing corporation a definite price for the securities and then bears the risk of selling the securities to the public at a price high enough to realize a profit. Besides purchase and sale of entire issues, investment-banking syndicates may participate in standby underwriting, in which the group underwrites the offering (usually of stockholders' rights) by agreeing in advance to buy at a specified price all securities which are not sold by the corporation itself. Another aspect of investment banking is best-efforts selling, or agency marketing, in which the investment banker merely markets a new security as the agent of the issuing corporation, but makes no agreement to underwrite the issue and assumes none of the risk of selling it. For additional details, see Henry P. Willis and Jules I. Bogen, *Investment Banking,* rev. ed., Arno, New York, 1975.

investment company (investment trust) An organization that combines the funds of many persons and invests them in a wide selection of securities. Although a few earlier companies resembled modern investment companies, the first real investment trust was the Foreign and Colonial Trust, which was established in London in 1868. Its purpose was to give small investors the same advantage—diversification—that large capitalists had. Today, along with diversification, investment companies give shareholders the advantage of professional managment. In the United States, the Securities and Exchange Commission (SEC) regulates investment companies under the Investment Company Act of 1940. Any company that falls within the act's definition of an investment company must register with the SEC. The SEC classifies investment companies under four types: management open-end (mutual funds), management closed-end, unit investment trusts, and face-amount certificate companies. As of December 31, 1979, there were 907 open-end investment companies, 163 closed-end investment companies, 386 unit investment trusts, and 5 face-amount certificate companies registered with the SEC. Their total assets were estimated at $156 billion. See Investment Company Act of 1940; U.S. Securities and Exchange Commission, *Annual Reports;* Irwin Friend, et al., *Mutual Funds and Other Institutional Investors: A New Perspective,* McGraw-Hill, New York, 1970.

investment plan The expectation of a business firm for investment in new plants and equipment. Most business firms have a program of investment projects which are expected to be carried out over the short or the long run. Since anticipatory investment information is valuable in forecasting business conditions, both company planners and government planners pay close attention to surveys of investment plans, such as the quarterly surveys of the

U.S. Department of Commerce and the annual surveys of the Department of Economics of McGraw-Hill Publications. The dollar value of investment plans for a specific time period often differs from the dollar value of actual investment in the same period. The difference arises because of the addition of new programs, the deferral of other programs, and the cancellation of still others. At the company level, the difference between planned investment and actual investment is very large, but as the data of individual companies are aggregated into industry totals and then into a total for all business, the differences tend to offset each other, with the result that total investment plans are very close to actual investment. For additional information on surveys of investment plans and the accuracy of investment plans, see National Bureau of Economic Research, *The Quality and Economic Significance of Anticipations Data,* Princeton University Press, Princeton, N.J., 1960, part IV.

investment trust   *See* **investment company.**

invisible-hand doctrine   The doctrine, introduced by Adam Smith in 1776, that individuals, all seeking to further their self-interest, will be led, as if by an invisible hand, to achieve the best good for all. The purpose of introducing the invisible hand was to demonstrate that any government interference with free competition would be harmful to society since such competition by itself was able to channel the selfish motives of individuals so that they automatically, though unintentionally, furthered the best interests of society. Since self-interest guides humanity as if each individual were "led by an invisible hand to promote an end which was no part of his intention," laissez faire was considered the best policy for the government to pursue in economic matters. A major limitation of the invisible-hand doctrine is that it works well only under conditions of perfect competition, and it is unrealistic to assume such conditions exist in the real world. For additional details, see Adam Smith, *The Wealth of Nations,* Random House, New York, 1937, p. 423.

IS-LM model   A standard representation of the Keynesian system in a form which is particularly suitable for comparative static analysis. Two curves (the *IS* and *LM* curves) are graphed, and the point of intersection determines the equilibrium income and interest rate in the economy. The *IS* curve is the graph of the equation which defines all combinations of income and interest rate for which the goods market is in equilibrium. Similarly, the money demand and supply equations are solved to obtain a single equation in income and the interest rate, graphed as the *LM* curve, in which the nominal quantity of money (base money) and the price level are taken as given. For example, an increase in government expenditures will shift the downward-sloping *IS* curve to the right, increasing both income and the interest rate. Also, an increase in the nominal supply of money will shift the upward-sloping *LM* curve to the right and increase income but reduce interest rates. Sir John Hicks first proposed the *IS-LM* model as an exposition of Keynes' central argument in *The General Theory of Employment, Interest, and Money.* It has in recent years lost much of its earlier dominance as a tool of macroeconomics. For additional information, see Michael R. Darby, *Intermediate Macroeconomics,* McGraw-Hill, New York, 1979.

isocost curve   A graphic line showing the various possible combinations of resources that can be purchased with a given quantity of money, on the assumption that the prices of the factors are in some fixed proportion. For example, let us assume that we wish to know the various combinations of steel at $80 per ton and of aluminum at $40 per ton with a given outlay of $320. The isocost line in the accompanying illustration indicates the possibilities of all purchase combinations (4 tons of steel, 8 tons of aluminum, or any combination between these two extremes). The isocost line, which represents the ratio of the prices of the two items, is used to determine minimum cost for a given level of output by choosing that combination of factor inputs which is cheaper than any alternative combination which could be used to produce the given output. This is done by using the isoquant, which represents the marginal rate of substitution between the factors, and its tangency to the lowest isocost line (the one farthest left). For a further explanation, see Donald S. Watson and Mary A. Holman, *Price Theory and Its Uses,* 4th ed., Houghton Mifflin, Boston, 1976.

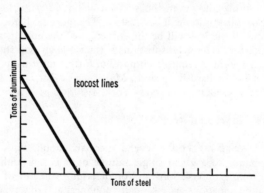

isoquant   A graphic line showing the various possible combinations of factors which will yield a given quantity of output. For example, let us assume that we wish to know the various combinations of steel and aluminum needed to build ten automobiles. The isoquant in the illustration on page 190 indicates the possibilities. The slope of the isoquant represents the marginal rate of substitution between the two factors at that particular point. Because of a diminishing rate of marginal substitution, the isoquant will usually be convex to the point of origin. This means that the greater the amount of one factor used, the less of the other factor is needed to replace a unit of the first factor.

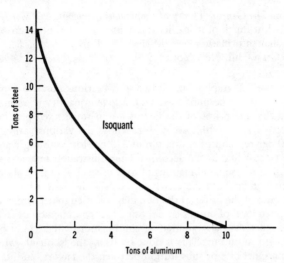

Thus, each additional unit of steel, past some point, replaces less than a unit of aluminum, and, correspondingly in the same area, less than a unit of aluminum can be substituted for more than a unit of steel. If the two factors are perfect substitutes, however, the isoquant will be a straight line, since the marginal rate of substitution will be constant. The more easily the two factors can be substituted, the less will be the curvature of the line. If, at the other extreme, the factors cannot be substituted, the isoquant will show a right-angle bend at the point of required output. For further information, see James M. Henderson and Richard E. Quandt, *Microeconomic Theory: A Mathematical Approach,* 3d ed., McGraw-Hill, New York, 1980, chaps. 4 and 5.

issued stock   *See* **capital stock.**

iteration (iterative method)   Several successive applications of a given statistical technique to a given single sample of raw data with a view to eliminating extreme observations and/or deriving estimates of parameters whose estimating equations are essentially nonlinear and of a type not suited for direct solution. In the case of estimating parameters, iteration refers to a sequence of approximations to the solution for a parameter that is obtained in such a way that the essential step in determining each approximation constitutes a linear function. For additional information, see Lawrence R. Klein, *An Introduction to Econometrics,* Greenwood, Westport, Conn., 1977.

iterative method   *See* **iteration.**

J

jawbone economics   Oral statements by political leaders on the economic health of the nation as they see it, together with a series of suggestions on economic action which should be carried out in order to improve the situation. For example, it has been suggested at various times by "experts" of this type that business is entering a deep recession when it has already started rising from the bottom of a very mild recession. Such amateur economists might also suggest that the way to cut the high unemployment rate to the so-called full-employment unemployment rate is to reduce taxes, which obviously may not provide a complete solution to the unemployment problem. They might also suggest that the only cure for a rapid rate of inflation is wage-price controls.

joint demand   Demand for two or more products which are generally used together, sometimes because of necessity and sometimes because of preference. Joint demand is demonstrated when the purchase of a greater quantity of one good leads to the purchase of a greater quantity of another. This concept, which was originated by Alfred Marshall, is used in the analysis of both demand for factors of production and consumer demand. In the case of factors of production, the joint demand for inputs, such as graphite and wood, is derived from the demand for pencils, the good which they combine to produce. Because there is a demand for pencils, there is a joint demand for wood and graphite. In the case of consumer demands, the joint demand results from the combinations, such as record players and records and automobiles and tires, in which consumers wish to use their goods. The theory of joint demand is used to help explain the course of demand for one good when the demand for another changes, as for example, through a price change. For the classical presentation of joint factor demand, see Alfred Marshall, *Principles of Economics,* Macmillan, London, 1920; for a more modern analysis, see Joan Robinson, *The Economics of Imperfect Competition,* 2d ed., St. Martin's Press, New York, 1969.

joint venture   An association of individuals or firms formed to carry out a specific business project. Although a joint venture is very similar to a partnership, it differs in that it is limited to the success or failure of the specific project for which it was formed. As in the case of the partnership, a joint venture is formed by a contract agreement in which each partner assumes unlimited liability for the organization's debts. For joint ventures in developing countries, see W. G. Friedman and G. Kalmanoff, *Joint International Business Ventures,* Columbia University Press, New York, 1961.

Juglar cycle   A business cycle of intermediate duration. Named for Clement Juglar, who was the first to isolate the major industrial business cycle, Juglar cycles are fluctuations of prices, production, employment, etc., over a period of nine to ten years. They are classified as major nonseasonal cycles. Juglar cycles, used by Joseph A. Schumpeter in his three-cycle analysis of business cycles, were explained by the mechanism of capitalist development innovations. They are superimposed on the Kondratieff cycles of fifty to sixty years, so that each Kondratieff cycle contains six Juglar cycles. For additional details, see Joseph A. Schumpeter, *Business Cycles,* 2 vols., McGraw-Hill, New York, 1939; Carl Dauten and Lloyd Valentine, *Business Cycles and Forecasting,* 5th ed., South-Western, Cincinnati, 1978.

Keogh plan   A plan created by the Self-employed Individual Retirement Act of 1962 and considerably enhanced by the Economic Recovery Act of 1981. It is also known as an H.R. 10 plan. Keogh plans can be established by people who are entirely self-employed or who earn and declare income from self-employment while at the same time working for others. Earnings from self-employment that are placed in a Keogh plan are exempt from taxation for the tax period during which they are earned, as are the earnings of the funds accumulated in the plan. All money is, however, subject to taxation when funds are withdrawn, presumably at a lower tax rate than that paid by the taxpayer during the time when contributions were made. By the act of 1981, the limit for contributions into a defined-contribution plan was raised to $15,000 or 15% of earned income, whichever is less, in any tax year. Assets being accumulated must be held in a plan that satisfies Internal Revenue Service requirements. Assets in Keogh accounts may be transferred from one type of investment program to another at any time. Keoghs can also be set up as self-directed trusts, in which assets are held by a qualified custodian but the account holder makes all decisions as to the placement of funds. Assets that may be held in Keogh accounts includes stocks, stock options, bonds, government securities, mutual funds, savings certificates, and annuity contracts. Laws covering Keogh plans were revised in 1982 to exclude collectibles such as gold, silver, and diamonds from approved plan assets. Contributions to a defined-benefit Keogh plan (a plan that establishes a formula by which a participant's benefits at retirement are to be determined, with contributions geared to provide the benefits specified by the formula) are not subject to the limit of $15,000 or 15% of earnings applicable to the defined-contribution plan described above. Instead, the limit is stated in terms of the maximum benefit that may be provided under the plan. For the typical case, the annual benefit payable at retirement under a defined-benefit Keogh plan may not exceed the lesser of $75,000 or the average of the contributor's highest three years' earnings while covered by the plan. Therefore, the maximum amount that may be contributed to a defined-benefit Keogh in any one year may be higher, or lower, than the maximum contribution allowed under a defined-contribution Keogh plan depending on such factors as the contributor's age and earnings. For further information, see Economic Recovery Tax Act of 1981; L. L. Unthank and Harry M. Behrendt, *What You Should Know about Individual Retirement Accounts,* Dow Jones–Irwin, Homewood, Ill., 1978.

Keynes-effect theory   The theory that a reduction in the overall price level leads to lower interest rates and to increased investment. It is based on the following line of reasoning: (1) Individuals establish a desired relationship between the money balances that they hold and their expenditures on goods and services. (2) Price reductions raise the real value of their money holdings; that is, the quantity of goods and services that can be bought with a given amount of money rises. (3) Thus, the desired relationship between real balances and expenditures is disturbed, and individuals have an excess supply of liquid assets. (4) Individuals are willing to lend part of this excess supply. (5) An increase in the supply of funds in the loan market lowers the rate of interest. (6) With a lower rate of interest, greater investment takes place. The Keynes effect operates only in the market for bonds; in this respect, it differs from the Pigou effect, which operates only in the market for goods and services, and from the real-balance effect, which operates in both the bond market and the market for goods and services. For the original statement of the Keynes effect, see J. M. Keynes, *The General Theory of Employment, Interest, and Money,* Harcourt Brace, New York, 1936, p. 257; for a further analysis, see Don Patinkin, *Money, Interest and Prices,* 2d ed., Harper & Row, New York, 1965.

Keynesian economics   The body of economic thought developed by John Maynard Keynes and his followers. The central theme of Keynesian economics is an analysis of the causes and results of variations in aggregate spending and income. Total income equals total consumption plus investment. If every increase in savings is not offset by increased investment, income will fall and unemployment will rise. The level of consumption (and saving) is said to depend on the individual's propensity to consume, which is a function of income. The amount of business investment is set largely through the marginal efficiency of capital or business executives' expectations as to future returns on capital investment. The interest rate is seen not as a factor tending to equalize the supply of savings and the demand for investment but rather as an independent element, depending on the extent of the individual's desire to hold savings in cash (the liquidity preference). Thus, savings and investment will not necessarily tend toward equilibrium; instead, the level of savings will generally be higher than investment, and the result will be frequent unemployment and stagnation. Keynes therefore proposed, for the first time in economic theory, the possibility of an underemployment equilibrium. To prevent mass unemployment in the depression phase of the business cycle, he argued that the central government should compensate for the deficiency in aggregate demand by using deficit financing to stimulate spending and to create investments which would raise income to the full-employment level, aided by the operation of the investment multiplier. The basic elements of the Keynesian theory of economics were introduced in 1936 by Keynes in his major work, *The General Theory of Employment, Interest, and Money*, and were further developed by his disciples, such as Alvin H. Hansen in the United States. Soon accepted in most academic circles, this "new economics" remains the most significant force on modern economic theory. For a fuller exposition of Keynesian economics, see J. M. Keynes, *The General Theory of Employment, Interest, and Money*, Harcourt Brace, New York, 1936; Brian Morgan, *Monetarists and Keynesians*, Wiley, New York, 1978.

Kitchin cycle   A short, rhythmic fluctuation in business activity. Named for Joseph Kitchin, who was the first analyst to study it in detail, the Kitchin cycle is a regular, forty-month fluctuation of prices, production, employment, etc. Kitchin cycles, used by Joseph A. Schumpeter in his three-cycle analysis of business cycles, are explained largely by changes in inventory investment and by small waves of innovations, especially in equipment which can be produced fairly quickly. They are superimposed on the longer Juglar and Kondratieff cycles, so that there are three Kitchin cycles to every Juglar cycle and eighteen Kitchin cycles in every Kondratieff cycle. For additional information, see Joseph A. Schumpeter, *Business Cycles*, 2 vols., McGraw-Hill, New York, 1939. For a brief criticism of the Kitchin cycle, see Carl A. Dauten and Lloyd M. Valentine, *Business Cycles and Forecasting*, 5th ed., South-Western, Cincinnati, 1978.

Kondratieff cycle A series of long waves of economic fluctuation. Named for N. D. Kondratieff, a Russian economist, Kondratieff cycles consist of waves in prices, production, and trade lasting from fifty to sixty years. According to Kondratieff, these cycles are due to processes inherent in the nature of capitalism, especially that of capital accumulation. He argued that changes in techniques of production, wars and revolutions, the opening of new markets, etc., are not random occurrences affecting the cycle, but rather are part of the rhythm of the long waves. For example, the expansion into new markets does not start a long-term upswing; instead, the upswing makes the expansion into new markets possible and necessary. Similarly, the declining phase of the long wave leads to important discoveries which are utilized on a large scale only at the beginning of the next major upswing. The upward phase of the wave, producing high tension in the expansion of economic forces, is a major factor in provoking wars and revolutions. Joseph A. Schumpeter, in adopting the Kondratieff cycle as part of his three-cycle analysis of business fluctuations, considered that the long cycle was closely linked to the waves of innovations, predominantly of a definite type, by which the long wave in question was characterized. Thus, the Kondratieff wave from about 1780 to 1840 was that of the industrial revolution; the next, from 1840 to 1890, was that of steel and steam; and the one from 1890 to 1950 was that of electricity, chemistry, and motors. For additional details, see N. D. Kondratieff, "The Long Waves in Economic Life," *Review of Economics and Statistics,* November 1935; Joseph A. Schumpeter, *Business Cycles,* 2 vols., McGraw-Hill, New York, 1939; Carl A. Dauten and Lloyd M. Valentine, *Business Cycles and Forecasting,* 5th ed., South-Western, Cincinnati, 1978.

Kuznets cycle Secular swings in economic growth rates with a duration of approximately fifteen to twenty-two years. Simon Kuznets studied U.S. economic development for the period prior to World War II and found evidence of such long swings in many kinds of economic activity, particularly in the construction industry. The Kuznets cycle is by no means confined to the construction industry nor to the United States, but is regarded as a phenomenon visible in growth rates in most major industrial sections in the forty years prior to World War II. The distinctive feature of Kuznets cycles is that they are cycles in growth rates rather than in absolute expansion and contraction of the level of activity. It was believed that demographic factors, particularly immigration waves, were important in explaining the long swings in economic growth rates prior to World War II. But this is debatable, as is the notion that these swings continue in the post-World War II period. For additional information, see Simon S. Kuznets, *Secular Movements in Production and Prices,* Houghton Mifflin, Boston, 1930; Brinley Thomas, *Migration and Economic Growth,* 2d ed., Cambridge University Press, Cambridge, 1973.

L

labor In economic theory, the human effort or activity that is directed toward production. As a factor of production, labor is distinct from raw materials, capital, and management and includes only the efforts of hired workers. In another sense, labor comprises all persons who work for a living. This definition refers to the labor force of a nation, which includes all the employable population over a certain age. In a somewhat more restricted sense, labor signifies the whole working class or organized employees as opposed to employers; it thus includes all nonsupervisory workers (workers below the rank of production supervisor) in all kinds of public and private employment. The term has also come to mean the organized labor movement. See R. B. Ekelund and R. F. Hebert, *A History of Economic Thought and Method,* McGraw-Hill, New York, 1975.

labor agreement A written contract between an employer and a freely chosen representative of the workers, setting forth the terms and conditions of employment. Since the employer is the sole buyer of labor for a particular plant, the typical employee is in a relatively weak position when dealing individually with an employer. So that they, too, can gain a degree of monopoly power, employees are therefore organized into strong unions. When agreement has been reached through collective bargaining and the approval of the workers has been obtained, the contract is signed. Such a contract covers the terms of agreement and lasts for a specified period of time. If agreement cannot be reached, labor can use its chief weapon, the strike, to induce the employer to agree to the union's terms. See Arthur R. Sloan and Fred Witney, *Labor Relations,* 3d ed., Prentice-Hall, Englewood Cliffs, N.J., 1977.

labor force According to the concept of the U.S. Department of Labor and the U.S. Bureau of the Census, the noninstitutionalized population, sixteen years of age or older, that either is employed or is not working but is looking for work. The labor force of the United States, which totaled nearly

100 million in 1980, includes members of the armed forces as well as civilians. Most persons in the civilian labor force are employed in business or in industrial establishments working for wages and salaries, but self-employed persons, unpaid family workers on farms or in stores, and the unemployed are also included. The labor force is measured monthly by the Bureau of the Census for the Department of Labor. In a survey conducted in the week containing the twelfth day of the month, census interviewers ask questions of 50,000 households in 449 areas to learn which persons are in the labor force in that week. For further information, see A. J. Jaffe and Charles D. Stewart, *Manpower Resources and Utilization: Principles of Working Force Analysis*, Wiley, New York, 1951; Guy Standing, *Labor Force Participation and Development*, International Labor Office, Geneva, 1978; current statistics are found in U.S. Department of Labor, *Employment and Earnings*, monthly.

labor-management relations   A term used interchangeably with labor relations or industrial relations. The labor-management relations function developed as a result of the legitimation of the trade union. The growth of this field in the 1930–1945 period is directly related to labor laws that were designed to balance the relative bargaining power of employers and employee representatives engaged in collective bargaining of labor agreements. The first of these laws was the Railway Act of 1926. Then in 1932 the Norris-La-Guardia Act severely restricted the use of court injunctions in labor disputes. But the Wagner Act, passed in 1935, was the most important law that eventually led to labor-management relations. The evolution of labor-management relations as a legitimate field of practice and study required the important element of strong employee representation in cooperation with management. Trade unionism and collective bargaining are the cornerstones of effective labor relations in the United States. For additional information, see John T. Dunlop, *Industrial Relations Systems*, Henry Holt, New York, 1958.

Labor-Management Relations Act of 1947   *See* **Taft-Hartley Act.**

labor mobility   The ease with which workers are able to change jobs and occupations. There are two types of mobility, horizontal and vertical. Horizontal mobility refers to the degree to which workers shift from job to job at the same level of skill. This type of movement, which may occur between geographical areas or within a single location, is due primarily to differences in the terms of employment, such as wages, hours, and working conditions. The main barriers to this type of mobility are certain characteristics of the workers themselves, such as lack of information concerning job opportunities and the psychological and financial difficulties of moving into a new area, and the characteristics of certain jobs which prevent workers from moving even though they desire to do so, such as restrictive union practices and preferential hiring. Vertical mobility refers to the degree to which workers are able to acquire education and new skills which permit them to move up (or down) the occupational ladder. This type of mobility is an index of the relative openness of a social structure, representing the mobility within income, prestige, and other structures. For further information on labor mobility, see Lloyd G. Reynolds, *Labor Economics and Labor Relations,* 7th ed., Prentice-Hall, Englewood Cliffs, N.J., 1978.

labor monopoly   The ability of strong labor unions to exert monopoly power through their ability to regulate the supply of labor and thus significantly affect the price of labor (wage rates). There is considerable disagreement over the extent and effect of this power and whether or not it is in need of additional public control.

labor theory of value   The theory that the entire value of all reproducible commodities stems from the labor that produces them, whether this labor is applied directly or is used to improve the land and build the machines that contribute to the productive process. Developed by the classical economists of the late eighteenth and early nineteenth centuries, the theory was soon modified to take account of the relative scarcity of goods and services that also determines market value. Karl Marx adopted the labor theory of value in full and used it to explain why he thought that workers were being exploited whenever capitalists sold products for more than their labor costs. His argument, the touchstone of communist economic theory, has frequently led the managers of the Soviet economy to place too low a value on capital, an error which many western economists believe has resulted in a considerable misuse of resources within the U.S.S.R. There are a number of shortcomings to the labor theory of value. Among them are the facts that it does not incorporate interest and that it does not take into account the length of the productive process. For a general discussion of the labor theory of value, see Mark Blaug, *Economic Theory in Retrospect,* 3d ed., Cambridge University Press, New York, 1978, chaps. 2, 4, 6, and 7.

labor turnover   The movement of wage and salary workers into and out of employment. This movement is divided into two major categories, hirings and layoffs. These two categories of labor turnover are generally considered leading indicators of national economic activity, since they provide early indications of turning points in business cycles. For U.S. industry statistics on labor turnover, see U.S. Department of Labor, *Employment and Earnings,* monthly.

Laffer curve   A mathematical indication, originated by Arthur B. Laffer, that there are normally two different tax rates that will bring in a particular amount of revenue. For example, a zero tax rate will bring in no revenue, and a 100% tax rate will also bring in nothing because, in effect, it would stop taxable activity. Laffer, believing that U.S. tax rates were very high on the Laffer curve, showed that lower tax rates could so stimulate business, shifting income from tax shelters to taxable activity, that lower tax rates would bring in higher revenues. Laffer believed that tax cuts would actually pay for themselves through increased revenues. But for this relation to hold mathematically, a tax cut would have to generate a supply response three times larger than itself. Critics also refuted the basic notion that the United States had reached the upper portions of the Laffer curve, which would mean that reductions of U.S. tax rates could actually enlarge revenues. For additional information, see Arthur B. Laffer and Jan P. Seymour (eds.), *The Economics of the Tax Revolt*, Harcourt Brace, New York, 1979; Jude Wanniski, *The Way the World Works*, Basic Books, New York, 1978.

lagging indicator   A measure of economic activity that usually reaches a turning point of the business cycle after the overall economy has turned. The use of statistical indicators of this type was developed by Wesley Mitchell, Warren Persons, and Arthur F. Burns, members of the staff of the National Bureau of Economic Research, to indicate historical changes in the general course of business. Geoffrey H. Moore and Julius Shiskin, also staff members of the bureau, have carried forward the indicator method of business-cycle analysis, and they consider the timing of the laggards necessary to round out the picture of the changing business scene. Increases in lagging series, such as unit labor costs, interest rates, or finished goods inventories, can help bring about declines in leading series, such as profit margins, capital investment commitments, or additions to materials inventories. Some economists pay little attention to the lagging indicators, suggesting that they do not represent a significant contribution to business forecasting. *Business Conditions Digest,* a report of the Bureau of Economic Analysis, lists seven lagging indicators, but there is no special division into related groups. For the development and analysis of lagging indicators, see Geoffrey H. Moore (ed.), *Business Cycle Indicators,* Princeton University Press, Princeton, N.J., 1961; for current statistics of the indicators, see Bureau of Economic Analysis, *Business Conditions Digest,* monthly.

laissez faire   The doctrine that government should limit itself to the maintenance of law and order and remove all legal restraints on trade and prices. It was developed in the atmosphere of the highly regulative monarchies of France and England in the late seventeenth and early eighteenth centuries, when there were many local and national barriers to business activity. The first use of the phrase is attributed to a French manufacturer named Legendre, who, in reply to a question by the minister Jean Baptiste Colbert on how government could help business, said "laissez nous faire" (leave us alone). Adam Smith, the great eighteenth-century English economist, and his followers argued that a laissez faire policy would promote individual freedom, the best use of economic resources, and economic growth. The doctrine reached its popular height in the late nineteenth century, but it lost influence thereafter as demands for government regulation grew. Nevertheless, some economists have continued to advocate positive programs of laissez faire in which government would avoid direct interference with prices and trade, but would be charged with the heavy responsibilities of (1) the maintenance of competitive conditions in industry, (2) the control of the money supply, and (3) certain social welfare activities. The classic statement in favor of laissez faire is Adam Smith, *The Wealth of Nations,* Random House, New York, 1937; for a discussion of the doctrine's decline in popularity, see J. M. Keynes, *The End of Laissez Faire,* Woolf, London, 1926; see also Murray N. Rothbard, *Power and Market,* Institute for Humane Studies, Menlo Park, Calif., 1970.

land   With labor, capital, and entrepreneurial ability, one of the four major factors of production. Land, in an economic context, represents the productive power of natural, untransformed resources, receiving rent as its factor payment. In this sense it exists only if it is in its natural state. The primary feature that differentiates land, except agricultural land, as a natural resource from the other factors of production is that it is exhaustible (depletable). The distinction which has been made between land and capital is in terms of their supply curves. Since the amount of land is fixed by nature, its supply curve is vertical while the supply curve for capital has the traditional upward slope. For additional information see R. B. Ekelund and R. F. Hebert, *A History of Economic Theory and Method,* McGraw-Hill, New York, 1975.

large-scale production   *See* **mass production.**

Laspeyres index   A statistical method for computing weighted aggregative index numbers, named after its originator and most frequently used in the construction of price indices. The formula assigns to each current price relative a quantity weight that is appropriate for the base year. The quantity weight for each commodity is held constant for a number of years' computations. Therefore, the index allows for no changes in tastes or environment. Price indices derived by this means are said to have an upward bias because they cannot allow for shifts in quantity in response to price increases. A modified form of the Laspeyres index is used in computing the U.S. Bureau of Labor Statistics' wholesale and consumer price indices:

$$P = \frac{\Sigma \, p_n q_o}{\Sigma \, p_o q_o}$$

For additional information, see Karl A. Fox and Tej K. Kaul, *Intermediate Economic Statistics,* Krieger, Melbourne, Fla., 1980.

leading indicator   A measure of economic activity that usually reaches peaks or troughs of business activity before total business does. The use of statistical indicators of this type was developed before World War II by Wesley Mitchell, Warren Persons, and Arthur F. Burns, members of the staff of the National Bureau of Economic Research, to indicate historical changes in the general course of business. Geoffrey H. Moore and Julius Shiskin, also staff members of the bureau, have carried forward the indicator method of business-cycle analysis so that many business and academic economists consider that the leading indicators provide significant clues in making early judgments about future shifts in the general course of business. Many economists use the leading indicators as merely one tool in a large kit of forecasting devices. *Business Conditions Digest,* a report of the Bureau of Economic Analysis, lists thirty leading indicators and divides them into five major groups for analysis: (1) sensitive employment and unemployment indicators, (2) new investment commitments, (3) new business incorporations and business failures, (4) profits and stock prices, and (5) inventory investment, buying policy, and sensitive prices. For the development and analysis of leading indicators, see Geoffrey H. Moore (ed.), *Business Cycle Indicators,* National Bureau of Economic Research, Princeton University Press, Princeton, N.J., 1961, vol. I; for current statistics of the leading indicators, see Bureau of Economic Analysis, *Business Conditions Digest,* monthly.

lead-lag relationship   A term which describes the timing of changes in one statistical series in relation to changes in another series. It is frequently used in sales forecasting, which makes use of the timing pattern between a company's sales and a particular economic indicator. The economic indicator must consistently lead the company's business in order to make it useful as a forecasting device. This relationship can be determined by plotting the historical movements of a particular indicator and the company's sales on the same graph. For example, the sales of construction-material companies follow the fluctuations of F. W. Dodge's data on contracts awarded, which are found to lead such sales by six months. Thus, by use of a mathematical relationship, a prediction of sales six months ahead can be made with a fairly high degree of accuracy. For further information on sales forecasting and the use of lead-lag relationships, see Vernon G. Lippitt, *Statistical Sales Forecasting,* Financial Executives Research Foundation, New York, 1969.

leaseback   A business deal in which a company owning land, buildings, and equipment sells all or part of its property to another company or to a private investor and simultaneously leases the property back under a long-term lease. The purposes of such a deal are to obtain funds for working capital or investment and to convert occupancy costs to rent, which is tax deductible as a business expense. The advantage to the investor is a relatively safe investment at a good rate of return. For a detailed discussion of sale and leaseback, see J. Fred Weston and Eugene F. Brigham, *Essentials of Managerial Finance,* 5th ed., Holt, Rinehart and Winston, New York, 1979.

least squares   In statistics and econometrics, a method of estimation that involves the choice of an estimate such that the sum of the squares of the deviations of the data from the estimate is a minimum. A least-squares estimate has a smaller variance than any other linear estimate and is unbiased: the average of many least-squares estimates is likely to differ only slightly from the true value. For additional information, see Karl A. Fox and Tej K. Kaul, *Intermediate Economic Statistics*, Krieger, Melbourne, Fla., 1980.

leverage   The effect of the use of senior capital (bonds and preferred stocks) over junior capital (common stock) in capitalizations. Leverage enables a relatively small issue of common stock to benefit from the earnings of a much larger capital fund, since the total capital fund will usually earn more than the cost of the borrowed capital. Thus, the rate of return on the equity capital will be higher than the rate on the entire capital stock. As the rate of earnings on total capital increases, leverage will produce a magnified increase in the earnings of common stock. On the other hand, as the rate of earnings on capital decreases, leverage will cause a proportionately larger fall in the common-stock earnings than would have been the case without capital investment. The earning power of highly leveraged stocks can disappear entirely even if the capital fund is earning profits as a whole. Leverage is thus a speculative factor, increasing possibilities for both gain and loss. For more details, see Benjamin Graham et al., *Security Analysis*, 4th ed., McGraw-Hill, New York, 1962, chaps. 40 and 48; J. Fred Weston and Eugene F. Brigham, *Essentials of Managerial Finance*, 5th ed., Holt, Rinehart and Winston, New York, 1979.

liabilities   The debts or amounts of money owed by an individual, partnership, or corporation to others. Considered from another point of view, liabilities are the claims or rights, expressed in monetary terms, of an individual's or a corporation's creditors. In accounting, liabilities are classified as either short-term or long-term liabilities or as secured or unsecured liabilities. Short-term liabilities are those which will be satisfied, or paid, within one year's time. Examples are payroll obligations, accounts payable, taxes due, accrued interest, and short-term notes (maturing within one year). Long-term liabilities are those which will not be satisfied within one year, such as mortgages, long-term notes, and bonds. Secured liabilities are claims that have specific assets pledged to ensure satisfaction; unsecured liabilities are debts which depend on the general resources of the firm for satisfaction. See Harold Bierman, Jr., and Allan R. Drebin, *Management Accounting*, 3d ed., Dryden Press, Hinsdale, Ill., 1978.

likelihood function   The mathematical statement (formula or measure) of the probability of drawing (observing) a particular sample. The formula says that the probability of the particular sample is equal to the probability that the error term of the estimating equation will have taken the particular values associated with the particular sample multiplied by a factor det *J*. The term det *J* equals 1 in all single-equation cases. Assuming that the particular sample drawn *is* the most probable, precise estimates of unknown parameters can be obtained by manipulating the likelihood function. Maximizing the likelihood function generates maximum likelihood estimates of the unknown parameters. For additional information, see Lawrence R. Klein, *An Introduction to Econometrics,* Greenwood, Westport, Conn., 1977.

limited-information methods   Econometric methods for estimating parameters that do not use all the available information. Such methods include, for example, using instrumental variables, reduced forms, and limited-information–maximum-likelihood. They make it possible to avoid the formidable computations of the maximum-likelihood method. The term is usually used in reference to methods that yield consistent estimates, that is, estimates that tend to approach the population value as sample size increases. For additional information, see Lawrence R. Klein, *An Introduction to Econometrics,* Greenwood, Westport, Conn., 1977.

limit order (limited order)   An order that a customer gives to a broker to buy or sell a certain amount of stock at a stated price or better. For instance, if a customer places a limit order to buy 100 shares of ABC Corporation at $50, the broker can buy ABC only at $50 or at a price below $50; the broker cannot pay more than $50 no matter what happens. Limit orders to buy must always be at a price lower than the current market price; limit orders to sell must always be at a price higher than the current market price. An example shows why customers place limit orders. Let us suppose that a customer believes that a stock's true value is $40, but the stock is currently trading at $45. This customer can place a limit order to buy at $40. If the price of the stock declines to the level that the customer thinks it is worth, the broker will buy it; if it does not, no trade will occur. The disadvantages of limit orders are that a person can miss the market (that is, never buy a stock that is rising because the limit price is too far below the market price) and will have difficulty in deciding at what price to set the limit. See George A. Christy and John C. Clendenin, *Introduction to Investments,* 7th ed., McGraw-Hill, New York, 1978.

linear programming   A mathematical technique of optimizing (maximizing or minimizing) linear objective functions subject to constraints in the form of linear inequalities. It is designed to select from among alternative courses of action the one most likely to achieve a desired goal, such as producing a product or group of products at the lowest possible cost. A decision-making tool of business management, linear programming has been employed on a variety of problems, ranging from the selection of the ingredients appropriate to producing the cheapest cattle feed of a given nutritional value to the determination of profitable sites for plant location. See William J. Baumol,

Economic Theory and Operations Analysis, 4th ed., Prentice-Hall, Englewood Cliffs, N.J., 1977; for the classic reference, see George B. Dantzig, *Linear Programming and Extensions,* Rand Corporation Research Studies, Santa Monica, Calif., 1963.

linkage   The ability of one industry to induce the establishment and growth of other industries. It develops through the interdependence of inputs (raw materials) and outputs (semifinished or finished goods). The first industry buys inputs that can be made by other domestic industries instead of being imported (the effect that this inducement has on other domestic industries is called backward linkage). It can sell some or all of its output to other domestic industries for use in production instead of exporting it or selling it as a finished product (the effect that this inducement has on other domestic industries is called forward linkage). An example of an industry with both backward and forward linkage is the iron and steel industry. It creates a market for such raw materials as iron ore and coal for other industries, such as machinery and power, and the iron and steel which it makes can be used by other domestic industries in their production. See C. P. Kindleberger and P. H. Lindert, *International Economics,* 3d ed., McGraw-Hill, New York, 1977.

liquidity   The ability of an individual, group, business, or any organization to meet its financial obligations. Liquidity is usually measured by examining the organization's balance sheet and relating some or all of its current assets to some or all of its current liabilities. For example, the current ratio (current assets to current liability) is a measure of a firm's liquidity. Or, in the case of a commercial bank, the ratio of loans to deposits is the most commonly used measure of bank liquidity. Liquidity is, however, a nebulous concept. Fundamentally, a firm's liquidity rests not so much on its balance sheet as on whether or not it is doing well and earning money. A strong balance sheet with a large current ratio simply postpones liquidity problems for a short while if the firm is losing money. Moreover, liquidity is a relative concept because there is no specific level of any balance-sheet ratio that indicates that the firm is no longer liquid. For instance, what is considered a dangerous loan-deposit ratio has changed over time, varies in different countries in the world, and ultimately depends on what bank managers and the monetary authorities *think* is too high. For additional information, see J. Fred Weston and Eugene F. Brigham, *Essentials of Managerial Finance,* 5th ed., Holt, Rinehart and Winston, New York, 1979.

liquidity preference   The desire to hold cash or checking accounts rather than assets, such as stocks and bonds, that earn a return and are less easy to convert to cash. There are three motives for liquidity preference: the transactions motive, or the common desire to have a supply of money available to carry out everyday transactions; the precautionary motive, or the need to keep a cash reserve for emergencies; and the speculative motive, or the belief that interest rates may rise, thereby reducing the value of earning assets. If only the last motive is affected by public policy, it may be futile for the monetary authorities to raise interest rates in times of a business recession in order to reduce liquidity preference and bring a larger amount of funds into the capital markets. Instead, John Maynard Keynes suggested a policy of low interest rates, which, by encouraging capital investments and quickened business activity, would support the general level of demand for production and output of goods, thus reducing the danger of falling prices and countering the speculative motive. The notion of liquidity preference is important at times when people decide to hold liquid assets rather than make investments because it is then that investment funds are likely to shrink and capital investment to decline. In the inflationary atmosphere of the post-World War II years, liquidity preference has not been a problem. The American public has proved to be very conscious of interest-rate levels: it has shifted large sums of savings to California savings institutions that offer a higher return than their eastern counterparts, and it has given unprecedented support to individual government-security issues that have promised a high return. For a more detailed discussion, see Paul A. Samuelson, *Economics,* 11th ed., McGraw-Hill, New York, 1980; J. M. Keynes, *The General Theory of Employment, Interest, and Money,* Harcourt Brace, New York, 1963.

liquidity trap In liquidity-preference theory, the idea that at some low interest rate, the speculative demand for money becomes infinitely elastic. John Maynard Keynes argued that it is possible that if the interest rate declined to, say, 2%, people would be on the margin, indifferent between holding bonds or money. Thus, interest rates could fall no lower because no one would purchase bonds at the implied higher prices. If the economy were caught in the liquidity trap, monetary policy would be ineffective. The monetary authorities could expand the money supply during a depression, which tends to lower interest rates and therefore encourages investment and consumer spending. But if interest rates dropped low enough to reach the liquidity-trap level, further increases in the money supply would not lower rates any further and would simply pile up as idle bank balances. (See figure on page 206.) For additional information, see John Maynard Keynes, *The General Theory of Employment, Interest, and Money,* Macmillan, New York, 1936; Gardner Ackley, *Macroeconomics: Theory and Policy.* Macmillan, New York, 1978.

listed security A stock or bond that has been registered with a stock exchange and is eligible for trading on that exchange. Corporations that want to list their securities on an exchange must meet its listing requirements and comply with all its rules and regulations. Of the thirteen stock exchanges in the United States, the New York Stock Exchange has the most stringent listing requirements. Its requirements are such that only large corporations, the stock of which is widely held and which have demonstrated earning power, are eligible for listing. The other exchanges have similar but less

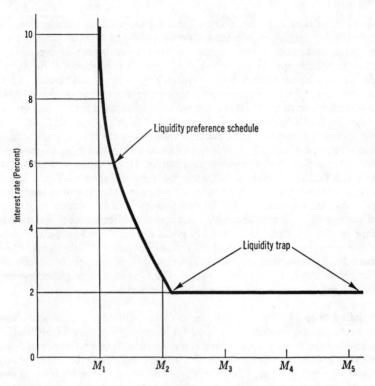

stringent listing requirements. Corporations list their securities on stock exchanges because (1) they want to broaden the market for their securities, (2)
capital might be raised more cheaply if the company were more widely known,
and (3) corporations like the prestige attached to having their stock traded on
a national exchange. As of December 31, 1979, about 3,400 issues of preferred
and common stock and 3,212 bonds were listed on the stock exchanges of
the United States. Of these, 2,195 stocks and 2,939 bonds were listed on the
New York Stock Exchange. For further information, see Securities and Exchange Commission, *Annual Reports;* George A. Christy and John C. Clendenin, *Introduction to Investments,* 7th ed., McGraw-Hill, New York, 1978.

loanable funds   The supply of funds available to the money market. It
consists of three parts: current savings; dishoarding, i.e., a decrease in cash
balances; and any increase in the money supply. The demand for such funds
is made up of dissavings by consumers, representing the financing of consumption expenditures from idle balances previously accumulated and from
newly created bank credit; hoarding, representing the increase in idle balances;
and investment demand. The loanable-funds theory of interest is based on

the relationship between the demand and the supply of these funds. According to this theory, the interest rate fluctuates with the relative supply of, and demand for, funds available for lending. For a brief description of the loanable-funds analysis, see Lawrence S. Ritter and William L. Silber, *Principles of Money, Banking and Financial Markets,* 3d rev. ed., Basic Books, New York, 1980; for major criticisms of the theory and for a treatment of loanable funds as opposed to liquidity-preference theories, see W. W. Smith, "Monetary Theories of the Rate of Interest: A Dynamic Analysis," *Review of Economics and Statistics,* vol. 40, 1958, pp. 15–21.

loanable-funds theory of interest   *See* **loanable funds.**

location theory   An economic theory of the factors influencing the location of firms. According to the analysis of location theory, firms will locate at the point at which their total transportation costs are minimized, all other things being equal. A firm's transportation costs include the procurement costs of materials and the distribution costs of finished products. Whereas procurement costs can be reduced by moving the plant closer to supplies, distribution costs are lowered by moving the plant closer to a point with good access to markets. Since these two considerations are likely to point in different directions, the producer must balance the relative advantages of each cost factor in deciding on the location for the plant. In some instances, the problem is simple; for example, the location of agriculture and mining is determined by the location of the relevant resources. Similarly, selling and many other services must be located near purchasers. In manufacturing, however, the determination of the optimum location is more complex. If the manufacturing process results in a considerable loss of weight or some other lowering of distribution costs in relation to procurement costs (e.g., smelting or cotton ginning), it is cheaper to locate the plant near the source of the raw material. On the other hand, if the finished product may spoil or if transportation costs for the product are relatively high (e.g., bread or compressed gases), the firm will locate its plant closer to the market. For a more complete exposition of location theory, see Melvin L. Greenhut and H. Ohta, *Theory of Spatial Pricing and Market Areas,* Duke University Press, Durham, N.C., 1975.

locked-in capital   Securities which the owner has held for six months or more and continues to hold because they have greatly appreciated in value and because, if they were sold, the realized capital gain would be subject to tax. In seeking reductions in the U.S. capital gains tax, the New York Stock Exchange argues that the rate of the tax deters many investors who have unrealized capital gains from selling their securities. This factor immobilizes capital movements (particularly after periods of rising prices) and accentuates stock price movements, both of which are detrimental to the public interest. Critics argue that many investors retain securities for investment and not for tax reasons; that there is no evidence that price movements are accentuated because of the capital gains tax and available data indicate that the opposite might be true; and that, even though some persons are "locked in," they are actually insulated from the tax because the gain will never be taxed unless they sell before they die. See Richard A. Musgrave and Peggy B. Musgrave, *Public Finance in Theory and Practice,* 2d ed., McGraw-Hill, New York, 1975.

lockout A device by which an employer refuses to admit workers to their jobs. The antithesis of a strike, the lockout is used primarily to avert a threatened strike. Employers rarely resort to a lockout. At the expiration of an agreement, employers can always announce their terms unilaterally and give the union the choices of striking, reaching an agreement, or working without an agreement during further negotiations. Almost the only occasion for a true lockout arises when a union calls for a strike against a member of an employers' association; the other emloyers may then close down their plants to support the struck employer. The term lockout and others referring to various forms of work stoppages are grouped under the heading strike. See Lloyd G. Reynolds, *Labor Economics and Labor Relations,* 7th ed., Prentice-Hall, Englewood Cliffs, N.J., 1978.

logarithmic chart A graph in which one or both axes are scaled in terms of logarithms. Where only the vertical scale is so scaled, the graph is known as semilogarithmic. Where both axes are scaled in terms of logarithms, the graph is known as double-logarithmic. In both cases, natural numbers are plotted on the logarithmic grids. This method of plotting is used to depict relative changes in statistical variables since equal slopes mean equal rates of change. For additional information, see John E. Freund and Frank J. Williams, *Elementary Business Statistics,* 3d ed., Prentice-Hall, Englewood Cliffs, N.J., 1978.

logarithmic transformation The conversion of a statistical variable stated in natural numbers into the logarithms of those numbers. This transformation is frequently used in statistics to reduce a curvilinear relationship to a linear relationship in regression analysis. For additional information, see Gerhard Tintner and Charles B. Millham, *Mathematics and Statistics for Economists,* Holt, Rinehart and Winston, New York, 1970.

long run A period of time that is long enough for a firm to vary all factors of production. In the short run, a producer can vary its output only by using its existing plant and equipment more or less intensively; it cannot adjust the size, or scale, of the plant and equipment. In the long run, however, a firm can change its output not only by using existing plant and equipment more or less intensively, but also by altering the scale of the plant. For example, a firm plans to build a new plant and purchase new equipment. This is a long-run situation because the firm can vary the scale of the plant and other factors of production to achieve the optimum size for anticipated output. Once the plant has been finished, costs of building and equipping it are fixed, and variation in output is limited by the plant scale. The concept of the long run is important to microeconomic theory because the "equilibrium" in much of the analysis occurs only in the long run. See Alfred Marshall, *Principles of Economics,* St. Martin's Press, New York, 1956; Donald S. Watson and Mary A. Holman, *Price Theory and Its Uses,* 4th ed., Houghton Mifflin, Boston, 1976.

long-term forecast A business forecast which extends at least five years ahead of the current period, although such a forecast is often made for a period extending as far ahead as fifteen years. Thus, a forecast using 1982 data as the starting point could extend to 1997. Long-term forecasts are not as popular with business economists as those for the short-term outlook, but they are more popular than medium-term forecasts. A 1962 survey of the membership of the National Association of Business Economists showed that 72% of those who made forecasts projected long-term prospects, 66% prepared medium-term forecasts, and 95% assessed the short-term outlook. One reason why fewer economists prepare long-term projections than short-term outlooks is that the former are of less immediate importance to their companies. Moreover, in long-term projections a small error accumulated over five, ten, or fifteen years can seriously affect the estimate. In the 1962 survey of business economists, most used the historical trend for long-term forecasts. Judgment was the second-ranking method, and the full-employment approach was the third-ranking method in terms of usefulness for long-term forecasting.

Lorenz curve A curve used in depicting the nature of any distribution— wealth, for example. It is, however, usually used in depicting the income distribution of a country. As shown in the illustration on page 210, the Lorenz curve is derived by plotting the cumulative proportion of people (ranked from the poorest up) against the cumulative share of total income which they receive. If there were perfect equality in the distribution of income, with everyone receiving the same amount of money, the Lorenz curve would be a 45° straight line. On the other hand, for the hypothetical case of absolute inequality, with one person earning all the income, the Lorenz curve would form the bottom and right side of the square. Any actual income distribution falls between these two hypothetical extremes and is thus represented by a sagging line. The greater the sag of the Lorenz curve, the greater the inequality of the income distribution. A statistical method of stating the degree of inequality shown by the Lorenz curve is to divide the area between the curve and the diagonal (A in the illustration) by the total area under the diagonal (A plus B). This measure, the proportion of the triangular area which is between the curve and the diagonal, is known as the Lorenz coefficient or the Gini index. See James N. Morgan et al., *Income and Welfare in the United*

**Lorenz Curves for Some
Measures of Income**

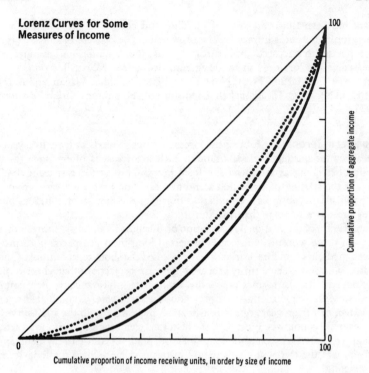

Cumulative proportion of aggregate income

Cumulative proportion of income receiving units, in order by size of income

States, McGraw-Hill, New York, 1962, chap. 20; M. Bronfenbrenner, *Income Distribution Theory,* Aldine, Atherton, Chicago, 1971.

Luddite   One of a group of English rioters who, between 1811 and 1816, attacked and destroyed much of the machinery introduced by manufacturers on the ground that it was causing economic distress and unemployment. The term is now sometimes used in an invidious sense to characterize a person who opposes the introduction of automated or other advanced types of machinery.

macroeconomics Modern economic analysis that is concerned with data in aggregate as opposed to individual form. It concerns itself with an overall view of economic life, considering the total size, shape, and functioning of economic experience rather than the workings of individual parts. More specifically, macroeconomics involves the analysis of the general price level rather than the prices of individual commodities, national output or income rather than the income of the individual firm, and total employment rather than employment in an individual firm. For further information on macroeconomics, see Gardner Ackley, *Macroeconomics: Theory and Policy,* Macmillan, New York, 1978; Thomas F. Dernburg and Duncan M. McDougall, *Macroeconomics,* 5th ed., McGraw-Hill, New York, 1976; R. J. Gordon, *Macroeconomic Productivity,* Harper & Row, New York, 1969.

Malthusian doctrine The theory, developed by Thomas Robert Malthus, a British economist and clergyman, that the world's population tends to increase faster than its means of subsistence. In *An Essay on the Principles of Population,* published in 1798, Malthus said that population tends to grow at a geometric rate (for example, 1, 2, 4, 8, 16), while the food supply grows only in arithmetic progression (1, 2, 3, 4, 5). He argued that only the positive checks of vice, pestilence, famine, and wars could curb the tendency of population to outstrip the food supply. In a later edition of his essay, however, he placed less emphasis on precise growth ratios and suggested that preventive checks (continence and late marriage) could help alleviate the problem. Malthus's gloomy prediction has not come to pass in the industrial nations of the world because of rapid increases in agricultural productivity and the tendency of upper-income groups voluntarily to limit the size of their families. Many Asian, African, and Latin American countries, however, still have difficulty in expanding agricultural production as fast as their population grows. Malthus has been attacked from many sides, but the post-World War II population explosion has revived interest in his ideas even in advanced industrial countries. For additional information, see Mancur Olson and Hans H. Landsberg (eds.), *The No-Growth Society,* Norton, New York, 1973.

Manchester school A school of classical economic thought which emphasized free trade. It arose in England in the middle of the nineteenth century because of the Corn Laws. The primary interest of its leaders, Richard Cobden and John Bright, was the repeal of the Corn Laws and eventual free trade for England. Because Manchester was the center of opposition to these laws, the English economists who believed in this reform were called the Manchester school. This group advocated laissez faire, or completely unhampered private initiative and competition, as the best means of achieving prosperity and growth. They opposed the commercial policy of protection, public care of the poor, the Factory Acts, compulsory education, and similar measures. For additional details, see W. D. Grampp, *The Manchester School of Economics,* Stanford University Press, Stanford, Calif., 1960.

manufacturing industry A general term encompassing all plants, companies, and industries which produce or assemble manufactured goods. Manufacturing industry is generally broken down into two major categories, durable goods and nondurable goods. The single most important industry in the United States, manufacturing ranks first in number of employees, capital investment, and contributions to the national income. Nevertheless, it has been declining in relative importance. For additional information, see Gunnar Alexandersson, *Geography of Manufacturing,* Prentice-Hall, Englewood Cliffs, N.J., 1967.

Maoism The application of Marxism-Leninism to the Chinese Revolution and the contemporary international scene, developed chiefly by Mao Tsetung. Mao's notion follows the usual Marxist idea of modifying the economic base and superstructure and also emphasizes the progressive role given the peasant in the revolutionary dynamics and the exploitation of naturalistic and patriotic values and sentiments. His strategy includes prominent egalitarian, populist, and voluntarist elements. Maoism considers people more significant than machines in the process of making China a powerful industrial society. In its economic aspects, Maoism evolved into a clearly definable model by 1966, after rejecting the Soviet model in the late 1950s. Because of China's dearth of capital, scarce arable land, and abundant but unskilled labor force, agriculture was given the highest priority. Heavy industry and other sectors were to grow along with agriculture and to economically make use of scarce capital resources. New capital was allocated through state budget revenue-sharing, with advanced capital accumulators feeding capital to backward ones. Labor was tightly controlled and allocated by a placement system rather than the payment of wages. After Mao's death in 1976, the model was modified by Mao's adversaries, who favored mechanizing agriculture before collectivization. For economists, the Maoist model provokes a range of questions relating to growth theory, labor allocation, industrial organization, and planning. For additional information, see John R. Gurley, *China's Economy and the Maoist Strategy,* Monthly Review Press, New York, 1976.

marginal cost The additional cost that a producer incurs by making one additional unit of output. If, for example, total costs were $13,000 when a firm was producing two machine tools per day and $18,000 when it was producing three machine tools per day, the marginal cost of producing one machine tool was $5,000. The marginal cost may be the same, higher, or lower in moving from three to four machine tools. The concept of marginal cost plays a key role in determining the quantity of goods that a firm chooses to produce. The purely competitive firm, which faces a given price set in the market, increases its output until marginal cost equals price. That point is the firm's best-profit output point. The imperfectly competitive firm equates marginal cost to marginal revenue (additional revenue) to obtain the highest profits. For most firms, marginal costs decline for a while and then begin to rise. The pattern of the marginal-cost graph depends on the nature of the firm's production function and the prices of the goods that it buys. Understandably, if a firm grows to a very large size relative to its industry, its purchasing decisions may strongly influence the prices of the goods that it buys. The emphasis placed in the United States on maintaining competition is due in large part to the efficiency of a firm that equates marginal costs to price. Only when a firm so equates marginal cost is it producing as much as possible for society from the relatively scarce resources of labor and capital that are available. George J. Stigler, *The Theory of Price,* 3d ed., Macmillan, New York, 1966, presents a complete explanation of the way in which marginal costs depend on the production function; see also William J. Baumol, *Economic Theory and Operations Research,* 4th ed., Prentice-Hall, Englewood Cliffs, N.J., 1977; Fritz Machlup, *The Economics of Sellers' Competition,* Johns Hopkins Press, Baltimore, 1952.

marginal cost of acquisition (marginal-factor cost) The additional cost to a purchaser when buying one more productive factor. When a buyer purchases a good in a highly competitive market (one with many small buyers and sellers, each of whom is too insignificant to influence the price), the additional cost of purchasing one more unit of the product remains constant. For example, if bolts are selling at $3.73 per gross, the additional cost of purchasing an additional gross will remain $3.73. If, on the other hand, the market is not characterized by many small buyers and sellers, sellers may demand a higher price as they sell additional items. In this case, the additional cost of buying a unit rises. Since perfect competition is a relatively rare phenomenon, it is not surprising that price increases as demand rises over the course of a business cycle and, conversely, that the prices of many items tend to decline as the quantity sold decreases. The theoretical concept of the rising marginal cost of acquisition is usually associated with monopsony (a market structure with a single buyer of a commodity or service). Obviously a single buyer of a good or service influences the market considerably, and will tend to restrict the amount bought in order to keep costs down. The monopsonist will equate the marginal cost of acquisition of goods with marginal revenue.

For an elementary treatment of the concept, see Donald S. Watson and Mary A. Holman, *Price Theory and Its Uses*, 4th ed., Houghton Mifflin, Boston, 1976.

marginal-factor cost *See* **marginal cost of acquisition.**

marginal-productivity theory of wages A theory that explains the overall level of wages and wages in different industries with reference to (1) the additional output that can be produced by adding one more worker (the marginal productivity of labor) and (2) the number of workers. It is based on the assumption that employers, in order to make the greatest possible profit, will hire additional workers at any given wage as long as the value added to the total product by the additional worker is at least equal to that worker's wage. In this theory, wages can rise through (1) reductions in the number of workers or (2) increases in the marginal productivity of labor, which may arise through higher worker skills, increases in the quantity of capital used in production, or technological improvements. Thus, unlike the earlier subsistence and wages-fund theories, the marginal-productivity theory allows for short- and long-run increases in both wages and the number of workers. The theory has been subject to two widespread criticisms: (1) It assumes perfect competition in the labor and product markets. (2) It is a partial-equilibrium analysis. Adherents of the theory, however, argue that both the theory and the analytical techniques used in conjunction with it are fully capable of dealing with monopoly and unemployment. For the classical statement of the theory, see John Bates Clark, *The Distribution of Wealth,* Kelley and Millman, New York, 1956; for another discussion, see J. R. Hicks, *The Theory of Wages,* Macmillan, London, 1932; for a detailed description of the analytical techniques employed in the theory, see Donald S. Watson and Mary A. Holman, *Price Theory and Its Uses,* 4th ed., Houghton Mifflin, Boston, 1976.

marginal revenue The additional revenue that a seller receives from putting one more unit of output on the market. The price, obviously, is the average revenue that the seller receives. The following table indicates the manner in which marginal, or additional, revenue is calculated:

Price	Number sold	Total receipts	Marginal revenue (additional receipts)
$3	2	$ 6	
4	3	12	6
5	4	20	8
6	5	30	10

The marginal-revenue concept is important because producers maximize profits (and minimize losses) when they continue to produce until their marginal revenue equals the additional cost of producing an additional unit of output. This is the profit-maximization point for any firm in any type of industry structure. The logic is obvious: if it costs $5 more to produce a good and only an additional $3 will be received, no producer who is intent on making a profit will produce the additional unit. See Donald S. Watson and Mary A. Holman, *Price Theory and Its Uses,* 4th ed., Houghton Mifflin, Boston, 1976.

marginal-revenue product (marginal-value product) The additional amount of revenue produced by using one additional unit of a productive resource while holding other productive inputs at the same level. The additional amount of receipts depends on two factors: (1) the amount of additional output that the additional resource helps produce and (2) the selling price. If the selling firm is not in a perfectly competitive industry, it faces a downward-sloping demand curve, which means that as it sells additional output, the price that it receives will fall. To maximize profits, a firm will hire additional productive resources (human and material) as long as the amount added to receipts is greater than the amount added to cost. See Donald S. Watson and Mary A. Holman, *Price Theory and Its Uses,* 4th ed., Houghton Mifflin, Boston, 1976.

marginal utility The additional satisfaction that a purchaser derives from buying an additional unit of a commodity or service. Since the unit of measurement is different for each individual (as different as the various moods of a single individual), marginal utility is a psychological phenomenon rather than an objectively measurable concept. To induce consumers to buy larger quantities of a good, the price must be lowered, other things remaining the same. The notion of diminishing marginal utility is an often-cited explanation (among others) for the downward-sloping demand curve. The hypothesis is that consumers receive less and less additional satisfaction from buying more and more of a particular commodity. The observed necessity for lower prices to induce buyers to make additional purchases would be expected if consumers received less and less additional satisfaction from additional purchases. Relatively little use is now made of the marginal-utility concept in economic theory. Another approach, in which it is assumed that any consumer can recognize the combinations of various goods that render the same satisfaction (the indifference-curve approach), now finds favor in advanced price theory. For further information, see Alfred Marshall, *Principles of Economics,* St. Martin's Press, New York, 1956; see also George J. Stigler, *The Theory of Price,* 3d ed., Macmillan, New York, 1966.

marginal-value product *See* **marginal-revenue product.**

margin requirement That part of the total purchase price of securities which must be put up in cash. Because excessive use of credit was one of the factors that led to the stock-market crash in 1929, the Congress of the United States empowered the Federal Reserve Board to limit the amount of borrowed funds that can be used to purchase and carry securities. The Board prescribes the maximum-loan value (the amount of money that can be borrowed as a percentage of the purchase price of the security) of securities registered with the Securities and Exchange Commission (SEC). Obviously, this amount also sets the minimum amount of cash that must be put up when buying securities. The Board changes the maximum-loan value as conditions warrant. For example, if borrowings to purchase securities are increasing, the Board may lower the loan value (raise margins) of securities; conversely, if borrowings are decreasing, it may raise the loan value (reduce margins) of securities. Since the beginning of 1974, the margin requirement for stocks has been 50%, and the margin for convertible bonds has been 60%. Although the Federal Reserve Board does not set margins on securities exempted from registration with the SEC (municipal bonds and U.S. government securities), the New York Stock Exchange sets a margin of 5% on U.S. government securities and 15% on municipal bonds. In addition to this official and semi-official regulation of credit, many brokerage houses set higher margin requirements on some securities. For further information, see George L. Leffler and L. C. Farwell, *The Stock Market*, 3d ed., Ronald, New York, 1963.

market-directed economy A mode of economic organization in which the forces of supply and demand are relied upon to solve the problems of the selection of which goods to produce, the method of producing them, and the persons who will receive them once they have been produced. For example, in the United States supply and demand, supported by individual initiative, self-interest, and the state of technology, determine how many automobiles will be produced in relation to the number of refrigerators, the production techniques that will be employed, and the relative incomes of the people and capital used in production. The United States is thus primarily a market-directed economy. Nevertheless, there are in the United States many elements of non-market-directed activity, such as the output of numerous agricultural products, which is determined by government-decreed acreage allotments and price supports.

marketing research (market research) The systematic gathering, recording, computing, and analyzing of data about problems relating to the sale and distribution of goods and services for certain time periods. It includes various types of research, such as the size of the potential market and potential sales volume, the selection of the consumers most apt to purchase the products, and the advertising media most likely to stimulate their purchases. Marketing research has been developed as a tool to aid management in solving its increasingly difficult and complex problems. Research may be carried out by business firms, consultants to business firms, or impartial agencies. Nearly every medium-sized and large corporation in the United States has a market research department or an individual who is responsible for market research. For additional information, see Robert Ferber, *Handbook of Marketing Research,* McGraw-Hill, New York, 1974; John G. Myers, William F. Massy, and Stephen E. Greyser, *Marketing Research and Knowledge Development: An Assessment for Marketing Management,* Prentice-Hall, Englewood Cliffs, N.J., 1980.

market share The ratio of a company's sales, in units or dollars, to total industry sales, in units or dollars, on either an actual basis or a potential basis for a specific time period. For example, General Motors' share of the U.S. passenger-car market, in units, was 40% in 1980. In order to increase their market shares, companies often carry out sustained advertising campaigns or expand their sales forces. Obviously, if General Motors planned to increase its 1980 share of 40% to a potential share of 60% by 1986, it would have to devote a greater amount of time and money to selling and advertising than it did before, or it would have to introduce new products which would have an extraordinarily high consumer acceptance in relation to its competitors' new products. See Louis E. Boone and David L. Kurtz, *Contemporary Marketing,* 3d ed., Dryden Press, Hinsdale, Ill., 1980.

market structure The organizational characteristics of an economic market. The most important organizational aspects are those which influence the nature of competition and pricing within the market. Perhaps the key element in the structure of a market is the degree of seller concentration, or the number and size distribution of the sellers. The number of sellers may be one (monopoly), few (oligopoly), or many (atomism), and the sellers may be relatively equal in size or unequal, with a few large firms and many small ones. Just as the degree of seller concentration affects the intensity and effectiveness of competition among the sellers, another important factor, the degree of buyer concentration, influences the nature of buyer competition. The degree of product differentiation, or the degree to which buyers can distinguish the quality, design, reputation, etc., of the products of different sellers, is another important element in market structure. The more homogeneous the products of different sellers, the more vigorous the price competition can be expected to be. The barriers to entry, characterizing the advantage that established producers have over potential entrants, also play a role in determining the effect of potential competition on the market conduct of sellers. For additional details on the actual market structures of American industry, see Walter Adams (ed.), *The Structure of American Industry,* 5th ed., Macmillan, New York, 1977.

markup The difference between the cost and the selling price of an article. It may be expressed as a dollar amount or as a percentage of cost or retail price. In retailing, the markup is usually based on the retail price. Thus, if an article sold for $8 and the cost was $5, the markup would be 3/8, or 37.5%. Based on cost, the markup would be 3/5, or 60%.

Marshallian economics   A school of economics named after Alfred Marshall, who was professor of economics at Cambridge University in England from 1884 to 1908, generally regarded as the founder of Cambridge economics. Marshallian economics has been described as neoclassical. It is not to be regarded as a set of theories or hypotheses to explain the working of a market or capitalist system; rather, it is a framework within which economies can operate. Marshall emphasized that an economic system is one of perpetual change and evolution. There are two basic notions which are the hallmark of Marshallian economics and which remain basic to contemporary economics. The first is his concept of the breaking down of complex interrelationships and the second is his handling of time. For additional information, see Mark Blaug, *Economic Theory in Retrospect,* 3d ed., Cambridge University Press, London, 1978, chaps. 9 and 10.

Marxism   Originating with Karl Marx, a social science representing a unified set of principles and policies concerning philosophy, history, economics, sociology, and political science. Marx viewed society as one unified organism having political, economic, and other aspects. Marxism is completely opposed to economic determinism, which maintains that the superstructure is determined by the economic base but denies that the base is also determined by the superstructure. According to Marxism, on the other hand, the superstructure of ideas and sociopolitical institutions fully determines the economic base. Marxists look to a future of classless, strifeless society reached by a series of economic stages. In its early stage of socialism, there is cooperative or collective ownership but there are still differential wages according to the level of work done. In the latter stage of communism, there are collective ownership and collective use according to need. One of Marx's basic theories deals with surplus value, which is the worth of a product over and above the value of the worker's wage. In a capitalistic economy, this surplus value becomes the source of all profits, rent, and interest. According to Marx, the capitalist system causes poverty not only because employers pay low wages but also because periodic depressions occur along with high unemployment. For additional information, see Karl Marx, *Capital,* 3d ed., International Publishers, New York, 1972.

mass production (large-scale production)   The use of technology and mechanization to turn out a large volume of standardized products. A large volume of production permits the efficient application of modern technology and the division of the productive process into a number of steps that can be mechanized. The economies of mass production are realized by substituting cost-cutting machinery for high-priced labor. Mass-production methods are used in industries in which the product and production process can be standardized and the market is large enough to absorb the high volume of output. Mass-production techniques were first applied in the automobile industry in the early twentieth century. Since then, nearly every large-output industry has adopted mass-production methods in one form or another. Postwar advances in mass-production technology include transfer machines, which automatically move parts from one machine to another, and automatic-control and feedback devices for the self-regulating control of the production process. For further information, see William G. Shepherd, *The Economics of Industrial Organization*, Prentice-Hall, Englewood Cliffs, N.J., 1979.

materialistic concept of history   *See* **economic interpretation of history.**

matrix   A rectangular array of economic data written in columns and rows, in which the rows represent the distribution of an economic variable, such as output, and the columns represent the distribution of another economic variable, such as input. A column vector is a matrix with one column, and a row vector is a matrix with only one row. The matrix is simply a device to facilitate the study and solution of problems, such as the investigation of the importance of steel in the production of machinery.

mature economy   An economy that has reached the final stage of growth, in which the rate of population increase begins to decline, a greater-than-average proportion of the national income is devoted to consumer exenditure, and a smaller-than-average proportion is devoted to business investment. Specifically, three things happen when a nation moves toward maturity: (1) The working force changes it composition. In the underdeveloped stage of an economy, about 80% of a nation's population is engaged in agriculture, living at a near-subsistence level; by the mature stage, this proportion has fallen below 20%. Along with a shift to an industrial, urban population in a mature economy, there is an increase in the level of skill and education of the workers. (2) The nation's leaders change from rugged individualists to an efficient managerial class and a bureaucratic machine. (3) The outlook of society changes from one of the individual's pride in the quality of work to one of complacency toward industrial and scientific advances. The chief question that faces the mature economy is the use of its wealth. For further information, see Walt W. Rostow, *The Stages of Economic Growth: A Non-Communist Manifesto*, 2d ed., Cambridge University Press, New York, 1971.

mature-economy thesis   *See* **secular-stagnation thesis.**

maturity   The date at which a loan, bond, note, etc., comes due and must be repaid in full by the borrower. Most securities have a definite maturity date (e.g., ninety days, one year, ten years), but common stocks (equities) have no maturity date, since they represent ownership rather than indebtedness. Securities which have only a short time before maturing are considered more liquid than those with longer maturities, and short-term interest rates are thus lower than long-term rates. Securities maturing in the near future also present less risk, since a change in interest rates will cause a smaller price change than in longer-term securities, and they will thus be less affected by future contingencies. For these reasons, the shorter the maturity of a bill or bond, the less it will fluctuate in market value. As a bond approaches maturity, however, its value approaches its original face value. At redemption, the maturity value of a security equals its face value plus any unpaid interest. For additional details, see George A. Christy and John C. Clendenin, *Introduction to Investments,* 7th ed., McGraw-Hill, New York, 1978.

maximum-likelihood method A method of estimating a parameter of a population that maximizes the probability of a sample. The maximum-likelihood criterion is based on the assumptions that the most likely factor or factors have generated the most probable sample and that the parameters of a relationship are unknown constants. The likelihood function reveals what values of the parameter (or parameters) attach the greatest probability to an observed event and the degree of reliability of such values. For additional information, see Karl A. Fox and Tej K. Kaul, *Intermediate Economic Statistics,* Krieger, Melbourne, Fla., 1980.

means test The requirement that applicants for public assistance must prove their need before they become eligible to receive benefits. The needy must present adequate proof that they are unable to provide even a meager living for themselves and their families. The purpose of the means test is to establish the existence of need as defined by law and to determine the amount of benefit necessary to relieve that need. It is argued that the means test, used in many states of the United States for the distribution of public relief, is degrading to individuals in that it treats them as second-class citizens. There has, however, been a trend toward administering the means test in a more humane way; individual circumstances are investigated, and the applicants are not required to exhaust all their savings or to sell their homes before becoming eligible for assistance. The means test is not used in programs of social insurance, such as the social security program in the United States, the benefits of which are considered a right of the individual whether the individual is shown to be in need or not. For further information, see Eveline M. Burns, *Social Security and Public Policy,* Arno, New York, 1976.

mediation (conciliation) The intervention of a third party in collective bargaining. Usually, mediation is performed by a governmental agency whose purpose is to keep discussion moving constructively, to achieve a resumption of discussion if it has broken down, to search for areas of agreement, or to devise compromises and induce both sides to accept them. This is the weakest form of intervention, for the mediator has no power to force a settlement.

The U.S. government provides most of its mediation services through an independent agency, the Federal Mediation and Conciliation Service, which was established in 1947 under the Taft-Hartley Act. This agency can intervene at the request of either party or on its own motion, although its intervention is mandatory under the emergency provision of the act. The Railway Labor Act provides for a three-person national mediation board to handle disputes over new contract terms. Most states and even some larger municipalities provide analogous services on the local level. For further information, see Gordon F. Bloom and Herbert R. Northrup, *Economics of Labor Relations*, 8th ed., Irwin, Homewood, Ill., 1978.

medicare program   A nationwide health insurance program for the aged and for certain disabled persons. The program is a part of the nation's income maintenance system. It became effective on July 1, 1966. Medicare consists of two parts: part A, hospital insurance, and part B, supplementary medical insurance. The financing of part A is derived almost entirely from payroll taxes paid by workers covered under the social security program. Persons insured under part B pay premiums amounting to less than one-third the costs of benefits and program administration; the balance is paid for by general revenues. To better meet the elderly population's out-of-pocket expenses, legislators have developed proposals to expand coverage through different methods of paying physicians and through a lowering of the 65-year age criterion. It has been suggested that a comprehensive national health insurance program would be the solution to medicare's expansion of coverage and financing issues. For additional information, see Richard H. Hoffman, *Medicare Issues and Problems,* paper for the National Commission on Social Security, Washington, D.C., December 1979.

medium-term forecast   A business forecast which extends from seven quarters to four years ahead of the current period. For example, a medium-term forecast made in July 1980 could cover the period from January 1982 through 1984. Forecasts for this time span are not as popular with business economists as those for short or long terms. A 1962 survey of the membership of the National Association of Business Economists showed that 66% of those who made forecasts prepared one for medium-term prospects, 72% projected long-term prospects, and 95% assessed the short-term outlook. One reason for the lack of popularity of the medium-term business forecast is that in times of rising business activity economists must pinpoint the next recession, and in times of declining business activity they must pinpoint the beginning of recovery. The principal guide for medium-term forecasters is the indicator technique developed by the National Bureau of Economic Research, with particular emphasis on the duration and amplitude of business cycles. Judgment is given about as much importance among medium-term forecasters as the indicator method.

member bank A bank which is a member of the Federal Reserve System. All banks with national charters must belong to the Federal Reserve System, and banks with state charters may join if they are qualified for membership and are accepted by the System. To become a member bank, an individual bank must subscribe a fixed percentage of its capital and surplus to the capital stock of its district reserve bank, must maintain legal reserves on deposit at its reserve bank, honor checks drawn against it when presented for payment at the reserve bank, comply with federal banking laws, and, if it is a state bank, be subject to general supervision and examination by the Federal Reserve System. The privileges of a member bank include the right to borrow from Federal Reserve banks, to use Federal Reserve check-clearing facilities, to obtain currency when required, and to participate in the election of six out of nine of the regional Federal Reserve directors. For additional details, see Lawrence S. Ritter and William L. Silber, *Principles of Money, Banking and Financial Markets*, 3d rev. ed., Basic Books, New York, 1980.

mercantilism An economic policy, pursued by almost all the trading nations in the seventeenth and early eighteenth centuries, which aimed at increasing a nation's wealth and power by encouraging the export of goods in return for gold. As part of the program, individual governments promoted large investment in export industries, built high tariff walls to encourage import-competing industries, and, in several cases, prohibited the sales of precious metals to foreigners. Since one country's gold gain almost always meant a gold loss to one of its trading partners, not all nations could succeed at the same time in their ambition—a fact that sharpened trade rivalries. When successful, mercantilist policies generally resulted in the full employment of a country's resources and led to rapid economic growth. As the later classical economists pointed out, however, these policies also produced inflation and a low level of consumption. For an early statement of mercantilist doctrines, see Thomas Mun, *England's Treasure by Foreign Trade*, Doubleday, Garden City, N.Y., 1953; for Adam Smith's criticism of the mercantilists, see *The Wealth of Nations*, Random House, New York, 1937.

merger The acquisition of one corporation by another, in which the one survives while the other loses its corporate existence. Basically, there are three methods by which a merger occurs: (1) One company, A, may buy the assets of another company, B, with payment being made either in cash or in securities issued by the purchasing company. (2) The purchasing company, A, may buy B's stock, becoming a holding company for B, which continues to operate as a separate company. (3) The stock of A may be issued to the owners of B rather than to the corporation, with A acquiring the assets and liabilities of B and B dropping out of existence; this arrangement is called a statutory merger. A merger differs from a consolidation, in which a new company is formed and the consolidating corporations lose their separate identities. For further information, see J. Fred Weston and Eugene F. Brigham, *Essentials of Managerial Finance,* 5th ed., Holt, Rinehart and Winston, New York, 1979.

microeconomics Modern economic analysis concerned with data in individual form as opposed to aggregate form. It is concerned with the study of the individual firm rather than aggregates of firms, the individual consuming unit rather than the total population, and the individual commodity rather than total output. Microeconomics deals with the division of total output among industries, products, and firms and the allocation of resources among competing uses. It is concerned with the relative prices of particular goods and the problem of income distribution. For further information, see George J. Stigler, *The Theory of Price,* 3d ed., Macmillan, New York, 1966; James M. Henderson and Richard E. Quandt, *Microeconomic Theory: A Mathematical Approach,* 3d ed., McGraw-Hill, New York, 1980.

minimax principle The notion that when a choice must be made among several possible actions, the decision maker should look only at the worst possible consequence of each action and choose the action for which the worst consequence is least injurious. In this manner, the decision maker minimizes the maximum harm which could result from the various actions possible. In many cases, this principle would lead to actions which an executive would reject on the basis that they would violate good business judgment. For further discussion, see T. R. Dyckman, S. Smidt, and A. K. McAdams, *Management Decision Making under Uncertainty: An Introduction to Probability and Statistical Decision Theory,* Macmillan, London, 1969, pp. 251–254.

minimum standard of living The level of consumption at which only those goods and services which a person regards as absolutely necessary are purchased. For large groups, it is approximated by calculating their budgetary breakeven point, or the income at which no saving occurs. Any reduction in the level of living below the minimum standard is strongly resisted, and this factor is important in the depression phase of a business cycle. Thus, consumption will not drop as fast as incomes but will be maintained at the minimum level even if it involves reduced savings or dissavings. Each society has a different minimum standard of living, and as a society grows more affluent, this minimum standard rises. The minimum standard for a North American therefore differs from that for an African. See Eveline M. Burns, *Social Security and Public Policy,* Arno, New York, 1976.

minimum wage The lowest wage rate allowed in the United States by federal, state, or local law. It was instituted on the federal level by the Fair Labor Standards Act of 1938, commonly known as the Wage and Hour Act, which set the minimum wage at 25 cents per hour for workers in industry engaged in interstate commerce, exclusive of agriculture and a few other types of industry. By 1981 the minimum wage had reached $3.60 per hour. As of

1980, thirty-eight states, including the major industrial states, and the District of Columbia had minimum-wage laws applying to intrastate industries; these were generally lower than federal minimums. Minimum-wage rates are set to eliminate extremely low wages without unduly disrupting the general wage and price level of the economy. The immediate effect of a minimum-wage law is to raise labor costs in industries employing labor paid below the minimum. In an effort to maintain wage differentials, however, this is eventually followed by an increase in all wages. If higher wages induce management to substitute machinery for labor, some technological unemployment may result. See Lloyd G. Reynolds, *Labor Economics and Labor Relations,* 7th ed., Prentice-Hall, Englewood Cliffs, N.J., 1978.

mixed economy   An economic system in which characteristics of both capitalism and socialism can be found. In a mixed economic system, both public and private institutions exercise a degree of economic control. In most free-world industrial economies, a mixture of governmental industries and private industries exists in varying degrees. Even in the United States, where free enterprise dominates the economic system, many forms of government enterprise and direct control can be found. The Post Office and the Tennessee Valley Authority are both operated by the federal government, and public transportation facilities are owned and operated by state and local governments. Federal, state, and local regulatory agencies exercise direct controls over the operation of much of private enterprise, substantially restricting its freedom of action. For further information, see Paul A. Samuelson, *Economics,* 9th ed., McGraw-Hill, New York, 1973.

model   In econometrics, an equation or set of equations depicting the causal relationships that are believed to generate observed data. Also, the expression of a theory by means of mathematical symbols or diagrams. For detailed discussions and formulas of various specific economic models, consult Lawrence R. Klein, *An Introduction to Econometrics,* Greenwood, Westport, Conn., 1977.

moment matrix   A matrix consisting of second-order moments; a matrix whose *i*th row and *j*th column are the product moment of x_i and x_j. A moment matrix need not be square. The notation and form of matrix algebra in this and many other instances are extremely convenient in computations. For additional information, see Lawrence R. Klein, *An Introduction to Econometrics,* Greenwood, Westport, Conn., 1977.

monetary base   A monetary aggregate consisting of currency held by banks and by the public plus member-bank deposits at Federal Reserve banks. The base may also be viewed as Federal Reserve credit (security holdings, loans to member banks, and float) plus Treasury accounts, the gold stock, and miscellaneous Federal Reserve accounts. The expansion of the monetary base determines the potential growth rate of the money stock. For additional information, see Beryl W. Sprinkel, *Money and Markets,* Irwin, Homewood, Ill., 1971, pp. 65–67, 80–84.

monetary policy Management by a central bank of a nation's money supply to ensure the availability of credit in quantities and at prices consistent with specific national objectives. In the United States in the mid-twentieth century, monetary policy, which is under the direction of the Board of Governors of the Federal Reserve System, has, like fiscal policy, been directed toward achieving the twin goals of price stability and full employment. Frequently, however, measures adopted to achieve one of these objectives have hampered the efforts to achieve the other. In addition, the task of monetary policy has been complicated by the nation's balance-of-payments difficulties. Among the tools of monetary policy directly available to the Board of Governors are the authority to alter the level of currency reserves that commercial banks must keep on deposit at Federal Reserve banks against their own deposits and the authority to alter the discount rate which is the payment that commercial banks make for borrowing from the Federal Reserve System. See Milton Friedman and Walter W. Heller, *Monetary vs. Fiscal Policy: A Dialogue,* Norton, New York, 1969; Board of Governors of the Federal Reserve System, *The Federal Reserve System, Purposes and Functions,* 6th ed., Washington, D.C., 1974.

monetization of the debt The process of increasing currency in circulation by increasing the public debt. The debt becomes monetized when new securities issued by the government are purchased by the banking system to expand reserves. The debt can also be monetized to create a greater amount of credit in the economy by using the newly created bank reserves to support additional demand deposits. Whereas the first method of monetization permits an increase in the money supply equal to the size of the new debt, the expansion of bank credit permits a much greater increase in the money supply (five times as much with a reserve requirement of 20%). For additional details, see John F. Due and Ann F. Friedlaender, *Government Finance,* 6th ed., Irwin, Homewood, Ill., 1977.

money Anything which serves as a medium of exchange and is generally acceptable for this purpose, or as a unit of value in terms of which the price of everything else is stated. Because of these uses, money makes possible the complex economic relationships necessary for an advanced economy, but since money tends to fluctuate in value, it has never performed these functions perfectly. Historically, many different commodities have served as money. Precious metals and paper notes were long the most important forms of money, since their quantity can be limited and they are durable, portable, and easily divided into different amounts. Today, however, they take second place to a system of bookkeeping debits and credits represented by demand deposits. See Lester V. Chandler and Stephen M. Goldfeld, *The Economics of Money and Banking,* 7th ed., Harper & Row, New York, 1977; for a comprehensive study of money and its role, see J. M. Keynes, *A Treatise on Money,* Macmillan, London, 1930.

money-flow analysis *See* **flow-of-funds analysis.**

money illusion The psychological valuation of currency without regard to its purchasing power. The money illusion arises when an individual associates money directly with its face value without considering its purchasing power. Thus, individuals subject to the money illusion feel better when their wages double even though prices also double and their real wage remains constant. Some economists believe that the effects of the money illusion are very strong, and that workers base their actions to a much greater extent on the level of their money wages than on the level of their real wage. Thus, workers may refuse to work when their money wages drop even if prices fall so that their real wage remains the same, but they will not stop working when their money wages remain constant even if prices rise so that their real wage is lower. The effect of the money illusion is to make the supply schedule of labor elastic to changes in the money wage (at a constant real wage) and particularly inelastic to changes in real wages caused by shifts in the price level. The money illusion also has an impact on consumption, an equal rise in wages and prices (leaving the real wage unchanged) having the effect of raising the real consumption level (at least in the short run). For additional details, see Irving Fisher, *The Money Illusion,* Adelphi, New York, 1928; Robert L. Crouch, *Macroeconomics,* Harcourt Brace, New York, 1972.

money market The term designating the financial institutions which handle the purchase, sale, and transfer of short-term credit instruments. The money market includes the entire machinery for the channeling of short-term funds. Concerned primarily with small business's needs for working capital, individuals' borrowing, and government short-term obligations, it differs from the long-term, or capital, market, which devotes its attention to dealings in bonds, corporate stocks, and mortgage credit. The money market is not a single, homogeneous market but consists of a number of distinct markets, each of which deals in a different type of credit. The most important of these markets are the commercial-paper market, which handles the short-term promissory notes of businesses; the collateral-loan market, which deals in loans granted on the security of bonds and other forms of property (also called broker's loans); the acceptance market, in which bankers' acceptances are traded; and the Treasury bills market, which handles short-term government securities. The major institutions operating in the money market are commercial banks, insurance companies, dealers in government bonds, commercial-paper dealers, finance companies, and factors. The money market may also be divided into customers' and organized markets. Most private short-term borrowing, especially by businesses, is carried out in the customers' market, in which commercial banks and finance companies play the largest roles. The organized short-term markets include those dealing in government obligations, commercial paper, acceptances, and federal funds. Most organized markets, such as the securities exchanges, investment banks, and the mortgage market, operate to a greater extent in the area of long-term financing. The New York money market is the largest and most important center for short-term financing in the United States, absorbing the surplus funds of the entire country. It plays a major role in financing the short-term needs of the federal government as well as the requirements of the entire business community. For additional information on the workings of the money market, see Marcus Nadler et al., *The Money Market and Its Institutions,* Ronald, New York, 1955; A. Polakoff et al., *Financial Institutions and Markets,* 2d ed., Houghton Mifflin, Boston, 1980; Marcia Stigman, *Money Market Calculations, Yields, Swaps and Breakeven Prices,* Dow Jones–Irwin, Homewood, Ill., 1982.

money stock   *See* **money supply.**

money supply (money stock)   The amount of money in an economy. Narrowly defined, the money supply (M1) consists of currency and demand deposits. Currency includes all coin and paper money issued by the government and the banks. Since the monetary authorities hold some stocks of currency, only circulating currency is included in the money supply. Bank deposits, which are payable on demand, are also regarded as part of the supply of money; in fact, they constitute three-fourths of the total money supply in the United States. Some economists also include near money, or cash liquid assets as commercial bank time deposits and deposits at savings and loan associations and mutual savings banks, in the money supply. The amount of currency in circulation is determined by the public. If individuals want a greater amount of cash, they withdraw it from their bank accounts; if they want to hold a smaller amount of cash, they deposit surplus cash in their accounts. The volume of demand deposits is determined primarily by the commercial banks. By increasing their loans and demand deposits, the banks are able to expand the money supply within the limits of the reserve requirements set by the Federal Reserve. They cannot expand loans, however, unless businesses, consumers, and the government are willing to borrow. Thus, the total money supply is determined by the banks, the Federal Reserve, businesses, the government, and consumers. For further information, see Milton Friedman and Rose Friedman, *Free to Choose,* Harcourt Brace, New York, 1980, chap. 9, pp. 248–283.

money wage   The amount of money received per hour, day, week, etc., in payment for services rendered or work done. It differs from real wages, which represent the purchasing power of the money wage, or the quantity of goods and services that can be purchased with the money wage. At times, the movements of money wages and real wages may be diverse. In times of recession, money wages sometimes fall less rapidly than the prices of consumer goods, so that real wages rise. Current statistics on money wages (average hourly or weekly earnings) are given in U.S. Department of Labor, *Monthly Labor Review;* for further information, see J. M. Keynes, *The General Theory of Employment, Interest, and Money,* Harcourt Brace, New York, 1936.

monopolistic competition *See* competition, imperfect.

monopoly A market structure with only one seller of a commodity. In pure monopoly, the single seller exercises absolute control over the market price at which the goods are sold, since there is no competitive supply of goods on the market. The single seller can choose the most profitable price and does so by raising the price and restricting output below that which would be achieved under competition. Monopoly thus leads to a higher selling price, a lower output, and excess profits. Usually, the term monopoly is extended to include any firm or group of firms which act together to fix prices or output. Complete control of all production is not necessary to exercise monopoly power; generally, any consolidation which controls at least 80% of an industry's output can dictate the prices on the remaining 20%. Monopolies may be divided into two broad categories, public monopolies and private monopolies. Public monopolies are those undertaken by the government, such as the operation of the postal system. Private monopolies, held by individuals or business organizations, may originate from a privilege granted by the government, such as a patent or copyright, from the possession of a superior skill or talent, or from the ownership of strategic capital. The last-named factor is responsible for most of the private monopolies associated with big business. The huge capital investment necessary to organize a company in some industries, which raises an almost insurmountable barrier to entry in these fields, provides established firms in these industries with the potential of monopoly power. The use of such monopoly power may, however, lead to the development of substitute products, an attempt at entry into the field by new firms (if the profits seem high enough), or the possibility of public prosecution or regulation. Monopoly power is not widespread in U.S. industry, partly because of the antitrust policies of the federal government, which have prevented the domination of an industry by one firm or even by a few firms. The U.S. Supreme Court, in the 1937 Alcoa case, ruled that the antitrust laws were intended not only to regulate business practices, but also "to perpetuate and preserve for its own sake, and in spite of possible costs, an organization of industry into small units which can effectively compete with each other." For further information, see Joan Robinson, *The Economics of Imperfect Competition,* 2d ed., St. Martin's Press, New York, 1969; Alfred E. Kahn, *The Economics of Legislation: Principles and Institutions,* Wiley, New York, 1970–1971.

monopsony A market structure with a single buyer of a commodity. Pure monopsony, or buyer's monopoly, is characterized by the ability of the single buyer to set the buying price. In the case of a monopsonist who maximizes profits, both the buying price and the quantity bought are lower than they would be in a competitive situation. Pure monopsony is not very common, but it may occur, as in the case of the demand for labor in a company town. Monopsonistic elements can arise in the market for a homogeneous product, in which a large number of competitive sellers offer their goods to a few large buyers. In such a case, no seller can influence price, but the price can be determined by the monopsonistic buyers. Such a situation arises in the wholesale markets for crude petroleum, tobacco, and sugar beets. For additional details, see Joan Robinson, *The Economics of Imperfect Competition,* 2d ed., St. Martin's Press, New York, 1969. Donald S. Watson and Mary A. Holman, *Price Theory and Its Uses,* 4th ed., Houghton Mifflin, Boston, 1976.

mortgage A legal transfer of ownership but not possession of property from a debtor to a creditor. The transfer becomes void upon payment of the debt for which the property has been put up for security. Thus, certain property is conditionally transferred when a debt is incurred, but ownership is regained upon completion of all obligations. In legal terms, there are two types of mortgages: (1) the common-law mortgage, which gives the creditor title to the property serving as security for the debt, subject to the conditions of subsequent payment; and (2) the legal-lien mortgage, which entitles the mortgagee merely to a legal lien upon the property. The advantage of a mortgage arrangement is that the debtor retains possession of the property and is thus able to operate it. The advantage to the creditor is the protection against nonpayment by retaining ownership until the debt has been repaid. See John P. Wiedemer, *Real Estate Finance,* 3d ed., Reston Publishing, Reston, Va., 1980.

mortgage buydown A disguised discount offered on the sale of a house, introduced to compensate for periods of mortgage money scarcity. The seller of the home offers a discount by arranging for financing at rates below market instead of reducing the purchase price. This technique may have advantages in marketing for the builder. A buydown works as follows: Suppose financing is needed for $75,000 (75%) on a $100,000 home and the prevailing rate is 16%. At this rate the annual mortgage payments would be $12,141. The seller may offer financing at 14% and lower mortgage payments of $10,710. However, at the prevailing rate the lower payments are equivalent to a present value of $66,160, or $8,840 less. The 2-percentage-point cut on the rate is equivalent to an 8.84% reduction in the cost of the house.

mortgage debt The amount of long-term debt of individuals, businesses, institutions, and nonprofit organizations that place mortgages on their property in order to buy or repair it. Mortgage debt represents the amount of interest and principal to be paid. In 1963 it became apparent that individuals in the United States were taking out mortgages to obtain funds for the purchase of goods and services other than homes and home repair. These individuals were taking advantage of the relatively low interest rate of mortgages instead of using installment credit. A statistical series on mortgage debt outstanding on nonfarm properties housing one to four families is prepared by the Federal Home Loan Bank Board with the cooperation of the Federal Reserve Board. For a discussion of mortgage debt and mortgage interest rates, see John P. Wiedemer, *Real Estate Finance,* 3d ed., Reston Publishing, Reston, Va., 1980; for current statistics, see Federal Home Loan Bank Board, *Estimated Home Mortgage Debt and Financing Activity,* Washington, D.C., quarterly.

mortgage market A term comprising all financial institutions associated with the marketing of mortgages. The market in which the actual mortgage transactions are negotiated between the borrowers and the initial lenders is called the primary mortgage market. The purpose of this market is to bring together the seekers of mortgage funds and those willing to invest. The market in which the previously created mortgage securities are traded between investors is known as the secondary mortgage market. It provides a means for holders of mortgages who need funds to dispose of their holdings before maturity. The chief institutions of the mortgage market, participating in both the primary and the secondary markets, are the mortgage originators, construction lenders, interim lenders, brokers, and ultimate investors. The major suppliers of mortgage credit are savings and loan associations, life insurance companies, mutual savings banks, and commercial banks. Although there are no organized exchanges for the trading of mortgages, the large brokerage houses, which arrange transactions for most of the major types of institutions and transactions between these institutions, provide a bridge between the primary and secondary markets and offer the nearest approach to an organized trading place for mortgages. For additional details, see John P. Wiedemer, *Real Estate Finance,* 3d ed., Reston Publishing, Reston, Va., 1980.

mortgage money Funds for home construction. The amount of mortgage money available to home buyers varies because of fluctuations in general economic activity, particularly interest rates. There have been times when mortgage money was hard to secure and others when it was easy to obtain. In the early 1980s, mortgage money was generally available, but because of high interest rates it was very costly. For the future, however, it is expected that mortgage money should be adequate to support a high level of homebuilding activity in the United States. The numerous savings institutions, commercial banks, mutual savings banks, savings and loan associations, life insurance companies, mutual funds, and pension funds are all sources of mortgage funds. In addition, the federal government provides funds through the Federal National Mortgage Association and the Government National

Mortgage Association. For a discussion of mortgage money, see John P. Wiedemer, *Real Estate Finance*, 3d ed., Reston Publishing, Reston, Va, 1980.

mortgages, nontraditional The volatile interest and inflation rates of the 1970–1981 period led to the creation of various alternatives to the traditional fixed-rate mortgage that has dominated the residential housing market since the 1930s. There are four nontraditional mortgage concepts, even though actual mortgages may combine aspects of two of them. These are adjustable-rate mortgages (ARMs), graduated-payment mortgages (GPMs), price level–adjusted mortgages (PLAMs), and shared-appreciation mortgages (SAMs). In an ARM the interest rate is subject to periodic adjustment. Usually the adjustments are made semiannually or annually. Adjustments are often limited by the maximum size of a single move (e.g., no more than 1 percentage point) and by the total difference between the initial rate and the adjusted rates (usually 2 to 5 percentage points). The monthly payment may be adjusted to reflect changes in the rate. Alternatively, the shifting rate is accounted for by adjusting the amount of the payment applied to reducing the principal. If the payment is not sufficient to cover the interest due, the principal outstanding can be increased through negative amortization. In a GPM the interest rate is fixed. However, the monthly payments vary in size, usually increasing over the first few years and then remaining steady for the balance of the mortgage term. This mortgage is designed for situations where the borrower's ability to pay is expected to increase over time. Examples include young families buying their first home and borrowers in inflationary environments where increases in nominal salaries are anticipated. Under a PLAM the monthly payment and the outstanding principal are adjusted to reflect actual inflation. In the early years the outstanding principal will rise if the increase due to inflation exceeds the rate at which the principal is paid down. This results in increasing the potential cost to the lender of a default. The last variety of mortgage is the shared-appreciation mortgage (SAM). The lender shares in the appreciation in the value of the home, and in return offers a lower interest rate. The lender will receive a lump-sum appreciation payment either when the home is sold or after a fixed term of years. For the borrower, a SAM represents lower mortgage payments and may be the difference between not buying and buying a home. The lender, however, is subject to an increased risk. The lender is not only assuming the risks related to inflation and interest rates but also bearing some of the investment risk. Moreover, SAMs offer the lender an unfavorable pattern of cash flow. Finally, because the lender has an interest on the value of the home, the lender may find it desirable to impose restrictions on capital improvements, further complicating the mortgage.

most-favored-nation clause A provision in commercial treaties between two or more countries that protects them against tariff discrimination by each other. It guarantees that all partners to the agreement will automatically extend to each other any tariff reductions that they might offer to nonmember countries. For example, if a trade agreement between the United States and the Netherlands contained a most-favored-nation clause, any reduction of the import duty on bicycles that the United States might offer to Great Britain (perhaps in exchange for a reduction of the British tariff on American automobiles) would automatically be extended to the Netherlands. Since 1948, when the General Agreement on Tariffs and Trade (GATT) provided for multilateral tariff negotiations under international auspices, all signatories to this convention (forty-two countries, which together account for more than 80% of world trade) have agreed to adhere to the most-favored-nation principle. Consequently, the problem of tariff discrimination, formerly a burning international issue, has been much reduced although it still exists. Furthermore, GATT specifically exempts from most-favored-nation obligations those countries, such as members of the Common Market, that plan to complete a customs union (without tariffs at all) among themselves. See C. P. Kindleberger and P. H. Lindert, *International Economics,* Irwin, Homewood, Ill., 1978.

motivation research   A group of techniques developed by behavioral scientists (psychologists and sociologists) which are utilized by marketing researchers to discover the factors influencing marketing behavior, such as consumer attitudes, reactions, and preferences. A few motivation-research studies were carried out in the United States soon after World War II, but since 1950 there has been a marked increase of interest in learning why people buy. For general information on motivation research and surveys, see Joseph Newman, *Motivation Research and Marketing Management,* Harvard Business School, Division of Research, Boston, 1957; for a different view of the importance of motivation research in marketing research, see Robert Ferber et al., *Motivation and Market Behavior,* Arno, New York, 1976.

multicollinearity   The tendency of many economic time series (theoretically, independent variables) to expand or contract simultaneously over time as a result of a common cause. When this condition prevails, the statistician is not able to isolate each series' separate contribution to simple and multiple correlation. If multicollinearity is serious, the sampling errors of the individual coefficients become large in a linear correlation, and the coefficients will not be precisely estimated even though the correlation for the entire equation is high. Thus the presence of multicollinearity may seriously impair the significance of the overall correlation. For additional information, see Lawrence R. Klein, *An Introduction to Econometrics,* Greenwood, Westport, Conn., 1977.

multiforecasting   A forecast of the upper and lower limits that are expected for sales in a given period. Forecasting a precise value of sales for a period extending six months or a year ahead is extremely difficult. Multiforecasting provides the maximum range because it pinpoints the upper and lower limits within which sales may reasonably be expected to move. Naturally, the distance between the upper and lower limits is greater for periods further in the future than for the near term. If the multiforecast is revised regularly, the area between the optimistic and the pessimistic forecasts becomes smaller, and management may gear production, inventory, and other policies to a particular value of sales within the narrow range of expected sales for specific planning purposes.

multi-industry company   A company that operates in more than one industry, such as a major producer of military and space systems that also sells cement, drugs, and chemicals. Such diversification is precipitated by the desire of a company to participate in a greater number of markets. The so-called battle of materials, in which a product competes against all possible substitutes as well as against the same commodity, has been responsible for much of the diversification. Security against fluctuations in the demand for one product and new technology are other factors contributing to the growth of the multi-industry company.

multilateral negotiations and agreements   Negotiations and agreements between more than two parties. The term is generally used to refer to the intricate trading relationships developed by many countries. Since trade between any two countries normally is not balanced, a typical trading country usually deals with a number of countries, developing a crisscross network of trading relationships in the world economy. The General Agreement on Tariffs and Trade (GATT) is an example of an agreement which seeks to establish multilateral trade. For further information, see C. P. Kindleberger and P. H. Lindert, *International Economics,* Irwin, Homewood, Ill., 1978.

multinational company   A company that has (1) a manufacturing base or other form of direct investment that gives it roots in at least one foreign country and (2) a global perspective. A global perspective means that its management makes fundamental decisions on marketing, production, and research in terms of alternatives available to it anywhere in the world. For further information, see Sidney E. Rolfe and Walter Damm (eds.), *Multinational Corporation in the World Economy: Direct Investment in Perspective,* Praeger, New York, 1970; Raymond Vernon, *Sovereignty at Bay,* Basic Books, New York, 1975.

multiplier   A conceptual tool employed in the study of business fluctuations. Introduced by R. F. Kahn in 1931 and used a few years later by John Maynard Keynes, it deals with the magnified impact that changes in investment spending have on total income. The money spent in building a new plant, for instance, sets off a chain reaction. It increases the incomes of the workers directly engaged in its construction, the incomes of the merchants with whom the workers trade, the incomes of the merchants' suppliers, and so on. The dollars do not multiply indefinitely, however, for people do not ordinarily spend all their new income; instead, they spend part and save part. Theoretically, the multiplier's final effect, or value, can be calculated by dividing the numeral 1 by the percentage of new income saved. For example, if people on the average save 20% of their additional income, a $1 billion increase in investment will ultimately raise total income by $5 billion ($1/0.20 = 5$; $5 \times \$1$ billion = $5 billion). This basic idea has been developed into many specialized multipliers, such as the foreign-trade multiplier, which deals with the effects of changing imports, and the successive-period multiplier, which deals with the timing of the multiplier effects. There are so many unknowns at work in the economy, however, that it is virtually impossible to discover the precise impact of any multiplier. See J. M. Keynes, *The General Theory of Employment, Interest, and Money*, Harcourt Brace, New York, 1936; Gardner Ackley, *Macroeconomics: Theory and Policy*, Macmillan, New York, 1978.

municipal bond   A long-term debt obligation issued by local governments and other political subdivisions such as school districts, sewer authorities, and so forth. As commonly used, the term also includes bonds issued by state governments. Like other debt obligations, a municipal bond is a written promise to pay a specified amount of money (principal) either at a certain date in the future (usually more than ten years) or periodically over the course of the loan, during which time interest is paid at a fixed rate on specified dates. These obligations are frequently referred to as tax-exempt bonds because they are not subject to federal income taxes. Municipal bonds are classified as either general or limited obligation bonds. General obligation bonds rest on the "full faith and credit" of the issuing entity for payment of interest and principal—which simply means the taxing power of the issuer. Limited obligation bonds depend on the revenues gained from whatever asset (e.g., a bridge, turnpike, or tunnel) they financed for payment of principal and interest. For this reason, they are frequently called revenue bonds. Other things being equal, the risk of default is obviously lower for general obligation bonds. For further information, see Jules I. Bogen (ed.), *The Financial Handbook*, 4th ed., Ronald, New York, 1968; David Darst, *The Complete Bond Book: A Guide to All Types of Fixed-Income Securities*, McGraw-Hill, New York, 1975; Robert Lamb and Stephen P. Rappaport, *Municipal Bonds—The Comprehensive Review of Tax-Exempt Securities and Public Finance*, McGraw-Hill, New York, 1980.

mutatis mutandis   A Latin term meaning "with the necessary changes having been made." In economic analysis, it is generally assumed that all variables except those being studied are kept constant. A change in a variable might result in a change in some of the conditions which are outside the particular area being studied.

mutual fund (open-end investment company)   An investment company that has a flexible capital structure. Because in virtually all cases open-end investment companies continuously sell shares in mutual funds and because they will redeem any outstanding shares, their capital structures are almost constantly changing. Their capital increases when sales exceed redemptions and decreases when redemptions exceed sales. The price at which mutual funds will sell or redeem their shares is usually the net asset value of the fund per share. (Total assets minus total liabilities divided by number of shares equals net asset value per share.) A distribution fee or commission is added when the mutual fund sells shares. Mutual-fund share prices are determined solely by the prices of the securities held by the fund. Unlike the prices of the shares of closed-end investment companies, the prices of the shares of open-end investment companies are not directly evaluated by the market. Like closed-end investment companies, however, mutual funds can be classified by investment objectives. Common-stock funds invest money primarily in common stocks, although they reserve the right to hold cash or to invest in defensive securities, such as bonds. Some common-stock funds invest money in specialized fields, such as growth stocks, electronics issues, or blue chips. Others diversify their investments over a wide range of common stocks. Balanced funds invest in common and preferred stocks and bonds and generally try to hold the proportions of each type of security close to stated policies. Because they diversify not only the companies they hold, but also the kinds of securities, they are more conservative than common-stock funds. Fully managed funds are funds that invest money at the discretion of the management. They have no stated investment objectives. See *Fact Book,* Investment Company Institute, New York, periodically; Securities and Exchange Commission, *Annual Reports;* Irwin Friend, Marshall Blume, and Jean Crockett, *Mutual Funds and Other Institutional Investors, A New Perspective,* McGraw-Hill, New York, 1970.

mutual savings bank   A savings bank which is owned and operated wholly for the benefit of its depositors, who must all be individuals. Banks of this type differ from cooperative banks in that they are directed by a self-perpetuating board of directors. Depositors have no voice in their policies. The first mutual savings bank was established in Scotland in 1810; the first one in the United States, in 1816. For further information, see Lawrence S. Ritter and William L. Silber, *Principles of Money, Banking and Financial Markets,* 3d rev. ed., Basic Books, New York, 1980; statistics are presented monthy in *Federal Reserve Bulletin,* Washington, D.C., and in greater detail in U.S. Comptroller of the Currency, *Annual Reports.*

naive model Not a formal mathematical model but rather an assumption that whatever the forces were that produced an economic event, or a change in a time series, in the immediate past, the same forces will be present in the immediate future and will act in such a way as to produce a similar or identical event or change. The application of this assumption implies complete ignorance of all causal factors and other related information. Its use in econometrics cannot be justified under other circumstances. For comparisons of naive models with economic forecasts, see Victor Zarnowitz, *An Appraisal of Short-Term Economic Forecasts,* National Bureau of Economic Research, Occasional Paper 104, Columbia University Press, New York, 1967.

national bank A commercial bank chartered by the federal government. Established under the National Banking Acts of 1863–1864, national banks were authorized to issue bank notes on a large reserve of U.S. government securities. Since it was believed that national banks would provide a stable national paper currency, the federal government, in 1866, placed a 10% tax on state bank notes to drive them out of existence. With the passage of the Federal Reserve Act in 1913, all national banks were required to join the Federal Reserve System, but no bank was required to be a national bank. Since 1935, when national banks lost their note-issuing privilege, the main reason for a national bank's existence has been prestige. See Lester V. Chandler and Stephen M. Goldfeld, *The Economics of Money and Banking,* 7th ed., Harper & Row, New York, 1977; for statistics on national banks, see *Federal Reserve Bulletin,* Washington, D.C., monthly.

national debt The total indebtedness of a national government. It is generally smaller than the public debt, which includes the debt of local governments as well as that of the national government, and it is usually larger than the net national debt, which omits the portion of the debt that is owed to government agencies and trust funds. Although the U.S. debt increased in dollar terms in the postwar period, it actually declined in relation to the nation's total production. Many persons who worry about the increasing size of the federal debt are concerned (1) that an increasing burden is being passed on to future generations or (2) that a big debt will eventually bankrupt the government. Those who deny the first problem readily concede that the national debt redistributes income, but they do not believe that the burden is passed on to future generations as a whole. With regard to the bankruptcy problem, they argue that the government can never become bankrupt because it can either increase taxes or create additional sums of money to pay the debt. A more real concern regarding a mounting national debt is the threat of inflation. Detailed statistics on the U.S. national debt are published monthly in U.S. Treasury Department, *Treasury Bulletin.*

national income The total compensation of the elements used in production (land, labor, capital, and entrepreneurship) which comes from the current production of goods and services by the national economy. It is the income earned—but not necessarily received—by all persons in the country in a specified period. It consists of wages, interest, rent, profits, and the net income of the self-employed. National income can be classified according to the industry in which it originates, such as mining, construction, or manufacturing. The difference between national income and net national product (gross national product minus capital consumption allowances) is accounted for mainly by indirect business tax and nontax payments: federal excise taxes, customs duties, state taxes and fees, local property taxes. National income generally is considered a better series for income-distribution analyses than the gross national product, but national income data have been criticized because they include some items for which there are no formal records, such as the amount of food consumed by farmers which they have produced themselves. For a detailed discussion of national income data, see Richard Ruggles and Nancy D. Ruggles, *National Income Accounts and Income Analysis,* 2d ed., McGraw-Hill, New York, 1956; for detailed definitions of the techniques and terminology of national income accounting, see U.S. Department of Commerce, *Survey of Current Business: National Income Supplement,* 1954; for current quarterly data on national income, see U.S. Department of Commerce, *Survey of Current Business.*

national income and product accounts A statistical statement of national output or receipts, such as gross national product, net national product, personal income, and disposable income. The national income and product accounts consist of the following individual accounts: consolidated business income and product account; personal income and expenditure account; consolidated government receipts and expenditures account; rest of the world account; and gross savings and investment account. The early work in developing national income and product accounts was done by the National Bureau of Economic Research. In 1932, Congress directed the preparation of national income accounts, and a few years later the Department of Commerce began publishing its estimates. The monthly personal income series was initiated in the late 1930s. During World War II, the development of the gross national product series was greatly accelerated because of its value in planning the war effort and in instituting controls. In the postwar period, the accounts have gone beyond the scope of measuring the size and composition of national output. Through the use of income and expenditure accounts, an understanding of the factors that determine the output can be gained. For further information, see U.S. Department of Commerce, *Survey of Current Business: National Income Supplement,* 1954; Richard Ruggles and Nancy D. Ruggles, *National Income Accounts and Income Analysis,* 2d ed., McGraw-Hill, New York, 1956; Simon Kuznets, *National Income: A Summary of Findings,* National Bureau of Economic Research, New York, 1946.

nationalization   An act by which a government takes over the ownership and operation of an industry or a business previously in the hands of private citizens. It has been argued that nationalization increases productive efficiency by permitting the direct investment of public funds, by enlarging the scale of operations, and by coordinating operations more effectively. On the other hand, opponents of nationalization state that the record of private enterprise is such that governmental takeover and control are unnecessary, and that government ownership is usually characterized by excessive costs because of elaborate, overcentralized organization. Nationalization has been used by some countries purely as a means of eliminating foreign ownership of their basic industries. For additional information, see Albert H. Hanson (ed.), *Nationalization: A Book of Readings,* Macmillan, London, 1963.

National Labor Relations Act (Wagner Act)   The principal labor relations law of the United States. It applies to all interstate commerce except airlines and railroads, which are covered by the Railway Labor Act. The National Labor Relations Act, which was passed in 1935 and subsequently amended, guarantees employees the right of full freedom in self-organization and in the choice of representatives for collective bargaining; it also prohibits specific unfair labor practices by employers or by unions. In 1947 it was amended by the Labor-Management Relations Act (Taft-Hartley Act). One of the amendments changed the composition of the National Labor Relations Board to include five members instead of three and provided for a general counsel. In addition, the board's judicial functions were separated from its prosecuting duties by delegating to its general counsel final authority to issue complaints of unfair labor practices and to prosecute the complaints before the board. Major amendments in the law banned the closed shop and defined certain union actions as unfair labor practices. The Landrum-Griffin Act of 1959 also substantially amended the basic act. Among other things, it authorized the board to delegate to its regional directors power to determine representation questions, subject to review by the board.

national wealth   The aggregate value of all the tangible nonmilitary assets of a country. National wealth statistics are a measure of the economic stocks of an area. Whereas the common concept of national income stems from an income-statement approach to social accounting, the measurement of national wealth is derived from a balance-sheet approach. The simplest calculation of national wealth is gross wealth, summing the value of all of a country's assets on an undepreciated basis and ignoring their age, usefulness, etc. A more realistic measure is net wealth, for which assets are valued on a depreciated basis. National wealth includes both reproducible tangible assets (capital stock) and nonreproducible assets, such as land and natural resources. The value of reproducible assets is estimated by the perpetual-inventory method of accumulating past capital expenditures, depreciated in accordance with the life of the asset. The value of nonreproducible assets is estimated independently, often from census or tax data. As a measure of economic growth, reproducible tangible wealth, excluding land and other natural resources, is more appropriate than total wealth. In the postwar period, the real value of reproducible wealth in the United States has been growing at an annual rate of about 3.5%. For additional details on the concept and measurement of national wealth, see Raymond W. Goldsmith, *The National Wealth of the United States in the Postwar Period,* National Bureau of Economic Research, Princeton University Press, Princeton, N.J., 1962; for a study of the problems and possibilities of a meaningful national wealth inventory, see John W. Kendrick (ed.), *The Formation and Stocks of Total Capital,* National Bureau of Economic Research, New York, 1976; for annual data on national wealth, see U.S. Bureau of the Census, *Statistical Abstract of the United States,* Washington, D.C., annually.

nation's economic budget   A rearrangement of national-income-accounts data so that each of the accounts of the four sectors, government, business, consumers, and international accounts, balances in terms of receipts and expenditures. Users of this budget format ordinarily do not consider it a planning or programming device but rather a useful tool for economic analysis. The nation's economic budget was devised by Gerhard Colm and Grover Ensley in the 1940s. For additional discussion of this format, see Gerhard Colm, *The American Economy in 1960,* National Planning Association, Washington, D.C., 1952, pp. 26–29.

natural rights   Essential rights of individuals for the enjoyment of the fullest possible prosperity and happiness. According to François Quesnay, one of the eighteenth-century physiocrats, natural rights were determined by observation of the facts concerning actual human situations and relations. Quesnay observed the situation of particular individuals, the services that they needed from each other and were in a position to render each other, and the reciprocal rights and duties that they must recognize. He called attention to the rights and duties of parents and children as an example. Young children are unable to care for themselves and thus require various parental services. Parents are best situated to provide these services; hence, children have natural rights to the service in question while the parents have a natural duty toward their children. In later years, the situation is reversed. Grown-up children are in the best position to aid their aging parents and thus have the natural duty to do so while the parents retain the natural rights to such aid. It was believed that it was the business of government to make and enforce a system of positive laws to protect these natural rights. When such natural rights existed in economic dealings, the government was not to interfere with these rights but to endeavor to protect them. Quesnay's essay *Droit naturel* can be found in Auguste Oncken (ed.), *Oeuvres de Quesnay,* Jules Peelman, Paris, 1888, pp. 359–377.

near money   An asset whose value is fixed in terms of money and which can easily be converted into money, yet which cannot be spent directly. The most important forms of near money are time deposits and United States government bonds, both of which can readily be converted into a specific amount of money but which are excluded from the definition of money because they do not function directly as a medium of exchange. Near moneys often have an important effect on the consumption habits of individuals, since the greater the amount of wealth held in the form of near money, the greater is the willingness of consumers to make purchases from their money incomes. Furthermore, highly liquid near money can be converted very quickly into actual money, adding significantly to the money supply. Thus, it can pose serious problems in inflationary periods. For further details, see Walter W. Haines, *Money, Prices and Policy,* 2d ed., McGraw-Hill, New York, 1966.

negative income tax   A scheme in which all family units with incomes above the amount necessary for a subsistence level of living would pay a progressive income tax, while all other family units would receive a government subsidy sufficient to raise their incomes to subsistence level. The subsidy in this case would be the negative tax. Under this system, existing welfare programs would be abolished. Critics of this scheme point out that it would be impractical, reducing incentives to work and to save. For further discussion, see Margaret S. Gordon, *The Economics of Welfare Policies,* Columbia University Press, New York, 1963, pp. 117–118; Stanley Masters and Irwin Garfinkel, *Estimating the Labor Supply Effects of Income-Maintenance Alternatives,* Academic Press, New York, 1977.

neoclassical school   A school of economists which existed between 1870 and World War I. Members of the school reconstructed classical economic theory to take into account the changes that had occurred since the early nineteenth century. The founders of the neoclassical school were William S. Jevons in England, Carl Menger in Austria, and Léon Walras in France.

Subsequent leaders were Alfred Marshall in Cambridge, Eugen von Böhm-Bawerk in Vienna, Vilfredo Pareto in Lausanne, and John Bates Clark and Irving Fisher in the United States. Neoclassicists believed that the power of competition was the regulating force of economic activity which would establish equilibrium between production and consumption. Their theory was mainly a theory of price and the allocation of resources to specific uses under the incentives of utility maximization for the consumer and profit maximization for the producer. The innovations of the neoclassical school as compared with the doctrines of the classical school were mostly mathematical. Neoclassical theorists applied logical concepts of integral and differential calculus to the analysis of relationships between inputs and outputs. Their emphasis on mathematical economics resulted in economics becoming technical and, at the time, less acceptable to the general public and to government. This school of economic thought did not continue the work of classical theorists in developing the aggregative approach to the measurement of total economic output or income. John Maynard Keynes broke with orthodox neoclassical theory in the early 1930s, when he developed his anti-neoclassical point of view, which emphasized liquidity preference and the notion of an underemployment equilibrium. For further discussion of the neoclassicists, see William Fellner, *Modern Economic Analysis,* McGraw-Hill, New York, 1960; for theories of the neoclassicists, see Léon Walras, *Elements of Pure Economics,* W. Jaffé (trans.), Irwin, Homewood, Ill., 1954; Alfred Marshall, *Principles of Economics,* 8th ed., Macmillan, New York, 1948; Gary S. Becker, *Economic Theory,* Knopf, Chicago, 1971.

neo-Keynesian economics   The doctrines of a small but influential group of post-Keynesian economists centered at Cambridge University in England. They accept the basic ideas of Keynes, especially those of *The General Theory of Employment, Interest, and Money.* Neo-Keynesians and post-Keynesians distinguish sharply between their interpretation of Keynes and that of the orthodox Keynesians. During the 1970s when the influence of orthodox Keynesians waned, the neo-Keynesian answer to the problem of stagflation—incomes policy—appealed to those who disagreed with monetarism as well as with mainstream neoclassical economists. For additional information, see Mark Blaug, *The Cambridge Revolution: Success or Failure?,* Institute of Economic Affairs, London, 1975; J. M. Keynes, *The General Theory of Employment, Interest, and Money,* Harcourt Brace, New York, 1936; Joan Robinson, *The Accumulation of Capital,* 3d ed. St. Martin's Press, London, 1969.

neoliberalism   An economic philosophy which holds that, on the whole, the market mechanism works well in satisfying human wants and in allocating productive resources to alternative uses. An economy composed of small units (one as close as possible to pure competition) is essential to ensure that the price mechanism works well. In general, neoliberalists prefer as little governmental intervention in the economy as possible. Neoliberalism is the modern adaptation of the laissez faire doctrine of the 1800s. Among its current proponents, Ludwig von Mises advocates a return to the economic doctrines of laissez faire espoused by the nineteenth-century liberals. F. A. von Hayek, believing that the gradual growth of government leads to socialism and that freedom and democracy cannot exist under socialism, considers that the drift toward further governmental control should stop and that competition should be strengthened. Henry C. Simons advocates increased competition, dissolution of monopolies, and a minimum role for government. Milton Friedman favors a return to a rather extreme version of laissez faire in which market prices would determine a great many things now in government hands. For individual points of view, see Ludwig von Mises, *Human Action,* Yale University Press, New Haven, Conn., 1949; F. A. von Hayek, *The Road to Serfdom,* University of Chicago Press, Chicago, 1944; Henry C. Simons, *Economic Policy for a Free Society,* University of Chicago Press, Chicago, 1948; Milton Friedman, *Capitalism and Freedom,* University of Chicago Press, Chicago, 1962.

net cash flow *See* **cash flow.**

net national product The market value of a country's output of goods and services after deducting the capital that has been used up in the production process. Among the deductions to be made are depreciation charges, accidental damage to fixed capital assets, and outlays charged to current account. Net national product differs from gross national product because it excludes all business products used by business during the specific accounting period. For a detailed explanation of net national product, see U.S. Department of Commerce, *Survey of Current Business: National Income Supplement,* 1954; Richard Ruggles and Nancy D. Ruggles, *National Income Accounts and Income Analysis,* 2d ed., McGraw-Hill, New York, 1956.

net profits *See* **profits.**

net worth The excess of assets over liabilities. The net worth of a business represents the equity of the owners (proprietors or stockholders) in it. Thus, a statement of net worth shows the total investment of the owners in the business (capital) and the profits which have been allowed to remain in the business and increase the proprietors' equity (surplus). Net worth is affected by the owners' original investment, additional investments, subsequent profits and losses of the business, and withdrawals from accumulated profits or investments. Only tangible assets are included when net worth is calculated for the purpose of judging credit risks, but intangible assets, such as goodwill and patents, are included for an accounting computation.

New Economics of the 1960s The use of aggressive federal government intervention to bring about economic growth through manipulation of the federal budget position. The correct policy moves in any given economic situation will depend on how the economy is performing in relation to its potential performance at the theoretical full-employment level. The proponents of the New Economics have held that a full-employment economy, under present conditions, occurs when unemployment is at about the 4% level. Lower levels of unemployment would yield less real growth and higher rates of inflation. The difference between the actual gross national product (GNP) and the potential GNP at full employment is called the GNP or performance gap. Economic policy under the New Economics would consist of attempting to close this performance gap by taking appropriate actions to influence the government's budget position. For example, in a slack economy, federal government policy would generally require running a budget deficit to stimulate economic activity. The New Economics depends to a great extent on the abilities of government economists to forecast accurately the trends in economic activity and the likely responses to various policy measures. Actions taken under accurate assessments of future activity are often the cause of as much difficulty as the problems the actions were designed to eliminate. In addition to accurate forecasting, the New Economics requires pinpoint timing of policy actions to achieve desired objectives. For additional information, see Walter Heller, *New Dimensions of Political Economy,* Harvard University Press, Cambridge, Mass., 1966; Herbert Stein, *The Fiscal Revolution in America,* University of Chicago Press, Chicago, 1969, chaps. 15–17. For a different view, see George Terborgh, *The New Economics,* Machinery and Allied Products Institute, Washington, D.C., 1968.

new order   A commitment to buy goods, received and accepted by a company, for present or future delivery. Since a lag normally exists between receipt and shipment of an order, new orders usually serve as a leading indicator of future business conditions. An increase in new orders generally means that production will increase in the future, thus providing a greater number of jobs and higher incomes. Because data on new orders provide significant information to the business and industry forecaster, many trade associations collect and compile such data. For example, the National Machine Tool Builders Association collects data on new orders for machine tools, and the National Electrical Machinery Association collects industry information on new orders for various types of electrical equipment. The U.S. Department of Commerce provides a monthly series of new orders in manufacturing industries. For monthly data on new orders, see U.S. Department of Commerce, *Survey of Current Business;* see also Victor Zarnowitz, "The Timing of Manufacturers' Orders during Business Cycles," in Geoffrey H. Moore (ed.), *Business Cycle Indicators,* vol. I, National Bureau of Economic Research, Princeton University Press, Princeton, N.J., 1961, chap. 14.

nineteenth-century liberalism   *See* classical liberalism.

nominal price   A term used to describe a price that is estimated because no actual price exists. Nominal price refers to a price quotation that is given by a commodity or security specialist because a particular commodity or security is not traded often enough to establish a definite market price.

nonborrowed reserves   A reserve aggregate consisting of total bank reserves (deposits of the Federal Reserve and vault cash) minus borrowings by member banks from the Federal Reserve. For statistics on nonborrowed reserves, see *Federal Reserve Bulletin,* monthly.

nondurable goods   *See* **soft goods.**

nonflexible price   A price that is less flexible on the down side than on the up side. When demand increases for a product with a nonflexible price, the price rises to a smaller extent than the price of a flexibly priced product in the same situation. Nonflexible prices occur in the case of manufactured products turned out by an industry that is highly concentrated, such as steel and automobiles. They also occur in the case of products turned out by a few producers that dominate a local market, such as beer. See Gardiner C. Means, *Administrative Inflation and Pricing Policy,* Anderson Kramer Associates, Washington, D.C., 1959.

noninstallment credit   Credit granted in which future repayment is made in a lump sum. The term is used in contradistinction to installment credit, which is repayable in separate installments. An example of noninstallment consumer credit is the department store charge account, which requires one payment by a specified date for all purchases made within a certain period. For current statistics on noninstallment credit, see *Federal Reserve Bulletin,* Washington, D.C., monthly.

nonmember bank   In the United States, a bank that does not belong to the Federal Reserve System. Since all national banks are required to be member banks, the nonmember banks are either state banks or private banks. State banks choose to be nonmember banks either (1) because they do not meet the minimum requirements for membership in the Federal Reserve System or (2) because they prefer the generally less strict regulations of state laws to Federal Reserve regulations. For instance, nonmember banks can charge a fee for clearing checks, and state reserve requirements are frequently more lenient than those set by the Board of Governors of the Federal Reserve System. See Lawrence S. Ritter and William L. Silber, *Principles of Money, Banking and Financial Markets,* 3d rev. ed., Basic Books, New York, 1980; for statistics on nonmember banks, see *Federal Reserve Bulletin,* Washington, D.C., monthly.

nonprice competition   Methods of competition which do not involve changes in the selling price. The main types of nonprice competition are product differentiation and advertising. Through product differentiation, a firm tries to distinguish its product from that of its rivals. This may be achieved by improving the product's quality, efficiency, etc., and by periodic restyling. Besides changing its product to suit consumer demand, a firm may try to increase its share of the market by attracting consumers by means of advertising and sales promotion. Less important types of nonprice competition include favorable terms of sale and customer services. The result of nonprice competition, especially product differentiation, is that the consumer is given a wide variety of types, styles, and qualities of a given product from which to choose. Furthermore, such competition serves to accelerate technological innovation and product improvement. Nonprice competition is most prevalent in oligopolistic industries, such as automobile and cigarette manufacturing, in which the possibility of increasing a firm's market share through price competition is small. For additional details, see E. H. Chamberlain, "The Product as an Economic Variable," *Quarterly Journal of Economics*, February 1953, pp. 1–29.

nonresidential fixed investment Expenditures by private business and nonprofit organizations and institutions for new and replacement construction (buildings, stores, warehouses) and producer durable equipment (machinery, office equipment, motor vehicles). The basic purpose of nonresidential fixed investment is to increase and modernize the capacity to produce goods and services for future consumption. With residential investment it adds up to gross private fixed investment. The difference between the nonresidential-fixed-investment expenditures series and the series on business expenditures for new plants and equipment (capital expenditures) is that the former includes investment by farmers, private institutions (such as hospitals and colleges), nonprofit organizations, professionals (such as doctors and dentists), and real estate operators, while the latter series does not. Also included in the nonresidential series but excluded from the capital spending series are oil-well drilling costs charged to current expense and expenditures for passenger cars for business purposes by salaried workers who receive reimbursement for the use of the cars. For a detailed discussion of the concept, coverage, and sources of data for the major components, see U.S. Department of Commerce, *National Income Supplement*, 1954; see also Richard Ruggles and Nancy D. Ruggles, *National Income Accounts and Income Analysis*, 2d ed., McGraw-Hill, New York, 1956; for quarterly and annual data, see U.S. Department of Commerce, *Survey of Current Business*, monthly.

nonsingularity Within the general econometric problem of identification, a condition that exists for an econometric model involving several equations each of which represents a sector of the economy that is economically different from all the others. The equations may respond to exogenous stimuli identically or in any other manner. However, each equation must respond to endogenous stimuli in a different or unique way. When this condition is met, it follows that none of the involved equations is a linear combination of other equations in the model, and the model is complete. For additional information, see Lawrence R. Klein, *An Introduction to Econometrics,* Greenwood, Westport, Conn., 1977.

normal year A year in which the physical volume of goods and services and industrial production in the United States increase by between 3 and 4%, prices rise from 4 to 5%, consumer money incomes rise from 7 to 9%, and unemployment ranges between 5 and 6% of the labor force. No single year in the post-World War II period meets all these requirements, but the postwar average for each of these key economic gauges falls about midway between the limits. The criteria given above are used by many business economists in describing a normal business year.

normative economics A system of economics which concerns itself with how our economic lives ought to be arranged, what goods and services ought to be produced, how and by whom the production of such desired goods and services should be organized, how ownership of productive factors should be distributed among members of society, and how income and, therefore, consumption of goods and services should be distributed among members of the larger society including the nations of the world as well as unborn future generations. Modern normative economics has become concerned with how different axioms and assumptions lead to different rules for choice of outcomes. Several formulas for weighting or counting individual welfares in order to arrive at a social welfare function have been proposed. Among them are the Benthamite-Utilitarian formula, which attempts to identify the best alternative social state out of a given environment, and those formulas attributed to Bergson, Nash, Arrow, and Rawls. For additional information, see Kenneth E. Boulding, "Welfare Economics," in Bernard F. Haley (ed.), *Survey of Contemporary Economic Theory,* vol. II, Irwin, Homewood, Ill., 1952.

O

obligational authority, new   The total amount of grants enacted by the Congress of the United States to cover appropriations and other financial authorizations made available to federal agencies for a given fiscal year. New obligational authority is a direct measure of congressional action on the budget recommendations of the President. In a few cases, such as interest on the national debt, there is permanent authority under which additional sums of money are made available automatically from year to year without new congressional action. New obligational authority does not include the unspent balances of prior years which are still available for current obligations. The granting of new obligational authority is a key control over federal expenditures. For the fiscal year 1981, new obligational authority totaled more than $718 billion. For details of the process by which the federal government reaches decisions on expenditures, see Murray L. Weidenbaum, "The Federal Government Spending Process," in U.S. Joint Economic Committee, *Federal Expenditure Policy for Economic Growth and Stability,* Washington, D.C., 1957; for current statistics, see U.S. Office of Management and Budget, *The Federal Budget* and *The Budget Review,* annual reports.

obsolescence   The shortening of the life of a capital asset, such as a plant, machine, or piece of equipment, because of technological progress, such as an invention, improvement in processes, changed economic conditions, or legislation. Obsolescence differs from depreciation, which is the actual wearing out of plants and equipment because of use. For further information, see *How Modern Is American Industry?,* McGraw-Hill Department of Economics, New York, 1980.

Occam's razor (Ockham's razor)   The principle that the primary assumptions of a logical system should be as few as possible. It was first formulated by William of Occam in the fourteenth century. The principle of Occam's razor, now also known as the principle of economy or the law of parsimony, asserts that in any system (e.g., an economic model) the number of unconnected propositions and those for which there are no proof should be at a minimum. Thus, in deciding between two explanations for the same phenomenon, the one which requires fewer simplifying assumptions should be chosen. For further information, see G. N. Bueschen, *Eucharistic Teachings of William Ockham,* Catholic University of America Press, Washington, D.C., 1950.

odd lot An amount of stock that is less than the unit of trading established by a stock exchange. For example, the unit of trading, or round lot, is 100 shares for most stocks listed on the New York Stock Exchange, and any number of shares from 1 to 99 is therefore an odd lot. Brokers who want to buy or sell an odd lot for a customer must execute the order with an odd-lot dealer, a member of the exchange who stands ready to buy or sell odd lots. Odd-lot dealers charge a differential on orders that they execute. For instance, on the New York Stock Exchange the odd-lot dealer's price is based on the first round-lot transaction that occurs after the odd-lot order reaches the trading post. If that price were under $40, the odd-lot dealer would charge a differential of 12.5 cents per share; if the price were more than $40, the odd-lot dealer would charge a differential of 25 cents per share. See George A. Christy and John C. Clendenin, *Introduction to Investments,* 7th ed., McGraw-Hill, New York, 1978.

Okun's law In 1961, Arthur M. Okun evolved a rule of thumb relating changes in the unemployment rate to changes in the physical volume of national output (real gross national product). Winning early acceptance by leading economists, the relationship has since become known as Okun's law. At the beginning of the 1960s there was general agreement that, given existing technology and labor-market conditions, an unemployment rate of 4% was consistent with relatively full utilization of resources. With this 4% unemployment rate as a starting point, Okun's law indicates that each percent increase in the unemployment rate is associated with a 3% shortfall in real gross national product. Okun presented his findings in a scholarly paper that is reprinted in Arthur M. Okun, *The Political Economy of Prosperity,* Brookings Institution, Washington, D.C., 1970. For further discussion see Arthur M. Okun, "Potential Gross National Product," in D. Greenwald (ed.), *Encyclopedia of Economics,* McGraw-Hill, New York, 1982.

Old Age and Survivors Insurance (OASI) A federal program of retirement pensions in the United States, financed equally by contributions from employees and their employers. In 1981, employers deducted 6.65% from wages up to $29,700 per year for each employee and matched this contribution. The 6.65% rate is broken down into 5.35% for retirement survivors and disability and 1.3% for hospital insurance. The self-employed are subject to a 9.3% tax. The program, which was established by the Social Security Act of 1935, is administered by both the Treasury Department and the Bureau of Old Age and Survivors Insurance of the Social Security Administration.

Various basic types of benefits are paid either monthly or in a lump sum: (1) The primary insurance benefit, a percentage of the worker's average monthly wage, is payable to the fully insured retired worker at the age of sixty-five. (2) The wife's benefit is one-half of the primary insurance benefit, payable at the age of sixty-five to a retired worker's wife. (3) The widow's benefit is three-fourths of the primary insurance benefit, payable at the age of sixty-two to the widow of a fully insured worker. The same percentage is paid if the widow is under the age of sixty-two but has a child of an insured worker to care for. (4) The child's benefit is one-half of the primary insurance benefit, payable to a retired or deceased worker's unmarried children under the age of eighteen. (5) The parents' benefit is one-half of the primary benefit, payable at the age of sixty-five to the surviving dependent parents of a deceased fully insured worker if no other relatives are eligible to receive benefits. (6) The lump-sum death payment is three times the primary benefit, payable on the death of an insured worker if no other monthly benefits are immediately payable. Payments are also made in the case of total and permanent disability, subject to certain conditions and limitations. In mid-1980, the Social Security Administration paid old-age benefits to more than 36 million persons. The original coverage of the program, which was quite limited, has been expanded. The only exclusions now are part-time farm and domestic laborers, government employees, and workers in nonprofit organizations. See Eveline M. Burns, *Social Security and Public Policy*, Arno, New York, 1976; for monthly statistics, see U.S. Social Security Administration, *Social Security Bulletin*.

oligopoly A type of market structure in which a small number of firms supplies the major portion of an industry's output. The best-known examples in the U.S. economy are the automobile industry, the gypsum industry, and the aluminum industry. Although oligopolies are most likely to develop in industries whose production methods require large capital investments, they also cover such diverse items as cigarettes, light bulbs, chewing gum, detergents, and razor blades. In economic theory, the term oligopoly means a mixture of competition and monopoly, and the benefit or harm done to the economy at large by oligopolies remains in dispute. Prices in oligopolistic industries generally fluctuate less widely than those in more competitive industries; each seller hesitates to lower prices, knowing that the few competitors in that market will immediately match the cuts, leaving the seller with essentially the same share of the total market and lower profits. Nevertheless, other forms of competition, such as styling, quality, new features, marketing, and advertising, may be very keen. Moreover, the large size of oligopolists may permit greater investment in an industry than if the industry were composed of more competitive sellers. Although there is no way to measure the extent of oligopolies statistically, the prevailing view is that the number of oligopolies in the United States has grown since 1900, if only because the monopolies and near monopolies that once characterized many basic industries have become oligopolies (for example, the steel and petroleum industries). Furthermore, new processes and products have created new oligopolies in the computer, airline, synthetic-fiber, and other industries. For a discussion of classical and modern oligopoly models, see Donald S. Watson and Mary A. Holman, *Price Theory and Its Uses,* 4th ed., Houghton Mifflin, Boston, 1976.

oligopsony   A market structure with relatively few buyers. The high degree of buyer concentration results in a significant amount of interdependence, since the purchasing patterns of any one firm affect all the others. An oligopsonistic situation may lead to express or tacit collusion among the buyers to depress their buying prices, generally at the expense of the sellers who supply them. Often it is possible for a single large buyer, even without collusion, to individually exercise bargaining power to negotiate lower prices. An oligopsonistic market may face either an atomistic, competitive selling market or one with a significant degree of seller concentration. The first case, that of concentrated buying from a large number of small sellers, occurs in the United States mainly in some agricultural and mining markets, such as the leaf-tobacco market, the fluid-milk market, and the crude petroleum market. The second case, that of concentrated buying from concentrated selling, or bilateral oligopoly, occurs in some markets for manufactured goods in which manufacturers sell to other manufacturers or to large distributive firms. The markets for sheet steel, rails, and primary copper are examples of this type of oligopoly. For additional information, see Donald S. Watson and Mary A. Holman, *Price Theory and Its Uses,* 4th ed., Houghton Mifflin, Boston, 1976.

open economy   The economy of an area in which trade is unrestricted. In an open economy, any individual may have unhindered business and trade relationships with anyone outside the area. The term open economy usually refers to an economy in which there are no restrictions on imports, exports, or the movement of factors across boundaries.

open-end investment company   *See* **mutual fund.**

open-market operations   The buying and selling of government bonds by Federal Reserve banks in the open market for the purpose of implementing Federal Reserve monetary policies. The Federal Reserve, through private securities dealers, buys and sells marketable securities of the U.S. government. The purposes of open-market operations are (1) to contract or expand the supply of reserves of member banks, thus affecting the power of these banks to expand credit; (2) to influence interest rates through the quantitative effect on reserves; (3) to provide an orderly market for government securities; and (4) to exert an effect on exchange rates and international gold movements through the effect on interest rates. Open-market operations are considered the most flexible instrument of monetary policy. For example, to expand reserves the Federal Reserve buys government bonds from the public or other institutions. The commercial banks thus relinquish part of their security holdings to the Federal Reserve, which pays for the securities by increasing the reserves of the commercial banks by the amount of the purchase. If the bonds are purchased from a private individual, the seller's demand deposit is increased, and bank reserves also are increased. A contraction of reserves may be brought about by selling bonds to commercial banks. Open-market policy is decided upon by the Federal Open Market Committee and is carried out by the manager of the open-market account, a senior officer of the New York Federal Reserve Bank. For further information, see Lester V. Chandler and Stephen H. Goldfeld, *The Economics of Money and Banking,* 7th ed., Harper & Row, New York, 1977, pp. 179–284 and 521–609.

operating rate (capacity utilization rate) The ratio of physical output to physical capacity. The operating rate is a key factor in evaluating the short-run business outlook, especially with regard to investment in facilities for expansion. It correlates fairly well with profits, so that forward estimates of the operating rate provide a rough gauge of the future level of profits. Moreover, the direction of the operating rate, whether up or down, may have an impact on industrial prices. The operating rate is a rather difficult concept because it depends on the definition of capacity, which varies widely from industry to industry and from company to company. Data on operating rates in the United States are available for manufacturing industries and for the industrial sector of the economy. End-of-year operating rates for manufacturing and for major manufacturing industries since 1954 are found in *Annual Surveys of Business' Plans for New Plants and Equipment,* McGraw-Hill Department of Economics, New York; for various measures of the operating rate and evaluations, see *Measures of Productive Capacity, Hearings before the Subcommittee on Economic Statistics of the U.S. Joint Economic Committee,* May 14, 22, 23, and 24, 1962, Washington, D.C., 1962.

operating statement *See* **profit and loss statement.**

operation nudge *See* **operation twist.**

operations research The use of certain mathematical techniques in analyzing particular activities in order to provide a more or less scientific basis for a choice among alternative means of accomplishing a given goal. In carrying out an operations research (O.R.) project, a team of experts is organized, each member of which is familiar with one aspect of the problem and, generally, with advanced mathematical techniques. The introduction of electronic computers has made it possible to apply O.R. to problem solving. O.R. was first used widely during World War II, when it was employed to analyze complex logistical and other military problems. More recently, it has received considerable attention as a business-management tool. Among the business problems to which it has been applied are production and inventory control, transportation planning, and plant location. For the classic reference, see George B. Dantzig, *Linear Programming and Extensions,* Rand Corporation Research Studies, Santa Monica, Calif., 1963. A recent text is F. Hillier and G. Lieberman, *Introduction to Operations Research,* 3d ed., Holden-Day, San Francisco, 1980.

operation twist (operation nudge)   The attempt by the Federal Reserve and the Treasury in 1961 to raise short-term interest rates relative to long-term rates in order to reconcile international and domestic objectives. Federal Reserve and Treasury officials believed that short-term rates should be raised to minimize the outflows of speculative funds to other countries while holding down the costs of long-term funds to expand business's capital investment. Through Treasury debt management operations and Federal Reserve open-market operations, the supply of treasury bills and other short-term issues was increased relative to the supply of long-term government bonds. The end result was that the interest rate paid by commercial banks on time deposits was increased several times, and funds were redirected from short- to long-term objectives. For additional information, see Lester V. Chandler and Stephen M. Goldfeld, *The Economics of Money and Banking,* 7th ed., Harper & Row, New York, 1977.

opportunity costs (alternative costs)   The value of the productive resources used in producing one good, such as an automobile, instead of another good, such as a machine tool. With a relatively fixed supply of labor and capital at any given time, the economy cannot produce all it wants of everything. Thus, the real cost to society of producing an automobile is the value of the other things that cannot be produced because the same resources are not available to build them. The fact of alternative costs is most clearly demonstrated in wartime, when a nation can have guns and tanks or new automobiles and appliances but not both weapons and consumer durable goods. The principle of opportunity costs, which was developed by the neoclassicists in the nineteenth century, is based on notions of Jean Baptiste Say and Nassau William Senior of the classical school of political economy. The concept of alternative costs covers more than the conventional accounting costs encountered in a profit and loss statement. For example, a production worker in a plant earns $5,000 per year. The worker saves money to buy a machine shop for $3,000, but takes home only $4,500 per year in profits from the shop. According to the principle of opportunity costs, the machine-shop owner has made no profit because the alternative cost of the $5,000 yearly salary at the plant has not even been covered, to say nothing of the loss of interest on the savings. For further discussion, see James R. McGuigan and R. Charles Moyer, *Managerial Economics,* 2d ed., West, St. Paul, Minn., 1979.

option   A contract permitting the purchaser, at his or her discretion, to require the seller to perform his or her part of an agreement within a stipulated period. If the buyer of the contract does not choose to exercise this option, the buyer loses only the amount of money paid for it. Options are used in many businesses: in real estate, when, for example, tenants are given the temporary right to purchase the property that they are renting at a given price; or in the theater or films, when a producer buys an option to a particular actor's services for a certain time. In the securities industry, options take many forms, including puts, calls, spreads, straddles, stock options, and warrants, but they all have one feature in common: the option buyer has the right to buy or sell a specified amount of securities, at a stated price, for a certain length of time. For further discussion, see William F. Sharpe, *Investments,* Prentice-Hall, Englewood Cliffs, N.J., 1978.

organized labor   The association of workers for the purpose of improving their economic position by bargaining with employers. The sheer weight of numbers in organized labor places it in a better position than that of individual workers to bargain with employers. The activities of organized labor in the past, and especially in countries outside the United States, have often been political rather than economic, ranging from lobbying and the exertion of unified pressure through established political channels to occasional successful attempts to overthrow the established order. Organized labor came into existence almost immediately after the development of the factory system, under which wage earners worked with tools provided by employers. It became necessary for an individual to join with other laborers in order to improve bargaining power and maximize the fraction of the total value of the product which went to each wage earner in the form of wages. As of 1982, union membership in the United States was estimated at 17.5 million, the AFL-CIO having the largest membership. The extent of labor organization varies with the sector of the economy. In the construction, coal and metal mining, and transportation and public utility industries the great majority of wage earners are union members. A large majority of the wage earners in manufacturing also are union members, although in some manufacturing industries only a minority of the workers are organized. These four sectors—manufacturing, construction, mining, and transportation and public utilities—account for less than 80% of all union membership in the United States. In service and distributing industries unionism is generally weak, but certain skilled workers, such as musicians, bartenders, barbers, and meatcutters, have fairly strong unions in large cities. In government, union membership is growing rapidly. See Neil W. Chamberlain et al., *The Labor Sector,* 3d rev. ed., McGraw-Hill, New York, 1979.

orthogonal   In a strict mathematical sense this term means perpendicular, or right-angled, as, for example, orthogonal coordinate axes. The term is

output   **254**

used in the same sense in connection with orthogonal regression, where vertical deviations from the regression line are minimized. The term has also been extended to describe certain techniques of matrix algebra, e.g., linear orthogonal factor analysis. Occasionally in the literature of statistics, two variables are said to be orthogonal if they are statistically independent of each other. For additional information, see Lawrence R. Klein, *An Introduction to Econometrics,* Greenwood, Westport, Conn., 1977.

output Any commodity or service that a firm produces for sale. It could be a steel ingot, an automobile, a machine, or a financial service.

overidentification A condition that exists when more relations are given by a system of stochastic equations than are necessary to derive unbiased estimates of all parameters. This condition can be removed by abandoning reduced-form methods and resorting to longer computations. For additional information, see Karl A. Fox and Tej K. Kaul, *Intermediate Economic Statistics,* Krieger, Melbourne, Fla., 1980.

overpopulation A condition of excess population. Overpopulation is the existence of too many persons in a given area, with the result that their standard of living is at a subsistence or near-subsistence level. According to the theory of population formulated by Thomas Robert Malthus, overpopulation develops because population increases faster than the means of subsistence. Malthus claimed that population increased by geometric progression (1, 2, 4, 8, 16), while the means of food production increased by arithmetical progression (1, 2, 3, 4, 5). He therefore believed that unless population growth could be changed, human beings were destined to misery and poverty. According to Malthus, there are preventive checks (moral restraint, late marriage, celibacy) as well as positive checks (famine, war, plague) which serve to keep population at least at subsistence levels. See Warren S. Thompson, *Population Problems,* 8th ed., McGraw-Hill, New York, 1961.

overproduction *See* **underconsumption.**

oversaving theory The theory that when planned saving is greater than planned investment the result is oversaving. When oversaving occurs, the amount of money removed from the income flow is greater than the amount returned to it; income must therefore fall. Oversaving has long been used by such economists as Thomas Robert Malthus and John Atkinson Hobson to explain low or falling national income. The lack of a theoretical base led some economists to believe that the oversaving theory was also an overinvestment theory, reasoning that oversaving caused overinvestment. John Maynard Keynes pointed out, however, that the level of planned investment does not depend on the level of planned saving. He maintained that, in maturing economies, people desire to save a larger amount of money at full employment than can be profitably invested because of diminishing investment opportunities. Keynes expected that, in mature economies, unless oversaving was prevented or compensated for by the government, there would be high unemployment. See William Fellner, *Modern Economic Analysis,* McGraw-Hill, New York, 1960; see also J. M. Keynes, *The General Theory of Employment, Interest, and Money,* Harcourt Brace, New York, 1936

over-the-counter market   A market for securities which includes all transactions in securities that are not made on organized stock exchanges. Unlike a stock exchange, which is an auction market located in one place, the over-the-counter market comprises thousands of stock and bond dealers who negotiate transactions primarily by telephone. Trading takes place when a potential buyer or seller of a particular security (or the buyer's broker) canvasses securities dealers who trade in that security and is quoted an acceptable price. By most measures, the over-the-counter market is the largest securities market in the United States. In addition to common and preferred stocks, almost all U.S. government securities and municipal and corporate bonds are traded over the counter. Stocks that are traded over the counter range from those of smaller and usually more speculative companies to those of large, high-quality corporations, such as, for example, most U.S. commercial banks and insurance companies. Although the over-the-counter market is virtually unregulated by the federal government, the National Association of Securities Dealers, which was established in 1939, provides self-regulation of over-the-counter securities dealers and their trading practices. For a brief description of the over-the-counter market, see George A. Christy and John C. Clendenin, *Introduction to Investments,* 7th ed., McGraw-Hill, New York, 1978.

P

paradox of thrift   The principle, first proposed by John Maynard Keynes, that an attempt by society to increase its rate of saving may result in a reduction in the amount which it actually can save. This ironic conclusion is arrived at through the Keynesian savings-investment approach to the determination of national income, according to which the attempt to save (consume less) results in a reduced national income and in the inability of individuals.

because of their smaller incomes, to save as much. The paradox, that saving is a vice and spending a virtue, is an illustration of a contradiction in incentives; while thrift may be desirable from the point of view of the individual, it may have disastrous effects on total output and employment from the point of view of society. For further information, see J. M. Keynes, *The General Theory of Employment, Interest, and Money*, Harcourt Brace, New York, 1936; Gardner Ackley, *Macroeconomics: Theory and Policy*, Macmillan, New York, 1978; Armen A. Alchian and William R. Allen, *University Economics*, 3d ed., Wadsworth, New York, 1971.

parameter   In economics, a constant which is assigned a value or a set of values at the outset of a problem. A parameter thus differs from a variable, which can take on any value. The values of a parameter are restricted by the particular problem under study, and a parameter can vary only when there is a change in the entire system being studied. In statistics, a parameter is a summary measure, such as a mean, median, or proportion of a characteristic of members of a population.

parametric (regression) method, seasonal-adjustment   A method of seasonal adjustment. In the parametric method, the systematic (trend-cycle and seasonal) components of the series are estimated by regression techniques, using explicit mathematical expressions in the form of the general linear model.

Paretian optimum   A situation that exists when no one in a society can move into a preferable position without causing someone else to move into a position which that person prefers less. In other words, a situation is not a Paretian or social optimum if it is possible, by changing the way in which commodities are produced or exchanged, to make one person better off without making another person (or persons) worse off. The term is named for Vilfredo Pareto, who first defined the social optimum, or the standard by which an economy can be judged. Although N. Kaldor, J. R. Hicks, and T. Scitovsky have attempted to refine the Paretian optimum, it still sets the conditions that maximize the economic wealth of any given society and therefore remains one of the cornerstones of welfare economics. See Vilfredo Pareto, *Manual of Political Economy*, Kelley, New York, 1971; for a mathematical interpretation of this condition see Gerard Debreu, "Valuation Equilibrium and Pareto Optimum," in American Economic Association, *Readings in Welfare Economics*, vol. XII, Irwin, Homewood, Ill., 1969, pp. 39–45.

Pareto's law   A law that states that the distribution of income is the same everywhere. Formulated by Vilfredo Pareto after wide-ranging statistical investigations, it states that if A equals a given income and B equals the number of persons with incomes greater than A, then if the logarithms of A and B are plotted on the y axis and x axis, respectively, or if A and B are plotted on log paper, the resulting curve, no matter which country is examined, will always be inclined by roughly 56° from the *y* axis. This law, which Pareto induced from statistical evidence, describes the fact that incomes are not distributed equally. More important, because of the rigidity that Pareto thought existed (the curve is always within 3 to 4° of a 56° incline from the *y* axis), the distribution of income is always the same no matter what the average income level of a nation may be. The implication is that the only way in which the income of the poorer segment of a country can be increased is by raising the income of the whole nation; in short, it is impossible to redistribute income. For the original statement of the law, see Vilfredo Pareto, *Manual of Political Economy*, Kelley, New York, 1971; for a refutation of the law, see Arthur C. Pigou, *The Economics of Welfare*, Macmillan, London, 1932.

pari passu   A Latin phrase meaning "with equal progress." The term *pari passu* is used in economics to indicate a simultaneous and equal change. For example, the quantity theory of money holds that if the stock of money in an economy is increased by 5%, there will be a *pari passu* increase in the price level.

parity price   A price received by U.S. farmers for many commodities which are adjusted to provide the same relative purchasing power that farm prices had in the base period (1909–1914). At the beginning of each marketing year, the U.S. Department of Agriculture announces the levels at which farmers' prices for basic commodities will be supported, provided the marketing quotas are accepted by two-thirds of the eligible farmers voting in a referendum. If production is greater than can be sold at these prices, prices are supported by nonrecourse loans or purchase agreements with farmers. In the process, the Commodity Credit Corporation may purchase many commodities. Prices have been supported at 60 to 90% of parity. Parity prices for a selected list of commodities are published in U.S. Department of Agriculture, Statistical Reporting Service, *Agricultural Prices,* monthly.

parity ratio, agricultural   A measure that shows whether the prices received by farmers are higher or lower in relation to the prices that they paid in a base period. In the United States, this period is August 1909 to July 1914, when the prices that farmers received and the prices that they paid for goods, services, farm wages, interest, and taxes were considered in good balance. The parity ratio is calculated by dividing the index of prices received by farmers into the index of prices paid by them. Thus, if the prices received by farmers had doubled since 1909–1914 and the prices paid had quadrupled, current farm prices would be at 50% of parity (200/400 = 0.50). Occasionally, as in 1951, U.S. farm prices have exceeded 100% of parity, but usually they have been below parity, and in mid-1981 they were at 93%. Changes in the parity ratio actuate several government price-support programs. Price-support programs, which were begun in 1929 to protect farmers against violent price fluctuations, are criticized primarily because they discourage the most efficient use of productive resources. Monthly data on the ratio of current farm prices to parity prices are reported in U.S. Department of Agriculture, *Agricultural Prices.*

partial-equilibrium theory The theory that individual sectors of the economy are not related to other sectors in terms of price or production. It ignores the mutual interrelationships between the prices and outputs of various goods and factors, assuming that repercussions from one market to another will be slight enough to be disregarded. All partial-equilibrium analyses are based on the assumptions of *ceteris paribus.* The familiar supply-and-demand analysis is an example of partial-equilibrium analysis. Although its basic assumptions are quite restrictive, partial-equilibrium analysis is valid for the study of a wide range of problems. For example, in studying the effects of an excise tax on a particular commodity, e.g., tobacco, it is not very unrealistic to assume that prices are as given in all markets other than the tobacco market. Similarly, partial-equilibrium theory can be used to analyze the effect of a lower price of steel on the automobile industry. The total effect on the economy of the lower steel price cannot, however, be regarded simply as the sum of the effects on each individual market. For such an analysis, partial-equilibrium theory is inadequate, and general-equilibrium theory must be used. For an exposition of the major aspects of partial-equilibrium theory, see George J. Stigler, *The Theory of Price,* 3d ed., Macmillan, New York, 1966; for a discussion of the distinction between partial and general equilibrium, see Richard G. Lipsey and Peter O. Steiner, *Economics,* 5th ed., Harper & Row, New York, 1978.

participation loan A loan in which two or more banks take part. Such participation agreements are usually made between a country bank and a large city bank. In this way, smaller country banks can take better advantage of investment opportunities in the larger money markets of cities and thus have a ready outlet for available short-term funds. Actual loans are made and terminated by the larger bank at its convenience, the smaller bank merely turning funds over to the larger one. The larger bank also holds the collateral for the joint protection of the two banks. The term participation loan may also refer to a large loan in which several large banks participate jointly. Such a loan is sometimes referred to as a syndicate loan.

partnership A type of business organization in which two or more persons agree on the amount of their contribution (capital and effort) and on the distribution of profits, if any. Partnerships are common in retail trade, accounting, and law. Since the partners pool their capital, partnerships, in general, are larger than proprietorships, but they still are relatively small when compared with corporations. In many respects, however, partnerships are similar to proprietorships. They are subject to little government regulation and taxation. In addition, the partnership ends if any one of the partners dies, becomes insane, or goes bankrupt. A partnership is characterized by unlimited liability, which means that all the personal assets of the partners are available as security for their creditors. For a more detailed discussion of partnership, see Lyman A. Keith and Carlo E. Gubellini, *Introduction to Business Enterprise,* 4th ed., McGraw-Hill, New York, 1977.

par value   The value which is printed on the face of common and preferred stocks and bonds. In the case of common stocks, par value originally purported to represent the initial investment of cash, property, or services behind each share of stock that was issued. After the company was operating for a while, however, par value usually bore little relation to market value or even to book value. Over the years, the par value of common stocks has become a meaningless number. Recognizing this fact, many corporations now either issue no-par stock or issue stock with low par values because federal transfer taxes are based on par value. Par value is more important in the case of preferred stocks and bonds because dividend and interest rates are calculated on par value. For example, with a 4% preferred stock the company will pay $4 a year on each share with a par value of $100 (the usual par value for preferred stocks). Although the par value of preferred stocks and bonds is normally closer to market value than is true of common stocks, they rarely are equal, and they can differ widely. See William F. Sharpe, *Investments,* 2d ed., Prentice-Hall, Englewood Cliffs, N.J., 1981.

patent   A contract between the government and an inventor providing that, in return for full disclosure of the invention, the government grants the inventor an exclusive right to practice the invention for a period of seventeen years from the date of the grant. At the end of this period, the patent expires and becomes public property available to all. Patents are granted to encourage inventors to disclose their inventions to the public and thereby to "promote the progress of science and the useful arts." In 1623 patent laws were first enacted in England, where patents on inventions or new trades brought into the kingdom were limited to fourteen years. The first U.S. Patent Act became law on April 10, 1790, and the present statute dates from July 4, 1836. For a discussion of the U.S. patent system, see David M. Abernathy and Wayne B. Knipe III, *Ideas, Inventions and Patents: An Introduction to Patent Information,* 2d ed., Pioneer Press, Atlanta, Ga., 1974.

pattern bargaining   The technique of a union whereby it completes labor negotiations with one leading company in an industry and offers the same terms subsequently to all other companies in the industry, with the threat of a strike if the terms are not accepted. The International Union of Electrical, Radio and Machine Workers attempts to set a pattern for the electrical-machinery industry by selecting General Electric or Westinghouse as the primary target of its negotiations. After the settlement, the union proceeds to bargain with other electrical-machinery manufacturers on the same terms. For additional details, see Lloyd G. Reynolds, *Labor Economics and Labor Relations,* 7th ed., Prentice-Hall, Englewood Cliffs, N.J., 1978.

payoff period (payout period) A popular means of determining how quickly a company can get its money back from a capital investment. For example, if a new $1,000 machine increases revenue by $500 annually or permits savings in costs of $500 annually, its payoff period is two years. The average payout in U.S. manufacturing is about four years, but for an individual company the period ranges from less than one year to more than nine years. The major limitations of this method of assessing capital investments are that it gives no indication of the total return that a machine brings in over its entire life span, ignores the cost of making the investment, and does not tell whether investment in other assets (for instance, in inventory) might not produce a higher return. For various methods of evaluating the profitability of proposed equipment purchases, see J. Fred Weston and Eugene F. Brigham, *Essentials of Managerial Finance,* 5th ed., Holt, Rinehart and Winston, New York, 1979.

payroll tax A tax levied on the payroll of a firm. It is based on the amount of wages and salaries of the firm and is paid by the employer. Payroll taxes are used in the United States to finance the employer's part of the social security programs. Whereas all employers pay the same rate of payroll tax for the old age, survivors, and disability insurance programs, different firms may pay different rates of payroll tax for their unemployment insurance. Although the social security payroll tax cannot be deducted from wages, the final burden of the tax is generally believed to be borne largely by the employee and by the consumer. For further information on payroll taxes in the United States, see B. Lewis Keeling, *Payroll Records and Accounting,* South-Western, Cincinnati, Ohio, 1975.

peak The high mark of the expansionary phase of economic activity. It is usually a short interval lasting for one or two months. According to the National Bureau of Economic Research, in the eight recoveries from recessions, the peaks were November 1948, July 1953, August 1957, April 1960, December 1969, November 1973, January 1980, and July 1981. For more detailed information on peaks, see Geoffrey H. Moore (ed.), *Business Cycle Indicators,* Princeton University Press, Princeton, N.J., 1961.

pegging In finance, the fixing of the price of a security or securities. The most recent example of pegging in the United States occurred during World War II. To finance the war, the Treasury, over the Federal Reserve System's protests, decided to adopt a cheap-money policy. Forced to carry out this plan, the Federal Reserve announced in April 1942 that it would buy or sell unlimited amounts of treasury bills at ⅜ of 1%. This effectively pegged the short-term government securities market because no one would pay more or take less for bills, which they could always buy or sell at a member bank of the System for a fixed price. The Treasury was assured of obtaining all the funds that it needed at low interest rates. The Federal Reserve authorities went further and pegged the entire government securities market (2.5% of government bonds) for the duration of the war. In July 1947, the System began to remove the peg by ceasing to maintain the treasury bill rate. At first, the Treasury and Federal Reserve authorities agreed on policy, but eventually a conflict arose because the Federal Reserve, fearing inflation, wanted to tighten money while the Treasury wanted to maintain an easy-money policy. The conflict was finally resolved in the accord of March 1951. See Herman E. Krooss, *Documentary History of Banking and Currency in the United States,* Chelsea House, New York, 1980.

pension fund   A plan established and maintained by an employer to provide for systematic benefits to employees after their retirement. In effect, pension fund assets are a pool of capital set aside for the purpose of meeting future liability payments. Pension funds account for a significant share of personal savings and represent one of the largest and fastest-growing segments of institutional capital. There are two major types of private pension plans, the noninsured and the insured. In the case of noninsured pension plans, company contributions are generally paid into a trust fund at a bank or trust company, with the trustee holding and investing the accumulated funds. In turn, the trustee makes payments to the plan's participants. Under insured pension plans, pension obligations are funded by premium payments made by the sponsoring company to a life insurance company, with the insurance company guaranteeing that it will make specified annuity payments in the future. Public plans are generally established and maintained under complex laws which dictate in large measure the administrative and investment policy. These plans usually require that the employee, as well as the employer, contribute. The United States is entering a period when fewer and fewer young workers will be forced to support a growing population of retired workers. Actuaries indicate that, as a result, enormous stresses are building up in public employee systems, pay-as-you-go social security, and private pension funds. Favorable tax regulation has provided employer incentive to establish and maintain pension plans. In 1974, Congress passed the Employees' Retirement Income Security Act (ERISA), which provides protection for the pensions of workers in private industry. For additional information, see Roger F. Murray, *Economic Aspects of Pensions: A Summary Report,* National Bureau of Economic Research, New York, 1968; Daniel M. Holland, *Private Pension Funds,* National Bureau of Economic Research, Occasional Paper no. 97, Columbia University Press, New York, 1966.

people's capitalism   A type of capitalism in which the ownership of industry is shared by a large part of the population, including middle- and lower-income groups. The phrase is frequently used to describe the United States of the mid-twentieth century, in which stock ownership is widespread, and to contrast it with the United States of the late nineteenth century, when most big businesses were owned by a few wealthy individuals. For a discussion of people's capitalism in the United States, see Marcus Nadler, *People's Capitalism,* Manufacturers Hanover Trust Company, New York, 1956.

percentage depletion   *See* depletion allowance.

performance budgeting   A method of preparing a governmental budget in which items appearing in the budget represent functions to be performed or activities to be undertaken. Under other budgeting methods, proposed expenditures for particular functions tend to become scattered under various titles, making it difficult to control expenditures. The performance budget seeks to reach a reasonable compromise between general appropriations, which give an agency freedom to allocate funds to specific projects, and appropriations that are so specific as to prevent adjustment to changing conditions. The performance-budgeting method was recommended by the Hoover Commission.

peril point   The maximum cut in a U.S. import duty which could be made for a given commodity without causing serious injury to domestic producers or to a similar commodity. First included in the Trade Agreements Extension Act of 1948, the peril-point mechanism was in effect almost continuously until it was eliminated in the Trade Expansion Act of 1962. The peril-point provision stated that, before entering into any tariff discussions with other countries, the President must submit to the Tariff Commission a list of the commodities to be negotiated. The commission would then conduct an investigation on the effect of tariff reduction on these commodities, determine the respective peril points, and present a list of recommendations to the President. If in the subsequent trade agreement, the President did not follow the Tariff Commission's peril-point recommendations, the President was obligated to send Congress a message stating the reasons for this action. The threat of a congressional investigation usually was effective in inducing the negotiators to follow the advice of the Tariff Commission on peril points. The inclusion of the peril-point provision in tariff legislation was a victory for protectionist interests because it sought to prevent concessions which would really liberalize trade.

periodogram   A chart with time on the horizontal axis and a composite series on the vertical axis. This chart is expected to reveal turning points in a time series that can be related to one or more statistically consistent causal factors or sources of variation. The technique works fairly well if the series under study consists of periodic, trigonometric terms and a random component. It works poorly or not at all for economic time series that are autoregressive and stochastic and where little or nothing is known about the time cycles of the causal factors or sources of variation. For a detailed discussion and the necessary formulas, consult Lawrence R. Klein, *An Introduction to Econometrics*, Greenwood, Westport, Conn., 1977.

permanent-income hypothesis   A theory of the income concept most relevant for determining consumption. The permanent-income hypothesis has been highly regarded by economists because it helps explain apparent inconsistencies of empirical data on the relationship of saving to income. Cross-section data for a single year show that as income rises, savings account for an increasing share of income, while data for a long period of years show that even though total income rises over the years, total savings account for a fairly stable share of total income. Milton Friedman states that this occurs because a study of measured income and consumption involves inaccurate concepts of what income and consumption really are. For example, there are actually two types of income—permanent and transitory. Permanent income is the amount which a consumer unit expects to receive over a long period of time and to which it adjusts its permanent consumption—a certain fraction of permanent income which does not depend on the permanent-income level but on factors affecting the unit's desire for current consumption versus the accumulation of assets. Transitory income is that amount which a consumer unit receives unexpectedly. When transitory income differs from permanent income, the consumer unit saves or dissaves the difference between two concepts (consumer durables, according to Friedman, are savings and not consumption). Thus planned or permanent savings differ from measured savings, and increases and decreases in transitory consumption cause permanent consumption to differ from measured consumption. For this reason, annual data give a distorted picture of consumer behavior. Friedman indicates that the factors affecting the ratio of permanent consumption to permanent income are more significant than levels of income in analyzing consumer behavior. See Milton Friedman, *A Theory of the Consumption Function*, National Bureau of Economic Research, Princeton University Press, Princeton, N.J., 1957; Michael R. Darby, "The Permanent Income Theory of Consumption—A Restatement," *Quarterly Journal of Economics*, vol. 88, May 1974, pp. 228–250.

permanent saving   *See* permanent-income hypothesis.

personal consumption expenditures (PCE)   Expenditures that reflect the market value of goods—durables and nondurables—and services purchased by persons—defined as individuals and nonprofit institutions—or acquired by them as income in kind. For example, the rental value of owner-occupied dwellings is included but not the purchase of dwellings. In the national income accounts, consumer purchases of owner-occupied housing are treated as business investments, while consumer purchases of durable goods are treated as current consumption expenditures rather than investment and, thus, reduce consumer savings. In the national income accounts, the category "persons" includes individuals in their roles not only as consumers or households but also as unincorporated businesspeople because household and business accounts of retailers, self-employed professionals, farmers, and other individual enterprises have not successfully been separated. The category also includes nonprofit institutions such as private colleges and hospitals, private trust funds, and private pension, health, and welfare funds. For additional information, see Richard Ruggles and Nancy D. Ruggles, *National Income Accounts and Income Analysis,* 2d ed., McGraw-Hill, New York, 1956.

personal finance company   *See* **consumer finance company.**

personal income   According to the concept of the U.S. Department of Commerce, the amount of current income received by persons from all sources, including transfer payments from government and business but excluding transfer payments from other sources. Personal income also includes the net incomes of unincorporated businesses and nonprofit institutions and nonmonetary income, such as the estimate of the value of food consumed on farms and the estimated rental value of homes occupied by their owners. The major monetary components of personal income are labor income, proprietors' income, rental income, dividends, interest, and transfer payments. Personal income is a measure of income before taxes have been deducted. The statistical series on personal income is a useful indicator of general trends, although the inclusion of nonmonetary income and of the income of unincorporated businesses and nonprofit institutions makes it difficult to tell how much income actually is received by consumers only. For monthly estimates of personal income, see U.S. Department of Commerce, *Survey of Current Business.*

personal outlays   The disbursements made by individuals of that portion of personal income available after payment of personal taxes. It is composed of personal consumption expenses for goods and services, interest paid by consumers, and personal transfer payments. For quarterly and annual data, see U.S. Department of Commerce, *Survey of Current Business,* monthly.

personal property tax   A levy on the personal property of an individual. Personal property should not be confused with real property, or real estate, which consists of land and improvements. It includes all other possessions of an individual or firm and can be divided into two categories: tangible personal property, which consists of furniture, jewelry, merchandise, etc.; and intangibles, such as stocks, bonds, and money. A few states of the United States tax both tangible and intangible personal property, while many tax only tangible property. Some states, such as New York, do not tax personal property at all. Numerous municipalities also resort to personal property taxation, which supplies a substantial part of the tax base (sometimes as much as 15 to 20%). A personal property tax involves many problems of administration, especially those of valuation and evasion. Furthermore, as applied to businesses, the personal property tax discriminates against the merchant with a slow turnover and favors the chain store over the independent retailer. For additional details, see John F. Due and Ann F. Friedlaender, *Government Finance*, Irwin, Homewood, Ill., 1978.

Phillips curve   A hypothesis advanced by A. W. Phillips stating originally that, assuming a given annual increase in productivity, the percentage rate of the change of money wage rates in the United Kingdom can be explained to a very large extent by (1) the percentage of the labor force that is unemployed and (2) the rate of change of unemployment. He further concluded that not only is there a clearly observable relationship between these variables, but also the form of the relationship has been remarkably stable over a period of almost one hundred years (1861 to 1957). Samuelson and Solow conducted a similar study using U.S. data. The results, while not contradictory, are not as clear-cut as those obtained by Phillips. Richard J. Lipsey has also questioned the findings of Phillips and has suggested that the relationship does not hold over the entire period in question, but can be relevant for shorter periods of time. For further details, see A. W. Phillips, "The Relationship between Unemployment and the Rate of Change of Money Wage Rates in the United Kingdom, 1861–1957," *Economica*, vol. 25, November 1958, pp. 283–299; Richard J. Lipsey, "The Relations between Unemployment and the Rate of Change of Money Wage Rates in the United Kingdom, 1862–1957: A Further Analysis," *Economica*, vol. 27, February 1960, pp. 1–31; Arthur M. Okun, "Efficient Disinflationary Policies," *American Economic Review*, May 1978, pp. 348–352.

physiocrat   A member of a school of French economists of the mid-eighteenth century. Based largely on the idea of François Quesnay and Anne Robert Jacques Turgot, the physiocratic philosophy had as its central tenet an overriding belief in land as the single source of income and wealth. Land alone, the physiocrats held, has the power to produce an output in excess of the materials used up in the productive process. In contrast to the working of the land, which produces this *produit net* (net product), manufacturing and commercial activities, the physiocrats thought, are sterile, yielding no excess over the quantity of materials that they receive as inputs. Physiocratic doctrines thus contrasted sharply with those of the mercantilists, who stressed the importance of trade and commerce as the source of a nation's wealth. In addition, the physiocrats adhered to a firm belief in natural law (laissez faire, or freedom from government regulation) as the best possible means of regulating human affairs. The physiocrats classified society into four groups: (1) the "productive" class, or agriculturists; (2) the proprietors, or landowners; (3) the nonproductive class (*la classe sterile*), which included merchants, artisans, and professionals; and (4) wage earners or laborers. In their opinion, the first three classes are independent and play an active part in the national economy since they are in possession of some capital and also exercise some enterprise. The fourth class is dependent and passive and only a minor factor in their classification. Adam Smith, during a journey to France, came under the influence of physiocratic doctrines in the course of discussions with Quesnay and other members of the school. Among the leading spokesmen of the school was a member of the French government, Pierre Samuel du Pont de Nemours, who later went to the United States and laid the foundations for the vast E. I. du Pont de Nemours' interests. For further discussion of the physiocrats, see Mark Blaug, *Economic Theory in Retrospect*, 3d rev. ed., Cambridge University Press, London, 1978

Pigou-effect theory The theory that a reduction in the overall price level leads to increased spending on goods and services. It is based on the following line of reasoning: (1) Individuals establish a desired relationship between the money balances that they hold and their expenditures on goods and services. (2) Price reductions raise the real value of their money holdings; that is, the quantity of goods and services that can be bought with a given amount of money is increased. (3) Thus, the desired relationship between real balances and expenditures is disturbed, and individuals have an excess supply of liquid assets. (4) They spend part of this excess supply on goods and services. The Pigou effect operates only in the market for goods and services; in this respect, it differs from the Keynes effect, which operates only in the market for bonds, and from the real-balance effect, which operates in both the bond market and the market for goods and services. For the original statement of the Pigou effect, see Arthur C. Pigou, "The Classical Stationary State," *Economic Journal*, Cambridge University Press, London, 1943; see also Don Patinkin, *Money, Interest and Prices*, 2d ed., Harper & Row, New York, 1961; for a critique of the Pigou effect, see M. Kalecki, "Professor Pigou on the 'Classical Stationary State,' " *Economic Journal*, Royal Economic Society, London, 1952.

planned economy An economic system in which some or all of the decisions on allocation, production, investment, and distribution are made by a central governmental agency. The collective economic planning used in a planned economy is based on the assumption that social welfare can be recognized and pursued more ably under centralized control. The assumption denies the advantages of private enterprise, which is said to lead to chaotic disharmony between production and consumption. In a planned economy, the initiative for economic activities and decisions concerning them does not originate with the entrepreneur. Rather, the government starts with an overall plan of major objectives and then attempts to achieve the fullest possible utilization of available resources in line with the stated objectives. In a completely planned economy, the market mechanism in price formation is eliminated, and the government undertakes to replace the market functions. The planning agency sets all the goals for production, allocates scarce resources among competing uses, makes decisions on production and investment, and distributes the output to consumers. Because of this, the planned economy claims to achieve maximum social welfare. Examples of planned economies are those found in the U.S.S.R., France, Yugoslavia, and Poland. For further information, see C. R. Blitzer, P. B. Clark, and L. Taylor (eds.), *Economywide Models and Development Planning*, Oxford University Press, London, 1975.

planning, programming, and budgetary system (PPB)   A system to achieve long-term goals or objectives by means of analysis and evaluation of the alternatives. PPB is designed to solve problems by finding the most effective and most efficient solution on the basis of objective criteria. In the 1950s the Rand Corporation and others applied PPB to defense problems. In 1961 it was first used by the Department of Defense. In 1965 all major civilian agencies of the federal government were directed to install PPB. For additional information, see Charles L. Schultz, *The Politics and Economics of Public Spending*, Brookings Institution, Washington, D.C. 1968.

plant   Capital asset units, such as factory buildings, warehouses, stores, and other commercial buildings. Spending for plants accounted for roughly 20% of total capital expenditures by U.S. manufacturers in the 1970s. For estimates of annual expenditures on plants, see *Annual Surveys of Business' Plans for New Plants and Equipment*, McGraw-Hill Department of Economics, New York.

pork-barrel legislation   The appropriation of money by a legislature for local projects that are not critically needed. Pork-barrel projects, such as local highways, hospitals, and river and harbor construction projects, are sought by individual legislators for their districts as a means of demonstrating their service to the voters in their constituencies and of thus improving their chances of reelection. Much of the pork-barrel legislation is enacted through a system of logrolling under which the legislators do not question each other's pet local projects in order to ensure that their own projects will be approved.

post-Keynesian economics   The thinking of economists from the Keynesian and neo-Keynesian schools as well as of some right-leaning members of the socialist group. Post-Keynesians recognize that all theories represent abstractions and simplifications of reality; thus, they repeat the notion that any general-equilibrium system is the basic logical structure for the comprehension of real-world economies. All post-Keynesian models are based on five concepts: (1) Time is seen as a real-world phenomenon that prevents everything from happening at once; economic decisions made in the present will require actions which cannot be completed until some future date. (2) There is a difference between uncertainty and risks. Risks are incorporated into the expectations of economic decision makers in a world where the mathematical laws of probability do not apply. (3) Economic institutions such as the monetary system, markets for goods, factors of production, financial assets, and money contracts are influential in determining output, employment, and the price level of money. (4) The distribution of income (and power) is relevant. (5) Emphasis must be placed on the nonmalleability of real capital as well as on the difference between financial and real capital and the markets for each. For additional information, see Paul Davidson, *Money and the Real World*, 2d ed., Halsted Press, New York, 1978; S. Weintraub, *Capitalism's Inflation and Unemployment Crisis*, Addison-Wesley, Reading, Mass., 1978.

potential gross national product (full-employment output)   The output that the economy can produce under full-employment conditions. Potential gross national output (GNP) is maximum production without inflationary pressures. It is an imprecise measure of productive capacity, using a 4% unemployment rate as the criterion for full employment. Some economists doubt that potential GNP can be measured at all. Another method of computing potential GNP was offered by Arthur M. Okun, a former chairman of the Council of Economic Advisers, who measured the extent to which output is depressed by unemployment in excess of 4%. This relationship can be stated as follows: "On the average, each extra percentage point in the unemployment rate above 4% has been associated with about a 3% decrease in real GNP." For further discussion of the potential GNP, see Arthur M. Okun, "Potential Gross National Product," in D. Greenwald (ed.), *Encyclopedia of Economics*, McGraw-Hill, New York, 1982; George L. Perry, "Labor Force Structure, Potential Output, and Productivity," *Brookings Papers on Economic Activity*, no. 3, Brookings Institution, Washington, D.C., 1971.

poverty   A condition in which income is insufficient to meet subsistence needs. Thus, levels of living may be considerably lower than those that are deemed adequate standards of living. Despite gains in levels of living in the United States since World War I, there is still considerable inequality in the distribution of income and wealth, particularly in some areas in which pockets of poverty exist. It is possible to identify approximately where poverty exists by relating a comprehensive measure of income, including nonmonetary income, to the estimated budget needs of a family. In some cases, particularly with regard to older families and individuals, assets should also be taken into account in studies of poverty. It is almost impossible to measure poverty precisely because the definition hinges on varying living and social standards. For further information, see Sheldon Danziger and Robert Plotnick, *Has the War on Income Poverty Been Won?*, Academic Press, New York, 1980.

predetermined variable   An econometric variable whose values at any point in time may be regarded as known. A predetermined variable may therefore be either an exogenous variable or a lagged endogenous variable. For additional information, see Lawrence R. Klein, *An Introduction to Econometrics*, Greenwood, Westport, Conn., 1977.

preemptive right   The right of stockholders, under common law, to maintain their proportionate control of and equity in a corporation if and when the corporation issues additional stock. In practice, this usually means that a corporation must give its shareholders rights to subscribe to a new stock issue in proportion to their previous holdings. Thus, if a stockholder owned 10% of a corporation's outstanding stock, the stockholder would be entitled to subscribe to 10% of a new issue. In the United States, many state corporation laws prescribe the nature of preemptive rights, and most states allow corporate charters to deny these rights to stockholders. For further information, see Jules I. Bogen (ed.), *Financial Handbook,* 4th ed., Ronald, New York, 1968; William F. Sharpe, *Investments,* 2d ed., Prentice-Hall, Englewood Cliffs, N.J., 1981.

preferred operating rate   The percentage of its productive capacity that a firm or an industry believes to be most profitable. The industrial rate preferred, on the average, in the United States in 1980 was 90%. If a company operates above its preferred rate, it may be using obsolete facilities and incurring excessive costs. If it operates below its preferred rate, some efficient capacity remains idle. For statistics on preferred operating rates, see *Annual Surveys of Business' Plans for New Plants and Equipment,* McGraw-Hill Department of Economics, New York.

preferred stock   Capital stock issued by a corporation which has preference over the common stock of the corporation in respect to the payment of dividends. This preference means that before any dividends can be paid to the common shareholders, the preferred shareholders must be paid a stipulated amount of money. Furthermore, in the event of dissolution, reorganization, or bankruptcy, the preferred stockholders usually have priority over the common stockholders in the distribution of the corporation's assets. Since the preferred stockholders are owners and not creditors of the corporation, however, their claims to assets must wait until the claims of the bondholders and other creditors have been met. Preferred stock is less speculative than common stock of the same corporation, but it is more speculative than the corporation's bonds; typically, the fact is reflected in its yield. Preferred stock can be cumulative, which means that all dividends due preferred stockholders from past years must be paid in full before a dividend can be declared to the common stockholders. Noncumulative stock does not offer this provision. For further information, see George A. Christy and John C. Clendenin, *Introduction to Investments,* 7th ed., McGraw-Hill, New York, 1978.

price control   Government regulation of the prices of goods and services designed to prevent the cost of living from spiraling upward. Price controls are usually imposed during a war, but they have been imposed in peacetime in countries in which inflationary pressures have accumulated. The prices of goods and services at all distribution levels are fixed generally at the highest levels prevailing for some stated period, usually immediately before the date of the announced control. Transactions at prices higher than those that have been established are prohibited by law unless they have been demonstrated to be necessary. Prices were frozen for ninety days on August 15, 1971, in order to halt inflation. After November 13, 1971, the Price Commission attempted to hold price increases to no more than $2\frac{1}{2}$% per year. During World War I, the U.S. price-control program was less general than during World War II. The General Maximum Price Regulation of April 28, 1942, froze the prices of goods and services at the highest price prevailing during March 1942 at the specific selling unit. Thus, different stores of the same chain could charge different prices if they had done so in March 1942.

price discrimination The charging of different prices to different buyers for the same good. Price discrimination can occur only when the seller has a degree of monopoly power and when the seller's market is divided into segments which can be dealt with separately. Customers are charged as much as they are willing to pay. Price discrimination generally produces greater profits for the monopolistic seller, but it can also have some beneficial value if it results in a reduction of costs. The Clayton Antitrust Act of 1914 made it illegal in the United States "to discriminate in price between different purchasers of commodities . . . where the effect of such discrimination may be to substantially lessen competition or tend to create a monopoly in any line of commerce." This provision was strengthened in 1936 by the Robinson-Patman Act, which authorized additional controls on price discrimination resulting from large market power. For additional details, see Corwin Edwards, *The Price Discrimination Law,* Brookings Institution, Washington, D.C., 1959.

price-earnings ratio The current market price of a company's stock expressed as a multiple of the company's per-share earnings. It is computed by dividing the annual per-share earnings of a company into the market value of its stock. For example, if company A's stock is selling at $100 per share and the company earned $5 per share, the price-earnings ratio is 20. The price-earnings ratio is a highly regarded measure of stock value because it gives a good indication of corporate success as measured against the price of the stock. Stockholders buy stocks with high price-earnings ratios (generally growth stocks) because they anticipate higher earnings and dividends in the future. Investors interested in stable income are more apt to invest in stocks with lower price-earnings ratios and steady dividend records. For further information, see George A. Christy and John C. Clendenin, *Introduction to Investments,* 7th ed., McGraw-Hill, New York, 1978.

price-level-adjusted mortgages *See* mortgages, nontraditional.

prices-paid-by-farmers index   A measure of the change from month to month in the average prices of goods and services bought by U.S. farmers for family living and farm production. The index is based on a price series for 235 commodities and services in family living and 244 items used in farm production. It includes interest, taxes, and wage rates. Information on commodity prices is collected at chain and independent stores, while costs of electricity and telephone service are based on an annual survey of some 20,000 farmers. The base period is set by law at 1910–1914. The index is published at the end of each month by the Department of Agriculture. When the index of prices received by farmers is divided by the index of prices paid by farmers, the result is the parity ratio.

prices-received-by-farmers index   A measure of the change from month to month in the average prices received by U.S. farmers for their products. The index is based on the prices of 55 important commodities that accounted for 93% of total cash receipts from the sale of farm products in the years 1953–1957. The prices quoted are those received at points of first sale, local markets, or other centers to which farmers deliver their products. No specifications are made as to grades; instead, average prices for all grades and qualities are used. Most of the data are gathered from price reporters, who are scattered throughout the United States. The reporters are usually buyers of agricultural commodities and other persons well informed regarding the local price situation. For the official index, conversion is made to the 1910–1914 = 100 base, which is the base period prescribed by law. The index is published at the end of each month by the Department of Agriculture. When this index is divided by the index of prices paid by farmers, the result is the parity ratio.

price stability   Maintenance of the purchasing power of a currency at a level which encourages investment, production, and employment without inflationary or deflationary price movements. Together with full employment and balanced international payments, it is one of the major objectives of U.S. economic policy. During the eight-year period from 1958 to 1965, the United States experienced a period of relative price stability.

price-support program   A government program designed to keep market prices from falling below a minimum level. U.S. agriculture has been the object of such a program because farming is a fluctuating industry, the products of which are sold in a highly competitive market subject to rapidly changing prices. Farmers have little control over prices or production, which is subject to such factors as weather and crop diseases. Because of these conditions, a feeling developed that the U.S. government should guarantee farmers a standard of living favorable to some period in history. The years 1909–1914 were chosen as a period when farmers enjoyed a favorable purchasing power for their commodities. By the 1960s almost every commodity was supported at some level of parity. This complex system of price supports had been accomplished by three basic programs: (1) crop limitation designed to cut supply and raise prices, (2) purchase-loan storage programs that guarantee to support prices, and (3) a purchase-and-resale differential-subsidy plan. For a discussion of these price-support plans, see Paul A. Samuelson, *Economics,* 9th ed., McGraw-Hill, New York, 1973, pp. 413–416.

price theory The theory concerned with how the price system handles the problem of allocating scarce resources in market economies. It deals with the method of determining relative prices, not with the method of determining the general price level. Price theory can be divided into five categories: (1) demand and consumer behavior, (2) the business firm, (3) market organization, (4) distribution, and (5) general equilibrium and welfare economics. There has been a growing body of research that treats principles of price theory as the basis of all economic theory, including the macroeconomic issues of inflation, unemployment, and the business cycle. For additional information, see John P. Gould and C. E. Ferguson, *Microeconomic Theory,* 5th ed., Irwin, Homewood, Ill., 1980; Milton Friedman, *Price Theory,* Aldine, Chicago, 1976; E. Phelps et al., *Microeconomic Foundations of Employment and Inflation Theory,* Norton, New York, 1970.

prime rate of interest The rate charged by commercial banks for short-term loans extended to their best customers, the 100 or so corporations in the United States with the highest credit ratings. Thus the prime rate is generally low in relation to other commercial rates. It provides the base on which other commercial interest rates rest. The differential between the prime rate and any other rate of interest charged for a commercial loan is an approximate measure of the premium for the additional risk involved. For further discussion, see Lawrence S. Ritter and William L. Silber, *Principles of Money, Banking and Financial Markets,* 3d rev. ed., Basic Books, New York, 1980.

private bank An unincorporated bank. Private banks formerly constituted a very important part of the U.S. banking system. There were about 5,000 unincorporated banks in the country in 1900, but they declined very greatly in number and volume of business thereafter. Before the passage of the Banking Act of 1933, many important U.S. banks, such as J. P. Morgan and Co., engaged in both commercial banking operations and the underwriting of securities. The act forced private banks to relinquish either their deposit services or their investment services and to submit to periodic examination by federal or state authorities. The supervision and regulation of private banks are now left to the states. In some states, private banks are prohibited; in others, regulations are very liberal; and in a few states, such as New York, private banks are regulated as strictly as incorporated banks.

private debt, net   The net debt of private individuals, noncorporate business, and corporations. At the end of 1980 net private debt in the United States totaled $3.6 trillion, or nearly three-fourths of the aggregate net public and private debt. The debt of private individuals is usually in the form of mortgages, consumer credit, and bank loans.

private sector   That part of the economy composed of consumer expenditures for goods and services and business expenditures for plants, equipment, and inventories. The private sector excludes all government purchases of goods and services. When government employees act as consumers by purchasing consumer goods and services, however, these expenditures become part of the private sector. In 1980 the private sector accounted for about 80% of the U.S. economy. For a breakdown of items of goods and services in the private sector, see U.S. Department of Commerce, *Survey of Current Business: National Income Supplements,* July issues.

producer goods (producer durable equipment)   The machinery and equipment (newly produced) that are acquired by private business and nonprofit institutions. Producer goods include such items as machine tools, generators, blast furnaces, freight cars, and passenger cars purchased for business use. The three largest components of this category are electrical machinery; trucks, buses, and truck trailers; and office, computing, and accounting machinery. Not all producer goods are capital goods, for some items, such as jigs and dies used up in one year in the automobile industry, are not charged to capital accounts but to current expenses, in accordance with conventional accounting procedures. For historical statistics and methods of estimating producer goods in the national accounts, see U.S. Department of Commerce, *United States Income and Output: Supplement to the Survey of Current Business,* 1958; for the latest quarterly estimates, see *Survey of Current Business,* monthly.

producer price index   A monthly measure of change in prices charged by producers that is compiled by the U.S. Bureau of Labor Statistics. At its inception in 1902 and until 1978, the index was called the wholesale price index. The index includes a representative group of about 3,000 commodities ranging from crude rubber, cotton, and iron ore to tires, apparel, and machinery. The importance assigned to individual items depends on dollar shipments. Currently 1972 data are used, but weighting factors are frequently revised. The reference base period for the index is 1967, and current prices are expressed as a percentage of the 1967 average. Indices are prepared for stages of process, major industries, product classes, and individual items. The index does not take full account of quality changes nor is it based on true transaction prices. Indices are released in U.S. Bureau of Labor Statistics, *Producer Price Indexes,* monthly.

production function The various combinations of land, labor, materials, and equipment that are needed to produce a given quantity of output. The production function expresses the maximum possible output which can be produced with any specified quantities of the various necessary inputs. Every production function assumes a given level of technology; once technological innovations have been introduced, the production function changes. The quantities of the particular factors necessary to produce a unit of output may be fixed or variable, in which case one factor may be substituted for another in the production process. All production functions whose technological coefficients are variable are subject to the law of diminishing returns: The marginal productivity of a factor must eventually decline if the rate of its use is increased while the use of the other factors is held constant. Another characteristic of a production function is the nature of its returns to scale. If a proportional increase in the input rate of each factor increases output by the same proportion, the production function is subject to constant returns to scale; that is; it is linearly homogeneous. On the other hand, if a proportional increase in all inputs increases output more than proportionately, increasing returns to scale are present, whereas if output is increased less than proportionately, the production function is characterized by decreasing returns to scale. An example of a linearly homogeneous production function is the Cobb-Douglas production function, which is $Y = kL^aC^bN^{1-a-b}$, where Y is output, L is quantity of labor input, C is quantity of capital input, N is quantity of natural resources input, and k, a, and b are positive constants. For additional details, see James M. Henderson and Richard E. Quandt, *Microeconomic Theory: A Mathematical Approach,* 3d ed., McGraw-Hill, New York, 1980.

productivity The goods and services produced per unit of labor, capital, or both; for example, the output of automobiles per worker-hour. The ratio of output to all labor and capital is a total productivity measure; the ratio of output to either labor or capital, a partial measure. Anything that raises output in relation to labor and capital leads to an increase in productivity. For the U.S. private economy, the ratio of total output to total labor and capital grew by 1.5% per year from 1919 to 1980. What caused the rise? Economists disagree. Some point to improvements in technology, mainly in the form of more efficient machines, as the important factor. Others state that investment in education and improvements in the quality of the labor force are the major causes. The most commonly used measure of productivity is the ratio of output to worker-hours worked, called labor productivity. This does not measure the gains due to labor alone, however, because an individual working with a more efficient machine can produce a greater amount of goods without working harder or better than before. For the U.S. private economy, the ratio of total output to total labor grew by about 2.5% per year between 1950 and 1980. For additional information, see John W. Kendrick and Beatrice Vaccara (eds.), *New Dimensions in Productivity Measurement and Analysis,* vol. 44 Studies in Income and Wealth, University of Chicago Press, Chicago,

1980; for statistics on labor productivity see U.S. Department of Labor, *Index of Output per Hour for Selected Industries,* annually.

productivity clause   *See* annual improvement factor.

productivity of capital stock   Output per unit of capital input. The productivity of capital stock is the ratio of the physical productive capacity (output) to the current real value of the stock of capital facilities and equipment. It depends on the level of technology, the size and nature of the capital stock, organization and management, etc. The major sources of changes in the productivity of capital stock are changes in the quality of capital inputs, changes in the effectiveness with which capital goods are utilized, and technological improvements which increase the productive capacity of current investment in capital facilities. Increases in the apparent productivity of capital stock may not be due to the enhanced contribution of the capital factor, however, but may result from greater contributions by other input factors, such as labor. For a detailed study of the changes in the productivity of capital stock of the United States, see John W. Kendrick and Beatrice Vaccara (eds.), *New Dimensions in Productivity Measurement and Analysis,* vol. 44, Studies in Income and Wealth, University of Chicago Press, Chicago, 1980.

profit and loss statement (operating statement)   A summary statement of the revenues and expenses of an enterprise for a given period. It sets forth the dollar value and sources of revenue, the types and amount of expenses, and the resulting net income (profit) or net loss for the accounting period. One of the objectives of running a business is to make a profit and this statement shows the degree to which this objective has been realized. The profit and loss statement provides operating facts and figures, a study of which may indicate ways of increasing profits. Prospective sellers, buyers, creditors, and stockholders are interested in the profit and loss statement because, to some extent, operations in the past provide clues to future potential. For further information, see Walter B. Meigs and Robert F. Meigs, *Accounting: The Basis for Business Decisions,* McGraw-Hill, New York, 1980.

profit margin   The percentage that net profit from operations is of net sales or of capital invested. These percentages measure the efficiency of a company or an industry. Nevertheless, profit margins vary widely among industries and among companies within the same industry. Although the absolute level of profits may reach new peaks every year, profit margins do not. As a matter of record, profit margins were generally lower in the early 1970s than they were in former periods of prosperity. For statistics on profit margins of manufacturing corporations classified by industry and by size, see U.S. Federal Trade Commission, *Quarterly Financial Report for Manufacturing Corporations.*

profit maximization The level of output which will yield the largest total profit. A business firm that has as its sole objective the maximization of profits will seek the level of production that is most profitable. This can be accomplished by constructing a table on the costs at each level of output and the total revenue that the sale of this output will yield. The optimal, or profit-maximization, output will be located where the difference between total revenue and total cost is greatest. Another method of determining profit maximization is to learn whether the marginal revenue received from the sale of an additional unit of output is greater than the marginal cost of the same unit. If marginal revenue is greater than marginal cost, the additional unit will be produced and production will continue as long as the same conditions prevail. On the other hand, if marginal cost exceeds marginal revenue, output will be contracted. The best profit position is the point at which marginal cost and marginal revenue are equal. This is the optimal situation of maximum profits. For further information, see Pearson Graham and Diran Bodenhorn, *Managerial Economics,* Addison-Wesley, Reading, Mass., 1980.

profits The amount left over after a business enterprise has paid all its bills. In accounting, profits may be expressed as gross (the difference between sales and the cost of goods sold), operating (the difference between the gross profit and the operating expenses), and net (the difference between the operating profit and income taxes). Not all companies make profits every year. Profits vary from time to time, from company to company, and from industry to industry. In high-profit industries, workers receive high pay. By means of research and modern tools, high-profit industries provide consumers with a greater number of goods, of better quality, and in greater variety. Profits lead the economy. After profits begin to rise, employment and income generally rise as well; when profits fall, employment and income follow closely behind them. The National Bureau of Economic Research classifies corporate profits among its leading indicators. Profits motivate private citizens to put their savings into useful enterprises, and they provide the largest single source of funds for economic growth. For further discussion, see Norman Ture, *Corporate Profits in Company Financial Reports, Tax Returns, and the National Income and Product Accounts,* Financial Executives Research Foundation, New York, 1978.

profit sharing The receipt by workers of a bonus above their regular wage, geared in some way to the earned profits of their employer. The distribution of a proportion of a company's profits to employees through a profit-sharing plan is undertaken primarily to provide an increased incentive for productive efficiency. Since workers so rewarded have a keener interest in the successful operation of the firm, they will have greater incentives to reduce costs and increase their productive effort. It is also stated that profit-sharing plans improve employee morale and labor-management relations, promote wage flexibility, and prevent strikes. A profit-sharing program may be a current one, in which bonuses are distributed to workers immediately after the profits have been earned, or it may be of the deferred type, in which the shared profits are held in trust in a type of pension plan for the workers.

profit squeeze   The narrowing of profits caught between rising costs and stable prices. Although the absolute level of profits might be increasing and setting new records each year, the various relative measures of profits in the 1970s were lower than they had been in earlier periods. The profit squeeze is best demonstrated by considering profits as a percentage of sales or as a percentage of national income.

progressive tax   A tax that takes a higher percentage of high incomes than of low ones, for example, 5% of $1,000, 10% of $5,000, and 25% of $10,000. The federal income tax is the most progressive tax in the United States. In 1969 rates ranged from 20% of the first $2,000 of taxable income to 91% of incomes over $200,000. This did not mean that individuals who earned $250,000 of taxable income paid 91% on all their earnings. The rates are marginal; that is, they apply only to the additional dollars (in this case, only the taxable income over $200,000). Taken as a whole, the U.S. tax system is progressive but not as progressive as federal income tax rates make it appear. The system contains many regressive taxes, and there are numerous ways of escaping high rates, such as tax-free municipal bonds; capital gains, which bear a maximum rate of 25%; and marriage, which provides income-splitting privileges. Those who favor progressive taxes state that they are more equitable than regressive or proportional taxes in that they are levied according to the ability to pay. Those opposed to progressive taxes argue that too great a degree of progression discourages effort and risk taking. The rates for all federal taxes are set forth in *United States Internal Revenue Code,* U.S. Government Printing Office, Washington, D.C.; see also John F. Due and Ann F. Friedlaender, *Government Finance,* 6th ed., Irwin, Homewood, Ill., 1977.

propensity to consume, average (APC)   The ratio of consumption to income at any given income level. It differs from marginal propensity to consume, which refers to the ratio of changes in consumption to changes in income. For further discussion of the average propensity to consume, see J. M. Keynes, *The General Theory of Employment, Interest, and Money,* Harcourt Brace, New York, 1936, chaps. 8 and 9.

propensity to consume, marginal (MPC)   The ratio of the additional amount that people will spend for consumption from an additional amount of income. Graphically, the marginal propensity to consume is represented by the slope of the consumption function at any particular income level. It may be calculated simply as follows:

$$\text{MPC} = \frac{\text{change in consumption}}{\text{change in income}}$$

The theory has sparked a great deal of controversy. For many years it was believed that the marginal propensity to consume declines as income increases, but numerous economists now believe that it may be constant for the economy as a whole. For further information, see J. M. Keynes, *The General Theory of Employment, Interest, and Money*, Harcourt Brace, New York, 1936, chaps. 8 and 9; James S. Duesenberry, *Income, Savings, and the Theory of Consumer Behavior*, Harvard University Press, Cambridge, Mass., 1949; John P. Lewis and Robert C. Turner, *Business Conditions Analysis*, 2d ed., McGraw-Hill, New York, 1967.

propensity to save, average (APS)   The ratio of saving to income at any given income level. For any particular consumption function, the average propensity to save is equal to 1 minus the average propensity to consume. It differs from marginal propensity to save, which refers to the ratio of the changes in saving to changes in income. For further discussion of the average propensity to save, see J. M. Keynes, *The General Theory of Employment, Interest, and Money*, Harcourt Brace, New York, 1936, chaps. 8 and 9.

propensity to save, marginal (MPS)   The additional saving generated by additional income. It is the ratio of change in saving to change in income:

$$MPS = \frac{\text{change in saving}}{\text{change in income}}$$

For any particular consumption function, the marginal propensity to save is equal to 1 minus the marginal propensity to consume, or

$$MPS = 1 - MPC$$

The theory has engendered considerable argument. For many years it was thought that the MPS increases as income increases, but numerous economists now believe that it may be constant for the economy as a whole. For further information, see J. M. Keynes, *The General Theory of Employment, Interest, and Money*, Harcourt Brace, New York, 1936, chaps. 8 and 9.

property tax   A tax on the value of real estate, that is, on land and on such improvements on land as residential, commercial, and industrial buildings. The use of this tax is limited to state and local governments in the United States, and it is particularly important as a source of revenue for local governments. Nevertheless, revenue from property taxes has declined as a percentage of all U.S. state and local revenues. On a local-government basis, the property tax accounted for less than 50% of all tax revenue in 1980, whereas in 1929 it represented 98% of the total. On a state basis, the tax percentage dwindled from 59% in 1915 to 2% in 1970. The property tax has been criticized on the ground that property, such as a home or a vacant lot, which does not provide income is a poor measure of tax-paying ability. Some economists believe that a property tax in underdeveloped countries, where property is owned mainly by the wealthy, may be progressive. It may also be beneficial, for use of a property tax could result in the conversion of unproductive property to productive property. For property taxes in the United States, see John F. Due and Ann F. Friedlaender, *Government Finance,* Irwin, Homewood, Ill., 1978; for statistics, see U.S. Department of Commerce, *Compendium of State Government Finance;* for Henry George's views on a land-value tax, see Henry George, *Progress and Prosperity,* Random House, New York, 1938.

proportional tax   A tax whose rate remains constant as the size of the base increases. A proportional tax rate is usually stated as a flat percentage of the base regardless of its size. For example, the property tax usually operates with proportional rates, and the tax might be expressed as 1% of assessed property value. Sales and excise taxes, payroll taxes, and most customs duties are also levied on the basis of proportional rates. For additional details on types of taxes, see John F. Due and Ann F. Friedlaender, *Government Finance,* Irwin, Homewood, Ill., 1978.

proprietorship   A type of business organization in which one individual owns the business. Legally, the owner is the business. Proprietorship is the commonest type of business organization in agriculture and retail trade. Generally, proprietorships are small businesses because of the limited capital available. Among the advantages of this type of operation are the simplicity of starting a business, the absence of much state regulation, and the direct acquisition of profits by the owner. Because the owner and the business are inseparable, there are certain disadvantages to proprietorships: The business stops if the proprietor dies, becomes insane, or is physically unable to continue it. Moreover, a proprietorship is characterized by unlimited liability, which means that all the proprietor's personal assets are available as security for creditors. Because of the death or illness of the individual owner, proprietorships generally last for a relatively short time in comparison with partnerships or corporations. For more detailed information concerning proprietorship, see Lyman A. Keith and Carlo E. Gubellini, *Introduction to Business Enterprise,* 4th ed., McGraw-Hill, New York, 1977.

prosperity   A sustained period of high and rising business activity in which business and consumer optimism is high. Prosperity is characterized by increased production, high capital investment with an emphasis on new capacity, expansion of credit, rising prices, low unemployment, full employment, and a high rate of formation of new business enterprises. The longest sustained period of prosperity in the United States occurred between 1961 and 1969, with only a minor interruption in 1967.

protectionism A term used to describe any movement by a government to alter the flows of its international trade. Protectionism refers primarily to policies to tax or limit imports but it also encompasses such measures as direct subsidies or taxes on the production of traded goods and multiple exchange rates as well as all governmental intervention affecting trade flows. For additional information, see W. M. Corden, *The Theory of Protection,* Oxford University Press, London, 1971.

pseudo inverse of a matrix For some square matrices one can define an inverse matrix (denoted A^{-1}) such that the matrix multiplied by its inverse is the identity matrix. This is analogous to multiplying a number by its inverse or reciprocal. For nonsquare matrices there is no inverse. However, a series of pseudo inverses can be defined which have some of the properties of the true inverse. For a matrix A, the conditional inverse is a matrix Ac such that $AAcA = A$. If AAc is symmetric, then Ac is the least-squares inverse. If AcA is symmetric and $AcAAc = Ac$, then Ac is the generalized inverse as well. See Pheobus J. Dhrymes, *Introductory Econometrics,* Springer Verlag, New York, 1978.

psychic income Income that is reckoned in terms of pleasure, satisfaction, or general feelings of euphoria. It is to be distinguished from income that is received in money or in the form of goods and services. Psychic income is commonly said to accrue to professional persons and creative artists who take pride in their accomplishments or gain satisfaction from their prestige and status. It may also frequently accrue to workers who enjoy their work surroundings and the company of their fellow workers and find pleasure in a job well done. There is no standard measurement of psychic income. See Paul F. Gemmill, *Fundamentals of Economics,* 6th ed., Harper & Row, New York, 1960.

public debt, net Total net government debt, including net federal debt and net state and local government debt. In 1980 net public debt in the United States totaled about $1,250 billion, $914 billion of which consisted of federal debt and $336 billion of state and local debt. The greater part of federal borrowing has been undertaken for emergencies (wars and recessions), whereas state and local credit has been used primarily for capital construction, such as highways, schools, and other public works. Although the U.S. public debt has been increasing in absolute terms, its size in relation to the gross national product (GNP) has been decreasing. For example, the total net public debt declined from 72% of the GNP in 1952 to about 47% in 1980. For further discussion, see Richard A. Musgrave and Peggy B. Musgrave, *Public Finance in Theory and Practice,* 2d ed., McGraw-Hill, New York, 1978.

public finance In common usage, the financing of government. More broadly defined, the term encompasses all activities of government, including not only the economics of finance but also the social effects and consequences of governmental policies. Modern public finance is concerned with adapting economic principles to areas of both economic and social concern, such as economic growth, countercyclical measures, and unemployment. A recent text dealing with this subject is Richard A. Musgrave and Peggy B. Musgrave, *Public Finance in Theory and Practice,* McGraw-Hill, New York, 1978.

public ownership   Government ownership and operation of a business enterprise. Under public ownership, the government replaces the private owner as the capitalist. Thus, the government supplies the capital and determines the facilities to be provided. It chooses the management and assumes the responsibility of paying labor, purchasing supplies, setting the price for its goods and services, and reaping profits or meeting deficits if they are incurred. The governmental act of removing private ownership and assuming the operation of an enterprise is called nationalization. In the United States, the most outstanding example of public ownership is the Tennessee Valley Authority, which is concerned with conservation and power production in the Tennessee Valley area. For a general discussion of public ownership, see R. Turvey and H. Christie, *Economic Analysis and Public Enterprise,* Rowman, Towata, N.J., 1971.

public sector (government sector)   That part of the economy which is composed of federal, state, and local expenditures for goods and services. The public sector excludes spending by the private sector, but when government employees act as private consumers in purchasing consumer goods and services, these expenditures become part of the private sector. In 1980 the government sector accounted for about 20% of the U.S. economy. For a breakdown of items of goods and services in the government sector, see U.S. Department of Commerce, *Survey of Current Business: National Income Supplements,* July issues.

public service commission   A state commission regulating public utilities in the United States. A semi-independent agency operating under general legislative power, it controls the rates and services of public utilities within the state. The commission method of utility regulation is said to have the advantages of expertness, flexibility, and practicality. A commission often involves much bureaucracy and red tape, however, and it may be subject to political and private influence. It is sometimes charged that many public service commissions are inadequately financed, understaffed, and limited in power, so that the proper regulation of public utilities is impaired. The first state regulatory commission was set up in Wisconsin in 1907. Subsequently, the idea was adopted by other states, and there are now public service commissions in every state (a few are still known as public utility commissions). Most public service commissions consist of three members who serve staggered terms. They have jurisdiction over motor carriers, telephone and telegraph companies, and electric power, water, and gas companies. The greater part of public service commissions' work originates in complaints brought by consumers and can be handled informally through negotiations between the commissioners and utility officials. For further information, see Neru Hazarika, *Public Service Commissions,* Humanities Press, Atlantic Highlands, N.J., 1980.

public welfare payment A federal, state, or local government payment to an individual who qualifies for assistance because he or she is either unemployed, retired, or a dependent, such as a senior citizen, a widow, an orphan, or a physically incapacitated or mentally defective person. Welfare payments were relatively unimportant in the United States before the depression of the early 1930s, but under the Social Security Act of 1935 the framework of a broad assistance program was established for the aged, dependent, and unemployed. At the same time, the states, spurred by the federal government, set up unemployment compensation and old-age assistance plans. The present system of welfare payments is supported on both humanitarian and economic grounds. Society generally recognizes the need to help those who, because of circumstances beyond their control, are unable to support themselves. Public welfare payments not only protect unfortunate individuals but help stabilize the economy during recession. For a discussion of the major economic issues associated with public welfare programs, see Margaret S. Gordon, *The Economics of Welfare Policies,* Columbia University Press, New York, 1963.

public welfare program A government-sponsored social program designed to transfer income from earners to nonearners whose capacity for self-support has been damaged. Among programs of this type are social insurance, public aid, and such other welfare services as institutional care and school lunches, veterans' programs, and public housing. In European countries, public welfare expenditures account for a larger proportion of national income than in the United States, partly because of the relative importance of U.S. private welfare programs. For further discussion of the economics of public welfare programs, see Margaret S. Gordon, *The Economics of Welfare Policies,* Columbia University Press, New York, 1963

public works Government-sponsored building or development projects. U.S. outlays for public works since the 1930s have been aimed at smoothing out cyclical declines in business activity. Under the title of public works, the government has adopted all projects that would not be undertaken by citizens or private corporations but that are essential to the development of the country. Under this heading are included such projects as the building of highways, slum clearance, public housing, rural electrification, and regional development. For information concerning public works and their use in economic stabilization policy, see John F. Due and Ann F. Friedlaender, *Government Finance*, 6th ed., Irwin, Homewood, Ill., 1977.

pump priming   Federal government expenditures in the United States that are designed to stimulate business recovery and achieve full employment. Such expenditures have taken the form of federal public works, grants for state and local public works projects, and subsidies and grants to farmers. Pump priming is based on the notion that, when public funds in sufficient quantities are injected into the income stream before or during a business recession, the economy will be pulled out of the recession and full employment will be restored. The success of the operation implies the existence of a positive multiplier and accelerator and a change in the attitudes that influence decisions on both private consumption and business investment. The degree to which pump-priming techniques may be utilized successfully as an economic stabilizer is in dispute. Much depends on the advance planning of projects and on the volume of work which can be crowded into recession years. Those who oppose pump priming point out that, by the time government expenditures have actually been made, the economy has usually begun to recover. Proponents of pump priming maintain that it induces recovery only when additional funds are put into circulation. If expenditures were to be financed by taxing persons or businesses, funds would merely be transferred from one group to another. Pump priming requires that expenditures for recovery be financed by borrowing or by incurring a budgetary deficit. For further information, see John F. Due and Ann F. Friedlaender, *Government Finance*, 6th ed., Irwin, Homewood, Ill., 1977.

purchasing power   The amount of goods and services that a monetary unit can buy. The purchasing power of the U.S. dollar is the reciprocal of a price index. Thus, if prices were to double in ten years, the purchasing power of the ten-year-old dollar would be cut in half. Since there are indices that measure prices at primary markets, at the retail level, and for the economy as a whole, different measures of purchasing power may be calculated. For example, by June 1981, the producer-market dollar of 1967 was worth 37 cents, the consumer dollar was worth less than 37 cents, and the dollar for the overall economy was worth 41 cents. For further information, see Irving Fisher, *The Purchasing Power of Money*, Macmillan, New York, 1912; rev. ed., 1926.

purchasing-power-parity theory   A theory used to explain the proper rate of exchange between two currencies. According to this doctrine, the exchange rate between two countries should be the same as the ratio of the price levels of the countries. For example, if a representative bundle of goods cost $2 in the United States and 10 francs in France, the exchange rate should be $1 equals 5 francs. Thus, the theory holds that an equilibrium rate is one which equates the respective domestic purchasing powers of any two currencies that are being compared. The underlying assumption is that the reason for desiring a foreign currency is to purchase goods and services in or from another country. Proponents of this notion hold that deviations from the rate which equates domestic purchasing powers cannot exist for a very long time. If goods in the United States cost one-fifth as many dollars as they cost in francs in France, while the exchange rate was $1 equals 1 franc, everyone who held francs would exchange them for an equal number of dollars and be able to purchase five times as many goods. The demand for dollars would raise the rate of exchange until it reached the level of $1 equals 5 francs, or the ratio of their purchasing power. At this rate, a franc spent in France would buy as much as it would if it were converted into a dollar and spent in the United States. Unfortunately, the purchasing-power-parity theory does not explain the complete relationship between two currencies. If only commodities entered into international trade, the theory might come closer to the truth, but many services that influence exchange rates never enter into the price index. For example, unilateral capital transfers are not considered in the purchasing-power-parity theory, and yet they result in a large demand for foreign exchange. Thus, this theory applies to exchange rates in only a general way. For a discussion of the purchasing-power-parity theory, see Eli Shapiro, Ezra Solomon, and William L. White, *Money and Banking,* 5th ed., Holt, Rinehart and Winston, New York, 1968.

pure rate of interest   The interest rate on capital funds that would exist if all risk and administrative costs were eliminated. In effect, it represents the pure cost of being able to use someone else's funds instead of waiting to save one's own. The actual rate of interest paid by a borrower is higher than the pure rate, since it must include a risk premium large enough to cover possible default and the costs of processing the loan as well as the rate of interest for the use of the capital itself. The pure rate of interest is a conceptual tool in economic theory. An awareness of this concept assists the economist in isolating the factors that determine changes in interest rates as such from varying administrative cost or risk factors that are also inherent in every loan. For further discussion, see Irving Fisher, *The Theory of Interest,* Kelley & Millman, New York, 1954.

put   A contract which gives the holder the right to sell a certain amount of stock for a designated time period at a specified price. It is the reverse of a call. There are four parties to every put: the holder (buyer); the maker (seller); the broker who brought them together; and the endorser, a New York Stock Exchange member firm, which guarantees that the maker will comply with the agreement. Puts are usually written for thirty, sixty, or ninety days or for six months, but any time period longer than twenty-one days (which is a New York Stock Exchange rule) to which the parties agree is acceptable. For the right to sell the stock, the buyer pays a premium to the seller of the put. The seller, in turn, pays a small commission to the put and call broker.

Four factors affect the price of a put: (1) the time period covered by the contract, (2) the price of the stock at the time the put is written, (3) the ability of the put to be exercised at that price or at a lower price, and (4) the volatility of past price movements of the stock. For further information, see William F. Sharpe, *Investments,* Prentice-Hall, Englewood Cliffs, N.J., 1978.

qualitative interview (depth interview)   A personal interview, used to explain consumer behavior, in which there is no fixed list of formal questions and little interruption on the part of a trained interviewer. Through the use of a general guide, the interviewer attempts to obtain a complete reaction to a product or an idea from a freely talking respondent. The qualitative interview differs from the quantitative interview, which follows a fixed list of questions, the answers to which can be tabulated and quantified. For general information on qualitative, or depth, interviews, see Robert Ferber (ed.), *Motivation and Market Behavior,* Arno, New York, 1976.

quantitative trade restriction (quota)   A limitation on the number of units of a commodity that may enter a country during a specific period. There are five kinds of direct import quotas: (1) The tariff or customs quota allows a specified quantity of the commodity to enter the country under a special low tariff rate, but additional imports of the good are subject to a significantly higher duty. (2) The unilateral import quota sets an absolute limit on the importation of a commodity in any one period. (3) Import licensing prevents a rush of imports. (4) Bilateral quotas combat the monopolistic exploitation of importing countries by means of negotiation with foreign producers and administration by the exporting country. (5) Mixing quotas limit the amount of foreign-produced material that can be incorporated in domestically finished products. As in the case of a tariff, the effect is to reduce imports and to raise prices to consumers. Article XI of the General Agreement on Tariffs and Trade (GATT) contains an indictment against quotas, import restrictions, and licensing systems. The International Monetary Fund concurs. See Charles P. Kindleberger and P. H. Lindert, *International Economics,* Irwin, Homewood, Ill., 1978.

quantity theory of money   The theory that the level of prices in an economic system is directly proportional to the quantity of its money supply. The quantity theory is based on the equation of exchange, which is simply $MV = PT$, where M is the quantity of money, V is the velocity of its circulation, P the price level, and T the value of real output. The equation of exchange is a truism, stating that total demand (total money in circulation times its rate of circulation) equals total supply (price level times real output). The quantity theory of money assumes that V is determined by the spending habits of the population and tends to remain constant and that T is determined by the productive capacity of the economy. Thus, the equation of exchange for the quantity theory becomes $M = kP$, or, expressed in words, the price level depends only on the quantity of money and is directly proportional to it. For example, the quantity-of-money theorists, among them Irving Fisher, who popularized the theory in the United States, would argue that if the quantity of money in circulation suddenly doubles, the price level would automatically double also. The quantity theory of money is related to the problem of income and employment, that is, the extent to which productive capacity is utilized. The quantity theory also considers money only in its role of a medium of exchange and not in its role as a store of value. For additional details, see Irving Fisher, *The Purchasing Power of Money*, Macmillan, New York, 1926; Milton Friedman and Anna J. Schwartz, *A Monetary History of the United States, 1867–1960*, National Bureau of Economic Research, New York, 1963; Philip C. Cagan, *Determinants and Effects of Changes in the Stock of Money, 1875–1960*, National Bureau of Economic Research, New York, 1965.

queuing theory   A theory of operations research which determines the amount of delay and the length of waiting lines that will occur when service has to be provided in sequence for customers arriving at a random rate. Queuing theory can be applied to any operation in which the objects to be dealt with arrive at irregular intervals and in which the operating facilities are of limited capacity. Checkout counters at supermarkets, the landing of aircraft at airports, highway toll booths, and the placing of telephone calls are practical examples in which queuing theory can be useful. By analyzing the frequency distribution of customer arrivals, queuing theory helps determine average waiting time, the expected length of waiting lines at different times of day, etc. The theory is used by management to determine the amount of customer-servicing facilities that should be available. For a fuller explanation of queuing theory, see C. W. Churchman et al., *Introduction to Operations Research*, Wiley, New York, 1957, pt. VI; Walter E. Duckworth et al., *A Guide to Operations Research*, 3d ed., Methuen, New York, 1977.

quota   The proportional share assigned to a particular division, group, or individual when a specific limit is desired. There are import quotas to control the influx of foreign goods, farm quotas to control farm production, etc. In international trade, there are two basic types of quotas: (1) a tariff quota that admits a certain amount of goods under a certain schedule of duties and additional goods at a higher-schedule rate and (2) an import quota that places a definite limit on the total quantity of an article that may be imported from a particular country within a specified time. Apparently first used by France in 1931, import quotas have since been adopted by many countries. The General Agreement on Tariffs and Trade (GATT) has sought to eliminate such restrictive quotas. For information on import quotas, see Charles P. Kindleberger and P. H. Lindert, *International Economics,* Irwin, Homewood, Ill., 1978.

R

radical economics   A dissenting school of economic thought motivated by political opposition to contemporary capitalism and intellectual dissatisfaction with contemporary mainstream economics. It combines features of a radical and a political economic approach to the study of society. The growth of its appeal can be linked to the faltering performance of capitalism in the United States in the 1970s. Many mainstream economists have dismissed this school of thought as unscientific and polemical, while others have accepted elements of radical-political economics only as useful supplements to mainstream economics. For a general introduction, see Richard Edwards, Michael Reich, and Thomas Weisskopf, *The Capitalist System: A Radical Analysis of American Society,* 2d ed., Prentice-Hall, Englewood Cliffs, N.J., 1978. For a detailed critique of radical political economy, see Assar Lindbeck, *The Political Economy of the New Left: An Outsider's View,* 2d ed., Harper & Row, New York, 1977.

random noise   In a statistical or econometric study the actual results will often show small random deviations from the theoretical ideal. This arises because of numerous small disturbances—called random noise—which may affect economic behavior. In estimating an econometric model an error term is included to reflect this. If the error term exhibits no systematic behavior, the deviation between the ideal and the estimated results is said to be due to random noise. In most applications the error term is assumed to obey a normal distribution.

random variable In statistics and econometrics, a variable that can take any of an infinite number of different values, regardless of their magnitude, each having a certain probability and provided there are at least two such values. Random variables are also called chance variables or stochastic variables. For additional information, see Gerhard Tintner and Charles B. Millham, *Mathematics and Statistics for Economists,* Holt, Rinehart, and Winston, New York, 1970.

random walk hypothesis The notion that successive stock-price changes are identically distributed and independent random variables. Thus, past security-price movements cannot be used to forecast future prices, nor can trading on new public information, on average, earn profits in excess of what would be earned using a buy-and-hold policy. For additional information, see E. F. Fama, "The Behavior of Stock Market Prices," *Journal of Business,* vol. 38, 1965, pp. 34–105.

ratchet-effect theory The notion that at the beginning of a recession consumers and investors try to maintain the previous high levels of consumption and investment, respectively. High consumption standards and high investment levels are not easily reversed. The term is used to describe this economic situation because a ratchet, when it takes hold of a mechanism, holds it in a fixed position. The ratchet keeps the economy from slipping back and losing all the income gains attained during the preceding expansion. It takes hold when economic activity has passed the peak and influences its course throughout the recession and subsequent recovery until the previous peak level has been surpassed. For further discussion, see James S. Duesenberry, *Income, Savings, and the Theory of Consumer Behavior,* Harvard University Press, Cambridge, Mass., 1949, pp. 114–116; John P. Lewis and Robert C. Turner, *Business Conditions Analysis,* 2d ed., McGraw-Hill, New York, 1967, chap. 6.

rate of return on invested capital The ratio of profits to capital or assets. The return on capital employed may be expressed as turnover times profit on sales. Manufacturing companies make their rate of return on invested capital with a low turnover and a high profit on sales, whereas merchandising companies produce their return on capital invested by means of a high turnover and a low profit on sales. This ratio is a measure of the effectiveness with which a company uses its existing assets. The rate of return on invested capital for manufacturing companies may be found in U.S. Federal Trade Commission, *Quarterly Financial Report for Manufacturing Corporations.*

rate of return on new investment   An evaluation of the profitability of proposed equipment purchases. The rate-of-return method of evaluation is the converse of the payoff or payout method. It assumes that an investment must earn something in addition to the recovery of the cost of the capital invested. Excess earnings (annual savings minus annual depreciation of the new facility) are measured against the investment to determine the rate of return. Rates of return vary for each company and for each product line. This popular method of determining the advisability of an investment does not help a business executive find the real cost of the capital used up by investment in a new machine. For further information, see J. Fred Weston and Eugene F. Brigham, *Essentials of Managerial Finance,* 5th ed., Holt, Rinehart and Winston, New York, 1979.

rational expectations   A substantial body of economic thought has grown out of the traditional assumption of rational economic behavior that is part of the foundation of economic theory. To be more precise, the assumption has been made that economic people (hence, rational people) will draw upon past experience and knowledge and all available current market information plus their best guesses about future conditions in making an economic decision, with the hope of maximizing their benefits. It has long been recognized that the decision made is influenced by what the decision maker expects will happen; e.g., expecting a price to decline, a decision maker may defer a purchase. With the growing use of complex econometric models, more thought is now being given to the problem of estimating the future values of independent variables in models in such a way as to ascribe effect to the expectations of decision makers as well as to the conventional forces of supply and demand. Contemporary rational-expectations theory assumes the rational economic behavior described above and adds the necessary assumption of random, unpredictable error in expectations that are not always right. Theorists derive the nature of expectations by means of econometric models that employ lagged nonexpectational variables. The goal of the theory is to capture and measure the expectations that govern actions rather than those that govern intentions to act. For further information, see Robert B. Ekelund and Robert F. Helbert, *A History of Economic Theory and Method,* McGraw-Hill, New York, 1975; John F. Muth, "Rational Expectations and the Theory of Price Movements," *Econometrica,* vol. 29, no. 3, July 1961, pp. 315–335.

ratio-to-moving-average method of seasonal adjustment   A method of computing seasonal adjustment. A preliminary trend cycle is estimated by taking a moving average of the original data after any prior adjustments. Seasonal-irregular (SI) ratios are obtained by dividing the original series by the preliminary trend cycle. The SI ratios for each month or quarter are smoothed out by a moving average to provide an estimate of the seasonal. Finally, the original series is divided by the seasonal to obtain the seasonally adjusted series. For further discussion, see Julius Shiskin, *Electronic Computers* and *Business Indicators,* National Bureau of Economic Research, Occasional Paper 57, New York, 1957.

real-balance-effect theory   The theory that a reduction in the overall price level leads to an increase in both consumption and investment. A generic term that covers both the Keynes effect and the Pigou effect, the real-balance effect is based on the following line of reasoning: (1) Individuals establish a desired relationship between the money balances that they hold and their expenditures on goods and services. (2) Price reductions raise the real value of their money holdings; that is, the quantity of goods and services that can be bought with a given amount of money rises. (3) Thus, the desired relationship between real balances and expenditures is disturbed, and individuals have an excess supply of liquid assets. (4) They spend part of this excess supply on goods and services. (5) They are also willing to lend part of this excess supply, which results in an increase in the supply of funds in the loan market and a lowering of the rate of interest. (6) With a lower rate of interest, additional investment takes place. Thus, the real-balance effect raises both consumption and investment. For a thorough discussion of the real-balance effect, see Don Patinkin, *Money, Interest and Prices,* 2d ed., Harper & Row, New York, 1965; John J. Klein, *Money and the Economy,* 4th ed., Harcourt Brace, New York, 1978.

real-bills doctrine   A theory, held by members of the banking school, that all commercial bank loans should be short-term, self-liquidating loans so that the expansion and contraction of the money supply would be based mainly on the needs of business. Banks should issue credit only on the basis of real bills—self-liquidating, short-term notes based on goods in process. If this doctrine were followed, its proponents argued, the means of payment in an economy would expand or contract with the volume of goods produced. The real-bills doctrine was the basis of the Federal Reserve Act of 1913. For a study of the evolution of the real-bills doctrine through the nineteenth century, see Herman E. Krooss (ed.), *Documentary History of Banking and Currency in the United States,* Chelsea House, New York, 1980.

real-dollar value   *See* **constant-dollar value.**

real estate investment trusts (REITs)   An investment medium which allows the small investor to participate and share in the profits of a managed portfolio of real estate assets held by a REIT in the form of either properties or mortgages. There are two major types: (1) mortgage trusts which invest in short-term mortgages, and (2) equity trusts which own or finance real estate directly. In 1961, Congress attempted to provide real estate financing with a contracyclical intermediary. It granted the same type of tax treatment to REITs—no tax at the REIT level if virtually all income was passed along to investors as dividends—that was enjoyed by mutual funds. When interest rates came down in the late 1960s, most of the mortgage-lending REITs suffered seriously. The shakeout period for REITs occurred during the double-digit prime-rate period of 1974. For additional information, see Michael C. Halpin, *Profit Planning for Real Estate Development*, Dow Jones–Irwin, Homewood, Ill., 1977.

real income   The purchasing power of the income of an individual or a nation. Real income is computed by adjusting money income to changes in consumer prices. Thus, if the price index rises by the same amount as money incomes, real incomes remain unchanged, for consumers can purchase neither more nor less with their money incomes. When prices rise more rapidly than money incomes, real incomes fall, and, conversely, when prices rise less rapidly than money incomes, real incomes rise. For annual statistics of real income (real disposable income either on a national basis or on a per capita basis), see *The Annual Economic Report of the President*, Washington, D.C.

real wage   The purchasing power of a worker's earnings. The real wage is computed by adjusting the money wage to changes in consumer prices. At times, the movements of money wages and real wages may diverge. In times of recession, money wages sometimes fall less rapidly than the consumer price index, so that real wages actually rise. The possibility of such divergences over the course of business cycles was a major issue in John Maynard Keynes's *General Theory of Employment, Interest, and Money*, in which he disagreed with the view of the classical economists that a decline in money wages would result in a prompt solution of business recessions. Keynes believed that, if real wages were rising, a decrease in money wages might be ineffective in lowering costs and actually be very detrimental by lowering consumer demand. Omitting business-cycle changes, real wages in the United States are climbing slowly over the long run. Between 1939 and 1980, average weekly earnings in manufacturing industries, adjusted for changes in the consumer price index, rose by an average of 1.7% annually. See J. M. Keynes, *The General Theory of Employment, Interest, and Money*, Harcourt Brace, New York, 1936; for current statistics on real wages, see U.S. Department of Labor, *Monthly Labor Review;* for a discussion of the concept, see Lloyd G. Reynolds, *Labor Economics and Labor Relations*, 7th ed., Prentice-Hall, Englewood Cliffs, N.J., 1978.

recession   A decline in overall business activity. In the United States, the average post-World War II recession has lasted about eleven months. The average decline, as measured by the Federal Reserve Board's industrial production index, has been about 10%. When recessions are unusually short and shallow, such as the recession of 1960–1961, they are called mild. The 1981–1982 recession, which was longer and deeper than the average, was severe. For an authoritative historical account of U.S. business recessions prepared by the

National Bureau of Economic Research, Inc., see Geoffrey H. Moore (ed.), *Business Cycle Indicators,* Princeton University Press, Princeton, N.J., 1961.

Reciprocal Trade Agreements program A U.S. program of reciprocal tariff reduction. The Reciprocal Trade Agreements program was originated during the depression of the 1930s, and its main object was to help end the depression by expanding U.S. exports. It was first enacted into law in the Reciprocal Trade Agreements Act of 1934, which reversed the previous U.S. protectionist trade policy and empowered the President to negotiate treaties for the purpose of lowering or raising duties by as much as 50% of their 1934 levels. In 1945 this authorization was extended to permit reductions of 50% below the tariffs of that year, and in 1955 it was extended again to permit another 15% reduction. The President was to negotiate the treaties whereby duties might be lowered only if an equivalent tariff concession was made in return by another country. Once a tariff reduction was concluded, the new rate was then applied nondiscriminatively, according to the most-favored-nation principle, to all countries with which the United States has tariff agreements. To preserve its bargaining power, the United States generally follows the practice of making its most-favored-nation tariff reduction for a commodity only with the chief supplier of that good to the United States. Although the Reciprocal Trade Agreements program was a significant step toward liberalizing trade, it was weakened by the addition of two provisions in later extension acts: the introduction in 1947 of the escape clause, permitting the United States to withdraw concessions on imports which had caused unforeseen serious injury to domestic producers; and the attachment in 1948 of the peril-point clause, whereby the U.S. International Trade Commission would recommend the maximum permissible tariff reduction which would not cause serious injury. For additional details on the history and results of the Reciprocal Trade Agreements program, see U.S. International Trade Commission, *Operation of the Trade Agreements Program,* periodically; see also C. P. Kindleberger and P. H. Lindert, *International Economics,* Irwin, Homewood, Ill., 1978.

reciprocity The lowering of trade barriers by one country in return for similar concessions by other countries. The principle of reciprocity has been dominant in U.S. tariff policy since 1934, when the Reciprocal Trade Agreements program was originated. Reciprocal agreements make it economically safe for each nation to reduce its tariffs, since mutual reduction eliminates the threat of a balance-of-payments deficit inherent in unilateral reduction. They also make it politically feasible, since the tariff reduction is viewed not as a surrender but as an exchange (in which the home country is always presumed to have gained the most). For further information on reciprocity and its beneficial effects on world trade, income, and production, see C. P. Kindleberger and P. H. Lindert, *International Economics,* Irwin, Homewood, Ill., 1978.

recovery An increase in business activity after the low point of a recession or a depression has been reached. The recovery continues until business achieves approximately the same level that it had attained before the decline. After that point has been reached, the recovery moves into the expansionary stage. The rate of recovery is generally related directly to that of the preceding decline; that is, recoveries are more rapid after severe recessions than after mild ones. The average recovery rate, as measured by the index of industrial production, is faster during the period immediately following a recession than later on. Some sensitive barometers, such as new orders for durable goods, awards of industrial and commercial building contracts, the work week, and corporate profits, are early indicators of recovery. For an authoritative historical record of U.S. business recoveries, see Geoffrey H. Moore (ed.), *Business Cycle Indicators,* vol. I, National Bureau of Economic Research, Princeton University Press, Princeton, N.J., 1961.

recursive system A system of econometric equations having the property that when the values of the variables are fully determined up to time t minus 1, the equations yield the values of the variables for time t, one at a time. That is, the determination of the value of one variable at time t facilitates the determination of the value of another variable at time t, and so forth in some order or other. For additional information, see Karl A. Fox and Tej K. Kaul, *Intermediate Economic Statistics,* Krieger, Melbourne, Fla., 1980.

rediscount rate *See* discount rate.

reduced-form equation A method of estimating the parameters in stochastic systems. It consists of expressing the endogenous variables individually in terms of predetermined variables, i.e., variables that are determined independently of, or before, the endogenous variables in a causal sense. Since each reduced-form equation contains a single endogenous variable, it is possible to estimate the coefficients of each such equation by the method of least squares. For additional information, see Karl A. Fox and Tej K. Kaul, *Intermediate Economic Statistics,* Krieger, Melbourne, Fla., 1980.

reference cycle The succession of expansion and contraction in general business activity. The reference cycle is determined by the combined behavior of a group of economic indicators (roughly coincident indicators) which are regarded as defining general business activity: employment, income, production, prices, etc. The cycle for the individual indicators of general business activity need not coincide with the reference cycle. The term reference cycle is used synonymously with business cycle. For further discussion on reference-cycle patterns, see Geoffrey H. Moore (ed.), *Business Cycle Indicators,* vol. I, National Bureau of Economic Research, Princeton University Press, Princeton, N.J., 1961.

reflation   A type of inflation, occurring during a recovery from a depression or a recession, in which prices are restored to a so-called desirable level by decreasing the purchasing power of money. Reflation to a preexisting price structure is brought about through the use of governmental monetary powers. In periods of reflation, it is often difficult to distinguish the time at which reflation ends and inflation begins. The examples of reflation in the United States usually cited are for the periods 1917–1920 and 1933–1934. For details on the process of reflation, see G. F. Warren and F. A. Pearson, *Gold and Prices,* Wiley, New York, 1935.

reform liberalism (twentieth-century liberalism)   An economic philosophy which embraces the idea that intervention by the individual in some markets will improve economic welfare. Contrary to classical liberalism, which held that there is a natural harmony in the economic system with benefits for all when individuals pursue their self-interests, reform liberalism holds that free markets permit maldistributions of resources and grossly unfair earnings for some workers. The general philosophy has been popularly termed the New Deal, the Fair Deal, the welfare state, or most commonly, simply liberalism. The term liberal has come to mean almost exactly the opposite of what it meant at the turn of the twentieth century. Proponents of reform liberalism point to enormous monopoly profits, the rape of forests and other natural resources, polluted streams, booms and busts, and unequal distribution of incomes that may result from a hands-off policy on the part of government. The approach of reform liberals is pragmatic. They look at what is being achieved by the market. If it conforms to their general idea of what is best, they leave it alone, but if they find difficulties, they interfere. In some cases, the solution may be the improvement of competition by antitrust activity; in other cases, the solution may be government ownership. In combating business cycles, reform liberals are more likely to be concerned about the human misery caused by unemployment than by the burden of the federal debt. When John Maynard Keynes suggested that the U.S. economy might suffer from a chronic lack of demand, many reform liberals seized upon this suggestion as additional proof that a larger role for government was required. See John Rawls, *A Theory of Justice,* Harvard University Press, Cambridge, Mass., 1971.

regional account   An income and product account on a subnational basis. Limitations on data prevent the compilation of detailed regional accounts similar to the national income account. Nevertheless, accounts of this type offer a flexible framework for regional economic analysis by decision makers at all levels of government and business. For further information, see Walter Isard, *An Introduction to Regional Economics,* Prentice-Hall, Englewood Cliffs, N.J., 1975.

regional analysis   The study of comparative growth and development in a geographic area, emphasis being placed on the future role of the region in the national economy. Regional analysis requires data on the flow of regional products and the stock of regional resources. Since many data are lacking, comprehensive statements of the economics of regions are not available. Nevertheless, some regional data, such as personal income, population, employment, and industrial production, are available. For further information, see Walter Isard, *An Introduction to Regional Economics,* Prentice-Hall, Englewood Cliffs, N.J., 1975.

regional stock exchange   Any U.S. stock exchange except the New York Stock Exchange (NYSE) and the American Stock Exchange (ASE). As of December 1979, there were nine regional stock exchanges in the United States, eight of which were registered with the Securities and Exchange Commission as national securities exchanges. The regional stock exchanges registered as national securities exchanges were the Boston Stock Exchange, Chicago Board of Options Exchange, Midwest Stock Exchange, Cincinnati Stock Exchange, Intermountain Stock Exchange, Pacific Stock Exchange, Phialdelphia Stock Exchange, and Spokane Stock Exchange. The Honolulu Stock Exchange was exempt from registration. All the regional stock exchanges are organized and governed in a way that closely resembles the structure of the NYSE. The major difference is that their rules and regulations are not as stringent as those of the NYSE, particularly regarding the requirements for listing stock. Most seats or memberships on regional exchanges are held by brokerage firms that are also members of the NYSE and the ASE. The basic purpose and function of the regional exchanges are to give small, regional, or local corporations, which cannot meet the listing requirements of the NYSE and the ASE, an opportunity to be listed on an organized stock exchange. See George A. Christy and John C. Clendenin, *Introduction to Investments,* 7th ed., McGraw-Hill, New York, 1978.

regression line   A statistical term that indicates a relationship between two or more variables. The regression line was first used by Sir Francis Galton to indicate certain relationships in his theory of heredity, but it is now employed to connote many functional relationships. A regression, or least-squares, line is derived from a mathematical equation relating one economic variable to another. The use of regression lines is important in determining the effect of one variable on another. For example, an increase in disposable income results in an increase in consumption, and a regression line can be used to show such a relationship. The regression technique is useful in forecasting general economic activity or individual fields. For further information, see Karl A. Fox and Tej K. Kaul, *Intermediate Economic Statistics,* Krieger, Melbourne, Fla., 1980.

regressive tax   A tax whose rate decreases as the tax base increases. In this sense of the term, there are no actual regressive taxes in the United States. Frequently, however, the rate structure of a tax is compared not with its actual base but with the net income of the taxpayer. When used in this way, the term regressive refers to a tax which takes a larger share of income from the low-income taxpayer than from the high-income taxpayer. A tax which is technically proportional in terms of the tax base can often be considered regressive in terms of the taxpayer's income. Common examples of such regressive taxes are sales taxes, excise taxes, and property taxes. For example, an excise tax on cigarettes is based on the number of cigarettes sold and thus by definition is proportional. Since the number of cigarettes consumed may rise as income rises, however, the rate of the tax decreases with increasing income and thus can be called regressive. The effect of a regressive tax is to increase inequalities of income, placing a larger burden on the poor than on the rich. The accompanying chart illustrates the basic concepts. For additional details, see John F. Due and Ann F. Friedlaender, *Government Finance*, 6th ed., Irwin, Homewood, Ill., 1978.

Alternative Tax Rate Structures

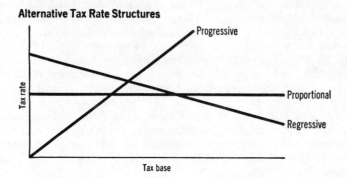

regulation of business   *See* government regulation of business.

Regulation Q   A banking regulation that determines the rates which the commercial banking system of the United States can pay on time deposits. First instituted in the Banking Act of 1933, it was amended in 1935. Because of the greater sensitivity in rates paid on time deposits in the 1960s, Regulation Q is playing a more important role in the Federal Reserve System's monetary policy. Between 1936 and 1957 only one change occurred in Regulation Q: in 1957 the maximum rate on savings was altered from $2\frac{1}{2}$ to 3%. Effective January 1, 1962, the rate was raised to 4%. Rates were raised still further in following years. Since the 1960s and early 1970s, Regulation Q has been used as a tool of Federal Reserve policy, its effect being to shift the flow of money without altering the supply. It increases the flow of funds into commercial banks, over which the Federal Reserve Board has more direct control than it has over other financial intermediaries. To meet the higher rates, the commercial banks reinvest these funds, and this, in turn, has an important bearing on the interest costs of other investment media. For a historical review of Regulation Q, see Albert H. Cox, Jr., "Regulation of Interest on Deposits: An Historical Review," *Journal of Finance*, vol. 22, no. 2, May 1967, pp. 274–299.

regulatory commission, federal A U.S. governmental administrative agency which regulates the conduct of certain business activities. There are five federal regulatory agencies with jurisdiction over the interstate operation of public utilities. These are the Interstate Commerce Commission, which supervises interstate transportation facilities; the Federal Power Commission, which has jurisdiction over interstate power transmission; the Federal Communications Commission, which regulates interstate telephone, telegraph, radio, and television operations; the Securities and Exchange Commission, which supervises the security markets; and the Federal Aviation Agency, which regulates the airlines. The regulatory commissions issue licenses, make inspections, conduct investigations, and enforce the law with respect to their special areas of operation. Since they are given broad discretionary powers by Congress, rule making and rule adjudication have become an important part of administrative regulation. Regulatory agencies often protect the public interest by their economic supervision, and their use permits continuing supervision of the regulated field and enables experts to handle the problems of regulation. On the other hand, regulatory commissions have been criticized as being bureaucratic. Moreover, the combination of rule making, prosecution, and adjudication under the aegis of the same agency has led to charges of unfairness and bias, although the Administrative Procedures Act of 1946 undertook to separate these functions in order to ensure impartiality. The quasi-judicial hearings of the agencies, which usually are not limited by strict rules of evidence, etc., have been attacked as arbitrary and unfair and as subject to possible abuse. All the commissions' decisions are, however, open to judicial review.

relative-income hypothesis The assumption that spending is related to a family's relative position in the income distribution of approximately similar families. Thus, for example, it would be expected that a black family earning $16,000 a year would save a greater amount than a white family earning the same sum, since the black family's position within its relevant income distribution would be considerably higher and more secure than the position of the white family. The relative-income hypothesis was conceived by James S. Duesenberry to help explain the differences found between consumption functions derived from data of families classified by groups and those derived from overall totals (time series). The accompanying three charts help illustrate

Relative Income Hypothesis

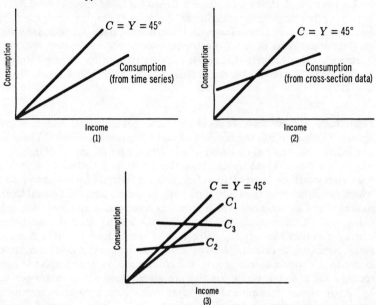

the problem. Chart 1 shows how the consumption function looks when it is derived from time-series data. Chart 2 illustrates the consumption function estimated from family-group data. Obviously, in chart 2 the dollar value of consumption exceeds the dollar value of income at low-income levels, whereas this is not true in chart 1. Duesenberry hypothesized that, at any given moment in time, consumption is not particularly sensitive to current income. People spend in a manner consistent with their relative-income position. With incomes rising or falling over the course of years, their spending patterns change if their relative position changes. Chart 3 points this hypothesis up as a series of short-run consumption functions which trace the long-run equilibrium path uncovered in the time-series studies of the consumption function. James Tobin showed that other factors could cause the effects that Duesenberry explained by means of relative incomes. Discussion of the relative-income hypothesis greatly diminished after Milton Friedman conceived his consumption-function theory, which relies on the notion of permanent income. Friedman's theory was based on extensive mathematical exploration. See James S. Duesenberry, *Income, Saving, and the Theory of Consumer Behavior*, Harvard University Press, Cambridge, Mass., 1949; James Tobin, "Relative Income, Absolute Income, and Savings," *Money, Trade and Economic Growth*, Macmillan, New York, 1951; Milton Friedman, *A Theory of the*

Consumption Function, a study by the National Bureau of Economic Research, Princeton University Press, Princeton N.J., 1957.

rent   In economics, the return to a unique factor used in production in excess of the amount which that factor (human or nonhuman) could earn in its next best alternative employment. For example, let us consider a female motion picture star with special attributes which permit her to earn $100,000 per picture. If the star could not earn her living in the performing arts, she might be able to earn only $4,000 over the same period of time. She therefore earned an economic rent of $96,000. While the concept of unique value is more easily understood with respect to land of unusual fertility or location, the notion is equally applicable to human talent. Rents are readily recognizable when they are paid by a firm or a single employer, but when they accrue to owners of firms (entrepreneurs), part of what is called profits may actually be rent. One of the features of economic rent that has long interested social reformers is the fact that it is not a cost of production. Some, notably Henry George, suggested in a corollary that the state could expropriate economic rent through a tax (single tax) without affecting production. For a general discussion of rents, see Paul A. Samuelson, *Economics,* 9th ed., McGraw-Hill, New York, 1973; for an antiquated expression of the economic doctrine of rent, see Francis A. Walker, *Land and Its Rent,* Macmillan, London, 1883.

representation controversy   A dispute between rival unions over the choice of the one union to represent a certain group of workers. Representation rivalry may involve unorganized workers or organized workers. When the workers are unorganized, the union must court the votes of the majority of the workers in the unit appropriate for collective bargaining. The U.S. National Labor Relations Board (NLRB) decides whether an employer unit, a craft unit, or a subdivision is appropriate in each case. The action of a union to attract workers who are already represented by another union is known as raiding. Under NLRB representation proceedings, the raided union has a better than 3 to 1 chance of defeating the raider. The NLRB has made raiding easier because it has systematized the proceedings whereby one union can take away the representation rights of another union. See Gordon F. Bloom and Herbert R. Northrup, *Economics of Labor Relations,* 8th ed., Irwin, Homewood, Ill., 1977.

required reserves   The percentage of their deposits that U.S. commercial banks are required to set aside as reserves at their regional Federal Reserve bank or as cash in their vaults. Reserve requirements vary according to the category of the bank. The purpose of required reserves is to give the central bank a method of controlling a member's behavior. Thus, Federal Reserve authorities are able to control the amount of bank money and demand deposits that the banking system can create. Banks that are not members of the

Federal Reserve System have no such requirements. For further information, see Lawrence S. Ritter and William L. Silber, *Principles of Money, Banking, and Financial Markets,* 3d rev. ed., Basic Books, New York, 1980.

research and development   According to the National Science Foundation, the basic and applied research and engineering, as well as the design and development of prototypes and processes, undertaken by business, governmental, and nonprofit organizations. The term research and development does not include quality control, routine product testing, market research, sales promotion, sales service, and geological or geophysical exploration. Many economists believe that research and development are the key to economic growth. Statistics on research and development expenditures are published in *Reviews of Data on Research and Development,* National Science Foundation, Washington, D.C., periodically; for additional information, see Richard R. Nelson (ed.), *The Rate and Direction of Inventive Activity: Economic and Social Factors,* National Bureau of Economic Research, Princeton University Press, Princeton, N.J., 1962.

reservation demand   In economic theory, the quantities of a commodity with a fixed supply which present holders wish to continue holding. Two important alternatives are open to holders of a commodity that has a fixed supply: (1) personal use or consumption and (2) sale at a future date. For example, a first edition of a book is a commodity that has a fixed supply. The owners at any given moment are seldom the only ones who desire the commodity for the next period. Population changes, changing income patterns, and changes in the prices of other goods lead to a continual redistribution of ownership. In an analysis of this type of demand, there are two classes of consumers: those who possess the commodity and those who do not. Let us suppose that, in the hypothetical case of a first-edition book, the consumer demand schedule for each of the two consuming groups look like this:

	Quantity demanded by	
Price	Owners	Nonowners
$20	70	15
$19	80	20
$18	90	40

If the total supply is 100, a supply curve can be determined. If those persons who presently own the first edition wish to hold x books at a price y, then they wish to supply $100x$ books at a price y. The supply schedule would look like this:

Price	Quantity supplied	Quantity held
$20	30	70
$19	20	80
$18	10	90

The equilibrium price is determined by equating the supply with the quantity demanded. In this case, the price would be $19. The quantities that present owners of the first edition wish to hold at each price is the reservation demand. The reservation demand is the willingness or reluctance of these potential sellers to sell their first editions or hold on to them. For a brief summary of this fixed-supply situation and how the reservation demand is transformed into the supply-and-demand analysis, see Alfred W. Stonier and Douglas C. Hague, *A Textbook of Economic Theory*, 5th ed., Longman, New York, 1980.

reservation price The price below which sellers will refuse to sell some of their stock of goods. For example, sellers cannot sell a greater quantity of goods than they have on hand, but they can sell a smaller quantity. The decision of whether to sell their entire stock or to hold some of it and wait for a more favorable price depends on the relationship between the market price and their reservation price. Sellers' reservation prices are controlled mainly by their estimate of future prices. If they believe that their prices will rise, their reservation prices will be high; if their expectations are for a price decline, their reservation prices will be low. Reservation prices are also influenced by the costs of storage, including rental, interest, and depreciation of goods. The higher these costs, the lower the reservation price. Moreover, if sellers need cash, their reservation prices will be relatively low regardless of other considerations. If they do not need cash quickly, they can afford to take a chance that prices will rise. Reservation price thus plays an important role in determining the supply schedule of an individual seller with a fixed supply of goods on hand. For further information, see Alfred W. Stonier and Douglas C. Hague, *A Textbook of Economic Theory*, 5th ed., Longman, New York, 1980.

residual In econometrics, an estimate of the error involved in a hypothecated econometric relationship. For any given equation, the residual can be calculated after estimates of the parameters of a relationship have been settled upon. For additional information, see Lawrence R. Klein, *An Introduction to Econometrics*, Greenwood, Westport, Conn., 1977.

restraint of trade Any agreement, collusion, or action between two or more individuals or firms which has the effect of impairing free competition. Collusive agreements restraining trade can be horizontal (made by firms at the same stage of production) or vertical (made by firms at different levels of production). Common examples of horizontal restraint of trade include agreements of sellers to fix prices or output at specified levels, to follow the price leadership of the largest firm, or to divide markets. Exclusive supply or purchase agreements are forms of vertical restraint of trade. Restraint of trade can develop through the explicit agreement of the firms involved, as is often the case in price fixing, or it may be the result of a tacit but unwritten agreement, as may be the case in price leadership. In the United States, the Sherman Antitrust Act of 1890 first prohibited collusive agreements among competitors which restrain or eliminate competition among them. While the Sherman Act applied to every contract or combination in restraint of trade no matter how insignificant, this provision was modified in 1911 by the "rule of reason," developed by the U.S. Supreme Court in the Standard Oil and American Tobacco cases. These decisions considered only unreasonable restraint of trade a violation of the Sherman Act. No concrete criteria for determining unreasonable restraint were supplied by the Court, however, and since then it has been up to the courts to determine the boundaries of reasonable and unreasonable restraint. In general, the courts have viewed all agreements to restrain competition as per se unreasonable, regardless of the beneficial effects which may have ensued. For further information, see Clair Wilcox and William G. Shepherd, *Public Policies toward Business,* Irwin, Homewood, Ill., 1975

retained earnings (undistributed profits)   The excess of a company's posttax income over all dividends distributed to stockholders. Retained earnings serve as an important internal source of funds for business expansion. Many companies prefer to finance their growth with internal funds because this procedure makes it possible for them to avoid dilution of stock equity or fixed interest obligations. For many years, the term earned surplus was used, but today numerous accountants believe that the term retained earnings is more descriptive and less subject to misunderstanding.

return on investment (ROI)   A measure of the yield or return on invested capital as, for example, in an existing business, or a measure of the expected return on prospective investments, as in the case of proposed plant or equipment purchases. The two principal measurements of ROI are rates of net profit to worth and net profit to total assets. There are three methods of weighing the relative profitability of possible purchases of new plant or equipment against alternative investment opportunities over a span of years. They are (1) payback, which represents the number of years of net attributable income to recover the investment; (2) average rate of return, which accounts, in a simple fashion, for the relative profitability of each project, and (3) discounted cash flow, which considers the cost of capital funds over the life of the project and allows for the differences in time, during which the investment generates cash, which itself yields income. For additional information, see J. Fred Weston and Eugene F. Brigham, *Managerial Finance,* 6th ed., Dryden Press, Hinsdale, Ill., 1978

returns to scale The relationship between equal proportional increases in all productive inputs and the proportional change in output using the same type of technology. If, for example, a doubling of all productive inputs results in a doubling of the firm's output, it is said that the firm's production function is characterized by constant returns to scale in that range of output. Returns to scale involve the relationship between physical amounts of productive inputs and salable output, not prices or costs, although costs are affected by returns to scale. It is possible to construct various production functions which exhibit constant returns to scale, such as output = $(L \times C)^{1/2}$. If output were related to factor inputs by the formula output = $L^2 + C^2$, the firm would experience increasing returns to scale. When discussing returns to scale, we are concerned with a *given* production function—that is, one which does not involve better technology at some levels of output than at others. In practice, we know that firms of very small size may not be able to take advantage of high levels of technology, but they will be able to do so as their output grows. Thus, most firms will actually have different production functions at different levels of output, and the various production functions may involve increasing, decreasing, or constant returns to scale. Returns to scale are not to be confused with the potential benefits of large-scale production, such as buying in carload lots, enjoying large size compared with suppliers, extensive division of labor with resultant economies, and other factors. A textbook treatment may be found in George J. Stigler, *The Theory of Price,* 3d ed., Macmillan, New York, 1966; for an explicit application for business firms, see John M. Heineke, *Microeconomics for Business Decisions,* Prentice-Hall, Englewood Cliffs, N.J., 1976.

revaluation The upward or downward change in a currency's value relative to gold or other currencies. As of 1981, for example, £1 could be purchased for $1.90, but the pound would appreciate relative to the dollar if its price rose to $2.00, or depreciate if its price fell to $1.80. When such changes in exchange rates are caused by the deliberate act of a government in buying and selling gold at a different price than it had previously, the currency is said to be revalued. The revaluation of a country's currency is an important tool in dealing with its balance of international payments. Chronic deficits may force a country to devalue its currency in order to return to equilibrium, while persistent surpluses may permit a country to let its currency appreciate and thus return its payments to equilibrium. For further information, see Eli Shapiro, Ezra Solomon, and William W. White, *Money and Banking,* 5th ed., Holt, Rinehart and Winston, New York, 1968.

revenue bond A limited obligation municipal bond, which is secured by the revenues produced by the facility it helped finance. Like all debt obligations, a revenue bond represents a promise to pay a specified amount of money (principal) at a certain date in the future, or periodically over the course of the loan, during which time interest is paid at a fixed rate on specified dates. Furthermore, since they are municipal bonds, revenue bonds are exempted from federal income taxes. Unlike general obligation municipal bonds, which are secured by the "full faith and credit" of the issuing government, revenue bonds depend on the income produced by the facility (bridge, tunnel, turnpike, and so on) they financed for payment of interest and principal. Therefore, other things being equal, revenue bonds carry a greater risk of default than general obligation bonds. For further information, see Julius I. Bogen (ed.), *The Financial Handbook*, 4th ed., Ronald, New York, 1968; David Darst, *The Complete Bond Book—A Guide to All Types of Fixed Income Securities*, McGraw-Hill, New York, 1975; Robert Lamb and Stephen P. Rappaport, *Municipal Bonds—The Comprehensive Review of Tax-Exempt Securities and Public Finance*, McGraw-Hill, New York, 1980.

revenue sharing, general   The earmarking of a portion of federal revenues for distribution to the states, in accordance with a formula. Local governments receive their share from their respective states. These funds are transferred automatically to the states to be used for any legitimate public purpose. They are not subject to annual appropriation by the Congress. It is one method of strengthening the fiscal position of state and local governments. It results in increased reliance on the federal income tax as a source of funds for state and local governments, and it allows them to have greater control over the ways these funds are spent. For additional information, see Charles L. Schultze et al., *Setting National Priorities: The 1972 Budget*, Brookings Institution, Washington, D.C., 1971, chap. 6.

revolving-credit plan   A method of providing credit to consumers so that they can purchase each month an amount of goods equal to the monthly payment made against their previous debt. The credit limit for the customer is based on the amount of monthly payment that is best suited to the customer's budget. In a twelve-month revolving-credit account, for example, a customer capable of paying $20 per month would have a limit on the account of $20 times 12, or $240. Thus, the monthly payment of $20 would permit the customer to charge up to $240 at any one time. The revolving-credit plan differs from the charge account, in which the customer is expected to liquidate the debt in a single payment. In revolving credit, the account is used almost as an open account for general shopping each month. The plan has many advantages over other methods of extending consumer credit. Unlike installment-credit contracts, which are usually limited to durable goods, revolving credit is extended to all goods in a store. It is a convenience for shoppers because it eliminates visits to credit departments in order to consolidate new balances with old balances. Because of the closer supervision by stores of this type of credit, it can be extended to somewhat poorer credit risks than is the usual practice. There is also a flexible revolving-credit account under which the customer does not pay a fixed monthly charge but rather a flexible amount which, when multiplied by 12 or some other figure, yields the present outstanding balance. Thus, the monthly payment changes with fluctuations in the unpaid balance.

ridge regression A possible solution offered for multicollinearity in regression analysis. When the set of independent or regressor variables exhibits a high degree of interdependence in a regression, the individual parameter estimates will not be statistically significant even though the overall regression will be. Ridge regression is one method which attempts to correct this problem by adding a diagonal matrix to the variance-covariance matrix of the regressors. Ridge regression estimates depend on the parameter of the diagonal matrix and must be interpreted with care. See Phoebus J. Dhrymes, *Introductory Econometrics,* Springer-Verlag, New York, 1978.

right-to-work law A state law which makes it illegal for collective bargaining agreements to contain union-shop, maintenance-of-membership, preferential-hiring, or other clauses requiring compulsory union membership. After state legislatures were permitted to pass laws of this type by the Taft-Hartley Act of 1947, about twenty states, mostly in the south and the midwest, passed right-to-work laws. Indiana, however, is the only major industrial state having a right-to-work law. The Taft-Hartley Act also provides that when a state prohibits the union shop, this prohibition shall be enforced even in establishments covered by federal labor relations laws. The major effect of the right-to-work laws has been to outlaw the union shop. In practice, such laws have proved relatively ineffective, however, and have merely given rise to bootleg closed shops. See Thomas R. Haggard, *Compulsory Unionism, The NLRB and the Courts: A Legal Analysis of Union Security Agreements,* Industrial Research Unit, Wharton School, University of Pennsylvania, Philadelphia, 1977.

risk The exposure of an investor to the possibility of gain or loss of money. The profit is the investor's reward for assuming the risk of economic uncertainty, such as changes in consumer tastes or changes in technology. The financial risk is based on natural, human, and economic uncertainties. The risk involved in the first two types of uncertainty can be minimized by ensuring oneself against them, but there is no insurance against the risk of economic uncertainty. For further information, see Jack Hirschleifer, *Investment, Interest and Capital,* Prentice-Hall, Englewood Cliffs, N.J., 1970.

risk capital *See* **venture capital.**

risk premium The incremental return required to compensate an investor in projects with uncertain outcomes. The risk premium, in percentage terms, is the difference between the rate of return required for a given project with risk involved and a specified risk-free rate of return. Measurement of the risk premium has practical importance for evaluating investment decisions in a world subject to random disturbances. For additional information, see Jack Hirshleifer, *Investment, Interest and Capital,* Prentice-Hall, Englewood Cliffs, N.J., 1970.

robust regression A regression which is relatively insensitive to situations where a few of the data observations may be in error. In regression analysis, the estimates can be sensitive to "outliers," single observations that do not appear to belong with the rest of the data. There are advanced techniques that assign lesser weight to these others to achieve more robust estimates. See Phoebus J. Dhrymes, *Introductory Econometrics,* Springer-Verlag, New York, 1978.

rolling readjustment The characteristic of a period of time when activity in some sectors of the economy is moving down and in others it is moving up, with the result that overall measures of economic activity do not change significantly. During a period of rolling readjustment, the various sectors of the economy begin their readjustment movements one at a time and not together; thus, a recession is avoided.

rollover A method of refunding used by the U.S. Treasury Department. By this method, a new security offering is subscribed for in terms of a maturing obligation. Thus, a new issue can be paid for merely by turning in maturing holdings for the new issue. In this sense, the maturity rolls over. The alternative to the rollover method of refunding is to pay off the holders of the maturing debt and offer new issues for cash.

roundabout production The use of less direct but more efficient means of production, usually first involving an investment in machinery or equipment. Robinson Crusoe might have nourished himself by wading out into the surf to catch fish bare-handed, but he found it more efficient to spend most of his time on shore, making and repairing fishing nets which did the catching unattended. A modern economy's production methods are increasingly roundabout; it has been estimated that only 10% of the U.S. work force in manufacturing industry is directly engaged in the production of consumer goods, while the rest either make the machines that produce consumer goods or make the machines that make machines. For the theoretical analysis of this trend, see Eugen von Böhm-Bawerk, *The Positive Theory of Capital,* G. E. Stechert, New York, 1923.

runaway shop A unionized business concern that moves to another state or another area to escape union demands. The question of whether any particular firm does or does not fit this category is frequently the subject of much debate. Labor leaders may insist that a particular firm is a runaway shop, while management insists that the primary motive behind the move was a tax concession, better access to raw materials, or greater proximity to markets. American trade unions have long faced great difficulties in establishing themselves in competitive industries in which firms can shift quickly from one part of the country to another. Firms in the garment industry, in which there is little capital investment, appear to have run away from union demands. Unless the union is alert it may suddenly discover that it has a large unemployed membership. The needle-trades unions, in particular, maintain efficient organizations to find runaway shops.

S

sales tax   A flat percentage levy on the selling price of an item. Sales taxes differ from excise taxes in that they are assessed on all, or almost all, commodities. They can be levied at any level of distribution. In some countries, France, for example, a tax (turnover tax) is collected each time that a commodity changes hands, but in the United States a sales tax is generally applied only once, usually at the retail level. The U.S. federal government levies excises on more than sixty different items, but it has no sales tax. Such taxes are, however, of great importance to state and local governments. In 1980 these governments raised over $50 billion from sales taxes or about 16% of total state revenues and more than 3% of local revenues. Sales taxes are frequently criticized as regressive, since they take a larger proportion of low than of high incomes, but when food is exempted, as it is in many states and localities, the regression tends to disappear. See Joseph A. Pechman, *Federal Tax Policy,* 3d ed., Brookings Institution, Washington, D.C., 1977; for annual data on sales tax collections, see U.S. Department of Commerce, *Compendium of State Government Finances* and *Compendium of City Government Finances;* for sales tax rates in individual states and communities, see *State Tax Reporter,* Commerce Clearing House, New York.

sampling   The process of selecting a segment of a population for the purpose of drawing inferences concerning the total population, or universe. The universe to be sampled, whether it is composed of people, payroll records, farms, or bank accounts, must consist of individuals so that sample units can be selected. The aim of sampling is simply to provide the required information with the minimum expenditure of time, effort, and money. In some cases, samples may provide more accurate results than a census or a complete enumeration if inexperienced workers take the census and make inaccurate reports. Two types of sampling are commonly used: (1) probability sampling, in which each unit is chosen with a known chance of being selected; and (2) nonprobability sampling, in which the selection of the sample may be based on convenience or judgment. There is always the risk that the selected sample may not be representative of the population, but only with probability sampling can the risk of relying on sample information be determined. For applications of sampling in business, see W. Edwards Deming, *Sample Design in Business Research,* Wiley, New York, 1960; John B. Lansing and James N. Morgan, *Economic Survey Methods,* Institute for Survey Research, University of Michigan, Ann Arbor, Mich., 1971.

sampling, convenience   The use of any handy group or chunk of the population or universe as the sample to be studied. Examples of convenience samples are workers in an office, houses in a block, a group of people interviewed on a street corner, or the top items in a carton. As an example of the last-named case, an aircraft manufacturer receives a shipment of 100,000 bolts, which to be usable must be strong enough to withstand a shearing force of 5,000 pounds. The manufacturer uses a convenience sample to test the strength of the bolts by selecting a few bolts from the top of each carton. It is conceivable, however, that the manufacturer of the bolts, knowing the testing procedures of the airplane manufacturer, placed all the strong bolts on the top of the carton. Thus, the convenience sample chosen by the aircraft manufacturer would not be representative of the complete shipment of bolts. With all types of samples, there is a possibility that the sample may not be representative of the population, but when convenience sampling is used, there is no way of knowing the extent of the risk of relying on sample information. Convenience sampling is often used in pilot studies and in studies in which sampling costs must be kept low. For applications of sampling in business, see W. Edwards Deming, *Sample Design in Business Research,* Wiley, New York, 1960.

sampling, judgment   The use of personal knowledge or experience in choosing a sample. Examples of judgment samples are the selection of a typical city's election results to determine the national trend or the choice of a group of companies considered representative of all companies, as in the McGraw-Hill Department of Economics' *Annual Surveys of Business' Plans for New Plants and Equipment.* Since probability theory is not employed in judgment sampling, standard errors of the sample estimates cannot be computed. For further discussion of judgment sampling, see W. Edwards Deming, *Sample Design in Business Research,* Wiley, New York, 1960.

sampling, probability   A method of sampling in which the likelihood of selecting each unit of the population or universe is known. Many methods are used in selecting probability samples. Let us suppose, for example, that a sample of factory workers is required for a study of income. When complete lists of factory workers are available, the sample units may be chosen randomly or systematically. Without such lists, we may select the sample in steps, first selecting a sample of areas from which to choose a sample of factories, which in turn yields a sample of workers. Whatever sampling procedure is used the selection of each unit is mechanical and has a specified probability. These probabilities are used as weights in calculating the income of factory workers and the standard errors of the estimated income. For applications of sampling in business, see W. Edwards Deming, *Sample Design in Business Research*, Wiley, New York, 1960.

sampling, quota   A method of sampling in which definite numbers are selected from each class of the population. The quota assigned to each class is generally proportionate to its share of the population being surveyed. In some polls, for example, interviewers may be assigned quotas by age group and sex from different social and economic classes. The interviewers then select the specified number of respondents in each quota. This selection procedure can produce biased results, since interviewers are likely to choose respondents who are easy to reach and willing to be interviewed. Because random selection methods are not used for quota sampling, tolerance or sample precision cannot be computed. See George Kress, *Marketing Research*, Reston Publishing, Reston, Va., 1979.

sampling, simple random (unrestricted random sampling)   A method of sample selection in which each individual or sample unit is drawn independently and each individual has an equal chance of being chosen for a particular study. Numbers might be assigned to all individuals in the population or universe, and the sample units might be selected by drawing them from a hat or, more likely, by using published lists of random numbers. Generally, simple random sampling is not very simple, particularly when the population is large and the individuals are not numbered. For further information, see W. Edwards Deming, *Sample Design in Business Research*, Wiley, New York, 1960.

sampling, stratified   A method of sample selection in which the population is first divided into a number of strata and sample units are then chosen from each stratum. The stratification is accomplished so that all units in a given stratum are as nearly alike as possible. Each stratum is represented in the sample, the sample units being chosen by random methods. In the sample used for the *Current Population Survey*, which is conducted monthly by the U.S. Bureau of the Census, for example, all 3,100 counties in the United States are classified into 333 strata, and sample counties or groups of counties are chosen from each stratum. In the stratification, such characteristics as geographic area, population, income, occupation, and race are taken into account so that the counties in any one stratum are similar. For further discussion, see W. Edwards Deming, *Sample Design in Business Research,* Wiley, New York, 1960.

sampling, systematic A method of selecting units from a population or a universe by means of an interval pattern. A sample unit is chosen from the first interval and thereafter from every nth interval. In this case, n denotes the length of the interval, which might be every tenth individual on a list of numbered individuals or every card every one-eighth of an inch, moving from front to back, in a file drawer of cards. For numbered or ordered populations, systematic selection is quick, easy, and inexpensive. For applications in business, see W. Edwards Deming, *Sample Design in Business Research,* Wiley, New York, 1960.

sampling, unrestricted random *See* **sampling, simple random.**

satisfice The process of resolving a problem as satisfactorily as possible, given the various constraints on choices. This is an alternative to maximizing or optimizing production and profits. Suppose, for example, that a firm wants to produce 100 units of a given product in a day but that its productive facilities allow it to produce only 75 units. In order to produce the extra 25 units, it would have to expand its capacity, work the labor force overtime, or farm the extra units out to be produced by some other firm. Thus, the firm analyzes all options open to it and the costs associated with them to decide on a satisfactory profit position. This is the point on the supply-and-demand schedule where it just pays to produce the last unit of output, given the constraints. For additional information, see Herbert A. Simon, "Theories of Decision Making on Economics," *American Economic Review,* vol. 26, no. 4, June 1959, pp. 243–283.

saving The amount of current income which is not spent on consumption. A decision to save is basically a decision not to use up income but to hold it—in a bank, in securities, or in the form of cash. An individual may set aside current income for future consumption for a number of reasons: to build a reserve for emergency purposes, to accumulate funds for old age, to protect the family, or to pay for a particular objective in the future, such as the education of children or the purchase of a home. A corporation also can save, usually by withholding part of its earnings from stockholders, in order to reinvest the money in the business. One of the most important factors influencing the level of personal saving is the size of family income; as income increases, the amount saved generally increases. Consumer saving also depends on expectations regarding future income; the greater individuals think their incomes will be in the future, the less incentive they have for rainy-day saving. The more certain this anticipated future income (e.g., from a safe job rather than from an uncertain one), the less motivation individuals have to accumulate a fund of savings. Furthermore, the degree to which present goods are desired over future goods and the care with which the future is anticipated also are important in determining individuals' saving habits. Another factor which may affect some types of saving is the rate of interest; the higher the rate of interest on invested funds, the greater the inducement to save. In the process of saving and providing for personal security, the individual is also providing a large part of the funds needed for business capital investment. For additional details on saving in the United States, see Raymond W. Goldsmith, *A Study of Saving in the United States,* National Bureau of Economic Research, Princeton University Press, Princeton, N.J., 1955; see also Lawrence S. Ritter and William L. Silber, *Principles of Money, Banking and Financial Markets,* 3d rev. ed., Basic Books, New York, 1980.

savings and loan association   A cooperative savings organization through which savers can accumulate funds to purchase homes and borrowers can obtain home-mortgage money. Its basic purpose is to make it easier for its members to finance the purchase and repair of their homes. When members put money in a savings and loan association, they are buying stock in the association; by law, the association cannot accept deposits. When members want their cash, they must ask the association to buy back their shares. The association is obligated to repurchase their shares only as long as sufficient funds are available, however, since members are stockholders and not creditors, as in a bank. The net earnings of the association are distributed to the stockholders as dividends on their investment. Savings and loan associations invest funds almost exclusively in home mortgages, especially for loans to members. They may receive charters either from federal or from state governments. Federal associations must join the Federal Savings and Loan Insurance Corporation and the Federal Home Loan bank in their district, while state-chartered associations may do so if they wish. The Federal Home Loan banks provide additional liquidity to savings and loan associations by making loans to them against mortgages as collateral. For additional details, see *Savings and Loan Fact Book,* U.S. Savings and Loan League, Chicago, annually.

savings ratio   The percentage that current savings is of current disposable income. Shifts and trends in the savings ratio are important in analyzing long-run trends in income and expenditures. Savings ratios that are based on data on consumer budgets provide information on savings patterns in different income and occupational classes at a given moment. For example, it has been found that the savings ratio is negative in the lowest-income classes but rises steadily as income increases. The savings ratio is also used in analyzing the economic growth of developed and underdeveloped nations. Underdeveloped nations typically have a very low savings ratio, which makes investment very difficult. For historical data on savings and income from which the savings ratio can be computed, see U.S. Department of Commerce, *Survey of Current Business*, July issues.

Say's law of markets   A principle which states broadly that an economy's productive activity always generates demand sufficient to absorb the goods produced. According to a translation of the writings of Jean Baptiste Say, the French economist who originated this idea early in the nineteenth century, ". . . a product is no sooner created than it, from that instant, offers a market for other products to the full extent of its own value. . . . Thus, the mere circumstance of the creation of one product immediately opens a vent [market] for other products." Say's law held that an excess supply of goods or an excess demand for money tends to be self-correcting. Thus, a generally insufficient demand for an economy's products could not exist. Taken with other assumptions of classical economics, such as wage and price flexibility, Say's law produced an equilibrium model of the economy that ruled out the possibility of an extended recession or unemployment. This principle aroused disagreement among economists that has persisted into contemporary discussions, partially because Say's precise meaning was unclear. Among those who strongly disagreed with the principle were Thomas Robert Malthus and John Maynard Keynes, but the prevailing thought of the nineteenth century supported Say. For a fuller statement of Say's economics, see Jean Baptiste Say, *Treatise on Political Economy*, Wells and Lilly, Boston, 1821; see also J. M. Keynes, *The General Theory of Employment, Interest, and Money*, Harcourt Brace, New York, 1936, chap. 2; for Malthus's opposing arguments, see Thomas R. Malthus, *Principles of Political Economy*, William Pickering, London, 1836.

scarcity   A limit to the availability of a productive resource during a given time period. In a system of voluntary exchange, a resource will be allocated to uses that return the greatest value to the owner. But in a market system, when property rights are conflicting or when distortion of incentives occurs due to taxation and regulation, resources may not be allocated efficiently, causing a scarcity. For additional information, see Paul Samuelson, *Economics*, 10th ed., McGraw-Hill, New York, 1976, chap. 1.

scedasticity (skedasticity)   A word denoting dispersion, particularly as it is measured by variance. If the variance of a variable x is not constant but varies with the magnitude of another variable or over time, variable x is said to be heteroscedastic. If, instead, the variance is constant, variable x is said to be homoscedastic. For additional information, see Lawrence R. Klein, *An Introduction to Econometrics*, Greenwood, Westport, Conn., 1977.

search theory of unemployment   The notion, associated with the monetarist school, that unemployment rises in a period of slowing inflation and wages because the unemployed wait and search longer for a job that pays the nominal wage they desire. This theory indicates that at any steady rate of inflation there is a normal or natural rate of unemployment. However, if the rate of inflation begins to slow down, wages will likely increase at a lower rate than expected and those people who become unemployed will have to take longer in finding a job that pays the nominal wage they want. For additional information, see Michael R. Darby, *Macroeconomics*, McGraw-Hill, New York, 1977.

seasonal adjustment   A statistical index of monthly or quarterly compensating factors used to correct a series of raw economic data for periodic climatic conditions and the existence of special holidays. Seasonal indices are expressed in terms of the percentage which each of the twelve monthly figures is of the average for the year. Seasonal adjustments are computed by various methods, such as the link-relative, monthly-means, and ratio-to-average methods. Seasonal adjustments may be stable (that is, they furnish a constant seasonal index for each month in every year) or moving (that is, they furnish a slightly different index for each month in every year). For additional information, see Arnold Zellner, *Seasonal Analysis of Economic Time Series*, Bureau of the Census, Washington, D.C., 1978.

Examples of Seasonal Indices

	Stable	Moving	Stable	Moving
	1980		1981	
January	71.9	74.7	71.9	74.9
February	76.3	80.2	76.3	79.4
March	101.3	100.5	101.3	99.2
April	113.9	115.7	113.9	116.2
May	118.7	117.6	118.7	118.6
June	116.3	114.8	116.3	115.2
July	112.2	110.5	112.2	110.1
August	112.9	111.9	112.9	113.5
September	106.6	105.2	106.6	104.2
October	105.4	103.3	105.4	103.3
November	89.7	90.1	89.7	89.9
December	74.8	75.5	74.8	75.5
Total	1,200.0	1,200.0	1,200.0	1,200.0

seasonally adjusted figures (seasonally compensated figures)   Economic figures that are free from normal seasonal influences. Allowance is made statistically for the underlying month-to-month or quarter-to-quarter swings in the raw data of an economic series. The advantage of seasonally adjusted data is that the cyclical movement is not obscured by purely seasonal variations. For comparisons of unadjusted and seasonally adjusted data and current methods of adjusting raw economic data, see Julius Shiskin, *Electronic Computers and Business Indicators,* National Bureau of Economic Research, Occasional Paper 57, New York, 1957.

seasonal unemployment Periodic loss of jobs caused by seasonal variations in the production of certain industries. The two main seasonal factors affecting output are weather and style changes. Certain industries, such as agriculture and building construction, are unable to operate during some periods of the year, while others, such as ice-cream and coal production, are subject to regular seasonal fluctuations in consumer demand. Fashion and trade customs, determining when the new year's models in automobiles, clothing, etc., are introduced, result in certain periodic slack periods. Peak seasons of general consumer demand, such as Christmas and Easter, also cause seasonal changes in employment and unemployment in specific industries. Although seasonal unemployment cannot be entirely eliminated, it is predictable, and thus the risks and hardships of seasonal layoffs can be reduced by planning ahead. Furthermore, although employees may be deprived of income in the off season, this type of unemployment is temporary, and employees are usually reemployed when the new season begins. Fixed annual wages and fill-in jobs are among the measures that are used to combat the effects of seasonal fluctuations. Changes in marketing policy, such as the staggering of introduction times for new annual models, are another approach to the problem. For further information, see Lloyd G. Reynolds, *Labor Economics and Labor Relations,* 7th ed., Prentice-Hall, Englewood Cliffs, N.J., 1978.

seasonal variation The more or less regular month-to-month or quarter-to-quarter fluctuations that occur in almost any economic series of data because of periodic climatic conditions and special holidays. For example, television-set production in July is usually smaller than in any other month of the year because of plant shutdowns, vacations, and programming of generally poorer quality during the summer. For a description of seasonal variations, the advantages of eliminating them, and current methods of adjusting new economic data, see Julius Shiskin, *Electronic Computers and Business Indicators,* National Bureau of Economic Research, Occasional Paper 57, New York, 1957.

second-best theory A theory that analyzes alternative suboptimal positions to determine the second best, when some constraint prevents an economy from reaching a Pareto optimum. In a general-equilibrium system, if one of the requirements for a Pareto optimum is unattainable, the other requirements, although attainable, may not lead to a second-best position. Thus, an optimum situation can be reached only by departing from all the Pareto conditions. For example, free-trade advocates have long argued that any reduction in tariffs will increase welfare, thereby getting closer to Pareto optimality. But a customs union that reduces tariffs between members can bring about production shifts that may reduce efficiency, thus moving further from Pareto optimality. See Richard Lipsey and K. Lancaster, "The General Theory of Second Best," *Review of Economic Studies,* vol. 24, no. 63, Cambridge, England, 1956–1957, pp. 11–32.

secular-stagnation thesis (mature-economy thesis) The theory that insufficient aggregate demand in advanced economies, such as those of the United States and Great Britain, is not merely a periodic, cyclical problem but a characteristic one. The secular-stagnation thesis, advanced by Alvin H. Hansen and John Maynard Keynes in the 1930s, was an attempt to explain the high unemployment and low investment of the depression period. It was argued that the ingredients needed for a high rate of growth in a mature economy (greater advances in technology relative to population growth) may also result in a deficiency of aggregate demand necessary for full employment. Hansen believed that the massive U.S. private investment undertaken in the nineteenth century had been a result of population growth, the western frontier, the industrial expansion associated with wars, and technical innovations. He thought that by the 1930s the United States had reached the status of a mature economy, with population growth declining, the frontier disappearing, the absolute volume of savings growing, and new technical innovations turning out to be capital saving. As a result, relatively few investment opportunities would be available, and a long-run trend of substantial unemployment would develop. Events since 1939 have proved that the depression of the 1930s was, in fact, only a deep cyclical contraction which ushered in decades of economic growth in even the most mature industrial economies. Nevertheless, fears of secular stagnation are revived during each downturn. In the early 1960s, secular stagnationists pointed to the prevailing high unemployment rate in the United States as a confirmation of the stagnation thesis. For further information on the secular-stagnation thesis, see Alvin H. Hansen, *Fiscal Policy and Business Cycles,* Greenwood, Westport, Conn., 1941.

secular trend (economic trend) A statistical term denoting the regular, long-term movement of a series of economic data. The secular trend of most economic series is positive, or upward, indicating growth, the angle of the trend depending on how fast or how slow the growth rate is. For example, since sales and production of chemicals grow faster than sales and production of food, the secular trend for chemicals is steeper than that for food, although the trend for both industries is upward. In a few cases, however, the secular trend of key economic series is important for business forecasting. For instance, after computing the secular trend for manufacturing production over a long period of years, it is possible to project the same rate of growth for a decade ahead and estimate the trend value of manufacturing output for that period. For the measurement of secular trend, see T. W. Anderson, *The Statistical Analysis of Time Series,* Wiley, New York, 1971.

selective credit control   A credit control designed to regulate the terms of a specific transaction. It differs from a general control in two fundamental respects. First, it applies to a specific transaction and is therefore personal in its effects, whereas a general control is impersonal. Secondly, a selective credit control curtails the demand for credit rather than the supply, as occurs under the application of more general controls. The primary purpose of controls of this type is to regulate areas that are not responsive to measures of general credit control. Thus, the high demand for stock-exchange loans in the 1920s, despite the high interest rates on such loans, revealed the necessity of having some sort of selective controls in this area. At the time of the U.S. entry into World War II and into the Korean conflict, when the prospect of war financing presented an obstacle to the vigorous application of general credit controls, selective measures were introduced to regulate consumer credit. Selective controls were necessary to curtail demand for consumer durables when the production of these goods was cut because of war production. In cases of consumer loans for stock purchases and for durables, the importance of nonbank lenders as a source of funds and the failure of high interest costs to dampen demand were of prime importance in favoring selective controls over general controls. A selective control operates by curtailing the use of credit in purchasing particular classes of goods. Among such controls were Regulation W for consumer credit, Regulation X for real estate credit, Regulations T and U for the financing of transactions in securities. The control operates by regulating specific aspects of the individual loan contract, such as minimum down payments and maximum maturity limitations. By raising the level of down payments and lowering the maximum maturity limitations, credit can be tightened. In the United States, selective controls now exist only in the regulation of stock-exchange credit. For further information, see *Credit Allocation Techniques and Monetary Policy*, Federal Reserve Bank of Boston, Boston, 1973, pp. 9–63.

sellers' market   A market situation in which demand is greater than supply at current prices. Because of the short supply, sellers have a favorable market position and can raise their prices and still sell their goods. Such a rise in prices will continue until supply and demand once again are equal at some price. When prices are relatively high in relation to past prices or producers' average costs, the existence of a sellers' market is indicated. In an extreme sellers' market, as during wartime shortages, it may be necessary to introduce rationing controls.

seniority rule   A provision in a labor contract that requires preferential treatment for workers having the longest service. One of the most common types of seniority rules covers layoffs and rehiring schedules: workers with the longest service are the last to be laid off during recessions and the first to be rehired in periods of recovery. An increasing number of U.S. labor contracts also make seniority a basis for promotion and transfer, workers who have the longest service being given first consideration for promotion or transfer to a more desirable job. Management frequently resists strict seniority rules on the ground that such rules promote inefficiency by preventing management from rewarding employees according to merit. Union officials, on the other hand, argue that seniority rules protect workers against arbitrary action and discrimination. For a discussion of the economic impact of seniority provisions, see Lloyd G. Reynolds, *Labor Economics and Labor Relations,* 7th ed., Prentice-Hall, Englewood Cliffs, N.J., 1978.

separation of ownership and control   The phenomenon of modern corporate structure in which the power to control a corporation's business is in different hands from those of the persons who collectively own the corporation. This divorce of ownership from control results primarily from the diversification of corporate ownership among many small stockholders. For example, in 1982, 3 million different persons were shareholders of American Telephone and Telegraph, and no single owner held even 1% of the total. In a typical giant corporation, all management (officers and directors) usually holds only about 3% of the outstanding common stock. Because of the lethargy of the individual stockholder, who either does not exercise voting rights or signs them over to the management by proxy, the control of management is largely unchecked in many corporations. This separation is not important if the actions of the control group (management) are in accordance with the wishes of the ownership group (shareholders). Management may, however, be less interested in maximum profits than in enhancing its own position and income through activities which are not in the interests of the corporation. Thus, separation of ownership and control may result in certain abuses by the control group.

serial correlation   The correlation between observations of a time series and other observations of the same time series that either lead or lag by a specified time interval. Serial correlation crops up when observations overlap or are derived by interpolation and when the time interval is too short. A statistical test, based on the ratio of the mean-square successive difference to the variance, guards against the presence of serial correlation; that is, it indicates whether or not it is present and significant. For additional information, see Lawrence R. Klein, *An Introduction to Econometrics,* Greenwood, Westport, Conn., 1977.

services   The component of the gross national product that measures the output of intangible items. Services include such items as telephone service; railway, bus, and air transportation; private education; and radio and television repair. Since World War II, services have constituted the fastest-growing area of the U.S. economy, rising by 232% between 1950 and 1980 as compared with an increase of 177% for the economy as a whole. Since, in the national income accounts, this component cannot be estimated by the normal commodity-flow method, it is built up from a variety of statistical sources. The reliability of this series is impaired by the heavy reliance on periodic and sometimes infrequent source material. Imputed services provided by financial intermediaries are computed from annual reports received from various government sources. Private sources provide annual data for the expenses of handling life insurance, local transportation, and public utilities. Comprehensive periodic information is available from the Census of Population and Housing, the Census of Business, the Census of Agriculture, the Census of Religious Bodies, and the Biennial Survey of Education. The Census of Population and Housing and the Census of Agriculture are used to estimate the rental value of homes. Private research organizations and trade organizations provide the miscellaneous sources of data on expenditures for services. For further information, see Richard Ruggles and Nancy D. Ruggles, *National Income Accounts and Income Analysis*, 2d ed., McGraw-Hill, New York, 1956; U.S. Department of Commerce, *Survey of Current Business: National Income Supplement*, 1954.

shared-appreciation mortgages *See* **mortgages, nontraditional.**

shifting of tax The transfer of the tax burden from the original payer to someone else. A tax on a manufacturer can be shifted forward to the consumer by increasing the price of the goods sold by the amount of the tax. For example, a tax on an automobile manufacturer can be shifted forward to the consumer by a rise in car prices. A tax can be shifted backward by reducing the price of raw materials and other factors purchased. Thus, by cutting wages an employer can shift the burden of a tax on the firm. The extent to which a tax can be shifted depends on the nature of the tax, the economic environment in which it is levied, and the taxpayers' practices in taking advantage of the possibility of shifting. The only way in which a tax can be shifted is by a change by business in the prices of goods and services that are bought and sold. Thus, a purely personal tax, such as a poll tax or an inheritance tax, cannot be shifted. Neither can a tax on an economic surplus, such as rent or capital gains, be shifted. Among the market factors favorable to shifting are a less elastic demand, a more elastic supply, and a long period of time. For further information, see Richard A. Musgrave and Peggy B. Musgrave, *Public Finance in Theory and Practice*, 2d ed., McGraw-Hill, New York, 1975.

short run A time period that is not long enough for the firm to vary all factors of production. One factor of production, usually plant and equipment, is fixed in the short run, and the firm can change its level of output only by more or less intensively using its existing plant and equipment. Since virtually all costs of production would become fixed if a sufficiently short time period were taken, the short run must be long enough for the firm to vary its output as much as technology permits without changing the scale of the plant. In the long run, all factors of production, including the size or scale of the plant, are variable. The concept of the short run is important to microeconomic theory because much of the theory of the firm and price theory uses cost curves and other analytical tools that assume a short-run time period. See Alfred Marshall, *Principles of Economics,* St. Martin's Press, New York, 1956; Donald S. Watson and Mary A. Holman, *Price Theory and Its Uses,* 4th ed., Houghton Mifflin, Boston, 1978.

short sale The sale of stocks, bonds, foreign exchange, or commodities that the seller does not own. Short sellers believe that the price of a security, commodity, or foreign exchange will decline. They sell it hoping to cover, or buy it back at a lower price, and thereby make a profit on the transaction. Dealers frequently are technically short sellers in the ordinary course of their business. This happens when a customer wants to buy a stock, for example, which the dealer temporarily does not own. To service the customer, the dealer sells the stock, covering this short sale as soon as possible. Short selling of securities differs from that of commodities and foreign exchange. Securities sold short must be borrowed by the seller in order to deliver them to the buyer. After the seller covers, the securities are returned to the lender. In the case of commodities and foreign exchange, short sellers need not borrow because they have merely promised to deliver a certain amount of the commodity or foreign exchange at a specified date in the future. Normally, short sellers cover their sales before the time at which they would have to deliver. For further information, see D. K. Eiteman, C. A. Dice, and W. J. Eiteman, *The Stock Market,* 4th ed., McGraw-Hill, New York, 1966, chap. 15.

short-term forecast A projection which usually extends as much as six quarters ahead of the current period. For example, short-term forecasts made in January 1981 could extend through the second quarter of 1982. Forecasts for the short term are more popular with business economists than those for the medium or the long term. A 1962 survey of the membership of the National Association of Business Economists showed that 95% of those who made forecasts prepared forecasts for the short run, 66% assessed medium-term prospects, and 72% studied the long-term outlook. One reason for the popularity of the short-run forecast is that the recent trend generally holds true over the short run. Occasionally, however, the economist making a short-term forecast must reckon with the fluctuations of the business cycle. Business forecasters most frequently use the indicator technique developed by the National Bureau of Economic Research. Not even judgment commands as much importance as indicators for short-run forecasts. Anticipations surveys rank third in usefulness in this type of forecasting.

simulation games for business Games used to provide experience for young executives by simulating the real-life operations of a business. Within the framework of a game, the executives are forced to cope with the same problems that face the top management of a company. The games are played with the help of computers, which make it possible to reproduce several years in the life of a business in one day. The rules of the game correspond as closely as possible to the realities of business economics. This type of gaming, which is referred to as operational gaming, attempts through simulation to provide a framework for trial-and-error decisions. The game's purpose is not to provide entertainment or a winner but to transfer the learning of a game situation to reality. For further discussion, see Theodore G. Lewis and B. J. Smith, *Computer Principles of Modeling and Simulation,* Houghton Mifflin, Boston, 1979.

simultaneous-equation estimation   A family of statistical techniques which proceed from the assumption that the disturbances in different equations of an economic model are, or are likely to be, correlated with one another. Prior to 1944, the assumption was universally made in economics that the disturbances in different equations of a model were statistically independent. Trygve Haavelmo and his associates concentrated on the implications of correlated disturbances in equations. Koopmans and Marschak helped extend, explain, and popularize Haavelmo's approach. In the 1970s, econometricians began to recognize the need for dealing explicitly with errors in variables. For additional information, see Trygve Haavelmo, "The Probability Approach in Econometrics," *Econometrica,* vol. 12 (suppl.), 1944, pp. 1–18; Henry L. Moore, *Economic Cycles: Their Law and Causes,* Macmillan, New York, 1914.

single tax   A levy on a single category, used by the government as its sole source of revenue. The term single tax is usually associated with Henry George's proposal for the special taxation of land rents. Such a land-value tax would be an annual levy (100% or close to it) on the economic rent received by landowners. The proponents of the single tax argue that economic rents are a completely unearned surplus and that they ought not to go to landowners but should be used to finance government services. According to George, the use of the single tax would remove inequality and eliminate poverty. A single tax on land is also an instrument of developmental tax policy, since it removes all taxes from capital and labor and thus encourages the growth of these productive factors. Land rents are not the only type of unearned income, however, for all deviations from pure competition in other markets result in some type of surplus. The opponents of the single tax argue that a single tax is unfair, since it places all the tax burden on landowners, especially rural landowners, who are not necessarily rich but may be poor farmers. The tax would be applied only to economic rents and not to business rents due to improvements made on the land. In practice, this distinction between land and capital is hard to make, so that the application of a single tax would be very difficult to carry out. For further information, see Henry George, *Progress and Prosperity,* Random House, New York, 1938.

skedasticity   *See* scedasticity.

sliding peg   *See* crawling peg.

sluggish year   A year in which the physical volume of goods and services and industrial production increase by less than 2%, consumer money income after taxes rises by less than 6%, and unemployment exceeds 6% of the labor force. In a sluggish business year, there are only modest purchases of consumer durable goods and capital goods. The criteria given above are being used by many business economists to describe a sluggish business year.

slump   A temporary decline in the volume of general business, a specific industry, a company, or a product line. Generally, a slump is not due to any basic economic change. At the national level, it may occur because of a shift in tastes, such as the sudden increase in purchases of small foreign-made cars and the decline in purchases of large U.S.-made cars in the United States. At the company or product-line level, a slump can occur when a company decides to curtail its sales effort on an overall basis or for a specific product line.

Slutsky equation   An econometric equation stemming from the demand calculus and dealing with economic value theory. It is often called the fundamental equation in the latter area. It separates the change in quantity demanded that is associated with a change in price into two parts: (1) the variation in quantity demanded that is due to income change and (2) the variation in quantity demanded that is a response to a price change for a constant level of utility. A final term in the equation depicts the substitution effect between two commodities. For additional information, see Lawrence A. Klein, *An Introduction to Econometrics,* Greenwood, Westport, Conn., 1977.

Slutsky's proposition   The moving average of a random series oscillates. This property is vital for the statistical analysis of business cycles. Since random time series are occasionally subject to runs similar to those encountered in tossing a true die (runs of fives or sixes), a moving average may reveal random oscillation that may be mistaken, for example, for a cyclical movement. This pitfall can be avoided by the use of correlograms and periodograms at an early stage of analysis. For additional information, see E. Slutsky, "The Summation of Random Causes as the Source of Cyclical Processes," *Econometrica,* vol. 5, 1937, pp. 105–146; Lawrence R. Klein, *An Introduction to Econometrics,* Greenwood, Westport, Conn., 1977.

small business   A business that is owned and operated by relatively few persons, has a relatively small sales revenue, and possesses relatively little capital. The U.S. Department of Commerce defines a small business as including "any manufacturing plant which employs 100 persons or less, wholesale organizations with annual sales of less than $200,000, retail stores, service establishments, hotels, places of amusement and construction concerns with sales or receipts of less than $50,000." Much has been done to help the development of small businesses. In 1953 the Small Business Administration was established as the first independent agency of the U.S. government charged with the duty of fostering the interests of small business. For further information, see Vincent P. Carosso and Stuart Bruchy, *The Survival of Small Business,* Arno, New York, 1979.

Smithsonian Agreement An interim agreement on currency realignment among the Group of Ten at the Smithsonian Institution on December 18, 1971. The agreement included an increase in the U.S. gold price from $35 per ounce to $38. In addition, there occurred a general realignment of currency values resulting in effective upward revaluation (in terms of the dollar price of foreign currencies) of 16.88% for the Japanese yen, 13.58% for the German mark, and 11.57% each for the Dutch guilder and the Belgian franc. The Swiss franc, which had been revalued in May by 7.07%, was adjusted to provide an additional 6.36% effective revaluation and the Italians adjusted the gold parity of the lira downward slightly so that the net revaluation against the dollar was about 7.48%. Also the bands of allowable fluctuations were widened to 2¼% above and below the new par values. For additional information, see Robert Solomon, *The International Monetary System, 1945–1976,* Harper & Row, New York, 1977.

socialism An economic and political system the basis of which is the abolition of private property and the public ownership and operation of the means of production. Whereas capitalism recognizes the relatively unrestricted right of private ownership of productive factors, socialism reserves the ownership of factors for the community as a whole. Since there is no private ownership of the means of production (capital), there is no class of employers and no separate class of employees. Without private employers, there is no private profit motive, and thus the classic market forces for organizing production are not present. Large-scale government planning is therefore necessary to ensure the smooth functioning of the system. Another major aspect of socialism is the redistribution of income for the purpose of achieving equality for all. This welfare consideration is summed up in the phrase "from each according to his abilities, to each according to his needs." As distinct from communism, socialism advocates the peaceful and democratic extension of government ownership and the gradual transition from capitalism to complete socialism. There are many varieties of socialist theory, including Christian, Fabian, guild, utopian, scientific, and Soviet socialism. For further information, see Ludwig von Mises, *Socialism: An Economic and Sociological Analysis,* Macmillan, New York, 1936; Maurice Dobb, *Welfare Economics and the Economics of Socialism,* Cambridge University Press, London, 1970.

social overhead capital *See* infrastructure.

social security program A public welfare program which seeks to reduce the threat to the economic security of the individual. Programs of this type attempt to reduce an individual's or a family's loss of income and welfare by providing cash benefits and needed services. There are three main categories of economic insecurity which social security plans try to eliminate. One is the risk of physical inability to work, leading to a loss of earning power. Examples of this type are sickness, accidents, old age, and death. The second category is economic risk, primarily that of involuntary unemployment. The third factor which reduces individual welfare is the economic burden of a large family. All social security programs involve a transfer of resources to increase total national welfare. If the program is financed by progressive taxation, the transfer is from the rich to the poor. If it is financed primarily by the payments of workers and employers, the resources are transferred within the same class of persons, from the more fortunate to the less fortunate. The actual benefits may be distributed through old age, survivors, and disability payments; unemployment compensation; public relief; family allowances; and public health services. Social security programs of one sort or another have been undertaken by most industrial countries. Some nations, such as Great Britain and New Zealand, have developed a much more comprehensive and unified system of social security than others. For further information, see Eveline M. Burns, *Social Security and Public Policy*, Arno, New York, 1976; Robert M. Ball, *Social Security Today and Tomorrow*, Columbia University Press, New York, 1978.

social welfare principle of taxation The principle that taxes should be levied in a way that will correct an unjust or improper distribution of income. The principle's adherents often argue that injustices may arise either through market forces or through inheritance, and they frequently favor progressive income taxes and inheritance taxes. See Richard A. Musgrave and Peggy B. Musgrave, *Public Finance in Theory and Practice*, 2d ed., McGraw-Hill, New York, 1975.

soft currency A national currency that is regulated by exchange control, thus limiting its convertibility into gold and other currencies. A nation places exchange controls on its currency because the official exchange rate overvalues the currency and it wishes to avoid the depreciation that would result from forced devaluation. Soft currency differs from hard currency, which is freely convertible. Nations export a smaller quantity of goods to a country when payment is in soft currency than if payment were in hard currency. For the same reason, prices of commodities often depend on whether payment is to be made in hard or soft currency. Nations with a soft currency find it difficult to make payment in hard currency because they must obtain most of their hard-currency balances through exports. Problems of this nature grow smaller as currencies become more freely convertible and as soft-currency countries increase their production of exportable commodities and exert greater control over internal inflation. Nations are sometimes willing to accept payment in soft currency because they desire to make payments easy for the debtor nation or because they receive some special trade benefit in return. See C. P. Kindleberger and P. H. Lindert; *International Economics*, Irwin, Homewood, Ill., 1978.

soft goods (nondurable goods) Consumer items which last for only a short time. Among soft goods are such items as clothing, shoes, and drugs. According to the U.S. Department of Commerce, an item is nondurable if it is used up in less than three years. The criterion of lack of durability cannot be applied in all cases, however; for example, although clothing is classified as soft goods, a fur coat, which is categorized as clothing, obviously is expected to last well over three years. Soft goods are usually purchased when needed. Expenditures for soft goods grow approximately in line with population growth. For a complete list of items classified as soft goods and U.S. consumer expenditures for each of them, see U.S. Department of Commerce, *Survey of Current Business: National Income Supplement,* July issues.

soft loan A foreign loan repayable in the receiving country's own soft currency. Soft loans were considered a compromise between hard loans and grants. Countries receiving aid in soft-loan form were expected to use the money in a responsible manner because they would have to repay it; however, it was easier for the needy country to obtain a loan. Soft-loan aid was not effective, however, because the donors accumulated large reserves of the debtors' soft currency without being able to use it. Most U.S. lending agencies now make foreign loans repayable in dollars and regulate the ease or difficulty of repayment by means of the maturity of the loan and interest rate. See C. P. Kindleberger and P. H. Lindert, *International Economics,* Irwin, Homewood, Ill., 1978.

special drawing rights (SDRs) A form of international liquid reserves used in the settlement of international payments among the member governments of the International Monetary Fund. The SDR system was established at the Rio de Janeiro conference of 1967, and the first allocation of SDRs was made in 1970. Drawing rights were allocated among the IMF members according to their already-established quotas in the Fund. SDRs were created to augment the total of international liquidity available to meet international payments arising through trade and investment between nations. The SDR augments gold, the key international currencies, bilateral borrowing arrangements between nations, and borrowing facilities of the IMF to meet the growing needs for world liquidity. SDRs may be used only by governments who are members of the IMF. For additional information, see J. J. Polak, "The SDR as 2 Baskets of Currencies," *IMF Staff Papers,* vol. 26, no. 4,

325   specific cycle

December 1979, pp. 627–653. For statistics on SDRs, see International Monetary Fund, *Annual Report.*

specialization The division of different productive activities among different individuals, industries, and regions. There is specialization, or division of labor, involved in the different operations needed for the production of a single good, as is the case in assembly-line production. Specialization can occur on the level of community production, as in the work of specialized artisans and trades people, and it can exist on a regional or national level, as in the concentration of one nation on the production of agricultural produce and another on the production of manufactured goods. Specialization is undertaken because it enhances productive efficiency and results in increased output at lower cost. It permits individual workers to take advantage of their different abilities, for individuals work in the area in which they are most productive. Division of labor also results in the acquisition of appropriate skills which increase efficiency. Devoting all of one's time to a single operation or occupation also eliminates the loss of time involved in shifting from one job to another. The simplification of function resulting from specialization within a single productive process lends itself to mechanization and the use of labor-saving capital. Moreover, the specialization of industry may facilitate the invention and efficient use of machinery. Specialization of production on a regional basis permits the nonhuman resources, land and capital, to be used in the most efficient way. Just as a different relative endowment of personal abilities makes some individuals better suited for certain types of work than others, differences in the relative endowment of productive resources among various regions make regional specialization more efficient. There are, however, limits to the extent of industrial and regional specialization. Increasing costs which accompany the rising output may reduce the comparative advantage gained by specialization to a point at which it is no longer profitable to specialize. Furthermore, specialization is limited by the extent of the market for the good being produced. Inherent in the existence of specialization is the existence of interdependence, or the need of the specialized worker, industry, and region to rely on others for the production of the goods and services needed for daily life. Thus specialization is the basis for all trade—local, regional, and international. For further discussion, see Adam Smith, *The Wealth of Nations,* Random House, New York, 1937, pp. 7–8. For further information, see Armen A. Alchian and William R. Allen, *University Economics,* 3d ed., Wadsworth, New York, 1971.

specific cycle Recurring alternations of expansion and contraction in individual business-cycle indicators. The specific cycle for an individual series may or may not coincide with the cycle in general business activity. For each indicator, the dates of the high and low points nearest the turning dates of the business cycle are selected as the specific turning dates. For further discussion of specific cycles, see Geoffrey H. Moore (ed.), *Business Cycle Indicators,* Princeton University Press, Princeton, N.J., 1961, vol. I.

specific tariff An import duty which is levied on the basis of a unit of quantity or weight. This type of tariff is levied as a specific charge per unit of the good imported, e.g., 10 cents per book or 3 cents per pound. It differs from the ad valorem tariff, which is based on value and not on units. Specific tariffs provide a fluctuating amount of protection, since the protection afforded varies inversely with changes in the prices of imports. When import prices are rising, the burden on imports with specific tariffs generally falls; when prices are falling, the burden increases. Specific duties are generally easier to administer than ad valorem duties because it is not necessary to estimate the value of the import.

spectral analysis In statistics and econometrics, a technique for isolating and estimating the durations and amplitudes of the cyclical components of time series. It results in separating the random from the systematic components of time series. For additional information, see Karl A. Fox, and Tej K. Kaul, *Intermediate Economic Statistics,* Krieger, Melbourne, Fla., 1980.

speculation The act of knowingly assuming above-average risks with the hope of gaining above-average returns on a business or financial transaction. Speculation is usually applied to the buying and selling of securities, commodities, or foreign exchange in the hope that a profit will be made because of price changes. With the exception of the transactions of persons who ordinarily need foreign exchange or commodities for their businesses, all transactions in these markets are speculative because neither of these items pays dividends or interest; thus, price movements are the only way in which a profit can arise. In the securities markets, speculation is distinguished from investment by the motives or attitudes of the person involved. The investor is interested in safety of principal, a moderate but steady income, and possibly some growth in principal. In contrast, the speculator, by assuming large risks, forgoes safety of principal in the hope of quick (in most cases), large gains. Successful speculation requires money, knowledge of the market that is speculated in, cool nerves (the ability to view losses with equanimity), and some luck. Even though the economic and social consequences of speculation have been debated for a long time, no firm conclusions have resulted. See George A. Christy and John C. Clendenin, *Introduction to Investments,* 7th ed., McGraw-Hill, New York, 1978.

spendable average weekly earnings Gross weekly pay of U.S. manufacturing production workers less federal social security and income taxes. This statistical series is the nearest measure to actual take-home pay but exceeds it by the amount of certain deductions, such as union dues and insurance payments. Spendable earnings are computed for two categories of workers, those with no dependents and those with three dependents. Estimates are published in U.S. Bureau of Labor Statistics, *Monthly Labor Review.*

spending unit   All related persons living together in the same dwelling who pool their incomes to meet their major expenses. In some cases, a spending unit may be only one individual. Wife, husband, and children under the age of eighteen living at home are always considered members of the same spending unit. Other related persons in the household are separate spending units if they earn more than $15 per week and do not pool their incomes. The number and characteristics of spending units are important statistics in establishing market potentials for consumer durable goods, such as stoves and refrigerators. For incomes, savings, and intentions to buy based on the spending-unit concept, see *Consumer Attitudes and Inclinations to Buy,* University of Michigan Survey Research Center, Ann Arbor, Mich., periodically.

spin-off method   A method used by a corporation to distribute to its own stockholders stock that it owns in another corporation. The term spin-off also refers to split-ups and split-offs. A spin-off occurs when company A transfers assets to company B for B's stock; then company A distributes its holdings of company B's stock to its stockholders. A split-up occurs when company A transfers some of its assets to company B for B's stock and the remainder of its assets to company C for C's stock. Company A distributes its holding of company B's and company C's stock to its stockholders in exchange for its own (company A's) stock. Thus, company A is liquidated. A split-off occurs when company A transfers certain assets to company B for B's stock, and then company A distributes B's stock to its own stockholders in exchange for some of its own stock.

spot market (cash market)   A market in which commodities are sold for cash and delivered immediately. The spot market, also known as the cash or physical market, consists of sellers who have the goods to be traded on hand, ready for immediate delivery, and of buyers who want the goods immediately. It is distinguished from the futures market, in which contracts for the future delivery of commodities are traded. Most ordinary trade takes place in spot markets. There are two main classes of spot markets, primary or local markets and central markets. Local markets develop in producing areas and center at local transportation points from which the commodities are shipped to the large central markets. Central markets, such as Chicago for grain or New Orleans for cotton, are the main centers of large-scale distribution of the primary commodities. In these central spot markets, trading is smoothed out by dealers, who act as intermediaries between the producers and the manufacturers who demand the goods. They bear most of the risk of exchange, buying and selling commodities in an attempt to make a profit from their transactions.

spot price (cash price)   The price quoted for the immediate sale and delivery of a commodity. The spot price is distinguished from the future price, which is the price quoted for the sale of commodities to be delivered at a future date. On grain markets, the spot price is also known as the cash price. Spot and future prices fluctuate together most of the time, since both spot and future markets respond to the same fundamental factors. The holders of futures can always convert their holdings into spot commodities if the price of futures falls in relation to the spot price and vice versa, and the future price will therefore generally be kept in line with the spot price. Often, dealers rely on the future market to determine the general level of spot prices and then express spot prices in terms of bids over or under the futures price; e.g., a spot price of wheat of "2 cents under September" means that if the future price of September wheat is $1.98, the spot price for wheat is $1.96. The interest of spot traders lies in obtaining the commodity on as favorable a basis relative to the futures as possible.

spread   A contract that gives the holder the right to buy or sell a specified amount of stock for a designated time period at prices that are above and below the market price of the stock at the time the contract is written. It is a combination of a put and a call, with the added feature that the buy and sell prices are the current market price at the time that the contract is written. As in the case of the straddle, both parts of the spread can be exercised during the life of the contract. For further information, see William F. Sharpe, *Investments,* Prentice-Hall, Englewood Cliffs, N.J., 1978.

spread effect   A stimulating effect which arises from international trade. The most important spread effect of a rise in the value of exports is its multiplier effect on per capita income in the other sectors of the economy. This is brought about by a rise in the demand for all the economy's goods. The higher the level of economic development that a country has achieved, the stronger the spread effects will usually be, since the export sector is more closely linked with the rest of the economy. Some economists have argued that the spread effects of trade for underdeveloped countries are very weak and are usually outweighed by the backwash (unfavorable) effects, so that on the whole underdeveloped nations have been hurt and not helped by international trade. For additional details on the spread effects in underdeveloped countries, see Gunnar Myrdal, *Economic Theory and the Underdeveloped Regions,* Duckworth, London, 1957.

stability   A condition of high-level economic activity with an absence of severe cyclical fluctuations. Basically, most economists would consider three aspects of economic activity relevant to the measurement of stability: production, employment, and prices. Since these three aspects tend to fluctuate together in a cyclical fashion, stability can be defined in terms of the absence of such fluctuations. Nevertheless, an absolute level of production cannot be consistent with full employment for more than a few days or months because it has to keep pace with growth and productivity gains; otherwise, the result would be a reduction in the employment level. At least in its physical aspects, economic stability does not mean constancy. Therefore, a norm of physical stability must be stated in terms equal to population growth and productivity increases while instability is stated in terms of deviations from potential production. This implies a growth norm in order to have economic stability in a growing economy. In contrast to the definition of stable physical activity, that is, a condition of growing employment and production, when economists speak of stable prices, they usually mean a constant price level. If stable physical activity is a long-run trend, determined by population and productivity, stable prices are desirable. Thus, it is obvious that the absence of severe cyclical fluctuations is the major criterion of stability. For further information, see Robert A. Gordon, *Economic Instability and Growth: The American Record,* Harper & Row, New York, 1974.

stages theory of economic development   A theory that describes economic growth as a succession of clearly defined processes. A stage must move progressively forward over time. The characteristics that distinguish each stage must be observable and measurable. The first major work of stages theorists was done by Karl Bucher, a representative of the German historical school, who divided the economic growth of nations into three stages: (1) the closed household economy, (2) the town economy, and (3) the national economy. Another influential stages theorist was Karl Marx, who thought that the forces of sociology, psychology, and economics, continually at work between the owners of capital and their workers, generate the evolution from feudalism to capitalism to socialism. Walter W. Rostow's work, *Stages of Economic Growth,* pointed up five stages: (1) the traditional, (2) the preconditions to takeoff, (3) the takeoff, (4) the drive to maturity, and (5) the age of mass consumption. For additional information, see Walter W. Rostow, *Stages of Economic Growth,* Cambridge University Press, London, 1960; Alexander Gerschenkron, *Economic Backwardness in Historical Perspective,* Harvard University Press, Cambridge, Mass., 1962.

stagflation   The condition of persistent and intractable inflation when the economy's resources are utilized at a level below its potential. The phenomenon of rising prices has occurred not only in periods of slow economic growth, but also in recessions. It is the initiating causes of inflation—rapidly expanding money supply and excess aggregate demand—which feed expectations of ever-rising wages and prices that are said to be essential and which precede the condition of stagflation. As long as overly optimistic and irrational expectations are retained, both prices and wages may continue rising even in recessions. For additional information, see Phillip Cagan, *The Hydra-Headed Monster: The Problem of Inflation in the United States,* America Enterprise Institute, Washington, D.C., 1974.

stagnation　An unsatisfactory rate of growth of real per capita product or income. Stagnation implies that real product or income is constant, declining or growing much less rapidly than it might. An economy may be subject to long-run or secular stagnation for two reasons. First, the growth rate of output may be less than the rate of population growth even though resources are fully employed. Secondly, although the economy may have the capacity for sufficient growth, insufficient aggregate demand may prevent the achievement of its potential. Some economists have argued that in a mature economy, such as those of the United States and Great Britain, a secular stagnation of the second type is setting in. The greater advances in technology relative to population growth are said to result not only in a greater capacity to produce, but also in an insufficient amount of aggregate demand, causing substantial long-run unemployment and stagnation. For further information, see Alvin H. Hansen, *Fiscal Policy and Business Cycles,* Norton, New York, 1941.

stagnation theory　A theory, originated in the late 1930s, which states that the United States and some other industrialized nations have become "mature" because investment outlets that could absorb savings are lacking and, therefore, that these nations' economies are stagnating. The most noted advocate of the stagnation theory was Alvin H. Hansen. Hansen argued that four factors caused a marked decline in U.S. investment outlets: (1) the rapid decline in population growth; (2) the closing of the frontier; (3) the lack of new industries, such as railroads, electric power, and the automobile, which could absorb massive doses of capital investment; and (4) the increasing importance of depreciation reserves which allowed corporations to finance their replacement capital needs without tapping new savings. Since expected savings would be greater than expected investment, national income would decline or, at best, remain stationary; the economy would not be growing but would be stagnating. This analysis led Hansen to recommend that government expenditures for such public works as slum clearance and education be increased to take up the slack and increase investment. Critics of the stagnation thesis argue that the rate of population growth had been declining long before the major economic slump in the 1930s, that the frontier had been declared closed before the twentieth century began, that there would be great new industries to absorb savings, and that depreciation allowances did not cover the capital needs of expanding corporations. See Alvin H. Hansen, *Fiscal Policy and Business Cycles,* Norton, New York, 1941.

Standard & Poor's composite index　An index of the prices of 500 listed industrial, railroad, and utility common stocks. The composite index is the best known of the 137 indices of securities prices computed and published by Standard & Poor's Corporation, the largest securities research organization in the United States. It is a weighted, aggregative index expressed in relatives with an average value for the base period, 1941–1943, equal to 10. Weighting is based on each stock's relative market importance, which is determined by the number of shares outstanding. Thus, the price of each stock in the index is multiplied by the number of shares outstanding, the products are summed, and the total is divided by the value of the base period; this quotient is multiplied by 10 to arrive at the index figure. The composite index, with other Standard & Poor's indices, is published in Standard & Poor's Corporation, *Outlook,* New York. Many newspapers publish the daily high, low, and close for the index. Standard & Poor's Corporation, *Security Price Index Record,* New York, annually, gives historical records of all the firm's indices as well as a detailed discussion of the method of computation; for further discussion, see D. K. Eiteman, C. A. Dice, and W. J. Eiteman, *The Stock Market,* 4th ed., McGraw-Hill, New York, 1966, pp. 182–187.

standard deviation   A measure of the spread of a set of values around the arithmetic average. It is the tendency of the individual values to vary from the mean. Operationally, the standard deviation is the square root of the sum of the squares of the deviations of observed values from the arithmetic mean of a series divided by the number of items. In general, about two-thirds of the individual values turn out to be less than one standard deviation from the mean, about 95% are within two standard deviations, and virtually all (99.7%) are within three standard deviations. The standard deviation is easier to interpret than the variance, another measure of spread, because the former indicates the spread in the same units as the variable itself. For example, the standard deviation for a set of family-income values would be expressed in dollars of income, whereas the variance would be expressed in dollars of income squared. For further discussion of variability, see John E. Freund and Frank J. Williams, *Elementary Business Statistics,* 3d ed., Prentice-Hall, Englewood Cliffs, N.J., 1978.

standard of living   A composite of quantities and qualities of goods, such as food, clothing, and house furnishings, and services, such as housing, transportation, and medical care, which an economic unit (an individual, family, or group) considers essential. The standard is usually expressed in monetary terms, since prices of the various goods and services making up the standard are usually available. Costs of attaining the same standard of living vary from place to place and from time to time. Because the actual levels of living of families and individuals often fall far short of the standards of decency and comfort, perhaps the standard of living is also a social aspiration or good for many persons. For a detailed discussion of standard and levels of living, see J. L. Hafstrom and M. M. Dunsing, "Level of Living: Factors Influencing the Homemaker's Satisfaction," *Home Economics Research Journal,* vol. 2, American Home Economics Association, Washington, D.C., 1973, pp. 119–132.

state bank A U.S. commercial bank operating under the authority of a state charter and under the supervision of a state banking commissioner. State banks outnumber national banks, which operate on federal charters, by nearly 2 to 1, but since most of them are small, they hold less than 40% of all U.S. demand deposits. State banks may belong to the Federal Reserve System (although most do not) and may participate in the Federal Deposit Insurance Corporation (most do). Annual state banking statistics are published in Federal Deposit Insurance Corporation, *Assets, Liabilities and Capital Accounts: Commercial and Mutual Savings Banks,* Washington, D.C.

statics That part of economic theory which analyzes equilibrium positions. Statics concentrates only on the definition of equilibrium positions and the requirements for equilibrium and is not concerned with the path by which the equilibrium position is reached or the time it takes for equilibrium to be achieved. For example, the familiar supply-and-demand analysis of price and output determination is an application of economic statics, since the problem is only to determine the equilibrium level of price and output. Comparative statics is the study of movements from one equilibrium position to another as certain of the given variables change. The economic thinking of David Ricardo and John Stuart Mill is best described as comparative statics. For a discussion of the nature of static analysis, see John R. Hicks, *Value and Capital,* Oxford University Press, Oxford, 1939.

stationary state An economic process which merely reproduces itself from one period to the next. Classical economists, such as David Ricardo and John Stuart Mill, believed that technological innovations would be insufficient to offset the effects of diminishing returns, and that therefore a developing capitalist economy would move gradually toward the stationary state of a mature economic system. As investment increases, the rate of profit decreases (as a result of diminishing returns) until profits have fallen so low that there is no longer any incentive for new capital accumulation. In the classical stationary state, wages are at a subsistence level (biological or customary), net capital formation is zero, and the economy's production has reached its maximum level. For further discussion of the classical concept of the stationary state, see Mark Blaug, *Ricardian Economics,* Yale University Press, New Haven, Conn., 1958.

statistician An individual trained in statistical methods. Statisticians are found in a variety of fields, ranging from biometrics to business. Business statisticians, in addition to having a working knowledge of statistical methods, must also possess an understanding of the economic principles involved in the operations with which they are concerned. The extent and character of their work are based on their position in the economic structure, that is, whether they work for a business firm, a trade association, a business research organization of a college or university, or the government; whether they are in a small or a large statistical department; and how far they have advanced up the occupational ladder.

statistics The science of the collection and classification of facts used to facilitate the interpretation of numerical data that have been obtained from groups of individuals or from groups of observations of a single individual. The individual can be nations, industries, firms, or consumers. Among the various statistical methods that are concerned with business and economics are measures of central tendency (averages), sampling and sampling error, correlation between two sets of related data, time series (business cycles), and game theory, which provides an optimum choice under different assumptions.

stochastic independence In econometrics, a condition in which the random term (or error term) in one equation is not correlated with the random term in any other equation of a given econometric model and over the same time period. It follows that stochastic dependence is the relationship between random variables that are correlated. For additional information, see Lawrence R. Klein, *An Introduction to Econometrics,* Greenwood, Westport, Conn., 1977.

stochastic model A formula or collection of formulas which describes the relationship between two or more economic variables, where specific statistical assumptions are made to allow for error. There is some probability that the model represents the exact but unknown relationship. Since the relationships are not entirely exact, an error term is specifically included in the equations of stochastic models to describe the special way in which the relationship between the dependent and independent variables is inexact. This relationship cannot be precise because models are necessarily incomplete; there may be errors in the basic data from which the stochastic models have been developed. Although many economists believe that there can be no specific representation of human interactions, which are subject to so many random disturbances, stochastic models are useful because they are shorthand representations of highly complex situations. For additional details, see Lawrence R. Klein, *An Introduction to Econometrics,* Greenwood, Westport, Conn., 1977.

stock A security which represents equity or ownership in a corporation. Stocks are an instrument used to bring savers and investors together, which is crucial for economic expansion. Preferred stock has preference over common stock with respect to payment of dividends and claims on residual assets in the event that the corporation liquidates. The most important right that an individual stockholder has is sharing in the corporation's earnings when dividends are declared. Equity financing via common or preferred stock historically represented a major source of funds to corporations, but in recent years corporations have conducted a relatively small amount of this type of financing. For additional information, see J. Fred Weston and Eugene F. Brigham, *Essentials of Managerial Finance,* 6th ed., Dryden Press, Hinsdale, Ill., 1978.

stock exchange An organized marketplace in which securities (mainly stocks) are bought and sold. In the United States, the term refers to eleven centrally located trading places where brokers and dealers regularly meet to transact business for their own accounts and for their customers. These stock exchanges must register with the Securities and Exchange Commission (SEC) as national securities exchanges unless they have been specifically exempted by the SEC. As of December 1982, there were eleven national securities exchanges in the United States; one stock exchange was exempted from registration. The SEC regulates the stock exchanges, the securities listed on the exchanges, and the brokers and dealers doing business on the exchanges. The New York Stock Exchange is the largest stock exchange in the United States, accounting for about 80% of the share-trading volume and nearly 84% of the dollar volume of trading on all national securities exchanges. For information on the SEC's regulation of stock exchanges, see U.S. Securities and Exchange Commission, *Annual Reports;* for statistical information on shares traded by exchanges, see Securities and Exchange Commission, *Statistical Bulletin,* monthly; for further information, see Frederick Amling, *Investments: An Introduction to Analysis and Management,* 4th ed., Prentice-Hall, Englewood Cliffs, N.J., 1978.

stockholders' equity Total capital stock and retained earnings in a corporation. In accounting for the elements of stockholders' equity, emphasis is placed on the source of capital, that is, the amount of the stockholders' equity that was produced by retained earnings. The ratio of net earnings to stockholders' equity is a popular measure of corporate success. Current statistics on stockholders' equity in manufacturing corporations appear in U.S. Federal Trade Commission, *Quarterly Survey of Manufacturing Corporations.*

stock option A contract which gives the purchaser the privilege of buying or selling a specified amount of stock at a certain price within a stipulated period. Although puts, calls, spreads, straddles, and warrants are all stock options, the term stock option is usually used to refer to a type cf compensation plan that corporations establish for some employees. Because U.S. personal income tax rates are sharply progressive, many corporations believe that the lure of higher salaries will not attract and hold key employees. Instead of giving such an employee a higher salary, a corporation gives the employee an option to buy the company's stock at the current market value (for example, at any time within ten years). Supposedly, the option gives the employee the incentive to work hard to help the company thrive because, if the company grows, the stock price will probably rise as well, thus increasing the value of the option. When key employees think that the time is most advantageous, they can exercise their options. Moreover, if they sell the stock for a profit, the profit is treated as a capital gain, which means lower tax liabilities for high-salaried employees. See William F. Sharpe, *Investments,* Prentice-Hall, Englewood Cliffs, N.J., 1978.

stock right   A privilege given to stockholders to purchase additional stock, in proportion to the amount that they own, at a price lower than that which nonstockholders must pay. As an example, a small corporation with 1,000 shares outstanding may wish to issue an additional 1,000 shares. The new issue can be sold through the distribution of rights, permitting, for each share presently held, the right to purchase an additional share, usually below the present market price. The premium between the market price and the subscription price (the lower price that existing stockholders pay for the additional shares) gives stock rights a definite value, and since the rights are transferable, the original holders may either use them or sell them to someone else. The value of each right can be determined by the following formula:

$$\frac{\left(\begin{array}{c}\text{Market price on old stock,}\\ \text{rights on}\end{array}\right) - \left(\begin{array}{c}\text{subscription price}\\ \text{of new stock}\end{array}\right)}{1 \text{ plus number of rights required to buy 1 new share}}$$

Stockholders of record receive the rights on the day of issuance. Thereafter, the stock is traded ex rights, and the formula for the value of the rights is:

$$\frac{\left(\begin{array}{c}\text{Market price on old stock,}\\ \text{ex rights}\end{array}\right) - \left(\begin{array}{c}\text{subscription price}\\ \text{of new stock}\end{array}\right)}{\text{Number of rights required to buy 1 new share}}$$

For the corporation, the issuance of rights is a method of raising additional funds from existing stockholders, but it is more costly than open-market financing, or the sale at the current market price through investment bankers. Moreover, it can be a hazardous method. Despite the discount price placed on the new stock, there is always the risk that the market price for the old stock may decline below the subscription price during the stock offering. This ruins the issue, since it is then cheaper to buy the stock on the open market than to exercise the rights. Because of these high risks, standby underwriting agreements are often made to assure the corporation of success. For further information, see Frederick Amling, *Investments: An Introduction to Analysis and Management,* 4th ed., Prentice-Hall, Englewood Cliffs, N.J., 1978.

stock split (stock split-up)   A division of the capital stock of a corporation into a greater number of shares without affecting the total capital account but reducing the par or stated value of 1 share. For example, a corporation with 1 million shares of $10-par-value stock (total capital equals $10 million) splits its stock 2 shares for 1 share. After the split, the company has 2 million shares of $5-par-value stock (total capital remains $10 million). The distinction between a stock split and a stock dividend is that the former does not affect the surplus, or retained earnings, account, whereas the latter capitalizes surplus. The market value of the stock in the above example would, *ceteris paribus,* be halved after the split. Essentially, corporations split their stock to reduce its market value for two reasons: (1) They plan to issue additional stock and want the price to be lower so that the stock will be more readily marketable. (2) They want wider distribution of share ownership so that outsiders would find it more difficult to concentrate enough stock and gain control of the company. See George A. Christy and John C. Clendenin, *Introduction to Investments,* 7th ed., McGraw-Hill, New York, 1978.

stop order (stop-loss order)   An order that a customer gives to the broker to buy or sell a certain amount of stock if the price of the stock rises to a certain price or higher (buy) or falls to a certain price or lower (sell). The main distinction between stop and limit orders is that the stop order becomes a market order if the price of the stock reaches the stated, or stop, price, whereas the limit order never becomes a market order. Stop orders are used to protect profits or to prevent large losses on either short sales or long purchases. An example of each on a long purchase follows: Let us assume that a person has bought stock at $20 per share. After a few months, the price has risen to $30 per share. To protect the greater part of this $10-per-share profit, the person puts a stop order to sell at $28. Now, if the stock begins to decline in price, the stop order becomes a market order at $28 per share, and the stock is sold at the best price available at that time. The bulk of the $10 profit is thus intact. If the price continues to rise, all that happens is that the person's profits keep increasing, and he or she can raise the stop price to protect the bigger profit. To prevent a large loss, a person can place a stop order to sell at $18 when buying a stock at, say, $20 per share. If the person buys at the wrong time and the stock's price starts to decline, a stop order can prevent a large loss; if the stock's price rises, nothing happens. There are two disadvantages to stop orders: (1) There is no guarantee that a person will be "stopped out" at the stop price because at that price the stop order automatically becomes a market order, which means that, if the price is declining rapidly, the actual sale price can be lower. (2) If a person places a stop order too close to the prevailing market price, a slight, temporary price dip can actuate the stop order, but subsequently the price may move upward. See Frederick Amling, *Investments: An Introduction to Analysis and Management,* 4th ed., Prentice-Hall, Englewood Cliffs, N.J., 1978.

straddle   A contract that gives the holder the right to buy or sell a specified amount of stock at a certain price for a designated time period. It is simply a combination of a put and a call. If the holder exercises either part of this option, the other is not invalidated. Thus it is conceivable that both parts could be exercised during the life of the contract. For further information, see Frederick Amling, *Investments: An Introduction to Analysis and Management,* 4th ed., Prentice-Hall, Englewood Cliffs, N.J., 1978.

strategic stockpile   Governmental storage of certain goods deemed strategic and vital to national defense. The purpose of stockpiling goods, set down in the Strategic and Critical Materials Stock Piling Act of 1946, was to "decrease and prevent wherever possible a dangerous and costly dependence of the United States upon foreign nations in times of national emergency." The determination of the degree to which a good is strategic depends on how vital it is to the defense effort, how it can be converted to military use, and whether its absence would cause a critical deficiency in the Soviet defense economy. For further information, see U.S. Office of Emergency Preparedness, *Stockpile Report of the Congress,* semiannually.

strike   A mutual agreement among workers to stop working in order to obtain or resist a change in working conditions. The workers do not quit their jobs but rather leave them temporarily. Strikes may involve a simple walkout or include picketing and, occasionally, even violence. They are most commonly caused by wage disputes. Many strikes result from unsatisfied demands for union recognition and from issues connected with union security or with working conditions, such as hours or work seniority or working rules. The number and duration of strikes at any time may depend on the financial condition of unions, the militancy of the labor movement, and the indifference of management. In addition, the number of strikes may depend on the machinery available for adjusting employer-employee disputes. Sitdown or stay-in strikes, in which strikers seize the property of the employer and prevent the use of it, are usually considered illegal. Lloyd G. Reynolds, *Labor Economics and Labor Relations,* 7th ed., Prentice-Hall, Englewood Cliffs, N.J., 1978.

structural equation   An equation making up all or part of the mathematical expression of an econometric model. Structural equations depict the pattern of relationships that is assumed to exist among the statistical variables involved in the model. Examples of structural equations accompanied by detailed explanations abound in most econometric textbooks.

structural unemployment   The loss of jobs resulting from changes in the economic environment. Among the more important structural changes believed to have a significant effect on employment are changes in consumer tastes, the level of technology, population growth, and government policies. Long-term variations in consumer tastes and technology may cause the creation or disappearance of industries, resulting in unemployment. Population growth can affect unemployment by influencing both the demand for production and the supply of workers. The effect of government spending and tax policies on unemployment is increasing in importance as government assumes a larger role in the economy.

subsidiary   A business enterprise which is controlled by another corporation. Its shares are owned by the controlling company (holding or parent company). A subsidiary differs from a branch of the parent company in that it has its own corporate entity and its own corporate charter. The parent company forms a subsidiary either by purchasing the controlling share of an existing corporation or by setting up a new corporation and retaining the controlling share of its stock. When all the outstanding stock of the subsidiary is owned by the parent company, it is called a wholly owned subsidiary. A subsidiary owned and operated by two or more other corporations is a joint subsidiary. For example, railroad stations used by several different railroads are joint subsidiaries of the railroads. See J. Fred Weston and Eugene F. Brigham, *Essentials of Managerial Finance,* 5th ed., Holt, Rinehart and Winston, New York, 1979.

subsidy   A payment to individuals or businesses by a government for which it receives no products or services in return. The purpose of such payments is to make available a particular service or product at a price that the public can readily afford, when the service or product cannot otherwise be profitably supplied at this price. The particular service or product is considered essential to the public welfare, and the government therefore finds it necessary to subsidize the enterprise in order to keep it operating and producing the service or product. In the United States, federal subsidies are given to airlines to carry mail, to railroads and other means of public transportation for the transportation of commuters, to farmers under the current agricultural program, and to the shipbuilding industry to build ships. The term subsidy has also been used to include governmental payments to other governments, now referred to as grants-in-aid. For further information, see Richard A. Musgrave and Peggy B. Musgrave, *Public Finance in Theory and Practice,* 2d ed., McGraw-Hill, New York, 1975.

substitute goods   *See* **cross elasticity.**

substitution effect   When the price of a good is changed, people buy more or less of it, depending upon whether the price has fallen or risen. The change in the amount purchased when the price changes (and therefore the elasticity of demand) is attributable to two separate influences upon the purchaser: the substitution effect and the income effect. The desire of a consumer always to purchase more of a cheaper product and less of a more expensive product is the substitution effect. A discussion of the general nature of the substitution effect and an indifference-curve analysis of it may be found in D. S. Watson and Mary A. Holman, *Price Theory and Its Uses,* 4th ed., Houghton Mifflin,

Boston, 1976; a mathematical discussion of the substition effect may be found in James M. Henderson and Richard E. Quandt, *Microeconomic Theory: A Mathematical Approach,* 3d ed., McGraw-Hill, New York, 1980.

super gold tranche   An automatic credit that can be drawn on by a member nation of the International Monetary Fund (IMF) in addition to its regular gold tranche position. A nation's gold tranche position is equivalent to the 25% of its quota in the IMF which it deposits in gold with the Fund. This may be drawn on at will by the country to meet payment imbalances. The other 75% of a country's quota represents the amounts of its currency paid into the Fund and is divided into three credit tranches. Permission from the Fund is needed to draw on the credit tranche position. With each succeeding credit tranche, it becomes more difficult to draw on the Fund's facilities without making explicit promises as to government policies to be pursued to right the balance-of-payments position. However, borrowings from the Fund of a nation's currency give rise to an additional credit to the nation whose currency is being borrowed. The credit is equivalent to the amount by which the Fund's holdings of the nation's currency fall short of the 75% of quota originally paid in. This credit is the super gold tranche and may be drawn on in a manner similar to that in which the gold tranche position is drawn on. For additional information, see International Monetary Fund, *Annual Report.*

supplemental unemployment benefit (SUB)   Any payment received by laid-off workers in the United States from private unemployment insurance plans in addition to benefits provided by state unemployment insurance plans. SUB originated in 1955 as a compromise between the positions of the United Automobile Workers, who demanded a guaranteed annual wage, and the Ford Motor Company. Plans of this type arise from collective bargaining agreements and are financed by employers. Typically, they increase a worker's income during a layoff from about 40 or 45%, the range most often provided by unemployment insurance, to 60 or 65% of base pay after taxes. In addition, SUB plans may pay the full 60 or 65% of basic take-home pay to workers whose rights to unemployment insurance have been exhausted. SUB plans increase the typical duration of unemployment benefits from 26 to 52 weeks. There are two basic types of plans: the funded, or insurance, type of plan; and the individual trust account or savings-arrangement type. Benefits are financed by the employer's contributions to the group or individual trust fund. When the fund is low, benefits may either be restricted to senior employees or be sharply curtailed for other employees. The introduction of SUB plans has made employers reluctant to hire additional employees and the unemployed less anxious to find new employment. See Gordon F. Bloom and Herbert R. Northrup, *Economics of Labor Relations,* 8th ed., Irwin, Homewood, Ill., 1977.

supply The ability and willingness of a firm to sell a good or service. The supply of a firm for a good or service is a schedule of the quantities of that good or service that the firm would offer for sale at alternative prices at a given moment in time. The supply schedule, or the listing of quantities that would be sold at different prices, can be shown graphically by means of a supply curve. The term supply refers to the entire schedule of possibilities and not to one point on the schedule. It is an instantaneous concept expressing the relationship of price and the quantity that would be willingly sold, all other factors being constant. Except for a monopoly market structure, adding the quantities offered for sale at the various possible prices, the supply schedule for all firms, or the market supply, can be derived. The monopolists' supply schedule is, in effect, the market supply schedule since there is no other seller. Supply schedules obviously depend upon the cost structures of firms. Assuming that firms attempt to maximize profits, the short-run supply curve is that portion of a firm's marginal-cost curve equal to, or greater than, average variable costs. In the long run (where all costs are variable) the supply curve is that portion of the marginal-cost-curve equal to, or greater than, average costs. In the short run, the supply curve will always have a positive slope because of the law of diminishing returns. That is, the higher the price for a good or service, the larger the quantity that will be offered for sale. In the long run, the supply curve will rise if there are internal or external diseconomies of scale, it will be horizontal if there are constant returns to scale, and it will fall (negative slope) if there are internal or external economies of scale. The latter case implies that larger output means more efficient production and, hence, lower costs. Thus a firm would be willing to supply more at a lower price. The level of costs of producing a good or service—and therefore the supply schedule—depends on the state of technology which is embodied in the production function for that good or service and on the prices of the required inputs. Any change in these determinants causes a shift in the whole supply schedule. For instance, if a technological advance results in the production of a larger output with unchanged inputs, the supply schedule shifts to the right; that is, at any given price the firm would be willing to supply a larger quantity for sale. If, on the other hand, the price of inputs increases, the supply schedule shifts to the left, and firms would be willing to supply smaller quantities at various prices. These changes should not be confused with a change in the quantity supplied, which describes merely the movement from one point to another along a given supply curve. See George J. Stigler, *The Theory of Price,* 3d ed., Macmillan, New York, 1966; William Baumol, *Economic Theory and Operations Analysis,* 4th ed., Prentice-Hall, Englewood Cliffs, N.J., 1977; Donald S. Watson and Mary A. Holman, *Price Theory and Its Uses,* 4th ed., Houghton Mifflin, Boston, 1977, chaps. 13 and 14.

supply-side economics A counterrevolution against both the theory and the related policy prescription of J. M. Keynes. In a broad sense, it is a return to the classical tradition of Adam Smith and Jean Baptiste Say. Although supply-siders do not call for a return to laissez faire, they advocate a framework for economic policy that replaces the Keynesian concept of demand management with a concern for the effect of government on supply. They charge that government attempts to offset temporary weakness in private demand by deficit spending have become a major source of economic instability. Just as Keynesian economics came into power because it offered a politically attractive remedy for unemployment, supply-side economics came into vogue in the late 1970s and early 1980s because it offered a politically attractive remedy for inflation. Supply-side economics holds that the proper approach by which to slow inflation is to stimulate production, generally by cutting taxes. According to supply-siders, a tax cut works by enhancing the incentives to produce rather than by increasing the capacity to consume. And since it stimulates supply more than demand, a tax cut will reduce inflationary pressures while at the same time allowing a more rapid rate of economic growth. To supply-siders, taxes have been rising much more rapidly than real incomes because of bracket creep, the interaction between inflation and a progressive income tax system. The tax increase has an adverse effect on incentives, thus reducing aggregate supply much more than restricting aggregate demand. This, in turn, aggravates the inflation problem. Representative Jack Kemp led a group of congressional Republicans in 1978 in arguing for a 30% across-the-board tax cut. The Laffer curve seemed to suggest that tax cuts could be so stimulative that they would acutally pay for themselves through increased revenue. But for this relation to hold mathematically, a tax cut would have to generate a supply response three times larger than itself. Supply-side economics is in some respects an offshoot of monetarism, and like monetarists, most supply-siders do not believe that the deficit has a direct impact on inflation. What counts is not the size of the deficit, but whether the Federal Reserve monetizes it. According to supply-siders, a tax cut has such a stimulative effect on personal savings that it creates the means of financing any deficit that it might generate. Critics of supply-side economics, who include some monetarists as well as most Keynesians, argue that it is based on an exaggerated notion of the incentive effects of taxes. See J. B. Say, *Treatise on Political Economy*, Elliott, Philadelphia, 1834; Thomas Sowell, *Say's Law; An Historical Analysis*, Princeton University Press, Princeton, N.J., 1972; Paul Craig Roberts, "The Economic Case for Kemp-Roth," *Wall Street Journal*, Aug. 1, 1978, p. 16.

surplus value   The difference between a worker's wages and the value of the goods that the worker produces during a certain period. The term was used by Karl Marx to define the capitalist's profit. Marx maintained that the value of a particular commodity is the result solely of the labor involved in its production. Thus, he viewed surplus value as a measure of the exploitation of the working classes. Modern economists recognize that labor, although extremely important, is not the sole factor in production. Capital and managerial skills are equally important elements in the productive process and, like labor, are legitimately entitled to a return. The fact that the U.S.S.R. now strongly emphasizes investment in plants and equipment suggests that the Russians have come to believe that capital as well as labor adds to value. See Karl Marx, *Capital*, 3d ed., International Publishers, New York, 1972; Paul M. Sweezy, *The Theory of Capitalist Development*, Oxford University Press, New York, 1942.

survey   A technique of gathering facts and attitudes related to various persons (consumers or business people) from a scientific sample of these persons that is considered representative of a larger group. The information is usually either of a quantitative nature or of a type which can be summarized in quantitative terms. The survey technique is one of the most advanced marketing-research practices. Nevertheless, with the introduction of panel-research and motivation-research techniques, it has become less important as a marketing-research method. Examples of surveys are those of the Conference Board and the Survey Research Center of the University of Michigan on consumers' plans to buy durable goods and those of the U.S. Department of Commerce, and McGraw-Hill Department of Economics on business's plans to buy new plants and equipment. For general information concerning surveys and survey methods, see John B. Lansing and James W. Morgan, *Economic Survey Methods*, Institute for Survey Research, University of Michigan, Ann Arbor, Mich., 1971.

sustainable growth   A rise in per capita real income or per capita real gross national product that is capable of continuing for a long time. A condition of sustainable economic growth means that economic stagnation will not set in. Sustainable growth will provide employment for a growing population as well as greater individual well-being, thus promoting the economic welfare of the country. Many economists put the rate of sustainable growth in the United States at 2.5% per year. According to Walt W. Rostow, the condition of sustainable growth in a developing country follows the takeoff stage in its economic development. With its radical changes in production techniques and distribution of income, the takeoff perpetuates a new scale of investment, which, in turn, fosters a rising trend in per capita output. For further information, see Walt W. Rostow, "The Take-off into Self-sustained Growth," *Economic Journal*, vol. 46, no. 261, Royal Economic Society, London, March 1956, pp. 25–48.

swap arrangement   An official arrangement between the central banks of two countries for standby credit to exchange holdings of each other's currencies. These standby arrangements help to limit potential problems caused by speculative runs on a nation's currency. The swap arrangement leads to a swap transaction when one of the two parties to the agreement requires a loan of the other party's currency. Swap transactions are generally temporary in nature, with the borrowing central bank generally pledged to repay the creditor within a three-month period. Swap transactions allow a central bank to intervene in the foreign-exchange market to defend its currency in the event of speculation on that nation's currency. The United States has by far the largest network of bilateral swap arrangements. For additional information, see Charles P. Kindleberger and P. H. Lindert, *International Economics*. Irwin, Homewood Ill., 1978; for data on swaps, see International Monetary Fund, *Annual Report*.

T

tableau économique A graphic picture of the general interdependence of the economic system introduced by François Quesnay for Louis XV in 1759. The *tableau économique* tries to show how the different sectors of the economy sell their goods to one another and how they spend the money received from these sales. It depicts the circular flow of goods in one direction and of purchasing power in the other direction, emphasizing the fundamental identity of output with income. Illustrating the mutual interdependence of industries, the *tableau* was based on the belief of the physiocrats that net production is derived only from the argicultural sector and that it all goes to the landlord

Tableau Economique, as Presented in Quesnay's Analyse (Millards)

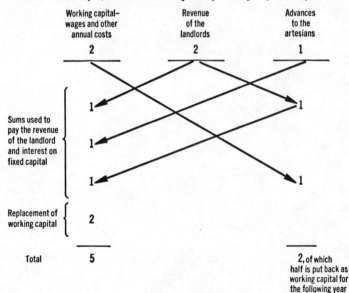

345 takeoff in economic development

in the form of rent. It was presented by Quesnay in the form of a numerical diagram (see the accompanying illustration). At the beginning of the period depicted, the farmers hold the entire money supply of 2 milliards. They pay this sum to the landowners for the rental of their land, and the landowners in turn spend the money on food (1 milliard) and other commodities (1 milliard). The artisans (producers of nonagricultural commodities) spend their total income of 2 milliards (1 milliard received from the landlords and 1 milliard received from purchases by farmers) on agricultural products. At the end of the period, the farmers have received 3 milliards of income and have spent 1 milliard, and they therefore hold the same amount as they started with. The 2 milliards are paid once more to the landlord as rent, and the cycle starts over again. For additional details, see Ronald L. Meek, "Tableau Économique," *Economica,* vol. 27, no. 108, November 1960 pp. 322–347.

Taft-Hartley Act (Labor-Management Relations Act of 1947) The primary federal statute regulating labor-management relations in the United States. The act attempted to establish a new balance of power in the collective bargaining process after the Wagner Act of 1936 had freed labor unions from many impediments and permitted them to grow without, in the later opinion of Congress, adequate safeguards for management and for the individual worker. Under the Taft-Hartley Act, the role of government in labor disputes is to safeguard the public interest and not to take the part of either labor unions or management in their disputes. To this end, the act reorganized the National Labor Relations Board (NLRB) and established the Federal Mediation and Conciliation Service. It also listed unfair labor practices of employers and of labor unions that might be directed against each other or against the individual worker, made extensive provisions for determining union representation and collective bargaining procedures, and provided for court review of actions of the NLRB and for suits by and against labor organizations. In 1959 the act was amended by the Labor-Management Reporting and Disclosure Act (Landrum-Griffin Act). For details, see Lloyd G. Reynolds, *Labor Economics and Labor Relations,* 7th ed., Prentice-Hall, Englewood Cliffs, N.J., 1978.

takeoff in economic development The critical point in the development of a national economy which marks the final disintegration of traditional society's resistance to steady economic growth and the liberation of the forces that establish expansion and progress as national goals. Walt W. Rostow, who views the takeoff as the most crucial period in a nation's economic history, indicates that it occurred in Great Britain in the two decades after 1783, in France and the United States in the several decades before 1860, in Germany in the third quarter of the nineteenth century, in Japan in the fourth quarter, in Russia and Canada at the turn of the twentieth century, and in India and China in the 1950s. In each case, the preconditions for rapid economic growth had been fulfilled; an adequate stock of social overhead capital had been installed, a surge of technological development had occurred in industry and agriculture, and dominant political power had come into the hands of persons who were committed to the pursuit of modernization and to a rapid rise of real output per capita as a major objective of national policy. Invariably, the takeoff is marked by an accelerated investment rate, the development of manufacturing industry, and the emergence of political, social, and institutional forces that favor continued growth as a means of raising incomes and the standard of living (always the overriding objective of underdeveloped countries). For a full discussion of this historical phenomenon, see Walt W. Rostow, *The Stages of Economic Growth: A Non-Communist Manifesto,* Cambridge University Press, New York, 1960.

tariff (customs duty) A tax on the importation and, rarely, on the exportation of particular goods, levied by a national government and payable to it when the item crosses the nation's customs boundary. Tariffs originated with the tolls that sovereigns collected on goods that moved into or through their territory. Instead of devices to raise revenue, import duties are now considered effective deterrents to imports that might endanger a domestic industry's sales or a nation's balance of international payments. Formerly, tariff schedules showed an absolute amount of duty to be paid on a variety of imported items, but, because of the frequent changes necessitated by inflation, the modern practice is to establish ad valorem tariffs, which show the duty as a percentage of the imported item's wholesale value. There is no question that an import duty tends to discourage imports; what is in doubt is whether this is in the interest of the tariff-levying country. Classical economists, beginning with John Locke and Adam Smith, have claimed that the artificial protection of certain domestic industries whose products could be bought cheaper abroad and the artificial limitation of the most efficient foreign producer's market result in a misallocation of resources that impedes the nation's and the world's economic welfare. This view is often disputed on political, military, and ethical grounds. The economic argument against it is generally based on one of three claims: (1) that a judicious tariff structure (the optimum tariff) can, if other countries do not retaliate by levying a tariff of their own, improve a country's commodity terms of trade, income terms of trade, or balance of payments; (2) that the concentrated injury to an important industry that loses its tariff protection outweighs the broadly scattered benefits of tariff reduction to the rest of the economy; and (3) that a new (infant) industry requires tariff protection while it is growing to the size and efficiency that will subsequently assure its success in a world of free trade. Since World War II, the trend has been away from tariffs as a tool of national policy. Most modern international tariff agreements aim at tariff reduction and generally provide for other means (especially international credits) to resolve the balance-of-payments, economic development, and other temporary national problems that once served as excuses for the introduction of higher tariffs.

See Charles P. Kindleberger and P. H. Lindert, *International Economics,* Irwin, Homewood, Ill., 1978.

tax anticipation notes   Short-term debt obligations issued by state and local governments to provide working capital until they receive funds from the payment of taxes.

taxation   The process by which governments secure funds to pay for government expenditures. Taxes, which are compulsory, may be imposed directly on individuals or on corporations. Direct taxes may be set in fixed amounts or based on income, wealth, or other measures deemed to represent the tax-paying capacity of those subject to the tax. Taxes may also be imposed indirectly on transactions or on objects, tangible or intangible, regardless of the parties or the ownership of the property involved. Income taxes are the most important form of direct taxation, while sales taxes are the principal form of indirect taxation. Fundamentally a tax system must provide adequate revenue. It must also be thought of as equitable. The principle of progressive taxation is widely accepted. Moreover, the tax system should be simple and economical, involving minimum waste and inconvenience for both the taxpayer and the government. For additional information, see Richard A. Musgrave and Peggy B. Musgrave, *Public Finance in Theory and Practice,* 2d ed., McGraw-Hill, New York, 1975.

tax avoidance   An attempt to reduce tax liability. It involves choosing legal forms and handling affairs in such a way as to take advantage of a legally permissible alternate tax rate or an alternative method of assessing income. Tax avoidance, in contrast to tax evasion, is considered by many to be a legitimate aim, since it is not illegal but consists of exploiting the discrepancies and loopholes in the tax laws to the fullest extent. Among the more common methods of tax avoidance are the manipulation of capital gains and losses, the formation of holding companies to create artificial deductions, and the creation of multiple trusts for relatives and dependents. For further information, see Joseph A. Pechman, *Federal Tax Policy,* 3d ed., Brookings Institution, Washington, D.C., 1977.

tax base   The objective basis on which a tax is imposed. The possible objects of taxation are almost endless, but some of the more common ones are income (income tax), property owned by the taxpayer (property tax), and the value of certain goods sold (sales tax). The specific nature of the tax base largely determines where the burden of each tax falls. Broadening the tax base refers to the application of the tax to a larger portion of the object already being taxed, usually by reducing previous exemptions. Erosion of the tax base refers to a narrowing of the tax base through an increase in the preferential treatment given to certain groups, usually by creating special exemptions and reducing tax rates.

tax burden   The final resting place of the tax levied. In effect, a statement of the tax burden is a statement of who pays the tax and in what amount. The problem of assessing the actual burden of a tax is complicated by the fact that the person who finally bears the tax is frequently not the person who pays it originally, since many taxes, especially those on businesses, may be shifted so that the real burden falls on the consumer. For further information see Joseph A. Pechman, *Federal Tax Policy,* 3d ed., Brookings Institution, Washington, D.C., 1977.

tax credit   A legal provision permitting U.S. taxpayers to deduct specified sums from their tax liabilities. A credit differs from a deduction in the following essential respect: It is subtracted after the total tax liability has been calculated, whereas a deduction is subtracted from the income subject to tax. Thus, a tax credit of a given amount is more valuable to a taxpayer than a deduction of the same amount. For example, if a U.S. taxpayer who is in the 50% bracket of the federal income tax is allowed a $50 tax credit, that taxpayer's total burden is reduced by $50. If it is a $50 deduction, however, the taxpayer's total burden is reduced by only $25. For a discussion of the tax credits allowed to individuals by the U.S. Internal Revenue Code, see U.S. Treasury Department, *Your Federal Income Tax,* annually.

tax deduction   A legal provision permitting U.S. taxpayers to deduct specified expenditures from their taxable income. A deduction differs from a credit in the following essential respect: it is subtracted from the income subject to tax, whereas a credit is subtracted after the total tax liability has been calculated. Thus, a tax deduction of a given amount is less valuable to a taxpayer than a credit of the same amount. For example, a U.S. taxpayer who is in the 50% bracket of the federal income tax reduces total burden by $25 if allowed a $50 tax deduction, whereas the total burden is reduced by $50 if the taxpayer is allowed a $50 credit. Examples of tax-deduction provisions in the U.S. Internal Revenue Code as of May 1, 1981, include (1) personal deductions for state and local taxes, interest on indebtedness, contributions to charitable organizations, medical expenses to the extent that these exceed 3% of adjusted gross income, and certain other specified items, such as losses from fire and theft and a part of the expenses of child care for working mothers; (2) business deductions for the ordinary and necessary expenses of carrying on any trade or business, including wages, salaries, interest, rent, and depreciation, which is the cost of plants and equipment either used up in production or rendered obsolete by time. For a detailed discussion of the deductions allowed to individuals by the U.S. Internal Revenue Code, see U.S. Treasury Department, *Your Federal Income Tax,* annually.

tax equalization An adjustment made by central U.S. governmental units, such as states or counties, to assure an equitable distribution of property assessments among tax districts. When these central units use property taxes as a large source of revenue, they generally resort to tax equalization to prevent competitive undervaluation by local districts. Such undervaluation may be used by local areas to reduce their share of the taxes paid to the central unit. Tax equalization is carried out by central assessment, under which each district as a whole is valued by a central board of assessment and within each district individual lots are assessed totally, so that the sum of all the assessed property values in a district equals the centrally fixed assessment for that district. For additional details, see John F. Due and Ann F. Friedlaender, *Government Finance,* 6th ed., Richard D. Irwin, Homewood, Ill., 1977.

tax equity A fair distribution of the tax burden. There are two aspects to tax equity: vertical equity, which is different treatment of persons in different relative positions; and horizontal equity, which is equal treatment for persons in equal positions even if they earn their income in different ways. Although equity is a universal goal in taxation, there is no unanimity of opinion as to the type of tax which results in the fairest distribution. There are three main approaches to achieving tax equity. The most common, the ability-to-pay doctrine, holds that an equitable tax is one under which the wealthy contribute proportionately more than the poor for government services. The obligation to pay is seen as a collective responsibility rather than a personal one. A different, more individualistic approach, the benefit theory, states that tax payments should be proportional to the benefits derived from government services. A third method, the sociopolitical method, would use the taxing power to redistribute income from the upper to the lower classes, placing almost all the burden on the rich and almost none on the poor. Political and administrative factors, however, require that other considerations, practicality and expediency, be added in placing the tax. The introduction of factors irrelevant to tax equity detracts from its fairness. For further information on the approaches to tax equity, see Richard A. Musgrave and Peggy B. Musgrave, *Public Finance in Theory and Practice,* McGraw-Hill, New York, 1975.

tax exclusion A legal provision that permits taxpayers to exclude certain specified types of income from their taxable income. As of May 1, 1981, the U.S. Internal Revenue Coded defined "gross income" as "all income from whatever source . . . except as otherwise provided. . . ." Among the most important exclusions as of that date were (1) veterans' pensions; (2) social insurance benefit payments; (3) workers' compensation; (4) life insurance payments by reason of death; (5) employer contributions to employee pension, accident, or health plans; (6) interest on obligations of state and local governments; (7) gifts and inheritances; and (8) dividends received up to $200 per year per taxpayer. For a detailed discussion of deductions allowed individuals by the U.S. Internal Revenue Code, see U.S. Treasury Department, *Your Federal Income Tax,* annually.

tax exemption A legal provision permitting taxpayers to deduct from their taxable incomes certain specified sums on a per capita basis. Exemptions in the U.S. Internal Revenue Code as of December 31, 1980, included (1) $1,000 for each taxpayer and each of the taxpayer's dependents, (2) an additional $1,000 if the taxpayer is 65 years of age or older, and (3) an additional $1,000 for blind persons. For a detailed discussion of exemptions allowed individuals by the U.S. Internal Revenue Code, see U.S. Treasury Department, *Your Federal Income Tax,* annually.

tax haven A foreign country which offers low tax rates and other special advantages to corporations of other countries. In the United States, tax laws formerly permitted a company to accumulate profits abroad tax-free, deferring the tax until the dividends were returned to the U.S. parent corporation. Thus, many large business firms formed foreign subsidiaries to take advantage of tax havens abroad. By shifting profits from one foreign company to another (e.g., through a holding company) and using companies in the low-tax countries to accumulate earnings, U.S. firms were able to save substantial amounts on taxes. Such tax havens as Switzerland, Panama, and Venezuela enabled corporations to accumulate capital more rapidly, made foreign financing easier, and allowed the use of foreign subsidiaries as a funnel for other investments. According to the Revenue Act of 1962, however, domestic corporations are no longer allowed a tax differential on dividend income received from foreign corporations in developed countries (this does not apply with respect to dividends received from corporations located in less-developed countries).

tax incentive The devising and arranging of taxes to provide positive encouragement to individuals and businesses and thus help achieve higher rates of economic activity for the nation. Such inducements in the United States take many forms, among which are exemptions and credits. For example, the 10% tax credit for investment in machinery and equipment, approved by Congress in 1975, was aimed at spurring capital investment. Thus, the tax system can be used to reward desirable economic conduct and penalize undesirable economic actions.

tax incidence The final resting place of the tax burden. By shifting the tax forward or backward, the burden of the original tax can be transferred from one person to another. The incidence of the tax falls on the person who cannot shift it any further. The only way in which to avoid the incidence of a tax is to remove oneself from its jurisdiction; e.g., to avoid the incidence of a property tax, one can sell the property. For further information, see Joseph

A. Pechman, *Federal Tax Policy,* 3d ed., Brookings Institution, Washington, D.C., 1977.

tax loophole   An unintentional and unforeseen avenue of tax avoidance. Often the term tax loophole is not used in this narrow sense of an inadvertent oversight in the drafting of legislation; instead, it refers to a tax provision which gives a special advantage to an individual or a group. Such intentional tax loopholes may have as their main purpose the promotion of certain fields of activity through special tax incentives or may merely represent the legislative influence of pressure groups or lobbies. Some provisions in U.S. tax laws that were generally considered in this category as of July 1, 1981, were capital gains, depletion allowances, and executive expense accounts. For further information on tax loopholes in the federal tax structure and proposals for reform, see Joseph A. Pechman, *Federal Tax Policy,* 3d ed., Brookings Institution, Washington, D.C., 1977.

tax-loss carryback   A legal provision permitting both corporations and unincorporated businesses to use the operating losses of one year to offset the profits of preceding years. Such provisions, it is argued, help reduce the tax-created risks of business, since a company that suffers a loss after having paid taxes in prior years can obtain a tax refund soon after losses appear. As of December 31, 1970, the U.S. Internal Revenue Code provided that operating losses, or ordinary losses, could be carried back for three years. For a full discussion of tax-loss carrybacks, see U.S. Internal Revenue Service, *U.S. Internal Revenue Code, 1954.*

tax-loss carryforward   A legal provision permitting businesses and individuals to use the losses of one year to offset the income of succeeding years. Such provisions, it is argued, help reduce the tax-created risks of business and investment and thereby promote business activity and private investment. As of December 31, 1970, the U.S. Internal Revenue Code provided that both capital losses and operating losses (ordinary losses) can be carried forward for five years. For a full discussion of tax-loss carryforwards, see U.S. Internal Revenue Service, *U.S. Internal Revenue Code, 1954.*

tax sharing   A practice whereby one level of government, such as a state, levies a tax and shares the proceeds with a lower level of government, such as a county or a town. Tax sharing has become a method of providing localities with sufficient funds for their growing needs. Usually, it is not accompanied by much central supervision, thus giving local units freedom to use the shared funds as they please. Two major problems arise in the distribution of the shared revenues. First, the apportionment of the funds among localities is often based on the origin of the tax receipts, but the origin sometimes cannot be determined accurately. Secondly, distribution based on origin often returns to the more wealthy districts a far greater proportion of the tax receipts than they can utilize efficiently while the poorer and more needy areas are somewhat neglected.

technical coefficient　*See* technological coefficient.

technical correction in stock price indices and averages　Brief decreases in stock-price indices and averages in a generally climbing, or bull market, or short-term rises in a declining, or bear market. Technical corrections are frequently associated with the Dow theory, which states that there are primary upward or downward movements in stock prices that usually last for more than one year. These trends, however, are interrupted by secondary, or intermediate trends, which are also known as technical corrections and are much briefer in duration. They occur whenever the primary trend has moved upward or downward too rapidly. For further information, see Robert D. Edwards and John Magee, *Technical Analysis of Stock Trends,* John Magee, Springfield, Mass., 1958.

technocracy　A program of social and economic reconstruction that proposed to place industrial engineers and scientists in control of economic life. The basic tenet of technocracy was that modern society with its technological advances was too complex to be run by politicians and entrepreneurs. According to the technocrats, control should be placed in the hands of those who had caused the revolution in technology, the engineers and scientists. The term technocracy, coined by William H. Smith in 1919, was defined as "a theory of social organization and a system of national industrial management." Others active in the technocratic movement were Walter Rautenstrach, Harold Loeb, and Felix Frazer. Technocracy had its greatest popularity in the later years of the depression, 1932 and 1933, and has since almost disappeared. For additional details, see Allen Raymond, *What Is Technocracy?* McGraw-Hill, New York, 1933.

technological coefficient (technical coefficient)　In input-output analysis, the ratio of units of inputs to units of output. If a given production function is a straight line, changes in factor costs do not influence the technological coefficient because there is no possibility of substituting one factor for another in response to price changes. For additional information, see Karl A. Fox and Tej K. Kaul, *Intermediate Economic Statistics,* Krieger, Melbourne, Fla., 1980.

technological unemployment　The displacement of labor by machinery and improved methods of production. Technological unemployment is an inevitable aspect of a dynamic economy which is constantly striving for increased productivity, higher living standards, and higher wages. It usually affects both the quantity and the type of labor needed in the industry involved, decreasing the number of workers employed for the particular operation and often requiring new and different skills for the remaining workers. Those most affected by technological change are semiskilled and unskilled industrial workers. Managerial employees, professional persons, and workers in the service industries are generally much less subject to technological unemployment. Not only may technological change cause considerable short-term unemployment, but unemployment may be prolonged if the new production methods do not lead to price reductions and new skills are not acquired by the displaced workers. To combat technological unemployment, many unions strongly oppose automation, condone featherbedding and make-work practices, and negotiate agreements that provide for generous dismissal benefits for displaced workers or the retraining and employment of displaced employees on new equipment. For further information, see Gordon F. Bloom and Herbert R. Northrup, *Economics of Labor Relations,* 8th ed., Irwin, Homewood, Ill., 1977.

technology   The science or body of knowledge applicable to the production of goods. It is generally acknowledged that modern technology was one of the most important conditions that led to the rise of the industrial system of modern capitalism. It was modern machinery, the product of technology, which made possible the rapid increase in the volume of production. The enormous increase in physical production is, in turn, the characteristic quality that has made capitalism a success. Thus, technology has made possible gains in individual and social wealth. For further information, see Nestor E. Terleckyj, *Effects of R and D on the Productivity Growth of Industries: An Exploratory Study,* National Planning Association, Washington, D.C., December 1974.

terms of trade   The relationship between the prices which a producer must pay and those which it receives for its products. An improvement in the terms of trade means that the producer's selling price has increased to a greater extent (or fallen to a lesser extent) than the price of the items that the producer needed, leaving it better off. This relationship is most frequently studied in the analysis of international trade. For instance, if the price of materials which Great Britain imports from Liberia declines while the price of products which it exports to Liberia rises (or falls to a lesser extent), the terms of trade are said to have moved in Britain's favor and against Liberia. Unless big changes in the volume of trade develop, such movements benefit the British balance of payments. The terms of trade can be calculated mathematically; if the relationship between export and import prices in the base year is taken as 100, any improvement in the terms of trade causes the index to rise and any deterioration causes it to fall. In some cases, government policy is set by such an index. For example, if the U.S. agricultural parity price index, which measures the terms of trade for farmers with 1909–1914 as a base period, falls to a predetermined level, a governmental loan program automatically goes into operation. Although terms of trade usually apply to price relationships and are more accurately labeled commodity terms of trade, it is possible to employ analogous methods to determine income terms of trade, which indicate whether economic changes affect the real earnings of income recipients in one country (or one industry or one firm) favorably or adversely when compared with another. For a full discussion of the terms of trade, see Charles P. Kindleberger and P. H. Lindert, *International Economics,* Irwin, Homewood, Ill., 1978.

thrift institutions Savings institutions whose primary objective is to attract savings from individuals and channel these funds into productive investment, largely mortgage instruments. There are two major types of thrift institution, savings and loan associations and mutual savings banks. In addition to ordinary passbook accounts, thrifts are currently authorized to offer accounts having specified maturities ranging from three months to eight years or more. Time-deposit contracts typically include: (1) the interest rate paid by the institution, (2) early withdrawal penalties which reduce the effective interest earned on the account, and (3) the conditions under which the deposit can be renewed when the maturity date is reached. In recent years the viability of thrift institutions in the U.S. financial system has been severely tested by a persistently rising interest rate and a highly inflationary environment. A fundamental reason underlying the current problems of thrift institutions in competing for savers' funds is the large numbers of relatively low-yielding mortgage loans remaining in their portfolios.

tied loan A foreign loan in which the borrower is required to spend the proceeds only in the country making the loan. The advantages of tied loans are that they stimulate employment and income in the creditor nation and do not affect the balance of payments of that country adversely. Underdeveloped countries, which are the main recipients of tied loans, however, sometimes resent limits on their freedom to use the money, especially when they are forced to pay higher prices in the lending nation than are available elsewhere. The chief U.S. agency offering tied loans to foreign countries is the Export-Import Bank of Washington. Whereas a considerable part of U.S. foreign aid has been tied, the trend is toward permitting borrowing nations to spend U.S. loans wherever they want. For additional details, see Robert Asher, *Grants, Loans, and Local Currencies,* Brookings Institution, Washington, D.C., 1961.

tight money (dear money) The term used to designate a policy of monetary restraint, conducted by the U.S. monetary authorities, which is designed to reduce the supply of credit, raise interest rates, and thus relieve inflationary pressures that have arisen because of excess demand. A change from an easy-money policy to a tight-money policy may take the form of positive actions, such as open-market sales, increases in required-reserve ratios, or increases in discount rates. Such a shift in policy can be passive, as in failing to increase reserves in the face of a rising demand for credit. As a result of open-market sales by the Federal Reserve System, the U.S. commercial banking system loses reserves and must make some adjustments in its asset portfolios. If there are no excess funds in the system, the banks must either borrow additional reserves from the Federal Reserve or restrict their earning assets by either curbing loans, disposing of securities, or adopting both measures. Long before they have exhausted their liquid assets and longer-term investments, however, most banks take measures to restrain the growth of their loan portfolios. They first satisfy requests for loans by good deposit customers with whom they have had a continuing relationship. Thereafter, restrictive measures include the reduction of the maturity of term loans that are granted, the stricter application of standards of creditworthiness, and the granting of less than the full amount of the loans that have been requested. The net free-reserve positions of Federal Reserve member banks, which are reported weekly by the Federal Reserve System and appear in Friday's newspapers, are an indication of the present monetary policy. For a discussion of tight money, see James M. Buchanan and Mary R. Flowers, *The Public Finances,* 4th ed., Irwin, Homewood, Ill., 1975.

time deposit Money held in the bank account of an individual or a firm for which the bank can require advance notice of withdrawal, usually a month to two months. Advance notice must be given for corporations' time deposits, but this requirement is almost always waived for individuals' deposits. Time deposits can be held in commercial and mutual savings banks. A 3 to 6% reserve on time deposits is required for all U.S. banks that belong to the Federal Reserve System. Reserves for other banks are subject to state law. See Lawrence S. Ritter and William L. Silber, *Principles of Money, Banking and Financial Markets,* 3d rev. ed., Basic Books, New York, 1980; for statistics on time deposits, see *Federal Reserve Bulletin,* Washington, D.C., monthly.

time series A set of ordered observations of a particular economic variable, such as prices, production, investment, and consumption, taken at different points in time. Most economic series consist of monthly, quarterly, or annual observations. Monthly and quarterly economic series are used in short-term business forecasting. Before these series can be made useful as forecasting tools, seasonal fluctuations must be removed. For a detailed discussion of time series and time-series analysis, see Karl A. Fox and Tej K. Kaul, *Intermediate Economic Statistics,* Krieger, Melbourne, Fla., 1980.

time-series analysis (time-series decomposition) The process by which the components of an economic time series, such as production, investment, and consumption, are separated and isolated in order to study the fluctuations peculiar to each of them. Economic series are generally assumed to be composed of three mutually exclusive and exhaustive components: (1) The trend cycle consists of cumulative and reversible movements characterized by recurrent and aperiodic intervals of expansion and contraction (the cycle) and by longer-run drifts underlying the economy (the trend). The trend is usually characterized by longer movements than those of the cycle. (2) The seasonal represents the composite effect of climatic and institutional factors and is represented by fluctuations which are repeated more or less regularly each year. (3) The irregular, the residual which is left when the trend cycle and the seasonal have been removed from the original economic time series, consists of erratic real-world occurrences and measurement errors and is characterized generally by movements of less than six months' duration. Most methods of time-series analysis assume one of two models: the additive model, in which the three components are related additively; or the multiplicative model, in which the three components are related multiplicatively. For a detailed discussion of time series and time-series analysis, see G. E. P. Box and G. M. Jenkins, *Time Series Analysis, Forecasting and Control*, rev. ed., Holden-Day, San Francisco, 1976.

time-series decomposition   *See* **time-series analysis.**

time-varying-parameter models   Models used in the econometric analysis of time series where the coefficients themselves may be functions of time. In the standard regression model, the coefficients to be estimated are assumed to be constants. In the time-varying-parameter model, this assumption is replaced by an alternative. One common assumption is the switching-regressions model. In this case there are two regimes (e.g., wartime and peacetime) and the regression parameters take on different values in each regime. Another assumption is that one or more parameters are linear functions of time. In this case both the regression functions and the parameter functions must be estimated. A general alternative assumption is the random-coefficients model where the coefficients are assumed to be random variables, possibly correlated with time. Some time-series cross-section models use this assumption. For additional information, see G. S. Maddala, *Econometrics*, McGraw-Hill, New York, 1977.

Tobin's *q*   The ratio of the market value of an asset to its replacement cost. The numerator of the ratio is the market value—the going price in the market for exchanging existing assets—while the denominator is the replacement or reproduction cost—the price in the market for newly produced commodities. According to James Tobin, this summary measure has considerable macroeconomic significance; it is the nexus between financial markets and the goods and services markets, particularly on the purchase of durable goods. In equilibrium, *q* has a nominal value—1—which sustains capital replacement and expansion at the natural growth rate of the economy. Values of *q* above 1 should stimulate investment in excess of requirements for replacement and normal growth, and values of *q* less than 1 discourage investment. In the short run, events, policies, and expectations move *q* up and down, creating or destroying capital-investment incentives. One way to consider *q* is as a representation of the comparison between, on the one hand, the marginal efficiency of capital, the internal rate of return on investment at its cost in the commodity markets, and, on the other hand, the financial cost of capital, the rate at which investors discount the future returns from such investment. The Federal Reserve affects the cost of capital and q in an indirect but powerful way, operating through a network of asset substitutions. Events and shocks, other than monetary policy, affect the cost of capital. The ratio q will vary independently of monetary policy as estimates of future earnings change. Business firms making investment decisions are interested in the q for specific incremental investments, not in the average q for the firm or for the economy. Marginal q's can differ from average q's, if, for example, capital investment is made for new processes or for products that would render existing capital obsolete. According to calculations of John Ciccolo, there is a good econometric relationship of investment to q's with lags distributed over eight quarters and with an elasticity of about 0.8. For additional information, see James Tobin, "Monetary Policies and the Economy: The Transmission Mechanism" *Southern Economic Journal*, vol. 44, no. 3, January 1978; John Ciccolo, "Essay III," *Four Essays on Monetary Policy,* Ph.D. dissertation, Yale University, New Haven, Conn., 1975; James Tobin and William C. Brainard, *Asset Markets and the Cost of Capital,* Cowles Foundation Paper no. 440, Cowles Foundation, New Haven, Conn., 1977.

tolerance A measure of the precision of survey estimates, based on probability sampling, that indicates how close the estimate is to the figure that would have been obtained from a complete census using exactly the same methods of data collection. Sample tolerance is generally reported in terms of standard errors. For example, the odds are 2 to 1 that the survey estimate will not differ from the census count by more than one standard error. The odds are 19 to 1 that the difference will be less than two standard errors. Tolerance can be calculated only for a probability sample. For further discussion, see W. Edwards Deming, *Sample Design in Business Research,* Wiley, New York, 1960.

trade barrier An artificial restraint on the free exchange of goods and services between nations. The most common types of trade barriers are tariffs, quotas, and exchange control. Such obstacles to trade are usually imposed by a country that wishes to protect domestic producers in their home market against foreign competition, better its terms of trade, reduce domestic unemployment, or improve its balance-of-payments position. The raising of trade barriers by one country often provokes other nations to retaliate with barriers of their own to maintain their overall trade position. Generally, the effect of a trade barrier is to reduce the volume of trade while increasing the domestic price of the protected good. Thus, it results in a relatively inefficient allocation of world resources and reduces the level of total world income and production. For further information, see C. P. Kindleberger and P. H. Lindert, *International Economics,* Irwin, Homewood, Ill., 1978.

trade union   An association of workers who do the same kind of work. It bargains collectively on behalf of its members with single employers, business firms, or associations of employers. Trade unions are generally limited to skilled or semiskilled workers who have learned crafts. A carpenter's union, for example, is made up exclusively of carpenters. Trade unions differ from industrial unions, which include workers in a given industry regardless of the type of work that they do. Early unions in the United States were formed on the trade-union basis, and skilled workers were thus the first to be organized. In Great Britain, the legal definition of trade union includes employers' as well as employees' associations. British trade unions have long emphasized a wide variety of educational activities. They also may take part in politics and the operations of government, and most of them provide their members with benefits for sickness, old age, unemployment, and work stoppages due to labor disputes. See Lloyd G. Reynolds, *Labor Economics and Labor Relations,* 7th ed., Prentice-Hall, Englewood Cliffs, N.J., 1978.

trade-weighted devaluation   Some countries peg their currencies to a basket of foreign currencies. If such a country chooses to revalue or devalue its currency, it will change the pegged value of the basket, resulting in trade-weighted devaluation. The exchange rate with each of the foreign currencies in the basket will be shifted.

tradition-directed economy   A mode of economic organization in which the problems of production and distribution are solved by procedures devised in the distant past and rigidified by tradition. For example, the production problem may be solved by the hereditary assignment of the father's job to his sons. Until recent times, most economies were tradition-directed, and even now tradition is of major importance in many backward societies. Even in highly industrialized and modern economies, such as that of the United States, tradition plays a major role in such things as tipping, allowances to minors, and bonuses based on length of service.

transfer payment   A government or business expenditure for which no goods or services are received in return. Most government transfer payments are of the nature of welfare payments, such as social security benefits, unemployment compensation, and relief payments. Certain other government subsidies, such as the farm price supports, are also considered transfer payments. Since they represent a return of revenue to individuals, government transfer payments are considered negative taxes. Their effect is to redistribute income (e.g., from employed to unemployed or from city worker to farmer), and thus they alter the composition of private goods production in favor of the recipients of the payments. Business transfer payments are usually gifts or donations, such as corporate gifts to nonprofit institutions; they amounted to $2.9 billion in the United States in 1981. For further information, see Eveline M. Burns, *Social Security and Public Policy*, Arno, New York, 1976.

transformation curve The locus of the output combinations of two goods that can be produced from a fixed total supply of resources. Each point on the transformation curve (also called the production-possibilities curve) depicts a possible distribution of output between two goods in a full-employment economy. The slope of the curve (always negative) is a measure of how much of one good *Y* must be given up to produce one additional unit of the other good *X*. The curve slopes downward to the right, indicating that to obtain more of one product *X*, a full-employment economy must always sacrifice some of the other product *Y*. The transformation curve is concave to the origin because of the law of increasing costs, since the factors of production are not completely adaptable to the two alternative uses. For additional details, see James M. Henderson and Richard E. Quandt, *Microeconomic Theory: A Mathematical Approach*, 3d ed., McGraw-Hill, New York, 1980.

transitory income *See* **permanent-income hypothesis.**

Transformation Curve

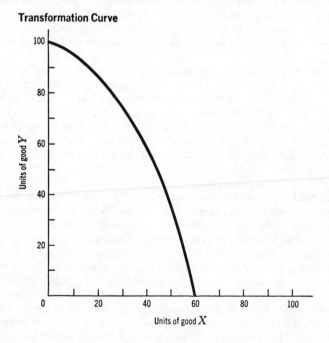

treasury bill   The shortest-term security issued by the U.S. government. Sold to the public at weekly auctions, treasury bills usually mature in 91 or 182 days, although tax-anticipation bills, a special type designed to attract funds set aside for tax payments, can be issued for a period as long as one year. The government's high credit rating makes treasury bills exceptionally secure investments. They are especially attractive to commercial banks, non-financial corporations, foreign central banks, and other investors who want to earn interest on temporarily idle cash without fear of default. Because of the short maturities, treasury bill prices do not fluctuate as widely as those of other U.S. securities, but price changes do occur. One reason for fluctuation is that the Federal Reserve System frequently buys and sells large quantities of treasury bills in order to affect the cost and availability of bank loans. Detailed statistics on ownership, maturities, and price are published in U.S. Treasury Department, *Treasury Bulletin,* monthly.

treasury note   A government security issued by the U.S. Treasury Department with a maturity of from one year to five years. It is thus an intermediate-term obligation of the Treasury. Short-term securities maturing in a year or less are called bills and certificates, and long-term securities maturing in a period longer than five years are called bonds. The reason for the issuance of securities with such different maturities is that the government wishes to be able to tap all potential sources of loanable funds. Statistics on treasury notes can be found in U.S. Treasury Department, *Treasury Bulletin,* monthly; ————, *Annual Report of the Secretary of the Treasury on the State of the Finances.*

trough   The low point of economic activity. Coming after a period of contraction and before a period of recovery, it is usually a short interval, lasting only a month or two. According to the National Bureau of Economic Research, the troughs in the eight U.S. postwar recessions occurred in October 1945, October 1949, May 1954, April 1958, February 1961, November 1970, March 1975, and July 1980. For a detailed discussion of troughs, see Geoffrey H. Moore (ed.), *Business Cycle Indicators,* Princeton University Press, Princeton, N.J., 1961.

trust fund   A fund of money or property administered by an individual or an organization for the benefit of another individual or organization. The trustee is the person or organization who is in charge of the fund, and the beneficiary is the person or group for whose benefit the fund was created. A trust fund can be established to provide income for beneficiaries during the life of the grantor or after the grantor's death, to benefit a charitable organization, to increase the value of property by placing it in the hands of a competent trustee, or to protect the trust property (e.g., for a minor). The primary duties of the trustee are to invest the principal of the fund and to distribute the benefits. The investment policies of the trustee may be specified by the individual setting up the trust, but if no specification is made, investment of trust funds in the United States is governed by state law. Although any adult may legally be appointed trustee of a trust fund, most trust services are performed by trust companies or commercial banks with trust departments.

turning point The point in a business cycle at which the direction of economic activity reverses itself. There are two distinct turning points in each cycle, the upper turning point (the peak), when expansion comes to an end; and the lower turning point (the trough), when contraction changes into the beginning of expansion. Actually, the term turning zone is more apt than turning point, since there is usually a critical period of a few months which marks the end of a phase of expansion or contraction. The upper turning zone is usually marked by a peak (or perhaps a slight decline) in output and employment, a fall in stock and commodity prices, a greater-than-normal increase in inventories, and a change of business optimism into caution and perhaps even into pessimism regarding the short-term future. In the lower turning zone, these factors are reversed. In the postwar period, according to the National Bureau of Economic Research, the United States experienced upper turning points in November 1948, July 1953, August 1958, April 1960, December 1969, November 1973, January 1980, and July 1981, and lower turning points in October 1945, October 1949, May 1954, April 1958, February 1961, November 1970, March 1975, and July 1980. For a fuller discussion of the theory, measurement, and forecasting of turning points, see Arthur F. Burns and Wesley C. Mitchell, *Measuring Business Cycles,* National Bureau of Economic Research, New York, 1946; Geoffrey H. Moore (ed.), *Business Cycle Indicators,* vol. 1, National Bureau of Economic research, Princeton University Press, Princeton, N.J., 1961.

turnover The number of times during a year that the inventory of a firm is sold. The annual stock turnover can be computed by dividing annual sales by the average inventory. Both inventory and sales figures should be valued consistently, that is, either at cost or at sale price. Generally, a firm with a higher annual rate of turnover has lower operating costs and earns a higher rate of net profit on its capital investment. It has been found that as the volume of sales of a firm increases, its rate of stock turnover also increases.

turnover tax A tax on transactions of goods and services at all levels of production and distribution. The turnover tax, also known as the general sales tax or the gross income tax, is more inclusive than the common retail sales tax, since it is levied every time that a good, whether finished or in the process of production, changes hands. Since the burden of any sales tax can usually be shifted forward by including it in the selling price of the good, the result of a general turnover tax is a tendency to pyramid the amount of the tax from one stage to another so that the final selling price of an article includes the sum of all the taxes paid on the good's materials during its production. Thus, when a turnover tax is in operation, it is to the advantage of producers to avoid as many independent transactions as possible in the process of producing a good. The turnover tax is an important source of revenue in the U.S.S.R. as well as in a number of European Common Market countries. It is also in use in a few U.S. states, such as Indiana, New Mexico, and West Virginia. For additional details, see Paul A. Samuelson, *Economics,* 11th ed., McGraw-Hill, New York, 1980.

twentieth-century liberalism   *See* **reform liberalism.**

two-stage least squares   An econometric technique facilitating the restatement of a set of equations in a simultaneous model such that each equation of the model specifies a single endogenous variable as a function solely of exogenous variables and/or first-stage least-squares estimates of other endogenous variables involved in any equation. In effect, this technique recognizes that some endogenous variables act as explanatory variables in some equations and overcomes barriers to their use as explanatory variables by restating them in the form of predetermined variables. For additional information, see Karl A. Fox and Tej K. Kaul, *Intermediate Economic Statistics,* Krieger, Melbourne, Fla., 1980.

unbalanced growth   The growth of capital investment in different sectors of a developing economy at a different rate. Whereas a number of economists have favored plans of balanced investment for underdeveloped areas, others have argued that the resources required for a program of balanced growth are so large that a really underdeveloped country cannot support such a plan. What is really needed is a deliberate unbalancing of capital investment, concentrating on strategic industries and sectors which will induce growth in other areas. A chronic imbalance of investment may produce a faster rate of growth than a balanced program because of the incentives and pressures that it sets up in nonstrategic industries. Investment should be concentrated in industries with the greatest amount of forward linkage (encouraging investment in subsequent stages of production) and backward linkage (inducing investment in earlier stages of production). For additional details on the purposes and programs of unbalanced growth, see Benjamin Higgins, *Economic Development*, Norton, New York, 1968.

uncertainty   In the real world a measure of uncertainty must always be expected for any actual investment project. Uncertainty is always with us. It makes innovation possible and creates positive and negative divergences between what investments expect to earn and what they actually earn. In a free enterprise system pure luck determines much of the dispersion of incomes. Frank Knight theorized that all true profit is linked with uncertainty. For additional information, see Frank Knight, *Risk, Uncertainty and Profit*, Houghton Mifflin, Boston, 1921; Werner Hochwald, "Economic History and Theory," in D. Greenwald (ed.), *Encyclopedia of Economics*, McGraw-Hill, New York, 1982, pp. 300–302.

underconsumption (overproduction)   The manufacture of goods in excess of consumer demand. Under the conditions assumed by the classical economists and their successors, general overproduction is impossible. These conditions included free competition among buyers and sellers, no significant limitations on the knowledge of market conditions. a high degree of mobility in the supply of labor and capital, and the use of money only as a medium of exchange. The classical economists recognized that local disparities between supply and demand could exist in particular markets, and under certain conditions, but these, they said, would disappear in time as a result of adjustments in the whole system. This doctrine, which is attributed to Jean Baptiste Say, is referred to as Say's law of markets. The law was criticized severely by opponents who believed that these conditions were unrealistic and that, given different postulates, a situation was likely to develop which could be described as a state of general overproduction. For example, Say's law assumed that each sale must provide the wherewithal to make a purchase; hence, supply creates its own demand. Money, which is received in exchange for a good, can serve as a store of value as well as a medium of exchange, however, and under certain conditions there is likely to be a rush for liquidity and a hoarding of cash, producing a situation in which there is a lack of demand. Thomas Malthus was one of the first to attack the Say doctrine, stating that it was theoretically unsound and contrary to experience because "we see in almost every part of the world vast powers of production which are not put into action." Eventually, Say's law was disregarded, and theories relating underconsumption or overproduction to business cycles developed. These theories maintained that the capitalist system would result in excess production which would exceed the ability of people to consume, in a decline of prices to unprofitable levels, in increasing unemployment, and in the existence of depressed conditions until the excess production was absorbed. For further information, see T. Sowell, *Say's Law: An Historical Analysis*, Princeton University Press, Princeton, N.J., 1972.

underdeveloped nation A country in which per capita real income is relatively low compared with the per capita real incomes of industrial nations. Thus, an underdeveloped nation is a relatively poor country with per capita income under $1,000, or less than one-tenth that of the United States. In general, there are several characteristics that are indicative of an underdeveloped area: (1) A very high proportion of the population is engaged in agriculture (usually between 70 and 90%). (2) There is evidence of considerable disguised unemployment and a lack of employment opportunities outside agriculture. (3) There is very little capital per individual, and the condition of low per capita income requires existence at a near-subsistence level. (4) For the large mass of people, saving is practically nonexistent, while the savings that do exist are accumulated by the land-holding class and do not further industry and commerce. For an examination of policies for economic development, see Benjamin Higgins, *Economic Development,* Norton, New York, 1968.

underidentification A condition that exists when it is not possible to estimate all parameters by means of the information supplied by a system of stochastic equations or when no parameters can be estimated. Most authorities equate underidentified and not identified. In special cases it is possible to eliminate underidentification by introducing additional restrictions into the analysis. For additional information, see Karl A. Fox and Tej K. Kaul, *Intermediate Economic Statistics,* Krieger, Melbourne, Fla., 1980.

underpopulation A condition of insufficient population for an area. In contrast to the case of an overpopulated area, an increase in population in an underpopulated area raises the standard of living by making it possible to utilize available resources more efficiently. In a nation experiencing underpopulation, there are a large land area and available resources in relation to the population. Person-land ratios, such as the number of persons per square mile or the acreage of arable land per capita, are crude measures of the degree of population concentration. Low person-land ratios or high arable-land–per capita ratios indicate underpopulation. Canada and Australia appear to be good examples of underpopulation.

undistributed profits *See* **retained earnings.**

unemployed person In the United States anyone sixteen years of age or over who is not working and is looking for a job. Also counted among the unemployed are (1) those who are waiting to be called back to a job from which they have been laid off, (2) those who are waiting to report to a new job scheduled to begin within thirty days, and (3) those who are out of work but are not looking for a job because of temporary illness or because of a belief that no work is available in their line or in their community. Monthly estimates of U.S. unemployment are obtained through personal interviews in a sample of 50,000 households in 449 areas. These estimates are always larger than the number of persons eligible for unemployment insurance, which does not provide complete coverage. The number of unemployed in the United States has ranged from about 13 million in 1933 to less than 700,000 in 1944. From 1950 to 1980, unemployment averaged about 4 million. U.S. unemployment statistics are compiled monthly by the U.S. Department of Labor, which uses figures gathered by the U.S. Bureau of the Census in a particular week of each month. See U.S. Department of Labor, *Monthly Report on the Labor Force.* For changes in unemployment from 1800 to 1960, see Stanley Lebergott, *Manpower in Economic Growth,* McGraw-Hill, New York, 1964, pp. 164–190.

unemployment benefit A benefit distributed under an unemployment compensation program. In the United States, the amount of the benefit and its duration vary from state to state. The number of unemployed U.S. workers who receive benefits has fluctuated between 40 and 60% of the total number of unemployed. The main factors associated with this relatively low rate of coverage are the increasing number of unemployed workers who exhaust their benefit rights, the entrance into the labor market of a growing number of new workers, who receive no benefits while first unemployed, and an increasing number of disqualifications for benefits. Although unemployment benefits have some countercyclical effect, they have averaged less than 3% of total consumption expenditures. Nevertheless, these benefits, which were not available during the depression of the 1930s, help offset losses in purchasing power. For additional details, see Richard A. Lester, *The Economics of Unemployment Compensation,* Princeton University, Industrial Relations Section, Princeton, N.J., 1962.

unemployment rate The number of jobless persons expressed as a percentage of the total labor force. The United States counts as unemployed anyone 16 years of age and over who is out of work and would like a job even if the person is doing little about finding one. Many other countries count as unemployed only those persons who are receiving unemployment compensation. These differences make international comparisons hazardous. Ranging from 3% in booms to 25% during the great depression of the 1930s, the U.S. unemployment rate since World War II has averaged about 5.5%. The U.S. rate is compiled monthly by the U.S. Department of Labor, which uses survey figures gathered by the U.S. Bureau of the Census. See U.S. Department of Labor, *Monthly Report on the Labor Force;* for rates of many other countries, see Statistical Office of the United Nations, *Monthly Bulletin of Statistics,* New York.

unfair competition Deceptive, dishonest, or injurious methods of competition. Originally, the law against unfair competition was aimed at halting the passing off of one's goods as the goods of a competitor, but it now includes both actions which hamper, injure, or exclude competitors and concerted action to suppress competition. Among the common forms of unfair competition are cutthroat competition, price discrimination among types of goods and among firms, false and misleading advertising, tying arrangements, bribery, spying, intimidation, and other direct interference with competitors. The Congress of the United States prohibited many forms of unfair competition in interstate commerce by adopting the Federal Trade Commission Act of 1914. In 1938 the jurisdiction of the Federal Trade Commission was extended by the Wheeler-Lea Act to protect customers against unfair business practices, primarily against misrepresentation of products. For additional details, see Jerrold G. VanCise, *The Federal Antitrust Laws,* American Enterprise Institute, Washington, D.C., 1975.

unfair labor practices   Actions on the part of employers which discourage or discriminate against union membership and actions on the part of unions which discourage or discriminate against nonunion personnel that have been outlawed by the National Labor Relations Act. Discriminatory hiring policies, the influencing of the choice of unions by their employees, and a refusal to bargain with union representatives are some of the practices forbidden to management. Forcing management to discriminate in favor of union members or of particular unions, engaging in secondary boycotts, and requiring featherbedding practices of the employer are some of the practices forbidden to unions. Complaints by either side are filed with the National Labor Relations Board, whose general counsel has sole power to investigate them and to prosecute. See Lloyd G. Reynolds, *Labor Economics and Labor Relations,* 7th ed., Prentice-Hall, Englewood Cliffs, N.J., 1978.

unified budget   A federal budget which covers financial transactions of two principal kinds of funds—federal funds and trust funds. It combines the receipts and outlays for both types of funds after deducting the transactions that flow between them. By and large, it measures the transactions of the government with the public. It is more comprehensive than either the administrative budget or the cash budget, the latter of which does not include all transactions of government trust-fund accounts. For additional details, see *The Budget of the United States Government, Fiscal Year, 1982,* Washington, D.C., 1981.

union shop   A plant or establishment in which all workers must join the union within a specified time after hiring (usually thirty days). The key distinction between a union shop and a closed shop is that the former gives the employer freedom to hire anyone, whereas the latter restricts the employer's choice to persons who are already members of the union. The union-shop arrangement is the only form of union-security provision that is growing rapidly in importance in the United States. There are two important reasons for the increase: (1) the Taft-Hartley Act of 1947, which prohibited the closed shop; and (2) the change in the steel industry from maintenance of membership to the union shop. For further discussion, see Lloyd G. Reynolds, *Labor Economics and Labor Relations,* 7th ed., Prentice-Hall, Englewood Cliffs, N.J., 1978.

unit banking system   A banking system in which banks are individual incorporated or unincorporated entities that are not affiliated with any other member of a system. The banking system of the United States was founded on the unit banking doctrine, but the credit needs of a growing country demanded that the system become more highly concentrated. Nevertheless, defenders of the unit banking system placed many obstacles in the path of greater concentration, such as laws which were intended to protect unit banks from the competition of branch banks. For example, the McFadden-Pepper Act of 1927 permitted national banks to establish branches in the metropolitan areas of the parent bank but forbade them to establish branches in towns of less than 25,000 population, permitting one branch in a town of 50,000 population and not more than two branches in towns of 100,000 population. Advocates of branch banking and unit banking still argue about advantages and disadvantages of each system. For further information, see Harry D. Hutchinson, *Money, Banking, and the United States Economy,* 4th ed., Prentice-Hall, Englewood Clifts, N.J., 1980.

urban economics   A branch of economics concerned with the patterns of locations of households, business enterprises, and other institutions in densely developed areas. As a recognized field of economics, it is less than a quarter-century old. The study of residential choice, where to live, and how much housing to consume, is a major component of urban economics. It is an extension of classical location theory, which deals almost exclusively with the location decision of the business enterprise. Given the key role of transportation costs in shaping urban form, it is not surprising that another major focus for research has been urban transportation. For additional information, see Edwin S. Mills, *Urban Economics,* 2nd ed., Scott Foresman, Glenview, Ill., 1980.

urban renewal   The redevelopment and improvement of urban areas in the United States. It involves the cooperative action of government and private business to reshape the structure of the nation's cities to meet the demands of a constantly growing and changing urban population. The most pressing problem being attacked by urban renewal programs is the spreading of slum areas in many large cities. Urban renewal includes slum clearance and rehabilitation, prevention of blight, relocation, low-cost public housing projects, and an attack on the city housing problem in general. It began with the passage of the Housing Act of 1949, which provided federal assistance to cities for the betterment of urban housing. In 1954 the act was amended to provide for a broader and more comprehensive approach to the problem of slums and urban redevelopment. Some states also have undertaken urban renewal programs, providing their cities with the funds and technical assistance necessary for urban planning and development. See Edwin S. Mills, *Urban Economics*, 2d ed., Scott Foresman, Glenview, Ill., 1980.

use tax A tax levied in the United States on the initial utilization of a good as opposed to one levied on its sale. It was devised by states to offset the loss of sales taxes through the purchase of goods outside their boundaries and to remove the disadvantage to local businesses of competing with out-of-state firms. The tax is imposed on taxable items which have been bought out of the state, and the amount is usually equal to the sales tax. Since a use tax is almost impossible to collect on small items, its applicability is generally limited to purchases of such items as automobiles, which are reported to the state by the owners in order to obtain licenses. Some cities levy use taxes, but the collection problem there is even more difficult than in the case of states. Revenue derived from use taxes is small, and their main importance lies in helping to make sales taxes effective. Since most reports on state and city tax revenues list the revenues derived from sales and use taxes together, it is difficult to determine the exact revenues derived from use taxes alone. See Joseph A. Pechman, *Federal Tax Policy*, 3d ed., Brookings Institution, Washington, D.C., 1977.

utility The ability of a good or a service to satisfy human wants. Utility expresses the relationship between goods and the individual's pleasures or pains. It is the property possessed by a particular good or service which affords an individual pleasure or prevents pain during the time of its consumption or the period of anticipation of its consumption. For example, a rib roast which a family is eating has utility for them, and so had the same roast when it was in their refrigerator before they cooked it. The utility of a good is said to vary in intensity with the intensity of the pleasure that it creates. The degree of utility of a good, however, varies constantly. For example, the first and second roasts may provide equal amounts of utility, but a third roast may result in diminishing utility and perhaps even in pain. Utility thus is not proportional to the quantity or type of the good or service consumed. For further discussion of utility, see W. Stanley Jevons, *The Theory of Political Economy*, 5th ed., Kelley and Millman, New York, 1965; Alfred Marshall, *Principles of Economics*, 8th ed., Macmillan, London, 1920; Nicholas Georgescu-Roegen, "Utility," in D. Greenwald (ed.), *Encyclopedia of Economics*, McGraw-Hill, New York, 1982, pp. 934–941.

V

value The price commanded by a good or service in the market. The concept of value is ordinarily used in economics to denote value in exchange. That is, the exchange value of a good is expressed as a quantity of other goods or money which must be exchanged to obtain one unit of the given good. The value of a commodity depends upon two elements: its desirability and its scarcity—the familiar factors of supply and demand. If a good is desirable (because of its usefulness, its aesthetically pleasing qualities, or any other reason), it has value for the individual. However, since the worth of a good to an individual decreases as it becomes more abundant (because of the law of diminishing marginal utility), value also depends upon the good's scarcity. To have value in exchange, a good must be both desirable and scarce. If it is not desired by anyone, no one will be willing to exchange any good or money for it no matter how scarce it is, and its exchange value will be zero. If the good is abundant, no matter how desirable it is (e.g., air), people have as much of it as they want, and no one will pay for it. Thus, it will have no exchange value. For further information, see J. R. Hicks, *Value and Capital,* 2d ed., Oxford University Press, New York, 1946; Mark Blaug, *The Cambridge Revolution: Success or Failure?*, Transatlantic Arts, Central Islip, N.Y., 1975.

value added by manufacture The difference between the value of goods and the cost of materials or supplies that are used in producing them. Value added is derived by subtracting the cost of raw materials, parts, supplies, fuel, goods purchased for resale, electric energy, and contract work from the value of shipments. It is the best money gauge of the relative economic importance of a manufacturing industry because it measures that industry's contribution to the economy rather than its gross sales. According to the 1977 *Census of Manufactures,* for example, the U.S. metal-cutting machine-tool industry had shipments of $2.8 billion, while the chemical preparations, n.e.c. (not elsewhere classified) industry had shipments of $4 billion. This would imply that the latter was of greater importance than the former, but the value added by the two industries was almost precisely the same: $1.87 billion for the metal-cutting machine-tool industry and $1.84 billion for the chemical preparations, n.e.c. industry. For detailed statistics on value added by manufacture, see U.S. Department of Commerce, *1977 Census of Manufactures.*

value-added tax (VAT)   A tax on the value added. The principle of this tax is that the person paying for goods or services pays tax thereon and collects tax on sales. The base of the tax measures essentially the value of the productive services claimed by the taxpayer in the conduct of business. The net effect is that taxes paid are credited against taxes collected, and only the balance is payable to the taxing authority. The tax is rebated on exports and imposed on imports. Border taxes in Europe are substantial and will grow in importance. Several members of the Common Market and EFTRA have value-added taxes. This type of tax is currently being proposed for the United States because of the balance-of-international-payments problem and the present heavy burden of income taxes. It is generally assumed that a value-added tax will be passed on to consumers and shifted forward. For additional details, see Richard W. Lindholm, *Value Added Tax and Other Tax Reforms,* Nelson-Hall, Chicago, 1976.

variable annuity   An insurance contract guaranteeing the annuitant—the individual covered by the contract—a periodic income, based upon the investment performance of an underlying portfolio of securities, in return for a single payment or periodic payments that go into the buildup of the portfolio. The main distinction between a variable annuity and the more common fixed annuity is that the present value of and the periodic payments from the variable annuity change with current prices and earnings of the portfolio while the fixed annuity is immunized from such changes. Development and growth of the variable annuity are closely related to prevailing perceptions of common stocks as a hedge against inflation. For additional information, see Paul A. Campbell, *The Variable Annuity,* Connecticut General Life Insurance Company, Hartford, 1969.

variable cost   Costs that vary directly in response to changes in the volume of production. Costs of this type include payments for labor, raw material, and all other variable resources. For many manufacturing firms, some portions of the electrical power consumption will be a variable cost. Other portions of the electrical consumption of the firm will represent fixed costs for lighting administrative offices, running accounting machines, and other purchases not associated directly with production. By definition, variable costs are zero when no output is being produced, and fixed costs are the only costs being incurred at that time. See D. S. Watson and Mary A. Holman, *Price Theory and Its Uses,* 4th ed., Houghton Mifflin, Boston, 1976.

variable proportions, law of   *See* diminishing returns, law of.

variable-span diffusion indices A collection of diffusion indices, each with a different time span, such as three months, six months, or nine months. For any given index, the time span is fixed. A diffusion index is usually computed over one-month spans, but similar measures can be computed over intervals of two months, three months, or any number of months. For further discussion, see Geoffrey H. Moore and Julius Shiskin, "Variable Span Diffusion Indexes and Economic Forecasting," paper presented at the Sixth Annual Forecasting Conference, American Statistical Association, New York Chapter, Apr. 17, 1964.

variance A measure of the spread of a set of values. It is the tendency of the individual values to vary from the mean. Operationally, a variance is the sum of the squares of the deviations of observed values from the arithmetic mean of a series divided by the number of items. For example, the variance for a set of family-income values would be expressed in terms of dollars of income squared. Since it is easier to interpret the measure of spread expressed in the same units as the variable itself, however, the statistical measure of spread generally used in economic analysis is the standard deviation, which is the square root of the variance. For further information on the subject of variability, see John E. Freund and Frank J. Williams, *Elementary Business Statistics,* 3rd ed., Prentice-Hall, Englewood Clifts, N.J., 1978.

variate-difference method A technique for the analysis of time series whose variations stem from a systematic and a random (error) component. If the systematic component (some smooth function of time) can be described by a polynomial, the systematic component can be eliminated by successive differencing, and thus the random component may be isolated. This method has rather limited applications largely because the mathematical solution of a system can rarely be described by a polynomial. For additional information, see Lawrence R. Klein, *An Introduction to Econometrics,* Greenwood, Westport, Conn., 1977.

veil-of-money concept The concept that money is neutral. Since goods are actually exchanged for goods, money transactions are only a veil that hides the underlying real processes. When people cannot see through the veil of money and consider money as having value in itself, a money illusion is said to exist. In the classical view, money was completely neutral, so that any changes in the money supply affected only the absolute price level and not any of the real variables of the system, such as the level of output. This concept, however, is valid only in comparing different full-employment equilibrium situations. When the economy is underemployed, money is no longer neutral and changes in the money supply can affect the real variables. For additional details, see Don Patinkin, *Money, Interest and Prices,* 2d ed., Harper & Row, New York, 1965.

velocity of money The number of times that an average dollar is spent during a specific period, usually one year. The velocity of money depends on the average length of time people hold their money, and it can be calculated by dividing the total dollar volume of sales by the total money supply in circulation. Since World War II, the velocity of money has been slowly rising. If the velocity of money rises, people are holding smaller cash balances and are spending their money sooner after they receive it. The transactions velocity is closely related to the level of economic activity; as economic activity expands, idle balances are reduced, increasing the velocity of money, and the expansion of loans puts the new money into the hands of active spenders. The reverse is true in terms of declining business activity. It has generally been found that the transactions velocity also varies directly with the level of interest rates. A concept closely related to the transactions velocity is the income velocity of money, which is the number of times that money moves from one income recipient to another. It can be derived by dividing the total national product by the money supply. For further explanation, see William L. Silber (ed.), *Financial Innovation,* Lexington Books, Lexington, Mass., 1975; Richard T. Selden, "Monetary Velocity in the United States," in Milton Friedman (ed.), *Studies in the Quantity Theory of Money,* University of Chicago Press, Chicago, 1956, pp. 179–275.

venture capital (risk capital) The money supplied by stockholders either from plowed-back earnings or from new stock purchases. It provides the bulk of the funds needed for industrial progress, either by developing new corporations or by financing new ventures for existing firms. Venture capital is also needed as a cushion to support business borrowing. Bankers and investors will not lend money to a company with an inadequate margin of equity capital. For further discussion, see Elvin F. Donaldson, *Corporate Finance,* 4th ed., Wiley, New York, 1975.

verification In econometrics, the process of setting up criteria for measuring the reliability of experimental results and using such criteria in deciding whether to accept or reject the economic theory or hypotheses being tested by means of the available data and an econometric model. For additional information, see Lawrence R. Klein, *An Introduction to Econometrics,* Greenwood, Westport, Conn., 1977.

vertical integration The operation of a single firm at more than one stage of production. The most comprehensive type of vertical integration would include productive stages from the processing of the raw material to the completion and distribution of the finished product. For example, some steel producers mine coal and iron ore, ship the ore in their own boats to their plants, make pig iron, convert the iron into steel, shape the steel into semifinished and finished products, and distribute and export the products to final consumers. A single company organized vertically can often carry out the entire production process more efficiently than a number of individual firms, each of which handles one stage of the process. One reason for this situation is that technologically complementary processes can be brought together in a single plant with a resulting gain in efficiency. Moreover, economies may result from the improved coordination of output rates at various production stages. Vertical integration may also eliminate substantial shipping costs and payments to intermediaries. It may not be economical in all industries, however, for the characteristics of the productive process and the nature of the demand for the goods produced at various stages play a large role in determining the suitability of vertical integration for a particular firm. For further information, see Frederick M. Scherer, *Industrial Market Structure and Economic Performance,* Rand-McNally, Chicago, 1978.

wage level The average level of wages of a given economic sector, of a single industry, or of the entire economy. The wage level can be expressed in absolute dollar terms, either in current or real dollars, over a period of time. It can be compared with wage levels in other sectors or industries, or in other countries or geographical regions. The wage level of an industry or an economy is an average of the wages paid to its various workers, and, as such, is an indicator of economic conditions. One use for average wage levels is to compare the current-dollar wage level with that adjusted for price changes for two or more time periods to determine the relative gain in dollar versus real wages. For example, it may appear that wages, on a current-dollar basis, have increased substantially over a five-year period. But when the figures are adjusted using an index of price change as a measure of inflation, it may turn out that real-wage levels, or the purchasing power of wages, has actually decreased over the period. A case in point is the period 1977–1981. Average weekly earnings in current dollars for the total private nonagricultural economy amounted to $255.20 in 1981, up 35% from $189 in 1977. However, when adjusted for inflation, and expressed in dollars of 1977 purchasing power, average real wages dropped 10% over the period to $170.13 from the $189 level of 1977.

wage rate The rate of pay received by a worker on the basis of some unit, such as an hour, a week, or a unit of product produced or sold. A schedule of established wage rates constitutes the basic wage structure of an individual firm or an industry. There are two basic types, time-rate structures and incentive-rate structures. Time-wage employees receive a fixed sum of money per unit of time, whereas incentive workers receive compensation that varies with output. For further information, see Lloyd G. Reynolds, *Labor Economics and Labor Relations,* 7th ed., Prentice-Hall, Englewood Cliffs, N.J., 1978.

wages and salaries Constituting a major component of the national income, wages and salaries represent the direct outlays paid to employees of business firms. Wages and salaries are classified as part of the larger category of national income, "compensation of employees," which includes, in addition to wages and salaries, various types of compensation not paid out directly to employees, such as paid vacation, paid sick leave, company-paid health and life insurance, and subsidized meals. In 1981, preliminary national income statistics showed that overall compensation of employees totaled $1,771.7 billion, or 75.6% of a total national income of $2,343.7 billion. Wages and salaries amounted to $1,482.8 billion, which represented 83.7% of employee compensation, and 63.3% of national income. For additional information, see Richard Ruggles and Nancy D. Ruggles, *National Income Accounts and Income Analysis,* 2d ed., McGraw-Hill, New York, 1956; for current data, see U.S. Department of Commerce, *Survey of Current Business,* monthly.

Wagner Act *See* **National Labor Relations Act.**

warrant An option which gives the holder the privilege of purchasing a certain amount of stock at a specified price for a stipulated period. There are two types of warrants, stock-purchase warrants and subscription warrants. Stock-purchase warrants (also called option warrants) are sometimes issued with or attached to bonds, preferred stock, and infrequently, common stock. They entitle the holder to buy common stock in the same corporation at a certain price. Some of these warrants limit the right to buy to a specified period; others are perpetual. Stock-purchase warrants are sometimes attached to the underlying issue and cannot be detached; their value is a part of the bond or preferred stock. Others are detachable, sometimes after a waiting period, and frequently have inherent value which depends on the current price of the common stock. These are traded in the same manner as other securities. This type of warrant is generally used to make the bonds or preferred stock more attractive to the investor; if the company thrives, the investor has an opportunity to gain through the purchase of the common stock. Subscription warrants are used with privileged subscriptions to new issues of common stock. Common stockholders in many corporations have preemptive rights to subscribe to that proportion of any new issue of common stock equivalent to the proportion of the corporation that they owned before the issue. Before the stock is issued, the common stockholders receive subscription warrants which indicate the number of rights that they have and which serve as evidence of their right to subscribe to the new issue. For further information, see William F. Sharpe, *Investments,* Prentice-Hall, Englewood Cliffs, N.J., 1978.

welfare economics A theoretical branch of economics which is concerned with the application of ethical standards of evaluation to economic systems. The actual socioeconomic goals are assumed and are not determined by economic analysis. For example, the primary social goals for a welfare evaluation of the operation of an economic system might be maximum freedom of choice for individuals, an equitable distribution of income, and optimum standards of living for all individuals as determined by their preferences and restricted only by available resources and technology. An optimum solution in welfare economics is usually considered one in which the welfare of the greatest number of people is maximized and not the profits of an individual or a firm. Much of the analysis of welfare economics has been accomplished in the area of maximizing consumer satisfaction. For any given distribution of income, the optimum allocation of resources occurs under competitive marginal-cost pricing. The optimum adjustment of production in terms of consumer preferences is obtained only if the marginal rate of substitution between each two goods that are consumed is equal to the marginal rate of transformation of the two goods in production. For a fuller statement on welfare economics, see Arthur C. Pigou, *The Economics of Welfare,* 4th ed., Macmillan, London, 1932; William J. Baumol, *Welfare Economics and the Theory of the State,* Harvard University Press, Cambridge, Mass., 1965; E. J. Mishan, *An Introduction to Normative Economics,* Oxford University Press, New York, 1980.

welfare state A private economy in which large-scale governmental action emphasizes social benefits. Welfare-state goals include maintenance of a minimum living standard for all citizens, production of social goods and services, control of the business cycle, and adjustment of total output to allow for social costs and revenues. Since the New Deal, the welfare-state aspect of U.S. government has been increasing. The growth in public services involves a transition from an individualistic economy to a mixed public-private economy. The welfare state is not socialistic; rather, it involves governmental expenditures and the use of fiscal policy to adjust aggregate demand to the productive capacity of the private economy. While the government makes large expenditures, private enterprise carries out actual production. Among the instruments of the modern welfare state are progressive taxation, social security, unemployment insurance, farm-support programs, and government-sponsored housing programs. Other nations, such as Great Britain and the Scandinavian countries, have moved further in the direction of the welfare state than has the United States. An example of this is the cradle-to-the-grave welfare assistance program operated by the British government. For further information, see Bill Jordan, *Freedom and the Welfare State,* Routledge and Kegan Paul, Boston, 1976.

withholding tax   A federal or state tax withheld by U.S. employers from the wages and salaries of workers at the time of payment. A fixed percentage is withheld from each pay check. This method of taxation has been characterized as "pay as you go," since the taxes needed to run the governments are paid from current earnings. Among the advantages of the withholding method of tax collection are prompt payment to the governments and lack of complaint on the part of the workers because they never possess the money that is withheld. Among the disadvantages are the additional paper work required of the companies withholding funds. For a more detailed discussion, see Richard A. Musgrave and Peggy B. Musgrave, *Public Finance in Theory and Practice,* 2d ed., McGraw-Hill, New York, 1975.

workweek, average   The number of weekly hours per factory worker for which pay has been received, including paid holidays, vacations, and sick leaves. In the United States, workweek figures cover full-time and part-time production and related workers who receive payment for any part of the pay period ending nearest the fifteenth of the month. Because of the increasing amount of paid holidays, vacations, and sick leaves, the paid workweek exceeds the number of hours actually worked per week. The average-workweek series compiled from payroll data by the U.S. Bureau of Labor Statistics differs from the series of weekly hours actually worked that is compiled from household surveys by the U.S. Bureau of the Census. It also differs from the standard or scheduled workweek because such factors as absenteeism, part-time work, and stoppages make the average workweek lower than the standard workweek. The average workweek for all manufacturing reflects shifts in importance as well as changes in the workweek in component industries. The average workweek is a significant indicator of overall business activity, which the National Bureau of Economic Research classifies as one of its many leading indicators. The workweek turns up or down more rapidly than employment because decisions about the length of the workweek are usually made by production supervisors who operate on a more flexible level than managements that determine shifts in hiring practices. For industry statistics and a more detailed explanation of the techniques of collection of workweek data, see U.S. Department of Labor, *Employment and Earnings,* monthly.

Y

yield   The percentage that is derived from dividing the annual return from any investment by the amount of the investment. For instance, a $10,000 investment in common stocks that pays $500 in annual dividends yields 5%. Similarly, a bond purchased for $1,000 that returns $40 a year yields 4%. The term yield is used to describe the rate of return on any investment. Current yield is a somewhat similar term that means the percentage derived from dividing the annual return from an investment by the current cost of that investment. For example, if a person buys a piece of real estate for $20,000 that returns $2,000 a year, the yield is 10%. If, however, it now costs $30,000 to buy this piece of real estate and there has been no change in the amount of the return, the current yield is 6.7%. For statistics on the yields on various securities investments, see *Federal Reserve Bulletin,* Washington, D.C., monthly; Securities and Exchange Commission, *Monthly Statistics Bulletin.*

yield curve   A smoothly drawn curve that shows the functional relationship between yield and time to maturity of fixed-income securities. To isolate this relationship, all other factors affecting yield—risk of default, liquidity, cost of acquisition, and so forth—are held constant. For this reason, yield curves are drawn for securities that are similar except for maturity—for example, U.S. Treasury securities, which are available in a wide range of maturities (from a few days to more than twenty years) and are virtually identical in all other respects. Different economic conditions result in yield curves with three basic shapes: upward-sloping curves, which indicate that long-term interest rates are higher than short-term rates; downward-sloping curves, which show that short-term rates are higher than long-term rates; and flat curves, which indicate that long- and short-term rates are similar. Because yield curves depict geometrically the term structure of interest rates, they are a useful analytical tool to monetary economists and financial analysts. For further information, see Burton G. Malkiel, *The Term Structure of Interest Rates,* Princeton University Press, Princeton, N.J., 1966.

yield to call The anticipated rate of return on a callable bond, based upon the assumption that it is called, which means that the bond is redeemed prior to maturity. More precisely, the yield to call is that rate of discount that equates all future interest, principal, and premium payments to the market price, calculated up to the call date. Although similar to yield to maturity, yield to call differs in two ways: first, for a given bond, the time to the call date is always shorter than the time to maturity; second, since the issuer in most cases must pay a premium if the bond is called, the redemption amount will be higher than the principal or face amount of the bond. For further information, see Robert Lamb and Stephen P. Rappaport, *Municipal Bonds— The Comprehensive Review of Tax-Exempt Securities and Public Finance,* Mc-Graw-Hill, New York, 1980.

yield to maturity The anticipated rate of return on a bond if it is held to maturity. More precisely, the yield to maturity is that rate of discount that equates the present value of all future interest and principal payments to the market price. Assuming the bond's principal, or face amount, is $1,000, yield to maturity can be expressed mathematically as follows:

$$P = \frac{I}{1 + r} + \frac{I}{(1 + r)^2} + \cdots + \frac{I}{(1 + r)^n} + \frac{1,000}{(1 + r)^n}$$

where P = market price of the bond
  I = annual interest payment
  n = number of years to maturity
  r = yield to maturity

The above equation can be solved for r by trial and error. Bond yield tables are available, however, that present yield to maturity for various combinations of the other three variables. Because yield to maturity accounts for gains or losses that will occur if the market price of the bond is below or above the face amount, it will differ from the current yield unless market price equals the face amount. For example, suppose a bond with a 5% coupon rate, maturing in nineteen years and one month, is selling for $970. The current yield on this security equals 5.15% (50/970); its yield to maturity equals 5.25%. For further information, see T. M. Simpson et al., *Mathematics of Finance,* 3d ed., Prentice-Hall, Englewood Cliffs, N.J., 1951; Edward I. Altman (ed.), *Financial Handbook,* 5th ed., Wiley, New York, 1981.

Z

zero economic growth   A concept of halting absolute growth in national economic output because of the deleterious effects of uncurbed growth on the nation's welfare. The no-growth advocates believe that continuous exponential growth in population, physical output, and material consumption in a finite world will lead eventually to a collapse of the ecological and socioeconomic systems. Most economists believe that the no-growth group is unreasonably pessimistic about the adaptive capability of our economic system as well as the potency of technological progress and that they have not adequately explored all available alternatives open to society to reduce the harmful effects often attributed to growth. Both sides agree that there is a price to pay for economic growth. The issue to be resolved concerns the relative magnitudes of costs and benefits involved in the pursuit of growth. For additional information, see Mancur Olson and Hans H. Landsburg (eds.), *The No-Growth Society,* Norton, New York, 1973.

zero population growth   A concept of bringing to a halt, at an early date, the growth of world population. Advocates of no population growth oppose further population growth not only for the low-income, less-developed countries, but also for the relatively rich industrialized nations. A continued rise in population would make it difficult to achieve and maintain a low level of environmental pollution as more and more people occupy a fixed geographical area. It would also accelerate the rate of use of nonrenewable natural resources. Most economists are more optimistic about the situation, believing that the advance of science and technology will certainly continue to allow more humans to live on earth with increased real material consumption per capita. For additional information, see Mancur Olson and Hans Landsburg (eds.), *The No-Growth Society,* Norton, New York, 1973.

Part Two
ORGANIZATIONS

Board of Governors of the Federal Reserve System A policymaking and supervisory agency of the Federal Reserve System of the United States. The seven members of the Board are appointed to fourteen-year terms by the President with Senate confirmation. The board determines general monetary, credit, and operating policies for the System as a whole and formulates the rules and regulations necessary to carry out the purposes of the Federal Reserve Act. It sets reserve requirements, margin requirements, and it reviews and determines the discount rates set by the district banks. The board has broad supervisory powers with respect to Federal Reserve banks and member banks. It acts as the chief representative for the Federal Reserve System, which it represents in most of its dealings with other governmental and congressional agencies. For further information, see *The Federal Reserve System: Purposes and Functions,* 1963. Its headquarters are located at Twentieth Street and Constitution Avenue, N.W., Washington, D.C. 20551.

Bureau of the Census A bureau of the U.S. Department of Commerce. It conducts censuses of population and housing every ten years and of agriculture, business, governments, manufacturers, mineral industries, and transportation at five-year intervals. Its sample surveys show current social and economic indicators in the fields of population and housing, construction, retail and wholesale sales and services, manufacturing, and governments. The Bureau also compiles detailed statistics on U.S. foreign trade from import and export firms, collects and processes data for other government agencies, and offers special tabulations of its data for thousands of users. A decennial census of the population, required by the U.S. Constitution as a basis for the allocation of representatives in Congress, has been taken by the federal government since 1790. U.S. marshals (reporting to the President in the first census and to the secretary of state in the next five censuses) and their assistants were the first enumerators (door-to-door counters). Specially appointed supervisors, who selected enumerators, first served in the 1880 census. From 1790 to 1900, temporary organizations were set up for each census. Then, in 1902, Congress established the first permanent Census office, making it possible to collect intercensal data. Even the first census in 1790 was not a simple head count. Data on the ages of men provided a measure of military and labor resources. The Congressional Census Act of 1840 directed census takers to collect "all such information in relation to mines, agriculture, commerce, manufactures, and schools, as will exhibit a full view of the pursuits, industry, education, and resources of the country." This was the first major step toward the Census Bureau's broad role as fact finder for the nation. The Bureau of the Census issues reports from its censuses and surveys and hundreds of special demographic and economic publications. Census reports are listed in a quarterly *Catalog of United States Census Publications,* and are available in most large libraries. A selected list of special publications follows: *Statistical Abstract of the United States,* annual one-volume basic reference source; *Pocket Data Book, USA,* a compact, easy-to-read reference book; *County and City Data Book,* a one-volume collection of data from major censuses and other sources; *Historical Statistics of the United States: Colonial Times to 1970,* more than 12,500 time series on major aspects of the nation's development, in two volumes; *County Business Patterns,* employment, payrolls, and reporting units, compiled from social security tax reports. Its headquarters are located in the Federal Center, Suitland, Md. 20233.

Bureau of Economic Analysis (BEA)   A branch of the U.S. Department of Commerce which engages in macroeconomic analysis, utilizing for this purpose primarily the economic accounts it develops, prepares, and maintains. BEA was formerly known as the Office of Business Economics (OBE). There is no other official source of the gross national product (GNP), national income, personal income, or U.S. balance of international payments. The economic accounts provide the framework for most macroeconomic analysis both by government and by business firms. BEA prepares several different kinds of accounts.

1. National income and product accounts provide a comprehensive view of the state of the economy and relationships among its major economic groups—consumers, business, government, and foreigners. GNP, the market value of the nation's output of goods and services, is the cornerstone of the national income and product accounts. The accounts show the kind of goods and services that make up the GNP, and the kind of income, such as personal income and profits, generated in its production. Measures of changes in the prices of the goods and services that make up the GNP are also provided.

2. Wealth accounts show the holdings of the nation's tangible wealth, including structures, equipment, inventories, residences, and consumer durables. Estimates of the structures and equipment owned by business are crucial to the analysis of the nation's ability to produce goods and services.

3. Input-output accounts show how industries interact—buying from and

selling to each other—to produce the GNP. These accounts provide a cross-sectional view of the economy that is especially useful for industry analyses and projections.

4. Income-size distribution accounts show how the nation's income is shared among families by income size and by age, sex, and race of head of family. This information is used by government in formulating tax policy and welfare programs and by business in marketing decisions.

5. Environmental accounts show the expenditures made by business, consumers, and government to protect the environment. These accounts show what portion of GNP goes to produce a cleaner environment.

6. Regional accounts provide detail on economic activity by region, state, standard metropolitan statistical area (SMSA), and county. Estimates of personal income by state and county are among criteria used to allocate federal revenue-sharing funds. BEA's projections of population, employment, personal income, and earnings are used by planners to forecast demand for goods and services.

7. Balance-of-payments accounts give details on U.S. transactions with foreign countries and on the international investment position of the United States. These accounts contain estimates of the major types of international transactions, such as exports, imports, travel, transportation, foreign aid, private investment flows, and changes in monetary reserves.

Of these accounts, the oldest is the U.S. balance of payments, which was developed from a concept into a working set of international economic accounts beginning in 1921. Hence, BEA derived its legislative authority through the Bureau of Foreign and Domestic Commerce, but it was established as a separate unit in 1945. Pursuant to a Senate resolution, national income became a Commerce Department responsibility in 1932. Since then, the scope, detail, and frequency of issue of both the whole set of accounts and each component part have been increased sufficiently to maintain the position of the United States not only as the pioneer but also as a world leader in this field. GNP was developed as a separate but coordinate aggregate in 1942, in response to the urgent need for such economic intelligence in the planning of the U.S. war effort. The monthly *Survey of Current Business,* the major vehicle for the dissemination of analytical data and results produced in BEA, was instituted about 1921. The forty pages of business statistics appearing in each issue are carried back, with explanatory notes, in a *Business Statistics Supplement* published in alternate years. To cast further light upon movements shown by the basic accounts data, BEA has developed auxiliary series in other more specific economic areas. One of these is the survey taken quarterly for about thirty years to report expected business expenditures for new plants and equipment. BEA is responsible for the statistical indicators program, including the issuance of *Business Conditions Digest.* BEA also publishes monographs to provide authoritative data on a comprehensive and timely basis. Recent titles include *National Income and Product Accounts of the United States, 1929–76: Statistical Tables; Definitions and Conventions of the 1972 Input-Output Study; The Detailed Input-Output Structure of the U.S. Economy, 1972; National-Regional Impact Evaluation Systems; Local Area Personal Income, 1974–1979;* and *U.S. Direct Investment Abroad, 1977.* BEA publications are available from the Superintendent of Documents, U.S. Government Printing Office, Washington, D.C. 20402. BEA's headquarters are located at 1401 K Street, N.W., Washington, D.C.

Bureau of Industrial Economics (BIE) A bureau of the U.S. Commerce Department that is the government's basic source for the industry-specific data, analysis, and research necessary for business planning and decision making, for the operation of federal programs, and for the development of federal policies. Established in 1980, the bureau provides industrial monitoring and forecasting, continuing assessment of current industrial trends, and an annual assessment of conditions in each of 200 industries, including forecasts of future output levels. It provides information and analytical support for industrial mobilization and for foreign trade expansion, and does basic economic research to support economic policy decisions. Its staff also analyzes and comments on the industrial impact of proposed legislation and regulations, responds to business and congressional requests for industrial data and technical assistance, and works to develop new sources of industrial data. Six units constitute the BIE: The Office of Basic Industries is responsible for monitoring metals and minerals, chemicals, construction and engineering, and forest products. The Office of Producer Goods covers industrial, transportation, and electronics equipment. The Office of Consumer Goods and Service Industries is responsible for consumer products, wholesale and retail trade, and services. The Office of Research Analysis undertakes the basic research needed to define the industrial environment over the next decade in light of demographic developments, patterns of natural resource supply, and trade pressures. The Office of Industrial Statistics compiles and maintains an industrial data base and econometric models, and provides or assists in acquiring specialized software needed for data processing. The Regulatory Analysis Division undertakes analyses of legislative, regulatory, and industrial policies and proposals that affect industrial growth and trade. BIE presents its analyses to the public through a number of publications. The bureau's major publication is the annual *U.S. Industrial Outlook,* a reference volume presenting economic developments and projections for 200 industries. Other annual publications include *Confectionary Manufacturers Sales and Distribution, Franchising Opportunity Handbook,* and *Franchising in the Economy.* The bureau also publishes three periodicals, *Forest Products Review, Printing and Publishing,* and *Construction Review;* and a number of one-time reports on various industries Its headquarters are located in Washington, D.C.

Bureau of Labor Statistics A bureau of the U.S. Department of Labor that serves as the federal government's principal fact-finding agency in the field of labor economics. Its major programs provide statistics and analyses of employment, unemployment, labor force, productivity and technological developments, wages, industrial relations, work injuries, price trends, costs and standards of living, and economic growth. The bureau obtains its information from workers, businesspeople, unions, and other government agencies, all of whom supply the data voluntarily because of their interest in and need for the analyses and summaries which ensue. The bureau's research projects, in turn, grow out of the needs of these same groups as well as the needs of Congress, federal and state governments, and the Department of Labor. Its research is oriented toward the Department of Labor's objectives of promoting the welfare of wage earners, improving their working conditions, and advancing their opportunities for profitable employment. A Bureau of Labor, predecessor of the Bureau of Labor Statistics, was established in the Department of the Interior by act of June 27, 1884, and organized in January of the following year. In 1913, after several changes in status, it became the Bureau of Labor Statistics in the newly created U.S. Department of Labor. The Bureau has eight field offices, located in Boston, New York, Philadelphia, Atlanta, Chicago, Dallas, Kansas City, and San Francisco. Its chief official, a nonpolitical Presidential appointee, is the commissioner of labor statistics. The bureau conducts a training program for economists, statisticians, and other labor officials from economically developing countries. This program is sponsored by the Department of State through the Agency for International Development. The information collected by the bureau through field surveys and other means is issued in special bulletins and reports, in several periodicals, and in press releases. The major periodicals are the *Monthly Labor Review* (which began publication in July 1915), *Employment and Earnings,* and the *Occupational Outlook Quarterly.* Another monthly periodical is *Current Wage Developments,* an *Occupational Outlook Handbook,* providing guidance material on major occupations, and a *Directory of National and International Labor Unions in the United States* are two biennial publications. Its headquarters are located at 441 G Street, N.W., Washington, D.C. 20212.

Congressional Budget Office (CBO) A nonpartisan organization mandated to provide the Congress with budget-related information and with analyses of alternative fiscal and programmatic policies. Its principal tasks are to present the Congress with options for consideration and to study the possible budget ramifications of these options. Its specific responsibilities include estimates of the five-year budgeting costs of proposed legislation, the tracking of congressional budgetary actions against budget targets preset in the concurrent resolutions, periodic forecasts of economic trends and alternative fiscal policies, analysis of programmatic issues that affect the federal budget, analysis of the inflationary impact of proposed legislation, and an annual report on major budgetary options. In 1974, the Congress enacted a comprehensive budget reform measure in which three new congressional institutions were created, the CBO and a committee on the budget in both the House and the Senate. The director of the CBO is appointed for a four-year term by the Speaker of the House and the President Pro Tempore of the Senate upon the recommendation of both committees of the budget. CBO is located at Second and D Streets, S.W., Washington, D.C. 20515.

Council of Economic Advisers   A three-member board which advises the President of the United States on national economic policy. Established under the Employment Act of 1946, the council has as its primary role "to develop and recommend to the President national economic policies to foster and promote free competitive enterprise, to avoid economic fluctuations . . . and to maintain employment, production and purchasing power." The council also assists the President in the preparation of the annual economic report, gathers information on economic conditions, appraises the economic programs and activities of the federal government, and makes economic studies at the President's request. It publishes each January the *Annual Report to the President by the Council of Economic Advisers*. See also Edward S. Flash, Jr., *Economic Advice and Presidential Leadership,* Columbia University Press, New York, 1965. Its headquarters are at the Old Executive Office Building, Seventeenth Street and Pennsylvania Avenue, N.W. Washington, D.C. 20506.

European Community   The European Community (EC) is an economic union formed in July 1967 and composed of three Communities (European Coal and Steel Community, European Economic Community, and European Atomic Energy Community) having common institutions: European Parliament, Council of Ministers, Commission and Court of Justice. The treaty establishing the European Economic Community (EEC), under which the main activity for the achievement of a European common market is carried out, entered into force on January 1, 1958. There are currently ten member states: Belgium, Denmark, Germany, Greece, France, Ireland, Italy, Luxembourg, the Netherlands, and the United Kingdom. The total population involved is approximately 270 million. Negotiations are taking place for the entry of Spain and Portugal into the Community. All customs duties and quotas on import and export of goods between member states have been abolished, and the Community works also to abolish nontariff barriers to trade through establishment of common standards for industrial products. Free movement of persons, services, and capital within the Community is foreseen, and arrangements exist to ensure that competition among manufacturers is not distorted. The member states pool resources to carry out a number of common policies, notably the common agricultural policy. Various funds are concerned with retraining of workers, with regional development, and with the encouragement of infrastructure projects; the European Investment Bank provides loans on favorable terms for certain economic development projects inside and outside the European Community. As part of its common trading policy the Community holds regular discussions with major trading partners in the industrialized world; maintains commercial agreements with countries of the European Free Trade Area; has association agreements with Turkey, Malta, and Cyprus; has cooperation agreements with over fifty countries forming part of the second agreement of Lomé for countries of Africa, the Caribbean, and the Pacific; and has cooperation agreements with eight countries of the southern Mediterranean area. General economic publications and those produced by the Community Statistical Office can be obtained from the Official Publications Office of the European Communities, Post Box 1003, Luxembourg. Headquarters of the European Community are located at 200 rue de la Loi, B-1049 Brussels, Belgium.

European Economic Community   *See* **European Community.**

Export-Import Bank of the United States (Eximbank)   An independent agency of the U.S. government whose purpose is to help finance and facilitate U.S. foreign trade. Established in 1934 as a District of Columbia banking corporation, it was reincorporated in 1945 and operates under the broad flexible provisions of the 1945 act, as amended. It was the first public agency, national or international, to arrange credits for the capital equipment required for large-scale economic development projects on a global basis. Primarily concerned with stimulating the sale of U.S. products overseas, Eximbank finances the purchase by foreign governments or private entities of U.S. capital equipment, materials, and services. Its loans must be spent in the United States and are repayable in dollars, plus interest on terms appropriate for the goods. In addition to dollar financing, the bank provides U.S. exporters with guarantees and insurance on their foreign accounts receivable. By its statutes, Eximbank is required, in all lending and guarantee operations, to assure itself of a reasonable ability of the borrower to meet commitments. In addition, the law directs the bank to supplement and encourage private capital interests and not to compete with them. To perform its functions, Eximbank has a capital stock of $1 billion, which is held by the U.S. Treasury, and, in addition, has been granted authority to borrow up to $6 billion from the Treasury. Since its inception, the bank has paid over $1 billion to the Treasury in dividends and accumulated reserves of more than $2.2 billion above operating expenses. In assisting the export sale of U.S. goods and equipment the bank authorized $5.4 billion in direct credits during fiscal year 1981. An additional $7.5 billion in guarantees and insurance was authorized which covered private financing of U.S. exports. Eximbank lending has financed a variety of U.S. industrial and agricultural equipment for every major geographical region of the world. Credits for the overseas sale of U.S. goods and equipment have supported electric power development, transportation, communications, mining development, agriculture, general industrial machinery, water-supply, and irrigation projects, among others. Further, a significant number of small transactions are included in Eximbank's activity. As the result of this activity, thousands of U.S. manufacturers and exporters have received overseas orders. Between the end of World War II and the establishment of the Marshall Plan, the bank administered the government's reconstruction program for Europe, which entailed the lending of billions of dollars for the purchase of U.S. goods. Eximbank's offices are located at 811 Vermont Avenue. N.W., Washington, D.C. 20571.

Federal Open Market Committee A committee of Federal Reserve System officials which governs the open-market purchases and sales of U.S. government securities and other authorized assets with a view to accommodating commerce and business and with regard for their effect on the general credit situation and the economy of the United States. The Committee's meetings constitute a forum for exploring all aspects of the economy's performance and discussing ways in which the Federal Reserve System's influence over the cost and availability of money and credit can be used most effectively to promote such national economic goals as a high rate of economic growth, high employment, reasonable price stability, and a favorable balance of international payments. Operations in foreign exchange, which are coordinated with the Treasury, are directed at counteracting disorderly conditions in the foreign-exchange markets. The Federal Open Market Committee developed from an informal investment committee set up by the Federal Reserve banks in early 1922 to centralize purchases and sales of U.S. government securities on behalf of the Federal Reserve banks. This committee began later in 1922 to make policy recommendations from time to time to the several Reserve banks, and the Banking Act of 1933 gave a successor advisory group statutory recognition as the Federal Open Market Committee. The Banking Act of 1935 gave the Committee statutory control over all open-market operations of the Federal Reserve System and provided that its membership include (as it does at present) the seven members of the Board of Governors of the Federal Reserve System, the president of the Federal Reserve Bank of New York, and four of the eleven other Federal Reserve bank presidents, serving in rotation. The Committee meets approximately eight times a year to discuss policy objectives for the period until the next meeting. The Committee's guidelines are embodied in a domestic policy directive. Under the Committee's direction, an account manager conducts domestic operations in U.S. government securities and bankers' acceptances. There is a separate account manager for foreign-currency operations. Both managers are appointed by the Federal Open Market Committee and are senior officers of the Federal Reserve Bank of New York, through which operations are conducted. A record of policy actions, which is a general review of economic and monetary conditions at the time of the meeting, the domestic policy directive, other policy actions considered by the Committee, the votes on the actions and dissenting views, if any, are made public a few days after the next regularly scheduled meeting. The policy actions are subsequently published in the *Federal Reserve Bulletin* as well as the *Annual Report* of the Board of Governors of the Federal Reserve System and the *Federal Register*. Additionally, the *Quarterly Review* of the Federal Reserve Bank of New York carries a regular article on the financial markets which covers open-market operations.

Federal Reserve System A nationwide system consisting of the Board of Governors, the Federal Open Market Committe, the twelve Federal Reserve banks and their twenty-four branches, the Federal Advisory Council, the Consumer Advisory Council, and depository institutions. Its purpose is to foster a flow of additional money that will facilitate orderly economic growth, a stable dollar, and long-run balance in U.S. international payments. Before the establishment of the Federal Reserve System, the United States suffered from an irregular flow of credit and money that contributed to unstable economic development. Following a monetary crisis of unusual severity in 1907, Congress appointed a National Monetary Commission to determine what should be done. After considering the results of the commission's study as well as the recommendations of other authorities, it passed the Federal Reserve Act on December 23, 1913. Because of experience in the late 1920s and early 1930s, the powers of the Federal Reserve System were strengthened materially by the banking acts of 1933 and 1935. At the top of the System's structure is a nonpartisan seven-member Board of Governors in Washington, appointed by the President with Senate approval. The Board's prime function is the formulation of monetary policy. It has the power to approve changes in the discount rates that Federal Reserve banks charge for loans to member banks. Its other responsibilities include the authority to vary the percentage of deposits that the depository institutions must keep as reserves, to set margin requirements governing credit for the purchase of securities. The Board administers the Bank Holding Company Act and supervises the operations of the Federal Reserve banks. The individual members are also members of the Federal Open Market Committee. Through the Federal Reserve banks and their branches, the Federal Reserve System performs a variety of services, including the distribution of currency and coin, the clearance and collection of checks, and the transfer of bank funds by telegraph from one part of the country to another. It also has broad responsibilities for the examination and regulation of the operation of its member banks. The Board of Governors publishes the *Federal Reserve Bulletin,* monthly; *Federal Reserve Chart Book on Financial and Business Statistics,* quarterly; and *Annual Report, The Federal Reserve System: Purposes and Functions.* These are all available from the Board of Governors of the Federal Reserve System, Washington, D.C. 20551. Each Federal Reserve bank publishes its own monthly review of business conditions, an annual report, and occasional pamphlets on topics of special interest.

International Bank for Reconstruction and Development An international banking institution affiliated with the United Nations. Known popularly as the World Bank, it operates primarily by making loans, in cases in which private capital is not available on reasonable terms, to finance productive investments in member countries. It also provides a wide variety of technical assistance to its members. The Bank may lend to member governments, governmental agencies, or private enterprises; if the borrower is not a government, the guarantee of the member government concerned is required for the loan. Founded at the Bretton Woods Conference in July 1944, the Bank began operations in June 1946. Its membership consists of the governments of member countries, each of which subscribes to its capital stock in accordance with the country's economic strength. As of June 30, 1980, 135 countries were members of the Bank, and the total subscribed capital was $39,959 million, of which 10% had been paid in. The paid-in capital, however, was never intended to finance all the Bank's operations. Lending funds have been drawn mainly from the sale of its bonds in the capital markets of the world, from the sale of parts of its loans, and from earnings and repayment of loans. By June 1980, the Bank had made 1,875 loans, totaling more than $59,341 million, to finance projects in 100 member countries. The distribution of World Bank lending was as follows: east and west Africa, $6,131 million; east Asia and the Pacific, $13,559.2 million; south Asia, $3,828 million; Europe, middle east, and north Africa, $16,890 million; and Latin America and the Caribbean, $18,932 million. Major publications are the *Annual Report; Summary Proceedings of Annual Meetings; The World Bank* (December 1977); *Catalog of Publications* (1980); and *Questions and Answers: The World Bank* (1981). The Bank's offices are located at 1818 H Street, N.W., Washington, D.C. 20433.

International Monetary Fund An international financial institution affiliated with the United Nations which provides funds to its member nations as they are needed to meet their balance-of-payments needs. It promotes a freer system of world trade and payments as a means of helping its members to achieve economic growth, high levels of employment, and improved standards of living. The Fund is a continuing forum for the consideration of members' balance-of-payments problems, in which members are encouraged to avoid the use of restrictive practices and to maintain an orderly and stable pattern of exchange rates. A request for Fund assistance is considered in the light of the member's fiscal and monetary policies and its cooperation with the Fund's principles. The Fund has also played a part in longer-range programs of fiscal and monetary reform, both in the planning efforts and in subsequent financing. Its financial assistance takes the form of a foreign-exchange transaction. The member pays the Fund an amount of its own money equivalent, at the par value agreed upon with the Fund, to the amount of foreign currency that it wishes to draw. The member is expected to "repurchase" its own currency from the Fund within three (at the outside, ten) years by a payment of special drawing rights (SDRs), dollars, or some other currency acceptable to the Fund. Each member of the Fund is assigned a quota which approximately determines its voting power and the amount that it may draw from the Fund. On April 30, 1981, the Fund's assets totaled more than SDR 65 billion. The first allocation of special drawing rights in the Fund took effect on January 1, 1970. On that date, nearly $3.5 billion worth of SDRs were distributed as a new reserve asset, supplementing gold and foreign currencies. Additional allocations were made on January 1, 1971, and again on January 1, 1972. On January 1, 1981, the Fund allocated SDR 4 billion to members, the third and final allocation under a board-of-governors' resolution under which allocations of SDR 4 billion were also made in 1979 and in 1980. In all, SDR 21.4 billion were allocated. The highest authority of the Fund is exercised by its board of governors, on which each member country is represented by a governor and an alternate governor. The board has delegated many of its powers to the executive directors. Six members each appoint one of the Fund's executive directors, and sixteen directors are elected by the other members, making a total of twenty-two. The articles of agreement of the Fund were formulated at the United Nations Monetary and Financial Conference held at Bretton Woods, New Hampshire, on July 1 to 22, 1944. The agreement has been in force since December 27, 1945, when it was signed by twenty-nine governments, representing 80% of the original quotas in the Fund. As of September 20, 1981, there were 141 member countries. The Fund's publications include the *Annual Report; Annual Report on Exchange Restrictions; International Financial Statistics,* a monthly statistical bulletin; *Balance of Payments Yearbook; Staff Papers,* three times yearly; and the weekly *IMF Survey* in three language editions. Its headquarters are located in Washington, D.C.

Joint Economic Committee   In the U.S. government, the congressional counterpart of the Council of Economic Advisers. The Joint Economic Committee of the Congress, created under the Employment Act of 1946, was established to assist the President in gathering authoritative information concerning economic trends, to appraise programs in the light of the declared policy of the act, and to recommend national economic policies, within the framework of the free competitive system, for avoiding economic fluctuations and diminishing the effects thereof. Its function is to make a continuing study of economic developments and national economic policies with a view to coordinating these programs in order to further the stated objectives of the act. This function is carried out through studies and reports on specific economic issues. At the beginning of each Congress, a report containing findings and recommendations with respect to the main proposals made by the President is filed with Congress as a guide to the committees dealing with legislation. The Joint Economic Committee, which was known under the original act as the Joint Committee on the Economic Report, is composed of ten members of the Senate and ten members of the House of Representatives, the majority party in each case being represented by six members and the minority party by four members. The committee issues *Economic Indicators* a monthly publication which is prepared for it by the Council of Economic Advisers and is supplied to each member of Congress and to subscribers throughout the United States who are interested in timely and authoritative information on economic trends; an annual economic report reviewing the President's economic program as presented to Congress; and reports of hearings on a wide variety of economic subjects. Typical of the reports of hearings are studies of the administration of monetary policy, the adequacy of government statistics, the problems of economic growth, the impact of foreign economic policy on the domestic economy of the United States, and the economics of public expenditure.

Organization for Economic Cooperation and Development (OECD)   An international intergovernmental organization, successor to the Organization for European Economic Cooperation (OEEC). The OECD promotes policies designed (1) to achieve the highest sustainable economic growth and employment and a rising standard of living in member countries, while maintaining financial stability, and thus to contribute to the development of the world economy; (2) to contribute to sound economic expansion in member and nonmember countries in the process of economic development; and (3) to contribute to the expansion of world trade on a multilateral, nondiscriminatory basis in accordance with international obligations. Recognizing that the OEEC, created in 1948 to implement the Marshall Plan, had successfully achieved the objectives of European recovery, and considering that broader cooperation would make a vital contribution to the peaceful and harmonious relations of the people of the world, the governments of twenty countries—Austria, Belgium, Canada, Denmark, France, the Federal Republic of Germany, Greece, Iceland, Ireland, Italy, Luxembourg, the Netherlands, Norway, Portugal, Spain, Sweden, Switzerland, Turkey, the United Kingdom, and the United States—signed the constituent convention on December 14, 1960. The convention was duly ratified by the required number of national parliaments by September 30, 1961. Since that time, the admission of Japan, Finland, Australia, and New Zealand has brought the number of member countries to twenty-four. The supreme body of the organization is the Council, which may meet at the level of ministers or at the level of their alternates (permanent delegations). Within the limits of the convention, the Council is in fact a permanent conference in which the economic problems of the member countries are constantly reviewed. The Council may establish such subsidiary bodies (committees, subcommittees, working parties) as may be required for the achievement of the aims of the organization. A secretary general, appointed by the Council and responsible to it, serves as chair of the Council meetings at sessions of the permanent representatives. The secretary general, with the help of the secretariat, assists the Council and the other bodies of the organization in the execution of the work by submitting proposals, conducting research, issuing publications, etc. The OECD prepares and distributes publications on general economics, statistics, trade, aid to less-developed areas, industrial sectors, energy, agriculture, basic raw materials, science, technology, etc. OECD headquarters are located at the Château de la Muette, Rue André-Pascal, Paris 16, France; the U.S. center is located at 1750 Pennsylvania Avenue, N.W., Washington, D.C. 20006.